# Heralds of Victory

# HERALDS OF VICTORY

A History Celebrating the 100th Anniversary of
The New York Staff Band & Male Chorus
1887-1987

by
Ronald W. Holz

ISBN 0-89216-065-9

©Copyright 1986 The Salvation Army

Co-published by:
                    The Salvation Army Literary Department
                    145 West 15th Street
                    New York, NY 10011

    and   The New York Staff Band
             120 West 14th Street
             New York, NY 10011

Cover design by: Warren Maye

Printed in the United States of America

# In Dedication

To the Men of the New York Staff Band
Who so Faithfully Served and Serve
Within Its Ranks

# Table of Contents

# Forewords

## *Foreword by the late Commissioner Richard E. Holz*

Most everyone has an innate longing to write a book about life's experiences, travels, or observations. My hope was that if I wrote a book it would be about the New York Staff Band and Male Chorus and its fascinating history and achievements. Other comrades, including former bandmasters and bandsmen have voiced similar desires. When Dr. Ronald Holz, music historian, indicated his interest in attempting to write a history of the band for the centennial celebration, we were happy to share our memories and memorabilia with him.

The resulting historical account and wealth of documental data in Dr. Holz's well-researched and artistic presentation has surpassed my imaginative dreams of what sucn a book could possibly reveal.

Once again the heroes of my boyhood have come alive; Gus Hillstrom with his ocharina (sweet potato); the humorous poet-drummer, John Stimson; Richard Von Calio and his one-man-band displays; Frank Fowler's magnificent bass voice and incomparable tuba playing; George Darby's imaginative interpretations; John Allan and Bill Parkins extending the limits of derring-do for cornetists; Bandmaster George Granger promoted to Glory with baton in hand: "Red" Sheppard's infectious enthusiasm; and Erik Leidzen's masterpieces being premiered.

Again I have been stirred by the accounts of the band's marches and meetings in the slums of our cities, its eloquence in the great churches, cathedrals and stadiums, its thrilling appearances on nation-wide radio and television, the nation-wide and world-wide tours, its 100-year battle to effectively survive despite economic disasters, organizational turmoils and intentional and unintentional persecutions.

These pages reveal more than historical adventures. They depict a reality of life that God's power and inspired music is a victorious combination. Not only were souls changed by such a ministry, but the men and women who participated in this idealistic effort were transformed. The ancient Greek philosophers declared that the first duty of music is to enoble the soul. For over 100 years these Salvationist musicians have demonstrated this miraculous life-changing force in God-glorifying sounds and the exemplification of the power and discipline of the Cross of Jesus Christ.

My composition for cornet ensemble and brass band entitled "Heralds of Victory" sought to capsulize this spirit. With fanfares and brilliant technical displays, the cornetists send forth cascades of trumpeting while the accompaniment reiterates the battle song, "We're a band that shall conquer the foe. We believe we shall win if we fight in the strength of the King." Quotations of Beethoven's victory motif from his 5th symphony are pyramided into a finale truly celebrating the spiritual victory of God and man uniting to save this beleaguered world.

This saga of the New York Staff Band is aptly named "Heralds of Victory." The five hundred bandsmen who bore this heroic mission through tragedy and triumph for over a century deserve our highest accolades. This history will remind us of their sacrifices and the heartfelt tribute we owe these pioneers of evangelical excellence.

May God grant that their achievements will be a prelude to even greater victories in the second century for these servants of the most-high God.

Commissioner (Bandmaster)
Richard E. Holz (R)*

*Commissioner Richard E. Holz was promoted to Glory on August 15, 1986 just days after writing this Foreword.

## Foreword by Commissioner Stanley E. Ditmer

Highlights of my musical and officership experiences must indeed place near the top my personal involvement on two separate occasions with the New York Staff Band, first as a playing member in the baritone section, and later as the executive officer. Most of us have had opportunity to enjoy the Staff Band's ministry in person. A relatively few of us have played and sung as members.

Dr. Ronald Holz has rendered a tremendous service in giving hours and hours of research and writing to bring to fruition this excellent history. It will rekindle the memories of many. It will bring much new information to all. It is stimulating and exciting reading, especially for those who have rubbed elbows at any time with the band. Most of all, it will reveal the dedication and commitment of a large number of Salvationists who, down through the years, have sacrificed personal and family activities in order to be part of its ministry, to the glory of God, the proclamation of salvation to the lost, and the setting of a musical standard of excellence worthy of emulation by every Army music group.

Thank you, Dr. Holz, for giving us this exciting story. Read on, friends, and enjoy the thrill of *Heralds of Victory.*

Commissioner Stanley E. Ditmer
Territorial Commander

# Preface

As a child, I frequently fell asleep to the sounds of New York Staff Band test-pressings wafting up the stairs of our Kearny, N.J., home. I know these records by heart, and I have the Staff Band in my blood, though I was never an official member. Stories of the band and its colorful personalities were frequently part of our family discussions.

No historian can be totally objective, and I must admit at the outset the background I bring to this study. That has been a tremendous asset, for the most part, in doing research. I was detached in a sense, yet also knowledgeable enough in the ways of Army banding and keenly aware of New York Staff Band heritage via the long-standing connection of my father, former Staff Bandmaster Commissioner Richard E. Holz. I pray that with this background I have done fair justice in shaping a history of this noble ensemble.

Ultimately I ask the reader to look beyond the human failings of the author and beyond the human failings of the band, which was not faultless, and beyond the human failings of its leaders, who were not infallible. What this band has wrought for the Kingdom of God and for the cause of all that is best in sacred music cannot be adequately measured by any human standard.

# Acknowledgments

This history exists in large measure because of the vision of the New York Staff Band Board. Before the author began his research some critical work had been accomplished by Major William MacLean and his appointed committee in compiling early band data. Three executive officers of the band gave their full-hearted support to the project: Commissioner Stanley Ditmer, under whom initial efforts were begun; Lt.-Colonel Wallace Conrath, who commissioned this current history; and the present leader, Lt.-Colonel Edward Fritz, whose encouragement has been most helpful. Concurrent with this has been the kind and gracious endorsement of territorial leadership from Commissioners William Goodier and Orval Taylor.

Three individuals of the band board must be singled out for their special help in the project: Major Charles Olsen (responsible for, among other things, band newsletters and the "Book of Memories" project which generated much response), Major Vincent Bulla (responsible for financial concerns), and Deputy-Staff Bandmaster Ronald Waiksnoris (for superb work in a host of details connected with the book).

The Salvation Army's Archives and Research Center, headed by Mr. Thomas Wilsted, proved invaluable in my work. Mr. Wilsted's staff, including Judith Johnson, Joy Rich, and Matthew Borman, were very cooperative and diligent in their assistance to me.

The Eastern Territorial Music Bureau, including Ronald Waiksnoris, Thomas Scheibner, and Peter Graham, gave tremendous support.

The staff of the library at Asbury College, Wilmore, Kentucky, has lent generous cooperation in several matters.

While a host of staff bandsmen, former bandsmen, spouses, relatives, and friends have helped in this project, I must list the following individuals for notable assistance in the lending of substantial material, in submitting to interviews, and/or contributing outstanding encouragement and advice in this venture:

Douglas Anderson (son of former Staff Bandmaster Charles Anderson)

The late Lt.-Colonel Charles Bearchell (former staff bandsman)
The late Lt.-Colonel William Bearchell (former staff bandmaster)
Colonel Brindley Boon (R) (Salvation Army music historian)
Brigadier Lawrence Castagna (R) (former staff bandsman)
Brigadiers Violet and Beatrice Fowle
Commissioner Richard E. Holz (R) (former staff bandmaster)
Mrs. Commissioner Richard E. Holz (R)
Colonel C. Emil Nelson (former executive officer)
Vernon Post (former staff bandmaster)
Colonel Paul D. Seiler (R) (former staff bandsman and historian/collector)
Derek Smith (former staff bandmaster)
Major Thomas V. Mack (Male Chorus leader)
Dr. Edward H. McKinley (Salvation Army historian)
Bandmaster Alfred Swenarton (former staff bandsman)
Commissioner William Parkins (R)
Major William Simons (former staff bandsman and former territorial music secretary)
Mr. Frank Borowy (for special assistance in researching the band's activities in Rockville, Ct., fall of 1887)

To Major Carol Sparks (R) and Mrs. Tille (Robert) Moore for technical assistance in the manuscript preparation when I was in need of extra help, I state a special word of thanks.

To Warren Smith Jr., staff bandsman, for his invaluable assistance on the computer in preparing the manuscript and the index.

Major Lloyd Stoops, literary secretary of the Eastern Territory, has faithfully and patiently served as editor of this manuscript. His attention to detail and his constant words of encouragement in the finishing of this book were matched by his professional skill, for which I am most grateful.

Finally, Beatrice Hill Holz, my wife, deserves the most special recognition for her excellent technical work in typing/editing the initial manuscript and for her gracious support of my work over a four-year period.

# Introduction

The 100 years of sacred music-making by the New York Staff Band and Male Chorus stand as testimony to a remarkable achievement in service to God and to man. The members of the band were the valiant servants who made this consistent and continuous musical force the superb organization it is today. It is their achievements and their triumphs that we celebrate.

The history is divided into three main sections: (1) a chronological account (Chapters 1-9), (2) topical features of a more technical nature (Chapters 10-15), and (3) supportive data in the form of appendix lists, endnotes and bibliography. I have tried to include as many primary source accounts as I felt would give the reader the character of each era.

More than 500 names are listed in Appendix D, the official Roster of Members, 1887-1987. No historical summary can possibly do justice to all these individuals. If the reader feels that some notable figures have been overlooked, particularly Army administrators indirectly related to the band, I plead both with limited space and my personal judgment as to those persons mentioned being of greatest importance. My perspective has, hopefully, been a balanced one. Higher rewards await those faithful soldiers whose names do not stand out in this account.

Chapters in Part I are grouped chronologically by bandmasters. The bandmaster has always shaped the band's character. He, and he alone, is ultimately responsible for what is or is not achieved by the band. The New York Staff Band has changed over the years in amazing ways, due primarily to the varying gifts of its conductors. This perspective will provide the focus of this initial portion of the book.

Chapter titles are taken from some of the important compositions featured by the band over the years. They were chosen to reflect a major aspect of the period under review or to act as a symbolic reference. For example, the quintessential Male Chorus item is Staff Bandmaster William Bearchell's "Rock of Ages"; therefore, I used this title for the chapter on the Male Chorus. Similarly, Erik Leidzen's cornet solo "Songs in the Heart," written for Derek Smith, is representative of the host of superb solos/

soloists connected with the band. Most of the choices, if not immediately clear, will become so as the reader browses through Chapters 10-15, the second section of this study.

The first five chapters of Part II deal with more specialized areas of the band's performance. Some readers may feel that a soloist, a composition, or a festival/event has been unduly ignored, but the limits of our project make that inevitable. Hopefully the illustrations and appendix lists will give at least some recognition, yet even in those sections I had to be selective, particularly in the highlights chronology. Not everyone can be mentioned who sang or played a solo with the band. Complete records of the band's schedule and programs, as far as I or the band have been able to collect them, are available for the more diligent scholar at the Salvation Army Archives and Research Center in New York City.

To the non-Salvationist reader I do not apologize for the emphasis placed on the spiritual side of the band's service. This is, after all, a *Salvation* Army brass band. Hopefully you will be spared too many confusions as I have tried to avoid Army jargon and, where possible, officer rank status, except where essential. Excellent histories of The Salvation Army are available to the uninitiated, as are technical dissertations concerning Army music. I mention, in particular, Dr. Edward H. McKinley's *Marching To Glory,* an insightful account of this denomination's first 100 years in America. My own doctoral work on the development of Salvation Army music and musical forms, *A History of the Hymn Tune Meditation and Related Forms in Salvation Army Instrumental Music in Great Britain and North America, 1880-1980* (Parts I and II), contains helpful aids in understanding the technical and administrative side of Army music.

Because these sources are available to the general reader or historian/musicologist, I have not retold Army history which has already been adequately explained elsewhere. Only where such major events interact with the band's history—our central focus— do I reshape such accounts from the band's perspective.

My final chapter, "Endless Day," is speculative in nature and should be read as such. It is a challenge to all who love the New York Staff Band and Salvation Army music in general. I am grateful to the leaders and members of the band who so openly discussed the concerns of a second century with me at their annual retreat, January 1986, at Ladore Lodge. This chapter is largely the result of that dialogue.

xviii

# PART I

# Bandmasters and Male Chorus Leaders of The New York Staff Band
## 1887-1987

## Bandmasters

| | |
|---|---|
| B/M Keep | 1887 |
| Major Wray | Dec. 1887 — 1888 |
| Charles Miles | 1888 — Sept. 1890 |
| Walter Duncan | Sept. 1890 — Jan. 1892 |
| William Bridgen | Jan. 1892 — July 1892 |
| Edward Trumble | Sept. 1892 — Mar. 1896 |
| Charles Anderson | Feb. 1897 — Mar. 1898 |
| Charles Straubel | Mar. 1898 — July 1898 |
| Charles Anderson | Sept. 1898 — 1907 |
| Robert Griffith | 1907 — Apr. 1912 |
| George Darby | Apr. 1912 — Apr. 1931 |
| J. Stanley Sheppard | Apr. 1931 — Nov. 1932 |
| William Broughton | Nov. 1932 — Sept. 1935 |
| George Granger | Sept. 1935 — Aug. 1945 |
| William Bearchell | Aug. 1945 — Jan. 1951 |
| William Slater | Jan. 1951 — Jan. 1955 |
| Richard E. Holz | Jan. 1955 — Oct. 1963 |
| Vernon Post | Nov. 1963 — Aug. 1972 |
| Derek Smith | Sept. 1972 — June 1986 |
| Brian A. Bowen | Sept. 1986 — present |

## Male Chorus Leaders

| | |
|---|---|
| George Darby | 1912 — 1931 |
| William Slater | 1935 — 1938 |
| William Bearchell | 1939 — 1947 |
| Richard E. Holz | 1947 — 1954 |
| Vernon Post | 1955 — 1972 |
| Derek Smith | 1972 — 1975 |
| Thomas Mack | 1975 — present |

# 1

## "Soldiers of the Cross"
### (Vernon Post)

## Bandmasters Keep, Wray, Charles Miles, Walter Duncan, William Bridgen and Edward "Trumpeter" Trumble
### 1887-1896

W hy a Staff Band? Marshal Ballington Booth, commander of The Salvation Army in the United States in 1887, knew the value of a brass band. His decision to form a "staff band" at his headquarters at 111 Reade Street in New York City was based on these pressing needs: (1) to attract more public notice of his troops' evangelistic efforts and to provide a morale boost for his recently reorganized Army,[1] (2) to provide a model of good music-making for developing bands across the nation and, as a consequence, to provide local New York City area corps with competent music leaders, and (3) to have an effective, mobile "back-up" force for major public appearances and fund-raising campaigns. For 100 years, no matter who was in command, no matter what the circumstances, these same concerns of Ballington Booth became the ongoing reasons for the New York Staff Band and Male Chorus to remain in existence. These functions have held firm over the past century as this remarkable ensemble has helped lead sinners to salvation, provided the standard of excellence in America for music and music leadership within The Salvation Army, and helped build a strong denomination through a variety of supportive roles.

1

Under the headline "What Next?" Ballington let the readers of *The War Cry* of June 25, 1887, have the following preview of this new band:

> *A large staff band has been started at our centre in New York with a sure prospect of success. All the bandsmen are saved. They are all commissioned and will wear a special white uniform helmet. Cheer up, you silent corps; with so many instrumentalists at headquarters you will soon have a boom.*[2]

Earlier that year, in a pamphlet entitled *Seventh Anniversary Songs and All About The Salvation Army* (April 1887), a defense was made for the Army's banding scheme:

> Can anything be said in favor of Colors, Bands of Music, Processions, and other sensational methods employed?
>
> *They are all explained by the first necessity of the movement, which is to ATTRACT ATTENTION. If the people are in danger of damnation of hell, and asleep in their danger, then the business of those sent to rescue them is—first, to awaken them— "to open their eyes." These and other methods attract their attention, secure a hearing for the Gospel, and thousands repent, flee to Christ from the wrath to come, and are saved. Many of the objections vanish on a little thought....*[3]

Ballington further addressed his plans to unite evangelical zeal with musical excellence in his annual report for 1887:

> *Now, thank God, the Army has discovered something more audible even than the crunch of cart wheels, more penetrating than the whistle of locomotives, in the time and melody of well-tuned voices in the salvation march—in the light, silvery calls of the cornet, in the jingle of the tambourine, and the steady pulse of the drum, wherefore we are making The Salvation Army advance a grand musical march, a melodious invasion upon the strife and discords of the world.*
>
> *To raise the standard of music from the mere ear-pleasing display of talent to a real useful end has been one of the Army's most visible motives. A sort of musical revival has taken place....*
>
> *The revival is greatly helped by the band of headquarters' staff. A day was given every week to practice. Special commissions, special uniforms, and other special encouragements were offered (to say nothing of the special blessings enjoyed in the*

*public meetings) and they began to attend as supports at the Lyceum holiness services.*

*We have had lads in the staff band, and in many of the corps' bands, who have taken a cornet in their hands for the first time and before three months could play in the band with accuracy and even with effect. So much for the power of enthusiasm and salvation as an awakener of slumbering genius.[4]*

The band's first official appearance was in Brooklyn, at the famous Lyceum, on Saturday June 18, 1887, at the close of that area's "Seventh Anniversary Gatherings":

*This was the first appearance of the Staff Brass Band, which, taking into consideration the short period it has been organized, and the very limited time at the disposal of its members for practising purposes, gave a good and creditable account of itself, each bandsman being crowned with a white helmet; said helmet being decorated with a narrow band of Army ribbon, and nickel badge in front.[5]*

Because this was Ballington's band (and it has remained identified with its commander, or later, territorial commander, ever since), he took "the boys" with him, their first out-of-town engagement being a weekend with the Marshal in Scranton, Pa., July 9-10. During the rail trip, "the Staff Band made things lively...by playing Salvation music in the cars, conductors and brakemen vying with each other in showing their appreciation of this variation of their usual hum-drum train ride."[6] By invitation of the Rev. Dr. Ellwood H. Stokes, first president of the Ocean Grove Camp Meeting Association, Ballington and the band made the first of many visits to that Jersey shore retreat August 13-14, 1887. They traveled by boat to Long Branch, N.J., and then by rail car to the Asbury Park depot, where their unusual appearance attracted a rowdy crowd.[7] The band then lined up and marched into hallowed Ocean Grove, a community built around a Methodist camp meeting grounds and auditorium.

A member of the band reported how he felt about this historic meeting and the band's service there:

*The hall was fairly well filled—not with the rough, unkempt mob this time, but with respectable upper-class visitors. "They play well" was the general remark, but we were determined in our own*

3

*hearts that before the time arrived for us to leave they should be made to say "They live well," for WE LIVE to make the world—the fashionable, dress-loving, ease-seeking world—believe in us; believing that God can empower us to LIVE what we sing and play and we talk about and profess.*[8]

The bandsmen, at this time each being a commissioned officer (clergy), was expected to be ready when Ballington called for a testimony, a solo or a story. Each young bandsman was, in the words of Ballington at a visit to Port Chester, N.Y., several weeks later, "not only a total abstainer from the use of intoxicating drink and tobacco, but a saved man, and willing at any time at the word of command, to exchange the office for a platform."[9]

The first bandmaster (B/M) we find mentioned in the October 22, 1887, *War Cry* report of the band's visit to Rockville, Conn., October 1-2: "B/M Keep and several others of the Staff Band spoke with liberty and effect."[10] The band was accompanying Major Keates, Ballington's chief-of-staff, to this manufacturing mill town. During this visit we have not only the first bandmaster identified as B/M Keep but also our first band piece recorded as "Roll on Dark Streams."[11] B/M Keep was lunged at by a drunken bystander but no permanent damage took place and the band's visit, as reported by Divisional Officer Edwin Gay, gave a real boost to the struggling comrades of Rockville's Army outpost.[12]

By December 1887, the band stood at seven strong under Band Manager Major Wray,[13] a converted minstrel and saloon-keeper. They were now veterans at backing their beloved leader in his successive campaigns. The year ended with National Staff Councils held in Brooklyn and New York City with the band, resplendent in new uniforms and new black helmets, playing a major role in the success of these celebrations.[14]

## Precursors

The Staff Band was not the first organized Salvation Army band in America. Frequently, "pick-up" bands were formed for regional rallies in the early 1880s with an incredible assortment of instruments the usual result. Colonel Joseph Pugmire insisted in an April 23, 1931, *War Cry* report that he had been part of a "staff band" at headquarters *before* the 1887 group was formed. He maintained that there were four members, including then Staff-Captain Hugh Whatmore (later Commissioner) as leader on the

4

"pocket cornet." Appropriately, the first tune "ever essayed by the Eastern Staff Band was 'If the Cross We Boldly Bear,'" as asserted by Colonel Pugmire.[15]

Whether or not that account can be considered official, it is true that organized bands were springing up. In 1883 the Kingston Silver Band (Canada) visited Syracuse, N.Y.,[16] and by December 1884, the famous East Liverpool (Ohio) Brass Band was in full swing.[17] Brass instruments began to be advertised in *The War Cry* in 1885 and bands can be confirmed as active that year in Oakland, Calif., Fall River, Mass., and Alliance, Ohio.[18] The "New York Brass Band" under Divisional Officer Wray appeared in early 1886 and so did the later-formed New York No. 1 Band under its first leader, B/M Halpin.[19]

During the various seventh anniversary demonstrations of 1887, new bands emerged in Boston, Mass., Lawrence, Mass., and Grand Rapids, Mich.[20] Nonetheless, laments began to appear early in the year about a possible loss in momentum in this new wave of brass banding.[21] The Staff Band formed by Ballington Booth in 1887 was a part of the effort to improve these fledgling forces. Recruiting from various bands which he had heard on his travels during 1888, Ballington brought such notable musicians as Edward Trumble, alias "Trumpeter" Trumble, and Walter Duncan to National Headquarters (NHQ) by November 1888.

Despite these early brass band efforts by the American Army, it could not yet be said that such bands were up to their British counterparts. A model was needed beyond the limited talents of the National Staff Band. It was provided by B/M Harry Appleby and the Household Troops Band from London, England.

## The Household Troops, Volunteer Brigade, and National Guards Bands

From March 2 through April 6, 1889, the Household Troops Band and their remarkable cornetist-bandmaster, Staff-Captain Harry Appleby, toured New England and the greater New York area. These 27 instrumentalists served as a fine example of what a disciplined ensemble could achieve:

*... one thing that perhaps made as great an impression upon the American public as anything else is the correct time kept in singing, playing and in all they do, and it speaks loudly and*

5

*impressively for the training that has been given them by their bandmaster.*[22]

This bandmaster, whose improvisational skills on the cornet "surprised and electrified audiences" during the band's grueling tour,[23] made sure his troops were also dedicated Christians. The effect was profound.

*Many recall, with keen interest, the memorable visit of the International Headquarters Household Troops Band many years ago. The accompanying spirit of revival that swept with it throughout the country was a great revelation of possibilities. As a result of the awakening and the harvest of souls gathered in it brought to us a strong incentive for bands, and quite a few throughout the country are the offspring from that memorable event in the eighties.*[24]

For the National Staff Band, 13 strong when they joined forces with Appleby's band for a farewell weekend in New York City, April 3-4, there was immediate benefit. A "Volunteer Brigade Band," modelled on the Household Troops Band, was formed a month later, under B/M Walter Duncan, to campaign in a much wider, freer way than was possible with the National Staff Band. For awhile, therefore, two bands existed at headquarters.

This new band was to be made up of single, non-officer soldiers.[25] They would maintain an intense schedule of evangelistic services throughout the eastern states, as their September 1889 tour itinerary shows.[26] The Staff Band, however, maintained its own pace-setting schedule with notable firsts: a wedding in June (really an evangelistic extravaganza or "demonstration" in which the ceremony played the central part), and the July 20-22 Old Orchard Beach Camp Meetings with Ballington Booth.

At Old Orchard Beach, Maine, the band paraded through the tourist throngs and stirred up such interest that one of the largest crowds ever (for that time) jammed into the grounds for the various meetings. The Lewiston, Maine, *Evening Journal* description of that hot Sunday afternoon program gives us a cameo portrait of the band under B/M Charles Miles:

*The Staff Band opened the exercises with a rendition of "Praise God from Whom All Blessings Flow." They play admirably together. They were dressed in neat blue uniforms with white*

6

*trimmings, and a double-knotted white cord across their breasts. Their caps resemble the fatigue caps of the government army officers, and over the visor of each were the letters "S. B. B." They were all intelligent looking men and well they might be, for they are the officials who conduct all the affairs at the Army Headquarters in New York.... Two of them edit* The War Cry, *the Salvation Army organ, another has charge of the composing room in the* War Cry *office, another is the Marshal's secretary, another the treasurer of the headquarters. Every one has responsible work to do at headquarters, and their musical genius is tested only on special occasions like this.*[27]

When the Volunteer Brigade Band joined the Staff Band for a Central District Rally in New York City in late August, Ballington knew his scheme to use bands to further the Salvation War was working. These bands joined together again in October at a great "Welcome Home" rally when Ballington returned with the touring band. Mr. Montigani of Brooklyn presented the Staff Band with a large silk parade banner which read "For God and America's Salvation."[28] One month later Ballington would warmly welcome back Colonel Richard E. Holz and a large group of officers in a major step toward final healing of the "Moore Split." Musical and spiritual revival were indeed underway.

Despite such triumphs, our heroes did not always have it their way. This banding life was a tiring one, and persecution awaited them around every parade corner. The frequency with which the Staff Band replaced its uniforms, instruments and personnel in its first decade is quickly explained in this graphic report from the hand of Staff-Captain Mantz:

*The Staff Brass Band received quite a stormy reception on the streets on the occasion of the farewell of Capt. and Mrs. Wilson, of the Men's Training Garrison, in Brooklyn. The devil and his hosts were out in full force and opened their batteries. Oh, my! what a shower! Talk about grape and cannister! Phew! it was muskmelon and tin cans, with a fair sprinkling of rocks and stones. In fact at times the air seemed full of all manner of missiles. An overripe musk-melon exploded on the cranium of a bandsman, covering his head and shoulders and scattering its slimy substance over several others. Rocks and stones rattled among the instruments, leaving their trademark. Our snare drummer's eye was put in mourning by some cowardly tough who struck him unawares. A soldier received quite a serious blow from a rock, rendering him insensible, and it was some time before he could be restored to consciousness....*[29]

Neither Ballington nor the band would be deterred! Combining the non-officer Volunteer Brigade Band with the National Staff Band in 1890 kept the ensemble strong. B/M Walter Duncan of the Volunteer Brigade Band assumed command in September and proceeded to build an effective band for Ballington's travels. So effective was it that Ballington formed another touring band, the National Guards Band, in August 1891, for the express purpose of the National Building Fund. Duncan and spiritual leader Ensign Hunter were to take the young members of the Staff Band plus recruits from the field and travel across the country, raising funds for both the new Memorial Headquarters in New York City and for the local corps they visited.

These seventeen instrumentalists, traveling lightly just like Appleby's Household Troops Band, stirred up the American Army musical world. The best Staff Band players were featured, like $E^b$ Cornetist Ed Trumble. Their preparation before tour included four hours a day of brass practice, two hours of marching, the remainder of daylight hours spent in devotion and recreation, and the evening spent in local area meetings. By the time they commenced their campaign, they were in fighting trim.[30]

During 1891-92 the National Guards Band visited 11 states (N.Y., N.J., Conn., Md., R.I., Del., Mass., Pa., Va., W.Va., and Ohio). An interim report from the April 2, 1892, *War Cry* cited 3,840 miles traveled since September, 90 cities visited, 96 souls confirmed, and many reconsecrations recorded as well as thousands of dollars raised. Their own expenses were listed at $937.34 for travel. Their schedule for October 1891 was as follows:

| | |
|---|---|
| 1-2 | — Perth Amboy, N.J. |
| 3-5 | — Plainfield, N.J. |
| 6 | — Bound Brook, N.J. |
| 7-8 | — Trenton, N.J. |
| 9-10 | — Philadelphia, Pa. |
| 12-13 | — Wilmington, Del. |
| 14-15 | — Elkton, Md. |
| 16 | — North East, Md. |
| 17-18 | — Havre de Grace, Md. |
| 19-21 | — Baltimore, Md. (3 corps) |
| 23 | — Norfolk, Va. |
| 24-25 | — Petersborough, Va. |
| 26 | — Richmond, Va. |
| 27 | — Manchester, Va. |

29     — Baltimore, Md.
30     — Anapolis, Md.
31     — Washington, D.C.

This kind of itinerary was the pattern followed from September 3, 1891, through July 1892. No wonder that B/M Duncan and "Trumpeter" Trumble were transferred to Chicago's Northwest Divisional Band in December 1891 and replaced by B/M William Bridgen and others. By March 1892 the group lay in exhaustion at the Long Branch, N.J., Rest Home for their one brief vacation of the 11-state campaign.

Colonel Evans, chief secretary at the time, praised this National Guards Band just before their break when they were supporting Ballington in Jermyn, Pa., where $500 was raised for the NHQ building and $355 for the local corps:

> *Never have I known the National Guards Band to play as well as it does now. The other night while in company with the Commander at Jermyn, I listened to music from it that I rarely heard surpassed in the Army. All it needs now is two or three more good musicians, cornetists preferred, to make it equal to any Army band going. Hurry up and apply, you that wish to join.*[31]

Armed with their own songbook produced especially for the tour, the National Guards Band proclaimed salvation and raised desperately needed money in an incredibly effective way. They were not without competition either, as a report from Fredonia, N.Y., in January 1892, relates:

> *...just imagine the National Guards Band on one corner of a street and a dog show band on the other corner. Both bands got good crowds, but we know we had the best time, for we were pointing sinners to heaven and the other was pointing sinners the way to hell.*[32]

**The Trumble Years**

August 25, 1892, was the last date of a National Guards Band engagement, when it combined with the National Staff Band in accompanying Ballington Booth to Jersey City. B/M William Bridgen had left by now for unknown reasons. By September the National Staff Band was reorganized under B/M Ed Trumble, the stalwart cornet soloist who had been associated with both the

9

National Staff Band and the National Guards Band. He faced a difficult task. While the National Guards Band had done its job well, its members were now scattered to various corps locations throughout the Eastern seaboard. Trumble's small band was still a musical rallying point. He used it to good effect in the November 21-23 Continental Congress as the nucleus of a massed band of nearly 150 bandsmen from six cities. Bands from South Manchester, Conn., Worcester, Mass., and Ansonia, Conn., helped swell that aggregation that sounded forth on the stage of New York's Carnegie Hall.[33] Featured among the reorganized Staff Band, resplendent in new uniforms, was Brother Garbutt, a recently converted drunk and former military drummer in an English Army regiment.

Ed Trumble was, in effect, the national bandmaster from 1892 to 1896. While his National Staff Band struggled during this period with severe personnel and financial problems, B/M Trumble did succeed as organizer of the music for Ballington's extravaganzas. At the congress in New York with General William Booth, October 20-27, 1894, "Staff Bandmaster" Trumble (the first use of this term) had "oversight of all the bands in the parades and public meetings."[34]

Born in Elyria, Ohio, in 1866, Trumble studied cornet as a high schooler, leaving school at age 18 to join a traveling minstrel band during the regular school year and playing solo cornet in the famed Elyria Town Band during the summer season. An encounter with Major J. J. Keppel in Elyria led to his conversion and subsequent use as a "Musical Marvel" in that part of the Army world. By 1888 Ballington had recruited him for NHQ where he held a variety of positions, including responsibility for the post office.[35]

Other than his cornet abilities, which, from all accounts, were considerable, Trumble was a limited leader. He would maintain for years that he was brought by Ballington to New York City to lead the band, yet despite his noble efforts at congress events, one of the poorest periods in the band's history is that of his official bandmastership from 1892-1896. There were some good achievements, however, including active Self-Denial and Building Fund Campaigns, a notable tour during October-November 1894, with General William Booth, and the landmark move of NHQ from 111 Reade Street to its new location on 14th Street in April 1895.

Accounts of the bandsmen of this era serve to illuminate the fascinating and sometimes whimsical events of the period. Staff

Bandsman Harry Taylor, BB♭ bass player (a circular helicon) in the 1895 band, was converted in Toronto, Ontario, at a regional Army rally. He was interviewed by a reporter for *The War Cry* on August 3, 1895. He told how his relatives had shunned him after he donned Army uniform, experimented with various brass instruments, and became a bandsman:[36]

> **Taylor:** *After visiting [his relatives], I saw an advertisement in the New York* War Cry *of bandsmen wanted, and I came to New York. Later I went into the Training Home for men, under Brigadier Miles. Leaving that, I again joined the Staff Brass Band. While on tour with them was taken sick with typhoid fever, and had a pretty tough time of it.*
>
> *After recovering I went into the field as a lieutenant. Was stationed at Troy, Cohoes, Schuylerville, and other places. At Glens Falls the Commander came along with the Staff Band, and another lieutenant was exchanged for me, and I again went along with the band boys. Made several trips with the band, and have been somewhere around New York since then. I was in the Food and Shelter Depot awhile; was also stationed at Newark No. 1 when it was a Men's Training Garrison, and for over a year have been constantly at NHQ here.*
>
> **War Cry:** *How did the old band which you used to travel with compare with the one of today?*
>
> **Taylor:** *Oh well, I don't know. The old one ought to have been the best, whether it was or not, for we were practicing all the time, several times every day, and I could play tunes I cannot now.*

The National Staff Band by 1896 had already experienced the full gamut of band activities that the present band now faces each year: congresses, welcome rallies (you name it, they welcomed it), commissionings (two a year then—and the crowd gossiped while the band played then, too), fund-raising events, festivals of music, local corps visits, appearances at large churches and camp meetings, building dedications, evangelical campaigns, marathon open-air meetings, and, particularly, parades of every variety. Within ten years Ballington's vision was paying off. Bands were established across America, his Army was strong, new buildings were springing up everywhere, and his Staff Band led the way with fighting zeal, even if they did lack, from time to time, musical acumen. They were among the best in the land, and he used them to great effect.

11

Ballington's decision to resign his command in January 1896—rather than follow the "farewell orders" given him by a stern father—nearly destroyed the Staff Band. Within weeks of his announcement, amidst the confusion and rumors, B/M Trumble resigned, too, as did some of the bandsmen, as a sign of respect and loyalty to the man they had followed so faithfully.[37] Trumble was soon appointed chief bandmaster of the new Ballington organization, the Volunteers of America, and was sent by his commander to Chicago to help rally more troops.[38]

Though a Staff Band could be mustered from the troops which had not defected, for Frederick Booth-Tucker's Carnegie Hall welcome in April, it was evident that a major disaster had not only befallen The Salvation Army in America but the Staff Band as well. Fortunately, the new commander, brother-in-law to Ballington, also recognized the value of this marvelous ensemble.

Hoping to act as if nothing had happened, Booth-Tucker soon began touring with the band in the greater New York area in an effort to rally local troops. The most skilled musicians had temporarily fled, however, and the efforts were short-lived. Despite the band's motto, "in continuous service since 1887," there ensued a brief period in the band's history when it ceased to function. A "Victory Boys Brigade" fulfilled National Staff Band functions during the summer months of 1896, and by late fall there was still only a NHQ "Officers Band" under the direction of Major Halpin.[39]

Booth-Tucker's "Plan of Campaign" for 1897, however, included specific remedies for the general plight of bands at this critical period. His call for the addition of 1,000 bandsmen to the ranks was the first official move of such magnitude in this direction by any American commander.[40] Booth-Tucker had the Trade Department secure more and less expensive instruments for his developing bands.[41] And he wisely chose Charles Anderson as the new bandmaster when he commenced the reorganization of the National Staff Band in January 1897.

# 2

# "American Melodies"
### (William Broughton)

## Bandmasters Charles Anderson, Charles Straubel, and Robert Griffith
### 1897-1912

The remarkable recovery of The Salvation Army in America after the loss of Ballington and Maud Booth was in no small part due to an equally, if differently, talented couple: Frederick Booth-Tucker and his wife Emma, the latter called the "Consul." Both were able speakers and skilled publicists for the Army's cause. Their enthusiasm for the work they faced was infectious. In spite of some desertions to the Volunteers of America, they were able to rally their troops quickly with a gift for choosing competent leadership in critical areas.[1]

For the National Staff Band, the choice of Charles Anderson for bandmaster was a happy one. His era would be marked by substantial improvement in musical standards, innovative programming, and a generally cheerful, positive approach to Christian banding. As a young man he served as an accountant for a Mr. Elsie, a Jersey City fishery director, and played cornet at Elsie Chapel, a religious institution also led by his employer. One of Anderson's duties included bailing out of jail young Army officers whose evangelical efforts were supported by Elsie. Five times Anderson visited the Jersey City Jail to release Lieutenant Alice Walden. As Douglas Anderson, his son, put it:

13

*So my father met my mother in jail. They fell in love and my mother did not want to leave the Army so Dad joined it and they were married. Dad was soon appointed to the NHQ Financial Department.*[2]

## Omnifarious Rumblings

*When you hear Thunnell's bass pom-pom-pom-pom,*
*Then you'll know that the Staff Brass Band has come,*
*To tell to sinners here salvation's glad, good news,*
*There'll be a big time in Newark to-night.*
*(To the tune: "There'll Be a Hot Time in the Old Town Tonight")*

*These words were those of Band Leader William Halpin and were used at various locations with concertina accompaniment. This particular song was quoted in one of several* War Cry *articles about the band entitled "Omnifarious Rumblings" during the 1897 season.*[3]

The National Staff Band (NSB) came to life again on Washington's Birthday, February 22, 1897, with new uniforms and under a new bandmaster, Charles Anderson. Fresh new ideas were in the air. Corps music festivals were flourishing, "traitors" like Trumble were returning to the fold, and bold new experiments were about to be attempted by this renewed band.

A festival, or concert, at the New York No. 9 (Bowery) Corps in March included humorous songs by J. J. Stimson and William Halpin, tin-whistle duets, a string band item, vocal quintet and a euphonium solo.[4] What the band lacked in musical ability it covered for with sheer showmanship and variety.

By spring, *The War Cry* could report: "Many novel innovations are introduced into the Staff Band festivals, and audiences are worked up to an exciting pitch of wonderment as to what is going to happen next."[5] In June, "Old-Battered B-Flat Cornet," the anonymous author of the "Omnifarious Rumblings" series, reported with humorous pride the mounting success of these adventures in Salvation Army music (after a visit to New York No. 4 Corps):

*The bandmaster's whistle sounded at 7:30 for march and open-air, and after falling in line, away we go down Lexington Ave. to 120th Street and the crowded Third Avenue, where an open-air ring was formed and ten minutes spent in pouring hot shot into the large crowd there assembled, and then up Third Avenue, stepping to the air of a lively march. The extreme modesty of the writer, who is a bandsman, refrains him from quoting some of the remarks of some of the spectators as we marched along; suffice it to say that they reflected great credit upon the way in which the bandmaster has brought the band up to its present efficient state. On arriving inside we found about 400 crowded into the hall, and this, too, at the admission price of 10 cents. It proved to be a very appreciative audience. The elaborate program provided by the members of the band stretched out until afer 10 p.m., although it was hurried as much as possible. The quality of the music can be judged when I inform our readers that only one individual fainted and another was seen to walk away on crutches....A good sum was cleared at this meeting [for corps building debt] and one young man knelt at the form for mercy.*

*Band sergeant: "Goodnight boys! Next engagements are band practice, Wednesday, at 4 p.m.; Thursday, at the Commander's holiness meeting, at 7:30 p.m.; Friday, practice from 4 till 9; Saturday and Sunday, at Morristown." And we separate, wondering whether or not "our boys" will recognize us even on Monday morning, if we go on at this rate long. But better "wear out than rust out."[6]*

Anderson had infused the band with a new enthusiasm for their duty. Anything was possible—even a female staff bandsman. Ensign Felicia Gircopazzi first played with the band as a guest at the Bronx Tremont Corps May 6, 1897.[7] As the famed "lady cornetist" she was frequently featured as a soloist with the band until her marriage to Staff Bandsman Harry Wright in 1900. Ensign Thompson, a vocal soloist with the band from 1898 to at least 1904, was Ensign Norma Thompson, later Mrs. Captain James Durand (he a staff bandsman also). Both women have been carried on the band's reunion rolls over the years, though official recognition can be found only under the *Disposition of Forces* band lists of 1899, where they are both listed as part of the cornet section, yet in italics so as to distinguish them from the "boys in the band."[8]

Charles Anderson's tenure as bandmaster was briefly interrupted during the spring and summer of 1898 when Charles Straubel was appointed head of a Headquarters Musical Department and staff bandmaster. Straubel succeeded in releasing the first *American Band Journal* of twelve items before he was inexplicably transferred into the Social Department in August of that year.[9] During Straubel's bandmastership General William Booth visited New York again. This time Booth's aides were armed with a 15-page pamphlet, "Regulations for Special Demonstrations Relative to the General's Visit in 1898." The item under "Miscellaneous—Bands" read:

> A decent band of say twenty instrumentalists is all that is required for an ordinary salvation or social meeting. When circumstances render it necessary to have united bands, there should be a good leader, who is held responsible for the whole. There must never be more than one good drummer, and he should be given to understand that he must beat loud enough, and with sufficient regularity to keep the congregation in good time, but not louder than is necessary for this. The drum must be kept going during every song and every chorus.[10]

Staff Band drummer and self-styled humorist J. J. Stimson soon ran afoul of the great leader when his performance was not up to this great saint's expectations. Stimson's only defense became a famous retort: "Once you've hit a drum you can't take it back."[11]

General Booth's arrival at 14th Street that year was marked by another humorous incident involving the band:

> A brass band [NSB] was stationed at the back of the lobby [120 W. 14th Street] with the mouthpieces of their instruments at their lips. A Salvation [Army] Colonel stood bareheaded outside, waiting for General Booth's carriage. Aides rushed back and forth. The great moment arrived. Word passed along the line. The band struck up immediately "Hail to the Chief"! General Booth entered the building....[12]

On another visit, October 1902, the National Staff Band was at dockside to greet the General when the Italian composer Mascagni, also on the same boat, waved vigorously to the band and large welcoming party, thinking that the demonstration was intended for him. The opera composer received a shock upon discovering that the entire proceedings, reporters and all, were actually held for eccentric fellow passenger William Booth, now a much more internationally famous celebrity than Mascagni could have imagined.[13]

## Moonlight Excursions

"A hallelujah physical and spiritual invigorator" is what Booth-Tucker labeled a Salvation Excursion (August 1897) of 1,600 Salvationists who traveled aboard the steamer *Taurus* from Pier No. 1, North River, to Long Branch, N.J., where they proceeded by rail to Asbury Park.[14] The National Staff Band played a major role in the festivities. B/M Anderson and William Halpin took up their Commander's lead and planned several "Moonlight Excursions" up the Hudson, one on board the *George Starr* on July 10, 1899, and another on the *Nassau* on August 2 of the same year. The chartered cruises were not merely diversionary in nature:

> The officers, soldiers and friends who thronged the decks of the George Starr did not strike one as being mere pleasure seekers, but rather a crowd of men and women, who, filled with the love of God, devoted one night to give praise to Him on a floating temple.
>
> Meetings were held, music was played, songs were sung and testimonies were given. Indeed, the tenor of the whole proceedings was such as the dear old Army is happily and blessedly accustomed to. Hallelujah!
>
> When the regular meeting was not in progress the comrades grouped together in small bands, and the air was made to vibrate with many of the Army's most popular choruses. Besides the singing of songs it was no uncommon sight to see sundry wearers of the Army uniform and others dealing personally with some of the ship hands, while followers of the various corps, who though not saved, could not keep away from The Salvation Army even for one night, were also bombarded about their souls.[15]

This band, with its energetic leaders Anderson and Halpin, was adaptable and flexible in its evangelical efforts. The bandsmen set the pace for other bands and they joined their commanders in further innovative programs. The year 1899, for example, in addition to band excursions, included:

> 1. Backing Emma Booth-Tucker in her Red Crusade, including a visit to New Haven, Conn., Feb. 4-5;

17

2. *Recording hymn tunes for play-back at Grand Rallies on the Graphophone Grand\* (April 22 Self-Denial Rally, part of Booth-Tucker's Holiness Meeting Series);*
3. *Developing an NHQ Orchestra, Singing Brigade, and Junior Staff Band (the latter in 1900);*
4. *Featuring band and orchestra at Madison Square Garden Christmas Day feeding of 20,000 (which became a yearly event);*
5. *Evangelizing in campaigns with noted preachers, like Samuel Logan Brengle.*

One highlight of the latter was the group's trip up the Hudson by boat to Poughkeepsie, N.Y., accompanying the inimitable Brengle in one of his "red hot" crusades. The men were "reckless for the best possible spiritual results" and supported the great holiness preacher to the limits of their endurance. By the end of that weekend, the men had "the joy of seeing more than 150 men and women kneel at the penitent form seeking grace and favor in the sight of their Lord."[16] These results, as Brengle admitted, were in no small way related to the personal efforts of the bandsmen in their dealing with the crowds that eagerly listened to the great preacher.

Anderson's men (and women!) were getting notice for their efforts; they were in demand for both musical and spiritual reasons, as *War Cry* editor Brewer pointed out:

> *We must say one word regarding the Staff Band of NHQ. For appearance, number, and excellence, it is certainly in the estimation of old timers away up in E. [Presumably meaning either "excellence" or "efficiency."] Adjutant Anderson is to be congratulated. The meetings of the band simply sweep everything. That corps is wise and far-sighted that secures its services for a night or weekend, and there is more varied and superior talent in the band than ever in its history.[17]*

Booth-Tucker agreed; his band was a fit fighting force to match the vision he had of a growing and vibrant Army.

For his 1901-1902 "Continental Campaign," Booth-Tucker

---

\**By 1894 The American Graphophone Co., under Bell-Tainter patents, was giving serious competition to Thomas Edison's products. The "10-Dollar" Graphophone, initially used for business dictation, used a vertically-cut, wax-composition cylinder. The recordings made of the band for this equipment are not extant.*

formed a "special staff brass band" of eleven players, under Anderson, but including soloists like Ed Trumble, vocalist Mrs. James Durand, and humorist J. J. Stimson. Nine-thousand miles were covered, many of them in a special train car called "Crystal."[18] The Mid-West (Chicago, St. Louis, St. Paul, Des Moines, Kansas City, etc.) and Far West (Seattle, San Francisco, Salt Lake City, Pueblo and Amity, Colo., etc.) were given special attention, and the sounds of this National Staff Band Ensemble supported Frederick and Emma Booth-Tucker in their historic whistle-stop campaign.

Back home, the other members of the National Staff Band were not idle. Major Gooding, interim bandmaster, kept them playing at a variety of locales in the New York City area and as far away as Wilmington, Del. A particularly rousing time was experienced by all the night of December 15, 1901, at the Newark No. 1 Corps as colorfully reported in bumpkin slang in a feature article entitled "Ruth Ann an' Me with the Staff Band." Here is a brief excerpt:

*Wall, we . . . went ter Newark ter see them band boys 'cause we heered sum uv thum boys whot went West with th'Commander say thare wan't goin' ter be any staff band when they wuz gone. I s'pose they thinked they wuz th'whole band. So they jist took th'good instruments and th'best music a long with thum.*

*"Law me!" sez Ruth Ann, "'ef thuther boys took all th'good music away these boys be able ter make music fur thairselves." Seems ter me it be a long site better nor whot they hed before.*[19]

The depth of the band at this period depended on employment opportunities available. For years the large Printing Department supplied many such jobs or appointments. The print shop of 1902 included the following luminaries of Staff Band fame: Brigadier Edward Parker, Corps Sergeant-Major Arthur Nason, Major Daniel Black, Captain J. J. Stimson, Staff-Captain Alfred J. Pike, and John Lock. Pressmen, compositors and clerks worked at a feverish pace, producing 3,200 copies of *The War Cry* per hour.[20] John Lock was representative of the many transformed men who worked at NHQ and played in the band. He and his brother George immigrated to America after John had a stint as a boy in the British Army band training program. His habits had not been the finest: gambling, drinking, etc. Saved at a New Year's Eve Watchnight Service, followed by an intense spiritual experience later that evening, John became a new man, able to resist the vices of his earlier life. Soon he was employed at NHQ as a porter in the press room. "During his first week on the job he was invited to sit in on a band rehearsal. From then (December 31, 1896) until New Year's Day 1931, he was a staff bandsman, being honored on that date for 35 years consecutive service."[21] These Lock brothers, whom Stimson rhymed with "mock" in his roll call song, little realized the far-reaching nature of their musical ministry when they first began to play in the National Staff Band. As they played their woodwind duet "Rain in Sunshine" on Anderson's innovative programs (George on flute, "Jack" on clarinet) in the small Army centers around the New York City area, how could they predict they'd soon be featured on the Thames Embankment bandstand in London?

**International Congress**

Preparations during the 1903-1904 season for the exciting International Congress included an intense schedule of corps visits and festivals. In the midst of it, tragedy struck. Consul Emma Booth-Tucker was killed in a train wreck on her way home from the Salvation Army farm colony in Amity, Colo. Her husband, the Commander was grief-stricken. The National Staff Band and Canadian Staff Band joined forces for the first time for the sad funeral procession, memorial service and interment. Marching up Fifth Avenue to 45th Street and Grand Central Station, the National Staff Band led the mourning crowd with Handel's "Dead March in Saul" and comforting hymns like "Abide With Me." The Canadian Staff Band headed up the second section of the largest parade New York City had seen in half a century. The bands combined at Woodlawn Cemetery.[22]

Commander Booth-Tucker put on a good face to disguise his devastated spirit during the next few months prior to the congress. Trivial decisions about what type of uniform the National Staff Band would wear (three were tried—minuteman outfits, Indian garb, and the finally chosen cowboy uniform) helped lighten matters. The band was practicing twice a week, once on the Army's time and once on their own, the latter on a weeknight from 7 to 9:30, 15 cents being supplied for supper money.[23] Prior to the June 14 departure, a June 12-13 campaign was planned for New York City in which all the special groups traveling to the congress could have a trial run. On Monday night, June 13, in Carnegie Hall the Commander presented his famed "The Landless Man to the Manless Land" speech and the following congress specials were featured:

— *The Colored Songsters: "You Fashionable People with Your Pomp and Pride"*
— *Chinese soloist Scheck of the San Francisco Converted Chinese: "Hold the Fort, for I Am Coming" (sung in Chinese)*
— *National Staff Band: Offertory (not identified)*
— *The Yankee Choir: "The Salvation Army Trinity"*
— *Colonel Holz and The Kentucky Mountaineers: Sacred Song to the tune "My Old Kentucky Home"*

The crowd encored every item; enthusiasm was at a fevered pitch. The next day, after a grand parade to the Cunard Dock, the National Staff Band played "Home Sweet Home" from the upper deck as the *S.S. Carpathia* with 400 congress delegates aboard glided slowly from the pier.[24]

The American delegation had an elaborate schedule of practices, Bible studies and public programs to be followed while on the *Carpathia*. The program for Tuesday, June 21, was:

| | |
|---|---|
| 7:45-8:45 | — Brass Band [NSB] in front of Smoke Room |
| 10:30-11:15 | — Bible reading and prayers in the saloon conducted by the Commander |
| 11:30-12:30 | — Yankee Choir in front of Smoke Room |
| 12:00-1:00 | — Brass Band in front of Library |
| 2:15-3:30 | — School of Prophets in front of Smoke Room; Subject—Books worth reading; Leader—Lt.-Colonel Brengle |
| 3:00-4:00 | — Colored Songsters in the saloon |
| 3:30-5:00 | — Brass band in front of Smoke Room |
| 8:15 | — Salvation concert in the saloon in aid of Seamen's Homes. Collection will be taken.[25] |

By the time the ten-day voyage ended at Liverpool, the band was playing very well indeed. Arriving by train in London's Euston Station, they were greeted by the International Staff Band! During the opening meeting of the congress, the National Staff Band marched in the 400-strong American delegation, playing a "national air," a feature of their congress repertoire. A brass band of 500 British bandsmen greeted each delegation with robust enthusiasm. The New Yorkers thought they had arrived in band heaven!

At the Thursday night Congress Music Festival, the National Staff Band joined these other bands: International Staff, French Staff, Canadian Staff, and a Norwegian band. An American *War Cry* reporter was dazzled by the unsurpassed execution and technique of the United Congress Band from the British Territory as well as the superb playing of the International Staff Band in such novelties as "Memories of Childhood." He let his American pride show through as he wrote: "The National Staff Band of New York has a turn, and with its quick, alert music brings the house down. B/M Anderson is to be congratulated."[26]

The National Staff Band was popular at the congress. By request of the London County Council the band was invited to play on the Thames Embankment. "American airs were rendered to the delight of thousands, who applauded heartily," said the [American] *War Cry* report. Bandsman John Allan was the hero of the day. His cornet solos, along with John Lock's clarinet solos, were highly acclaimed. The crowd was estimated to be the largest by far to date.[27]

On another outdoor program, B/M Anderson reported, "The crowds were so great that the militia had to be called forth; so great were the crowds in certain neighborhoods that people could not force a passage into their homes."[28] This was nothing compared to the estimated 70,000 that thronged into the massive Crystal Palace on the final day of the congress. At the 2:30 p.m. Brass Band Festival in the Palace Transept, 50 bands played under the direction of Commissioner Carleton. Eleven items were featured, including a solo spot by the National Staff Band. On reflection, many years later, B/M Anderson considered this triumph of Salvationism as being notable for the outstanding music and musical fellowship that everyone enjoyed. "On returning to the homeland and to our various duties, each delegate felt that truly he had tasted a bit of heaven on earth."[29]

Renewed by the congress, Booth-Tucker launched a "Tent Evangel" campaign under a large canvas tent at 57th and Broadway, New York City, using the Staff Band to draw large crowds. His use of popular songs like "Blue Bells," "Good Old Summer Time," "Sweet Bye and Bye," and "Down Where the Wurzburger Flows" (with new texts!) further endeared him to the public.[30] It was Booth-Tucker's last major campaign with the band, however. In December the National Staff Band welcomed their new leader, Commander Evangeline "Eva" Cory Booth, with a novelty selection that combined "The Maple Leaf Forever" (for her previous appointment in Canada) and "Yankee Doodle" (for her new command).[31] This commander would use "my boys," as she called her band, with a skill and effectiveness that would become legendary.

## Eva's Spectaculars

Evangeline Booth launched a "Siege" Spiritual Campaign in the winter of 1905 that concluded in a 25th Anniversary Congress, March 25-28. American audiences caught their first "production" item by this multi-talented woman, entitled "The Shepherd," in which the Commander, dressed in shepherd's garb, carried a small lamb and strode across the stage with a large shepherd's crook in hand. The Staff Band provided appropriate background music, brass and vocal, with special emphasis on Eva's opening processional with eight little shepherds as a supporting cast.[32]

The performance was spellbinding, but Eva was still not content. Somewhat of a perfectionist, she continually improved these spectacles. For a series of Sunday nights in Carnegie Hall, early in 1906, she reoutfitted the Staff Band in "crimson, black-slashed suits."[33] The band was reorganized for further efficiency, including the addition of Deputy B/M Robert Griffith, brother of her aide-de-camp, Richard Griffith.[34] By the May 1906 congress in the New York Hippodrome, Evangeline Booth's "Shepherd" and "Rags" presentations appeared on the same program along with her "Red Knights" Choir. The virtuoso efforts of cornetist John Allan, now internationally famous, were used as the finale. The following outline from the Congress Spectacular can serve as a good sample of these E. C. B. productions and show how the National Staff Band was used in these meetings:

**May 1906 Congress Spectacular in New York Hippodrome[35]**

The band [NSB] will play from 7:30-8:00 o'clock
1. Opening song "Rescue the Perishing"
2. Prayer by Colonel French
3. Introductory remarks, Commissioner Kilbey
4. The band will play
5. Entry of 50 slum officers
   The Commander Appears in Slummer's Costume
   Song
   The Commander's Address
   Song
6. "Love"—The Building of a Living Cross [By red and white-robed choir]
7. The choir— "Diadem"
8. Collection
9. Band selection
10. Choir— "When Mothers of Salem"

11. Dedication—Commander Booth
12. Marching in of children and shepherd
    Song— "Savior, Like a Shepherd Lead Us"
13. Cornet solo—Cadet Allan

Evangeline was to use the band for the next 30 years in similar ventures, with more and more sophisticated effects. Her efforts met with acclaim, growing in volume through the years as she and her musicians inspired the hearts and imaginations of a new generation. Wherever she went, from her Cherry Street Slum Settlement to the stage of Princeton University, and whenever she could (and when the cost was not prohibitive) she brought "my boys" with her.

**America's Best**

Major Charles Anderson's appointment to the position of the Commander's auditor and statistical secretary for the Social Department (previously he had been cashier in the Finance Department) brought demands that made Robert Griffith's bandmastership a logical step. The only other non-officer staff bandmaster (besides former Staff Bandmaster Derek Smith), Griffith held a job in the 13th Street print shop. He and his brother were competent musicians of the Canadian tradition. While the band made no large leaps forward under his baton it did experience some band "firsts" and triumphs: (1) the beginning of a prison visitation ministry, (2) the continued imaginative programming previously shown in such ventures as their POPS series, and (3) a successful tour of New York State and Toronto, Canada.

In December 1910, the band played in the lower corridor of the main block of the "Tombs," the City Prison of New York City, launching a marvelous phase of the band's service which has continued to this day. During the program, items like "Southern Melodies" and the finale "Auld Lang Syne" were heartily applauded. The usual crowd reactions included catcalls, a cockcrow, "Three Cheers for the Army," even a "Fire a Volley" called out, no doubt, from someone who had at one time attended the Army—"alas! without much to show for it."[36] The program became an annual event, and soon many prison wardens welcomed the band. The Staff Band became the first band or musical unit of this type ever allowed at Sing Sing Prison, Ossining, N.Y., when it first appeared there December 28, 1912.

The weekly Tuesday night "Popular" or POPS programs instituted by the band in November 1909, were held at the New York No. 1 Corps hall. During the next months and years all kinds of speakers and topics were explored. Here are a few of them:

1. Chalk Talk on "Nature" by "outside friend of the band" (November 1909)
2. Guest Speaker Rev. Dr. Smith (United Churches of New York City) and film by E. J. Parker, including shots of William Booth and National Staff Band in Washington, D.C. (November 1909)
3. Talk by Dr. Rankin, "How to Avoid Tuberculosis" (January 1910).

The meetings were preceded by an open-air meeting, with many "street people" brought into the meetings as a result.[37]

Further exploits of Griffith's band included Water-Wagon Parades and Ex-Boozer Demonstrations as Evangeline joined forces with the pro-Prohibition forces. The highlight of his bandmastership, however, was the band's 1909 tour. The itinerary of that 17-day trip, mostly to New York communities, follows:

| Aug. | 21-22: | Utica |
|------|--------|-------|
|      | 23:    | Rome |
|      | 24:    | Auburn/Seneca Falls |
|      | 25:    | Geneva/Canandaigua/Rochester |
|      | 26-27: | Toronto, Canada |
|      | 28-29: | Niagara Falls |
|      | 30:    | Buffalo |
|      | 31:    | Dunkirk/Johnstown |
| Sept. | 1:    | Olean/Wellsville |
|      | 2:     | Hornell/Corning |
|      | 3:     | Elmira |
|      | 4:     | Oswego |
|      | 5:     | Binghamton |
|      | 6:     | Port Jervis/Middletown |

In Toronto the bandsmen were greeted by Mayor Oliver, renewed fellowship with the Canadian Staff Band, and were treated like conquering heroes. The entire trip was as exhilarating as it was exhausting, with Griffith sick at the conclusion and Frank Fowler, featured as bass (voice) and tuba soloist, without a voice. Staff-

Captain Norris, *War Cry* reporter for the trip, gave this statistical review two-thirds of the way through the tour:[38]

| | |
|---|---|
| Miles traveled: | 878 |
| Open-Airs/Marches: | 33 |
| Indoor Meetings: | 32 |
| Estimated Attendance: | 19,350 |
| Souls: | 32 |

A summation or overview of the Anderson/Griffith Band was given by Commissioner Alexander M. Nicol in the May 1908 *Bandsman and Songster* (later reprinted in the American *War Cry* of June 13, 1908, p. 13). Nicol, visiting this country from Britain, gives what seems to be an unbiased appraisal of the band in Washington, D.C., during William Booth's 1907 tour of America. His evaluation of this young band, then entering its second generation, is as revealing as it is lengthy:

> The American Staff Band is essentially American. But some-one asks, What is that? Well, it is difficult to define—impossible to describe adequately unless one has studied the American in his own ample home.
> My first close acquaintance with the staff bandsmen was in Washington.... It was on the anniversary of the Consul's death, a beautiful Autumn day. I had seen them on parade—they don't use the word march on the other side—in the afternoon, from the balcony of a hotel. At the head of the band waved two huge banners—one the Blood-and-Fire, the other the glittering star-spangled emblem of American freedom and union.
> The uniform of "the boys" —an American term employed to describe the concern in its corporate capacity—is also Amer-ican. The Boys wore a well-made tight-fitting uniform, with panel-shaped epaulets. As they marched along, playing one of our popular airs, I observed that they had caught the art of making the very most of their numbers. They spread themsleves out, two yards apart in the rows and three yards between the lines. It is mightily imposing. In this over-crowded part of the world room is at a premium, and our streets are like alleys to the broad, boulevard thoroughfares in this great commonwealth. The Gen-eral studied them from the same window, and remarked, "The music of the Army is, or will be, everywhere!"
> In the evening I saw and heard the band at closer quarters in one of the most awkwardly-shaped, low-roofed halls I've visited in America since I was stewed in a Pittsburgh old store twelve years

*ago. It was about the worst place in the world for a musical festival. But these American boys were evidently as much at home in it as if they had been in the New York Carnegie Hall. An American is a dabster at adapting himself. It is in the blood, and you see the trait among commercial people. If they fail in business they either blow out their brains, or start afresh with a light, hopeful heart.*

## THE LEADER

*Bandmaster R. Griffith is the leader of the American Staff Band, a Salvationist who first sniffed the smoke of salvation warfare in Canada. Below average height, he slightly resembles the South Tottenham Bandmaster. His style is after Brigadier Grinsted, and, therefore, exact, unflurried, and grippy. He has charge of the engravers' section at the National Headquarters and is respected for his love of honor and uprightness. The members of the band are made up of various representatives of Headquarters life—just as those of the International Staff Band are.*

*The points of similarity between the London and New York Bands are few. It plays the same instruments and uses the same music, but there the similarity ends. New York has a distinctiveness of its own. It is behind in experience, technical knowledge, and general musical ability. It could not well be otherwise, though one or two instruments could supply even the International Headquarters with a few pointers.*

*But if the American Staff Bandsmen are weak in musical efficiency, they have more life, individuality and variety than those of the parent band. They waste no time; they are always ready. They have a free platform manner—not so conventional, you know. Their individual efforts in the program, such as solos, recitations, and dialogues, are all marked by a vim and quickness which are conspicuous by their absence in most of the British bands.*

## HARD WORKERS

*Their salvationism is also all right. There are no harder workers anywhere, though in this respect they but reflect the spirit of the nation. Americans not only work, but know how to work. Then they go for souls with glorious peremptoriness. "You just have to get right with God, friends, and right here and now. You will be left behind if you don't. You know it ain't no good fighting God."*

*But the Staff Band of New York is not perfect, and the younger portion of it is just like our own. It had to journey to Baltimore, if I recollect rightly, next day at a certain hour. The tickets were procured beforehand, and, naturally in the hands of one man. But two or three did not turn up—they slept in, and, one had mislaid his instrument. I mention the incident lest the above should suggest to some of our readers' minds here that human nature is not quite the same under the American flag.[39]*

# 3

## "Memories"
(John Allan)

## Bandmaster George Darby
## 1912-1931

George Darby was a self-taught, gifted musician from Cannock (Midlands), England. Immigrating to the United States just after the turn of the century, he first located in Fall River, Mass., soon becoming the bandmaster in the corps there. Called into officership from this post, he was soon recognized by Evangeline Booth as an able leader and she placed him in charge of the choirs at her "Living Tableau" demonstration at Carnegie Hall, November 1911. When Robert Griffith resigned as bandmaster in March 1912, Darby, as acting deputy-bandmaster, asserted his rights to the leadership of the band.[1]

For nearly two decades, Darby developed an increasingly proficient and sophisticated musical organization. His years of service are still unsurpassed. Among the most outstanding of his achievements would be the development of the Male Chorus into a consistently fine ensemble, the reorganization of the band board (making it, for the first time, truly efficient), the utilization of modern techniques of musical communication, including radio and recordings, and the insistence on high-quality musical repertoire and festival performances that would truly set the standard for other bands. (Darby's unique approach to the band's instrumentation and repertoire is dealt with at length in chapters 10 and 12, respectively.)

Above all, Darby had a vision for the finest sacred music that, if he did not always achieve it in reality, he constantly held up before his bandsmen as a goal. As a child I met the then Colonel Darby in Asbury Park, and I remember the respect and awe people had for this great man.

He summed up his philosophy of Army banding in an article published early in his career as staff bandmaster:

*Far more than any other religious body of people can it be said of The Salvation Army that we have a musical and singing religion. It was this that attracted me in my very early boyhood. I firmly believe that a great measure of the success of The Salvation Army has been brought about by its music.*

*Many Salvation Army bandsmen approach their music in the wrong spirit; they lack the deep reverence and worshipful attitude that is absolutely necessary. To some it is purely a selfish pleasure, and to others an opportunity to show off their ability.*

*Any success that has come to me personally I credit to the fact that as a young boy I recognized the sacredness of my calling. To me my music has always been just as much a service for Christ as any other part of a Salvation Army meeting. So deep was this feeling impressed upon my heart that I never once took my instrument to practice, or began my studies, without first closeting myself with God, seeking His assistance and guidance. This, with plenty of hard work, has made me what I am today, for I have never spent one cent in musical tuition, or ever had a teacher.*

*If we can get bandsmen to realize the sacredness of their calling we shall not have the careless playing, inattention and other evils that rob us of our power and usefulness. Can you imagine anyone giving his testimony or appealing to sinners in the half-hearted way that some bandsmen perform their duties?*

*The cause of Christ demands, and should have, the best. There was a time in our early experience when a few faithful comrades, with a drum and few old brass instruments did able service for the Master, although their musical efforts were far from being proficient, but what they lacked musically was more than equaled spiritually by their deep sincerity.*

*While I have the deepest reverence for the glorious old bass drum and tambourine, yet I feel the time has come when these are insufficient to attract all classes of people to hear the Gospel. Every organization that does not make progress soon begins to decline, and I feel that The Salvation Army has been a recognized organization long enough to show at least some degree of musical efficiency; in fact, the public are within their right in expecting this from us after forty years of continued effort along these lines.*[2]

## England, Again!

As an aggressive member of the band board, Darby argued for "Home Rule" for the band to allow it greater flexibility in scheduling and financial matters.[3] Soon two rehearsals per week were allowed, Tuesdays and Thursdays at noon, as Darby had already begun leading the Male Chorus during one of these by early 1912. The band's "first annual concert" was held on June 5, 1912, under its new leader who had organized the event by getting the support of bandmasters from Brooklyn No. 1, No. 7, and No. 9, New York No. 4, and Newark No. 1 Corps.[4]

The concert featured solos by Samson Hodges (trombone), John Allan (cornet), and Frank Fowler (bass voice); a "vanity" march entitled "Our General"; and, the hit of the night, Darby's Male Chorus feature "Bible Pictures."[5] These soloists, the Male Chorus and Darby's inventive program arrangements would be standout features of the band that traveled to the 1914 International Congress.

The band donned cowboy hats again for this congress but did not wear the full outfit they had in 1904. Saxophones, French horns, and a contrabass trombone were among the unique array of instruments they took aboard the *S.S. Olympic.* Fellow passenger Colonel Theodore Roosevelt thoroughly enjoyed posing with the band and full delegation for photos, on which some staff bandsmen made a profit.[6] Other bands on board included the Flint, Mich., Citadel Band, Chicago Territorial Staff Band, and Worcester, Mass., Band. The daily schedule was only slightly different from ten years before:[7]

7:30 Breakfast
8:45 Band Practice
10:15 Morning Prayers
10:45 Colored Songsters Practice
12:00 Lunch
2:00 Band Practice
3:00 Singing Practice (Male Chorus)
5:30 Dinner
7:00 United Band Practice
8:15 Evening Service

31

The International Staff Band again greeted the delegation as it arrived, this time at Waterloo Station, with "The Star-Spangled Banner." The NSB and Colored Songsters accompanied the chief secretary to a pre-congress weekend at Wood Green Corps where:

> ...The band could scarcely crowd into or out of the Citadel, so great was the crush at all times outside and marching was almost impossible. Never did our American crowds give the band such tumultuous and hearty applause at every occasion as did these Londoners. The Londoners are as far from being flatterers as is possible, so that we may be certain the applause was earnest and real.[8]

The Colored Songsters featured the music of Boston Salvationist Thomas Ferguson, whose "You Must Go Home by the Way of the Cross" would become a standard Staff Band Male Chorus feature.

Throughout the congress, reports on the singing of the National Staff Band Male Chorus stand out. To the amazement of British bandsmen, for example, the full band sang in four-part harmony, without accompaniment, at the Abney Park Cemetery where William and Catherine Booth were buried. Many honors came the band's way, including an Embankment concert (Temple Gardens, Victoria Embankment) and an appearance in the courtyard of Buckingham Palace for King George VI and Queen Mary (confirmed in *Jacobs Band Monthly,* March 1923).

At the Crystal Palace, five staff bands (International, Swedish, German, Chicago, and New York) united for a program in the Grand Transept, the only sad notes on this occasion being those unplayed by the Canadian Staff Band, the majority of whose membership had perished in the sinking of the *S.S. Empress of Ireland* while en route to the congress. John Allan, lauded as a superb soloist, experienced a personal tragedy as well when his father, also a congress delegate, passed away while they were in England.[9]

On the final weekend of the congress, the National Staff Band supported their Commander at meetings in the famous Congress Hall. A musicale was presented Saturday, June 27, to 2,000 and by some miracle 3,000 were squeezed into the hall on Sunday, with the addition of the Congress Hall Band in the evening service. In these meetings, Evangeline, "pleading with tears," led marathon prayer meetings while the Male Chorus provided items like

"Prepare Me to Stand Before Thy Throne." The official record of souls for June 28 stood at 180.[10]

Upon return to America, the band—though seriously in debt because of the congress—kept stride with the pace set by their energetic bandmaster. In 1915 they established a Friday noon concert series at Memorial Hall for working people in the 14th Street area, inviting them in to enjoy their sack lunches with some Salvation sounds. Central Province (New York area) Bandsmen's Councils were held in June of the same year with 250 brass participants. Young B/M Stanley Sheppard was leading the New York No. 1 Band and Ensign John Allan led a Life-Saving Scouts Band. The pattern of staff bandsmen supplying leadership in local bands was definitely established.[11]

Billy Sunday, the noted American evangelist, asked for and obtained the band's involvement in his September 1915 crusade in Paterson, N.J. This involved a Sunday school parade with 40 bands (the NSB "indisputedly the best musical organization in the parade") and open-air meetings that attracted 20,000 people.[12]

The annual concert of 1916 raised $2,250 in one program (an astronomical sum for those days) and that was enough to eliminate any congress debt. At this concert the ensemble was called "The National Staff Band and Male Chorus" for the first time, in recognition of the growing importance of the group's vocal program.[13]

Advertised as a band of "Sousa's class" during their 1917 spring tour of New York State, the band was in beautiful form. Solos by Hodges, Allan, Cooke, Arkett, Fowler, and Sheppard were in great demand. William Palmer's recitations were also being encored. In the Annual Report of 1917 to the Chief of the Staff at International Headquarters, a statistical summary of the tour was used as an example of the band's efficiency:

*Among the feats of the year, accomplished by the National Staff Band, was the special tour to Ogdensburg in connection with the dedication.... The trip took six days, and in this time they traveled over 900 miles, conducted 32 meetings, played 216 instrumental selections, and took, in many various other ways, part in the meetings, such as singing solos, praying, etc.*

*Taking this on an average, it would mean that they traveled 150 miles daily, held 5⅓ meetings and played 36 selections every day. This does not include the splendid work of the Male Chorus. The income from this trip was $2,000.[14]*

33

In June, the band was declining engagements frequently because they were so busy. However, the United States' entry into World War I changed all. By December 1917, this large effective musical troupe was "reduced by recent enlistments to famine proportions."[15]

## The War Years

There is nothing like a band to help fan the fires of patriotic spirit within an American. The record of the National Staff Band during World War I, and the years directly following the war stands among the finest of any American band. In May 1917, Evangeline Booth and the band were already being featured at patriotic rallies.[16] Despite personnel setbacks, Darby sought out band engagements of this sort, and in March 1918, the Liberty Loan Committee of New York City, perhaps the largest in the country, asked the NSB to be present for the launching of its fund drive at midnight, April 5, in Times Square.[17] Within the next few weeks the band was in constant use at noontime and evenings for Liberty Loan work.

Since Evangeline Booth needed her own funds for the Army's war work in France, a May 5, 1918, Hippodrome fund-raiser for the Army combined the National Staff Band with Constance Balfour, noted British soprano.[18] New York City's July 4th parade that year featured an amalgamated band under Darby, that included the NSB and bandsmen from local Swedish corps under the young Erik Leidzen.[19] To help fulfill Salvation Army engagements that the larger group could not oblige, a special brass quartet was formed, called the Naval and Military League Quartet, using Sheppard, Fowler, Griffith and Campbell.[20]

When the Armistice was announced November 11, 1918, Evangeline Booth led a spontaneous procession, with the National Staff Band, from 14th Street to the New York Public Library steps, for a service of thanksgiving.[21] The band was chosen by the mayor of New York for the city-wide Thanksgiving Day celebration in Madison Square Garden several weeks later.[22]

For the next two years, the reorganized band—its ranks swollen again by returning doughboys—would be called on for many patriotic and war-related fund-raising events.[23] Here are a few of them:

1919: March—Eastview, N.Y., Soldiers Hospital Program; Welcome Home Parade for President Wilson and War

34

Heroes in Washington, D.C. (Also programs in New-port News, Va., at hospitals, Red Shield Club, and on the battleship *West Virginia*).

April—Victory (Liberty) Loan Rallies at Public Library, City Hall, Sub-Treasury steps at Wall Street, "Liberty Altar" Madison Square Garden, Camp Merritt, N.J., and on the battleship *Wyoming*.

September—Camp Dix programs; Pershing Parade in Washington, D.C. with band given special bandstand on Pennsylvania Avenue.

1920: November—Band featured prominently in New York City Armistice Day Parade.

While things seemed to be returning to normal, Chaplain John Allan, home from meritorious service on General Pershing's staff, stated in an interview that the war had affected his perspective on things: "I am afraid my playing days are over—there are more important things than cornet-playing to be done."[24] Music, however, was something John Allan soon recognized to be a vital part of the revived Army he envisioned after the disillusionment of war. He was soon back in the band, joining them for soul-stirring music at the Eastern Congress, October 15-19, 1919, and he would soon start the first summer music camp for developing young bandsmen.

Captain John Horgan's article, "Eastern Territorial Staff Band Takes Charge of a Corps for a Week," from the April 1921 *Local Officers' Counselor* perceptively reported on the renewed zeal with which post-war bandsmen and their indefatigable Darby approached their banding:[25]

*For many years the National Staff Band, as it was formerly called—now the Territorial Staff Band—at National Headquarters in New York City has played and sung at every event of national importance in The Salvation Army in the Eastern Territory. Enjoying a nation-wide reputation not only among Salvationists but also in the outside musical world for artistic excellence in execution that puts it on a par with many of the high-class secular bands, this splendid body of consecrated players has always been an important factor in the making for the success of many meetings and the medium through which numberless hearts have been blessed and turned to God. Its splendid choral singing has* become equally famous as its fine playing. For years at big meetings, like the Boozers' Day meetings, when souls come forward in hundreds, or at the dedication of a new corps building in a small town, or some other event where they come by the twos or threes, the playing and singing of the band has been a feature and the attraction that drew many to the meetings.

But right here its usefulness seems to have stopped. Outside of the fishing and personal work of some of the members at some meetings, its functions seemed to be only the musical end of the program and the supporting of various leaders with its musicales and orchestral work during the meeting. And loyally and faithfully it has done its part and rejoiced with all at the seeing of many souls saved, but never during all these years has the Staff Band, as an organization, conducted a spiritual campaign it could call strictly its own affair.

There have been, and are still, some of the most spiritual officers on National Headquarters, who are members of the band who have a passion for souls for God, and so, when it was proposed recently that the band run its own spiritual campaign there was rejoicing not only among these, but in the heart of every member of the band. And as a result of the "old-fashioned revival," as they choose to call it, and which has recently finished at New York No. 5 Corps, 55 seekers have sought God for pardon, for the healing of thier back-sliding, and for the blessing of a clean heart. And this is only a small part of the blessings that have resulted, for hundreds who have stood around the spirited open-airs have had their souls blessed by the great singing, playing and testimonies of this fine body of men. The bandsmen themselves were blessed and their hearts filled with joy over the splendid success of the campaign.

It was a bandsmen's affair all the way through. A program and plan had been arranged by Adjutant Darby, the bandmaster, in which every member of the band had a part to take during the six days' meetings.[26]


## Motorcade 1: Old Orchard or Bust

Later that summer the band formed a special motorcade of five touring cars and a truck for an intense campaign to and from the Old Orchard Beach Camp Meetings:[27]

*The Eastern Territorial Staff Band, under Bandmaster Darby, motored no less than 400 miles to the camp at Old Orchard Beach, Maine, to lend a hand to Colonel McIntyre and take part in the great camp.*

*The editor-in-chief, Lt.-Colonel Sandall, accompanied the band and contributed several pages of racy notes to* The War Cry *concerning the same, accompanied by many snap shots.*

*All the way from New York to Old Orchard Beach the band left a trail of salvation music, song and testimony. Under the high-pressure leadership of Colonel McIntyre, the two and a half days occupied by the journey were packed full of engagements. The 12 programs that were given en route were all lengthy, the average duration being one hour, says Colonel Sandall, who continues: "When we say that the time available for the road, out of the 52 hours spent on the way, was not more than 20, while the distance covered was over 400 miles, those who know anything at all about such traveling will at once appreciate the good leadership, close attention to schedule and the hearty co-operation on the part of Adjutant Darby and his men that was exhibited.*

*A good deal of the success of the journey, from the standpoint of timekeeping, was due to the very kind attention given to the fleet by the police authorities. New York set the pace in this respect by providing an escort which took us up Fifth Avenue and out of the city at a rattling pace, while the traffic was held up for us to pass, the right-of-way thus granted through the entanglements of the city streets being worth an hour or more's start. And then, as we went along, city after city, hearing of New York's example, vied one with the other in providing like facilities within their boundaries.*

*The cities visited en route were: South Norwalk (first stop), Allingtown Hospital (near New Haven), New Haven, New London, Providence, Pawtucket, Fall River, New Bedford, Boston, Lynn, Salem, Beverly and Portsmouth, then on to Old Orchard.*

*All reached the camp ground in good trim and ready for immediate participation in the opening of the campaign, which in its entirety included the reaching of at least 175,000 persons, the giving of 52 musical festivals, and traveling something like a thousand miles through five states.*[28]

While in Maine the band also played in Portland and Bath. Their route home (the entire trip, in fact) was piloted by CSM Fred Foster of Cambridge Citadel, Mass., and included stops at Nashua, Rochester, Manchester and Dover, N.H.; and Putnam, South Manchester and Hartford, Conn. The old bands of the 1890s had nothing on the stamina of these comrades!

### Radio and Recordings: Into the Modern Age

During its May 20-22, 1922, Western Pennsylvania trip, the band was first heard over radio from the Emory Methodist

Episcopal Church in the 11:00 a.m. Sunday service and later that evening from the Pittsburgh Theatre.[29] John Allan, along with other New York Salvationists, was involved in short religious service broadcasts from WJZ in Newark by June 1922.[30] At Poughkeepsie, N.Y., that autumn the band was heard twice on the air waves.[31] Bands from Rochester, N.Y.; Toledo, Ohio; and Troy, N.Y., also had notable radio premieres during the summer of 1922.[32] Army banding in America had entered the electronic age.

The Aeolian Company of New York City approached B/M Darby in the fall of 1922 to produce a series of recordings on their Vocalion Records series. The first 12" double-sided disc was advertised in the December 30 issue of the Eastern Territorial *War Cry*. On side one it included three hymn tunes, and, on side two, a march medley with trumpet fanfare remarkably prophetic in its similarity to the ubiquitous Staff Band march "Golden Jubilee" of several decades later.[33]

On-location broadcasts were quite novel in 1923. The Staff Band was heard in two programs sponsored by different department stores in Philadelphia during a congress there in January. One was at Wanamaker's Department Store in the organ loft, the other at WFI-Radio (Philadelphia), paid for by Strawbridge Clothier.[34] The February 16 Annual Festival at Memorial Hall, 14th Street, was broadcast live on WOR (Newark) with resulting positive reports from listeners as far removed as Ohio, Kansas, Wisconsin, and Ontario. The band may even have played a part in establishing a tradition, as it signed off the air with "The Star-Spangled Banner."[35]

In March the band was recording a second album for Vocalion; the first release had proven so popular that 4,000 copies were sold in the first week of sales. The new disc contained more daring fare: John Allan in his own cornet solo, Air Varie "Memories," and "Gems from Haydn" *(GS 854)*.Modern listeners can verify the technical assurance and musical artistry of this famed cornetist. The unique aspects of Darby's band, including woodwinds and Von Calio's melody percussion are unmistakably present.

Soon radio and recording requests were commonplace, with requests from stations WEAF, WJZ, and WOR in the month of May alone. Regularly established programming would not commence, however, till the famed CBS series of the 1930s. The next officially-produced 78 rpm recording would have to wait until the days of B/M George Granger. One final pioneering broadcast venture should be mentioned. During a Salvation Army congress in

Washington, D.C., in November 1923, the band was asked by Postmaster-General Harry New to play in the court of the U.S. Post Office Building. As a result their Saturday night festival was broadcast on WCAP of the Chesapeake and Potomac Telephone Co.[36] Band compositions like George Marshall's "Olivet and Calvary," and Male Chorus features like "Jesus the Name High Over All," sounded forth from the nation's capital to homes across the country.

## Rags and Romance

The band of the 1920s was kept very busy, as a quick glance of these years in Appendix A will confirm. Traveling with Commissioner Thomas Estill, or Chief Secretary Colonel Richard Holz, the band or its ensembles crisscrossed the Eastern Territory several times. They visited deeper into the South as well, including two exciting trips with Holz during 1924. Evangeline Booth had not forgotten "her band" either. She took part of the Staff Band and Male Chorus with her for a special lecture at Princeton University in 1923. By 1925 she had revised several of her extravaganzas, complete with new cue cards, to help the band strategically place incidental music. Lyell Rader later devised an electronic signal board that she could manipulate from the podium, communicating discreetly with her bandmaster, pianist, and organist.[37]

In addition to "Rags," which she brought out in revised form in the spring of 1925, Evangeline Booth used the band in "Christ of the Doorstep" and "The World's Greatest Romance." We can still listen to her "Romance" lecture as preserved on a remastered recording produced by the Eastern Territory, with Male Chorus background and all, although it seems a sample of Evangeline beyond her prime. Background music was not the band's only function in these affairs. After the usual crowd warm-up (prefestival), special staff bandsmen would be singled out as features. At a Philadelphia performance of "Doorstep" the testimony of "Jack" Lock was notably effective.[38] Copying her much earlier use of John Allan as cornet soloist, Evangeline would feature "Red" Sheppard in the cornet solo version of her own song "O Teach Me to Love Thee" at the conclusion of the drama.[39] The Male Chorus may have been indispensable, however, because at a Washington, D.C., "Rags" presentation (1927), even though Evangeline had the U.S. Marine Corps Band as the duty band, she still featured the Male Chorus.[40]

In summertime the Commander would vacation at Lake George, N.Y., many times inviting soldiers and officers to join her for much-needed rest. Yet even then she would sometimes work with the band! In 1928 she brought the band up to Lake George via boat for a series of meetings at Bolton Landing. While Eva recovered from the weekend, the band continued its tour in Eastern New York the next Monday. That day they visited Comstock Prison, with some of the men grumbling about the tedium of the road. Deputy Bandmaster Sheppard cheered the group up with a story about the band's ministry that he had just received while with the Commander at Ballston Spa, N.Y. It seems a well-dressed man had come up to Sheppard that Saturday and asked if he recognized him. Sheppard couldn't place him. The man then related the story of his conversion in Dannemora Prison in a meeting led by Sheppard and the band three years before. Now a local leader in a large church, he could declare, "I am in business here now and have never lost the joy of salvation which I found that Sunday morning in prison."[41]

For Evangeline to call the spiritual warfare of The Salvation Army "The World's Greatest Romance" was not an exaggeration. "Her band's" music was intended to do more than delight the ear. It was meant to reach the hearts of listeners; as a result, lives were changed and directed by Christ's redeeming grace. From Carnegie Hall to the Brooklyn Academy of Music, from Busnell Auditorium in Hartford to the humblest roadside open-air meeting, these Evangeline Cory Booth appearances wrought "rags to riches" transformations in people's spiritual lives.

**The Golden Years**

This subheading was chosen not only because The Salvation Army had its 50th anniversary in the United States in 1930, but also because the period 1927-1930 can be labeled one of the most fruitful periods in the ovement's music in the country as well as in the New York Staff Band's history. Excellent strides were made by the New York Staff Band (NYSB) and corps bands in the New York area, particularly in tackling some of the new, more challenging music published by International Headquarters. Another attempt was made, as well, to establish a permanent Music Department in New York at this time, with more long-lasting results than the short-lived Straubel experiment of 1898. All this culminated in the grandly spectacular National Congress of 1930. At the congress, Americans realized they had a fine network of superb bands, choruses and composers who did not need to take second seat to any in the Army world at the time. Heading up this musical renaissance was George Darby, his Staff Band, Male Chorus, and newly reformed Staff Songsters.

"To champion the cause of bands and songster brigades in the Eastern Territory" was the definition given to Edgar Arkett's appointment as secretary for bandsmen and songsters in January 1928.[42] A member of the Staff Band since 1911, Arkett was a noted French horn player and an aspiring composer. Under his leadership, a new band journal began to be published regularly, a separate *American Festival Series Journal* was begun, and festivals/councils were heartily encouraged by upper administration.[43] Lt.-Commissioner Richard E. Holz, territorial commander in the East, had recommended the appointment and had already instituted programs designed to encourage the musical forces of his territory. The massive festivals of the November 12-17, 1927, Territorial Congress are good examples. Notable participants included local bands led by several staff bandsmen, including the Training College Band (William Maltby), New York No. 1 (George Granger), and Newark No. 1 (A. C. Laurie). Bands from Schenectady, Brooklyn No. 1, South Manchester (Scout Band) and songster brigades from Troy and the Scandinavian corps of the New York area joined the Staff Band and the newly reorganized Territorial Staff Songsters in presenting the latest and best from Army publications, or new manuscript items by Leidzen and Darby.[44]

At the Staff Band and Songsters Annual Festival, February 6, 1928, Holz officially installed Arkett to his new appointment. Appropriately, the concert began with a manuscript march by Arkett, entitled "The Conqueror." Soloists for the evening were George Wilmer, playing Hartmann's "Grand Fantasia on a Theme by Weber" and Euphoniumist William Slater. Commissioner Holz always reveled in hearing the classics played by Darby's band, and he was not disappointed. He had the pleasure of introducing, with his rich German accent, the band's famous arrangement of Beethoven's "Eroica Symphony." Other meaty fare included Bramwell Coles' meditation "Man of Sorrows" and a trio for cornet, trombone,and euphonium with band arranged from various Verdi opera arias.

Enthusiasts of vocal music were not disappointed either. The Male Chorus offered Walford Davies' setting of Kipling's "Hymn

Before Action," the Staff Songsters sang "How Beautiful Upon the Mountains" (Rathbone) and "Thou Wilt Keep Him in Perfect Peace" (arr. Darby). The grand finale was Darby's setting "Vespers" for women's voices with chimes and bells, handled expertly by Richard Von Calio (in addition to lighting effects) and the female section of the staff songsters.

The hall was packed as Darby continued to follow his scheme of involving the local music leaders on these occasions. Holz brought these soldiers to the platform to receive the applause of the enthusiastic audience. The list of men shows the depth of leadership then in the Metropolitan area at that time.[45]

B/M Erik Leidzen (Scandinavian Dept.)
B/M Tom Budd (Brooklyn No. 1)
B/M W. Abram (Yonkers)
Ensign W. Maltby (Training College)
B/M G. Charleson (Harlem—New York No. 4)
Adjutant A. Laurie (Newark No. 1)
Captain G. Granger (New York No. 1)

In November 1928, the final programs were held in the old Memorial Hall, 122 W. 14th Street. During 1929 the new headquarters and Centennial Memorial Temple were under construction on the south side of 14th Street between 6th and 7th Avenues. The band was forced to rehearse at the Bowery Corps, the men sacrificing both time and their lunch hours to maintain a reasonable standard during this transitional period.[46]

Notable first-generation staff bandsmen were going to their heavenly reward at a rapid rate during this time, as well. Back in 1922 the band had presented a Memorial Festival for ocarina specialist "Gus" Hillstrom. Four years later they played and sang at Herbert Booth's graveside, renewing friendship with their old leader Ballington Booth. In February the band laid to rest Karl Bergh and then in July, Colonel Gustav Reinhardsen, one of the great men of the early Staff Band.

Reinhardsen's story is typical of these valiant warriors but also unique. Born in Norway, September 8, 1866, he left home to be a sailor at the age of 15. A little over a year later, he was converted to Christ and "sworn in" with the first group of Scandinavian Salvationists in Brooklyn. He entered training in 1888, having worked as an office boy at NHQ before that. Reappointed to NHQ in March 1890 (Finance Department), he traveled with the National Guards

Band as one of the elder statesmen of the group. Playing in the band for many years and serving as "spiritual bandmaster" 1903-05, he finally laid down his trombone on account of heavier duties in the Finance Department. He was national auditor and financial secretary when he died on July 2, 1928.

Departed heroes were sorely missed; yet this Army was approaching its 50th anniversary and God was richly blessing both the Movement and the band. The American public now fully embraced the Army's cause. Even Town Hall, New York City (113 W. 43rd Street) opened its doors for a "Festival of Music and Song" by the Staff Band, Songsters, and Cadets' Band and Chorus on June 3, 1929.[47] Erik Leidzen conducted his popular "Home Sweet Home" meditation, and Bramwell Coles led the Staff Band in his challenging piece "Wareham," a meditation on "When I Survey the Wondrous Cross." Edgar Arkett, William Bearchell, and George Darby also led their compositions or arrangements. Ten bandmasters were present, including Bandmaster Abram, of Blackburn No. 1, England, whose son was bandmaster at Yonkers, N.Y., and whose grandson, serving as solo cornetist there, would soon join the Staff Band.

Captain Charles Williams, solo trombonist of the band, provided a sensitive review of the concert while also giving a description of the band and its conductor, George Darby.

*The Staff Band played two numbers during the evening, both meditations of well known themes and both conducted by the composers. The first was "Home Sweet Home," by Erik Leidzen, and the second, "Wareham," by Staff-Captain Coles. It was in these numbers the Staff Band displayed and proved its superiority over all other musical organizations. It played with clarity and feeling and smoothness of tone that was a treat to listen to, and they nobly overcame the difficult task of following strange conducting with little rehearsal. They were truly impressive performances of brilliant compositions.*

*A further word regarding this band and its leader. It is difficult to comprehend the marvelous amount of work accomplished by this great unit of our musical fraternity. Their concerts are filled with music at once uplifting and inspiring. It is at such times that one becomes aware of the artistry of the conductor, Brigadier George Darby. He is a convincing master of the baton, an interpreter who is jealous of the composer's intentions and dedicated with a scholastic seriousness to his own artistic privileges. Whatever he conducts is worth listening to, for he speaks with authority and singular clearness. The band's playing gave complete and eloquent testimony of the merits of the bandmaster's teaching. This can also be said of the Staff Songsters.*

*The final number of the program, "Memories," the soliloquy of a veteran bandsman, gave abundant evidence of Brigadier Darby's complete knowledge of all that is best and noblest in the realm of music. An arrangement as thrilling as it was beautiful, the Staff Band and Songsters assisted by the cadets in chorus, yielded themselves to the magnetic influence of the conductor. The audience, unable to contain themselves for sheer enjoyment of it, sent wave after wave of thunderous applause around the building, and as Colonel Palmer, who gave the recitative throughout the number, rose to give the final benediction, this writer could not help but feel the joy of playing and singing to such an appreciative audience and to vaguely imagine what a joy it must have been for them to listen to such a presentation.[48]*

The January 18, 1930, issue of the Eastern *War Cry* announced two notable musical events: (1) the formation of a "Metropolitan Ensemble" under Divisional B/M Erik Leidzen, and (2) a National Congress in New York City scheduled for May 16-22, to include composers' contests in various categories.

**Metropolitan Ensemble**

The team of Alexander Ebbs, divisional commander for the metropolitan area, and Erik Leidzen, both soon famous as the founders of the Friday Evening at the Temple Series (F.E.T.), brought exciting new ideas to Army programming at a critical time in the Movement's history. From the banding perspective, Leidzen's nine-piece ensemble, culled from staff bandsmen, represented one answer to the financial difficulties of moving around a 35-piece band. Not intended to replace the Staff Band, but to supplement its activities in the New York City area, the ensemble of virtuosi under the superb direction of Erik Leidzen soon became legendary. Leidzen's choice of instrumentation for the group included three cornets, two horns, one baritone, one trombone, one euphonium, and one E$^b$ bass.[49] Substitute another trombone for the baritone and you have the *American Band Journal* scoring ( "Yellow Book" or "Band Music for Evangelism" series) launched by Holz and Leidzen 17 years later.

Darby was not threatened by this development. In fact, Darby had been trying to get Leidzen into the band from as early as 1921, when he petitioned the administration in his behalf.[50] In later years these two men would correspond frequently. Here are some excerpts from Leidzen's note to Darby on the occasion of Darby's retirement from active service, September 30, 1948:

*The band I played in at the time, Stockholm I, also went to the congress, and the boys returned with glowing reports about the New York Staff Band and its outstanding director, George Darby [Leidzen could not attend due to studies]...*

*By a queer quirk of fate you and I, George Darby, never were allowed to work together for long, though goodness knows you tried valiantly and stubbornly to bring it about. When I think of the repeated slurs you received on account of me [Leidzen is referring to his break with Evangeline Booth and its consequences], I marvel at the steadfastness of your friendship. Rest assured it is all very deeply appreciated by yours truly.*

*Now when the smoke of the battle has lifted and the perspective is clear it is doubly precious to realize, that someone with ideals "beyond the call of duty," has shared my aspirations and dreamed the same dreams that animated me. So many of your plans for the development of music did not come true, but even in this respect you have fought the good fight, and I know that you have kept the faith.*[51]

## National Congress

Part of Darby's dream did come true at the National Congress of May 1930. On Sunday, May 18, 700 bandsmen representing 25 bands joined with 1,000 songsters of the Festival Chorus under Edgar Arkett to fill the Metropolitan Opera House in New York City with glorious music in a 3:00 p.m. "Mammoth Festival of Praise and Song." An estimated crowd of 8,000 heard John Philip Sousa praise Salvation Army music and then lead the massed bands in his new march, "The Salvation Army."[52]

The Chicago Staff Band and New York Staff Band shared the limelight at the congress. B/M Broughton had prepared his men on the prize-winning pieces that were to be announced during the festival, and he also took them through his setting of "Songs of the Evangel" and Marshall's "Army of the Brave." The New York Staff Band drew the accompanying duties for the large group of Festival Songsters and for Cornet Soloist J. Stanley Sheppard, who played a Herbert Clarke variation solo. The NYSB's solo spot was Eric Ball's "Adoration."

Arkett let Darby lead the massed songsters in Darby's vocal march, "The Spirit of the Army," but directed them himself in

Gounod's chorus, "O Turn Thee to the Lord," and in the grand finale setting of "The National Hymn," which united all the bands, chorus, and audience in the final verse. Another staff band, from the Southern Territory in Atlanta, Ga., (under B/M Albert Baldwin), also participated in the congress. They accompanied the NYSB's Richard Von Calio in a xylophone solo, "Russian Fantasia" (Levy), and played "Harlan" (Kitching) as their "solo" item.

Corps bands held their own at the congress as well. The band from Flint, Mich., under Bernard Smith, gave a smashing perform-ance of "A Soul's Awakening" (Ball). Their "cousins" from Detroit Citadel (B/M R. Herival) were not to be outdone and read clearly through the difficult selection "Visions" (Marshall). The New England bands contributed beautifully as well, with Cambridge Citadel (George Foster) offering Coles' "Wareham," and South Manchester (David Addy) offering another bouquet to their na-tional leader with the presentation of Turkington's march "The American Commander." Sam Toft led a Scandinavian orchestra and chorus in a piece called "King David" (but not the composition by Honegger) and some Hawaiian singers provided relief from the ponderous brass with two lovely native songs.

B/M Leidzen, who, along with Edwin Franko Goldman, William Broughton, and Bramwell Coles, had served as the adjudicators in the composers' contest, led the massed bands in George Mar-shall's march "Mighty to Save" and gave a demonstration on the use of new four-part brass arrangements of hymn tunes (with optional fifth part) that would later be released through the Central Territory's Music Department. Although this educational demon-stration was squeezed into this marathon event, it was an impor-tant aspect of the program, for so many small bands across America could not play the full orchestrations of the *Band Tune Book* released in 1928.[53]

Two New York staff bandsmen shared in the prizes awarded that day in the composers' contest. William Slater received third prize in the selection category, and William Bearchell received first prize for his songster selection. Major K. M. Fristrup of California was awarded a prize in nearly every category. The one award-winning piece still active in Army band repertoire today is Emil Soderstrom's first-prize march, "Army of God." Americans could not have been prouder of their musical groups and composers at this milestone event.

John Philip Sousa, in the September 1930 issue of *Etude Magazine*, restated his reasons for admiring the Army's music program:

> *If you want to know one of the very good reasons why the world needs bands, just ask one of The Salvation Army warriors, who for years has marched carrying the cross through the back alleys of life. Let him tell of the armies of men who have been turned toward a better life by first hearing the sounds of a Salvation Army band.... The next time you hear a Salvation Army band, no matter how humble, take off your hat.*

More difficult times were around the corner for Army musicians, for at the height of their landmark congress celebration in May 1930, the financial devastation resulting from the Stock Market Crash of 1929 and consequent Great Depression was close at hand. Leidzen's song on an Army social work motto, "A Man May Be Down, But He's Never Out," sung with such gusto by Olof Lundgren in later years, might well have characterized what would soon be one of the most challenging periods in the band's history. Right after the congress, however, Darby's band was at the peak of its skill.

When Bramwell Coles praised the playing of the 1930 band during the National Congress he also recalled "Memories" of past glories. He was deeply appreciative of Darby's interpretive skill and reminded the band and *War Cry* readers of a sensitive rendition the Staff Band gave of Coles' "Atonement" at the 1914 International Congress.[54] For Darby, this praise helped smooth a rough decision; for the band, it was some consolation—for they would not have their fine leader with them for very much longer.

*Musicians of the highest rank,*
  *Have held our standards high,*
*They passed to us a legacy*
  *We'll honor till we die.*
*We think of Colonel Darby*
  *And his work for twenty years,*
*We doff our hats—revere his name—*
  *And give three lusty cheers.*[55]

47

# 4

## "Songs of a General"
### (Stephen Bulla)

## Bandmasters J. Stanley Sheppard and William Broughton
### 1931-1935

W hen the Staff Band visited Philadelphia in January 1931, everyone in the group seemed in top form. "Billie" Parkins had joined the band as cornet soloist ("Happy Day" and "Hallelujah" were heard there), Fowler was back singing solos like "The Sea of Galilee," and the band was enjoying the new contest-winning music from the congress.[1] But Darby was having bouts of ill health.[2] By April his resignation was announced in the Easter edition of *The War Cry,* the reason cited as poor health.[3]

At the May 1-5 congress with General Edward Higgins (whose son had played in the old National Staff Band), George Darby, Charles Anderson, and "Trumpeter" Trumble were honored during the Congress Music Festival. Acting B/M J. Stanley "Red" Sheppard, who had only limited conducting experience, mostly filling in for Darby over the years, managed to take the band through "fine presentations" of "In the Firing Line" (Coles) and "King of Kings" (Ball).[4]

"Red" Sheppard's brief "caretaker" duties as bandmaster from April 1931 to November 1932 included some wonderful events in the band's story, including two motorcades of 1931 with Eva Booth, prison visitation work, joint programs with the Montreal Citadel

49

Band, and work among "the down-and-out" at the Army's Depression relief centers.

As a cornet soloist, Sheppard was known for a beautiful tone and lyrical legato style.[5] Not a flashy player, he was a solid end-chair section leader. His real gifts, however, lay in the development of Salvation Army prison work, one of the finest stories in the Army's history. While that part of Sheppard's life is told by others, mention should be made here that he was recognized for his outstanding efforts by being elected president of the American Prison Association in 1950 after 40 years of continuous work in correctional services. In 1962 the City of New York opened the J. Stanley Sheppard Rehabilitation Center (for delinquent youth), at 443 West 22nd Street, named posthumously in his honor.

### The Commander's Auto Tour Extraordinary (a *War Cry* headline)

Starting with a Times Square rally on June 3, 1931, Commander Evangeline Booth launched her 12-day motorcade with pomp and fanfare. A police escort led the Commander and her entourage through crowded streets to the Holland Tunnel after their brief program to cheering thousands at Times Square, the famous "Crossroads of the World." Evangeline was dressed in gray cloak and crimson hat for easy recognition. She was accompanied by her staff, who rode in several "roadster" or "scarlet Battery cars," and by the Staff Band in their "superbus" and accommpanying special van equipped with a "Hoovenaire Sound System" for portable amplification.[6]

With a speed and schedule that must have terrified the various local leaders in charge of protocol and arrangements along the way, Evangeline traversed 2,000 miles in 12 days, mostly in the states of Pennsylvania and Ohio. Staff Bandsman Richard Von Calio would be sent ahead, sometimes with Billie Parkins, to warm up the people gathered in a town square eagerly awaiting the chance to see the famous Evangeline Booth. His "one-man band" routines drew the crowds.[7] The band would arrive next, to add further excitement, and then the Commander would make her grand entrance. Each day concluded with a "high class" music festival, "but the climax" was "always...an address by the national leader."[8]

The people loved Evangeline and the crowds were enormous. Brigadier John Allan, at this time divisional commander for the

Central Ohio Command, had planned a reception at the state capitol in Columbus, Monday, June 8. Many considered this the peak engagement of the tour and for two hours, the thousands who had gathered with Ohio's civic, political and religious elite stood spellbound by a phenomenon described by *The War Cry:*

> *Later when it was dark and the Commander was uttering an address that must rank among her greatest open-air triumphs, the glaring floodlight lamps of the Capitol showed a sea of faces rapt, attracted, gripped, controlled by the eloquent oratorical spell of the Commander-in-Chief's message. It was a meeting of myriad blessing.*
>
> *In a marvelous way sustained of God the National Leader threw off the fatigue of yesterday, and was peerless, inexpressibly forceful, powerful and compelling in her presentation of the Army's international activities as in her impassioned delivery of eternal spiritual truths.... Artists, professors, lawyers, clergy, millionaires, all voiced their loud appreciation of the Commander's effort. It was the talk of the town.... In a varied musical prelude of vocal, instrumental and solo items, as well as during the Commander's address, the Staff Band rendered yeoman supporting service....[9]*

The statistical review of the motorcade's 12-day tour cited crowds of at least 125,000, 60 addresses by the Commander, 284 band offerings, 42 Male Chorus items and 45 cornet solos by Parkins.[10] One novelty event of the trip was the band's grand entrance into Butler, Pa., each member riding in a "baby" Austin automobile.[11]

If some of the bandsmen had grumbled about the motorcade, it did not phase Evangeline. She scheduled another one, much shorter this time, through Eastern New York on the July 4th weekend. Sheppard arranged for Evangeline and the band to perform for prisoners at Sing Sing and Comstock Penitentiaries, and 20 Army centers were given a great boost by the appearance of the Commander and her band.[12]

Next April the Montreal Citadel Band (B/M Norman Audoire) came to New York for the Easter weekend, the first non-American band to visit New York since the Household Troops Band. This 45-piece brass band (with one saxophone) was a terrific model for corps bands in the area. The NYSB and their Canadian friends shared several programs together, including a three-mile parade, most of it up 5th Avenue.[13]

Several weeks later Edwin Franko Goldman led the NYSB and massed bands at a Metropolitan Opera House United Appeal Fund meeting in Handel's "Largo" and Turkington's second-prize march, "Homeward Bound." He remarked that he "was delighted with the intonation, alertness, and quick response and general playing of the Army bands; we must do something to bring this music to the Mall [Central Park]." Something *was* done, but not until Holz's band of the 1950s.[14]

Yet the glamour engagements could not match the satisfaction received by the men when they would play every other month at the Army's Gold Dust Lodge or at the Ellis Island compound by request of the Commissioner of Immigration. The Gold Dust Lodge housed over 1,000 unemployed men hit hardest by the Depression. Here the Army struggled valiantly, sometimes futilely, to lift spirits and to find work for the desperate men. The effect of Frank Fowler singing "I Love to Tell the Story," accompanied by Bill Bearchell on the organ, or the influence a stirring march by the band had on the audience was immediate, and much good was accomplished during the 1930s as the band played and sang

## Hard Times

Evangeline Booth's decision to bring William Broughton to New York as staff bandmaster and territorial music secretary was a tragic mistake that hurt both Broughton and the band. She did not prepare Sheppard, the band nor Broughton for what would happen. In fact, Broughton was brought to New York City by the Commander without specific appointment; only later did it dawn on Edgar Arkett that he would soon be replaced as territorial music secretary.

Broughton was one of the leading Army musicians in America. He had had notable success as bandmaster of the famous Chicago "Rink" Corps Band, the Chicago Staff Band, and the Flint Citadel Band. Compositions of his were played throughout the Army world. Evangeline relied on his arranging skill in "Songs of the Evangel," and he reciprocated with flattering pieces written in her honor.

New York is a different place than Chicago or Detroit, however. The men of the NYSB had studied with the leading orchestral players in America; they had a long-standing heritage and skill to match it. Broughton was a domineering, forceful, perhaps bossy personality. The chemistry between the band and bandmaster was just not right regardless of all the talent present.

What follows is a series of entries from William Bearchell's diaries of this critical period, 1932-33.[16] We catch sight of Bearchell's esteem for Broughton as a musician but his sadness that the general situation was not working out:

| Date | Entry |
|------|-------|
| 10/11/32 | "Red" Sheppard in tears announced Broughton coming to the Staff Band. |
| 11/3/32 | Broughton arrived secretly. |
| 11/10/32 | Major Broughton introduced to Staff Band by Arnold [Chief Secretary]. What a frigid reception. |
| 11/13/32 | Festival at F.E.T. with Commander; 300 in overflow. "Red" Sheppard's "Swan Song." |
| 11/14/32 | Broughton's first day. Signing of the contract. |
| 11/15/32 | Commander off the Band for not signing "her" contract. [She was asking for them to sign a covenant of loyalty to herself and to Broughton.] How ridiculous—danger of formalities. |
| 11/17/33 | My first rehearsal with Broughton—he should do OK. |
| 11/24/32 | First broadcast (Thanksgiving) from Temple, WRNY. |
| 11/29/32 | Boys hid Broughton's briefcase; Broughton doing OK with music. |
| 1/17/33 | Broughton boasting added power given him by C.S. [Chief Secretary] to rule band. Poor fellows. |
| 1/23/33 | Band practices are terrible. Fellows just can't stand Broughton. |
| 2/7/34 | Rumors Broughton resigning. |
| 3/3/34 | Broughton walked out of band practice. (Also 5/8/34 and 6/12/34) |
| 8/26/35 | Broughton not objecting to farewell. |

Commander Evangeline Booth and Colonel William C. Arnold, then chief secretary, made it doubly negative by initially insisting on a signed covenant of loyalty to the Commander and her chosen bandmaster [later withdrawn]. Several bandsmen walked out at the first rehearsal when Broughton told the band, "If you do what I say, I will make you a good band."[17] There was no doubting

53

Broughton's musical abilities; he was not, in this instance, a tactful leader of men.

Broughton was a fighter, however, and he did not give up easily. There were notable achievements under his baton that are most important in the overall development of the NYSB. He eliminated the last traces of the old Darby woodwinds, standardizing the instrumentation along British band guidelines. The radio broadcasts that began on WRNY and then on the CBS nationwide network were shaped under his direction. The F.E.T ensemble was kept going in good form by Broughton after a disastrous confrontation of Evangeline Booth and Erik Leidzen in May 1933, which resulted in Leidzen disappearing from the Army festival stage for many years (see endnote #1 in Chapter 5). Even the Male Chorus, which had languished a bit after Darby left the band, was revitalized during Broughton's tenure, under the direction of William Slater.

The appointment of John Allan as "spiritual bandmaster" (executive officer) in March 1933, did much to help stabilize the situation. Broughton was soon also busy with widespread visits to corps around the territory. Every indication in the official records shows Broughton to be an energetic, hard worker. He even served on the formative staff that held a Bandsmen's Council at Star Lake Camp during an extended Labor Day weekend in 1935; this would blossom the following year into the famous Star Lake Musicamp.[18]

Appropriately, the last great event for Broughton as bandmaster was Evangeline Booth's farewell meeting at Madison Square Garden, November 1, 1934. Evangeline was now the General-elect of The Salvation Army. Eighteen thousand friends, Salvationists and dignitaries were there to bid farewell to their leader of three decades. The musicians on hand included the People's Chorus of New York, the Temple (F.E.T.) Chorus, the Associated Glee Club of America, and the Three Arts Club (all combined into a 700-voice choir under the direction of L. Cavilieri), the NYSB and the Military Band of the First Division, plus massed corps bands from the New York City area. Evangeline's great song "The World for God" was premiered by this mighty aggregation and the band under Broughton played a selection of songs composed by their new General [probably Broughton's "The Evangel" *(American Festival Journal #1)*].[19] The program marked the end of a remarkable era for the band. Their Commander was departing.

# Start of the COMMANDER'S Great 12 Day Motorcade

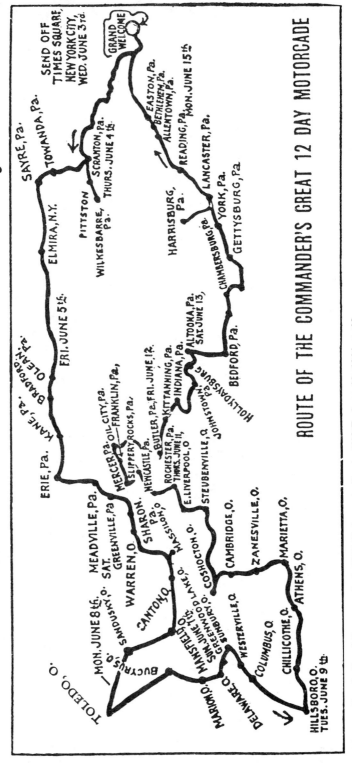

ROUTE OF THE COMMANDER'S GREAT 12 DAY MOTORCADE

4-1.    Facsimile of Commander's 1931 Motorcade Route, WC/E, June 13, 1931, p. 13.

# 5

## "A Soul's Awakening"
### (Eric Ball)

## Bandmaster George Granger
## 1935-1945

The "Friday Evening at the Temple" series was beginning its third season, November 1, 1935, when the New York Staff Band, under its new leader, George Granger, took the stage as the regular duty band. In spite of the tragic loss of Leidzen[1] and the equally sad outcome of Broughton's short-lived leadership, the meetings themselves were a success. Staff bandsmen had not only formed the basis of the Metropolitan Ensemble but had also served in the ranks of the Temple Chorus for the past two years. In fact, weekly spiritual meetings at headquarters in which the band was featured had been an element of New York Salvationist life since the 1880s.[2]

The decision to put the Territorial Staff Band on duty for the meetings—a service they perform to this day—was a wise one. Any possible remaining conflicts between Metropolitan Divisional Headquarters, Eastern Territorial Headquarters, and National Headquarters were, for the moment, effectively resolved by this appointment.[3] The musical aspects of the inspiring F.E.T. meetings were now on a normal schedule: the NYSB under a new bandmaster, George Granger, Temple Chorus under William Bearchell, and Mrs. Major William G. Harris, Licentiate Trinity

College London (L.T.C.L., a performance certificate), at the organ console.[4]

When Alexander Ebbs and Erik Leidzen had first conceived the idea of the Temple Fellowship late one night in Leidzen's West Side apartment, they envisioned outstanding music, great Bible preaching and Christian camaraderie that would make the resulting experience "an irresistible spiritual force and a means to the Holy Spirit of bringing revival into every corps and church throughout this vast Metropolis—and even farther afield."[5] Each program in the inaugural season began with 20 minutes of musical praise that was not relegated to the now-derogatory category of "Preliminary Music." The finest speakers, Army or otherwise, were sought out for the series. Music played a pivotal role, involving large numbers of people (who, in turn, brought other people). Whole evenings were given over to music, like the February 3, 1933, "Grand Soiree de Repertoire," a sacred concert that involved the 200-voice Temple Chorus singing Bearchell's setting of "Psalm 121," the Temple Ensemble (Band) playing Ostby's lengthy meditation "Princethorpe," and the full Territorial Staff Band sounding forth Eric Ball's "A Soul's Awakening."[6] Despite the Depression, New York Salvationists were experiencing a rejuvenation of their fighting spirit through these F.E.T. meetings.

Participation in the series has never been easy for the bandsmen. Friday became a long day, indeed, with such problems as finding child-care, transportation, and affordable meals being faced each week of the season. Still the NYSB rallied to support the cause of evangelism, and others took notice. Olin Downes, music critic of *The New York Times,* experiencing the F.E.T. at the Grand Finale of the 1935-36 season, wrote: "I see in the instrumentalists of The Salvation Army playing and singing to their fellow creatures who are often so heavy laden and knowing terror and want, the essence of music that echoes from God above."[7] Granger's band and Bearchell's chorus had been augmented on that great occasion by Tenor Soloist Manley Price Boone, the Florenda Trio (piano, violin, cello) and Concertina Virtuoso Gregory Matusewitch.[8] All of New York was invited to share in the enriching cultural and spiritual endeavor.[9]

In addition to providing music at each F.E.T. meeting, the Staff Band was given its own Friday night in the series. In 1940, for instance, Colonel George Darby was guest speaker for that season's "Staff Band Night" on the topic "The Cosmic Significance of Music for the Deepening of Spiritual Experience." Former Staff B/M Charles Anderson testified and gave accounts of the 1904 International Congress, while J. J. Stimson kept things lively with his humorous sketches of past and present foibles in the Army fight. Other greats of the band's past participated, including J. S. Sheppard, Robert Griffith, Claude Bates, and others.[10] Each year the F.E.T. planning committee searched for the best speakers and musicians while encouraging local duty groups as well as corps ensembles and soloists. The Staff Band added to the excitement by being on radio each week. (For awhile, part of the F.E.T. was broadcast.) People expected young, brilliant speakers, like Norman Vincent Peale who opened the 1938-39 series (October 21), and they anticipated hearing the best in sacred brass and vocal music when they made their way each Friday to the stunning hall on 14th Street.

## A Leader of Men

When Captain George Granger was bandmaster of the New York No. 1 Band of 1926, he submitted a paper to the *Local Officers' Counselor* entitled "A Tactful Bandmaster," which contained a prophetic statement about how he was to be chosen as Staff Bandmaster nine years later:

*I remember reading an article some time ago of a certain rubber firm in this country, who had a foreman's vacancy in one of their departments. In this department there was a man, a very skilled mechanic; in fact he was a master of every machine in that particular department. He was energetic, always on the job, and generally looked upon as the one to fill the vacancy; but to the surprise of all, and disappointment of this man, the position went to another apparently less capable man.*

*He at once made it his business to see the superintendent and aired his grievance with him. The superintendent, who was a very tactful man, listened attentively until he had said all he had to say, and then calling him by his Christian name, said, "Tom, you surely have the making of a good foreman, with the exception of one thing. You are not tactful enough to handle men, and get the best out of them."*

*Now, this is what we need in our bandmasters today—men who can be tactful enough to get the best out of the bandsmen for the Kingdom's sake.*[11]

59

After the stormy ego of a Leidzen or a Broughton, Granger was a much-needed relief. His men knew of his musical limitations but they rallied behind him for ten years in unswerving loyalty to this sensitive leader of men.[12] With John Allan as his executive officer and William Bearchell directing the Temple Chorus and soon to be Deputy B/M and Male Chorus Leader, Granger had a support system that would overcome his apparent lack of skill with the baton.[13] The New York Staff Band's camaraderie was restored under his leadership, excellent achievements and milestones were reached, and, in spite of a second world war that hurt the band much more than the first, the band's position in the history of Army banding took on almost mythical proportions.

When outstanding young people receive the Granger Memorial Scholarship at the Eastern Territory's Star Lake Musicamp each August, they are chosen because they represent the best in Salvationist and banding spirit. The man for whom the scholarship was named stood as an example of this balance of Salvationism and of excellence in the ministry of music that the scholarship winners are encouraged to uphold.

Granger first played in a Salvation Army band in Kingston, Ontario. By 1904 he was a member of the Canadian Staff Band, with which he traveled to the International Congress. He filled all band local officer positions at his home corps of Kingston within the next two years, including bandmaster, before being appointed bandmaster of the popular 146th Battalion Band, Canadian Army, serving four dangerous years overseas during World War I. Given citations for bravery, he was severely wounded in action in 1918 less than three months before the Armistice was signed. In 1922 Adjutant Nellie McGree asked Granger to move to New York and revitalize the old New York No. 1 Band (Temple Corps). This position he held with distinction, particularly in his demonstration of sensitive guidance to young bandsmen. When a leader was needed for the Staff Band in 1935, although more musically knowledgeable and technically proficient bandmasters were available, George Granger was just the man needed for this vital responsibility.[14]

## Over the Airwaves

If you ask old-timers about the band of the 1930s invariably they speak with pride about the CBS nationwide radio broadcasts of the band under Broughton and Granger. The series began in

November 1932, on WRNY with two half-hour programs per week (Tuesdays, 8:00-8:30; Sundays, 6:00-6:30). Occasional services were broadcast, such as the Thanksgiving Day Service in 1932, direct from the Temple. The weekly Sunday evening program featured Staff Bandsman Samson Hodges on the organ, along with short messages by guest speakers and vocal or instrumental soloists. The Staff Band and Staff Songsters were heard on a weekly Tuesday night series.[15] At the beginning of the 1933-34 F.E.T. series, WRNY decided to readjust the schedule and cover the opening part of the meeting only, omitting the sermon. A few months later WRNY became WHN, and this series was stopped.[16] During May and June 1934, the Staff Band was heard irregularly over the Columbia Broadcasting System network out of local affiliate WABC. By July of the same year, the band, with Emcee John Allan, had a weekly 15-minute series.[17]

William L. Devoto, publicity director for the Army in the New York area, worked diligently to maintain the band's program in the face of commercial opposition at CBS.[18] During the next few years, the time and day of their 15-minute segment kept shifting. WOR, WMCA, and WEAF also covered the band during this same period. The nationwide brooadcast came to a conclusion in December 1937, when, for financial reasons, CBS could no longer subsidize the project and neither could the Army afford the expensive air time.[19]

While the series lasted, it brought the joy of the gospel into millions of homes and boosted morale and pride among Salvationists who tuned in. The range, due to shortwave broadcast, was enormous. Mail came into the Public Relations Department at territorial headquarters at an enormous rate. One band secretary from Hastings, Sussex (England) wrote: "I listened to your program on 25-36 meters on Thursday last, Nov. 5th, which came in at great strength here. I tuned in just as 'The Old Rugged Cross' was being played, and the two marches came across excellently."[20]

By 1936 the responsibility for the broadcast was in the hands of Adjutant Harold Jackson (euphonium soloist) and Envoy Richard Holz, the latter recently arrived in John Allan's Public Relations Department as Allan's private secretary and as an E$^b$ soprano cornetist for the Staff Band. These men wrote the brief script and worked with B/M Granger in the musical choices/timings. One sample script survives, from a July 1936, 15-minute broadcast.[21]

Other than hymn tunes, the music was by staff bandsmen or former staff bandsmen. John Allan was the announcer:

**Fanfare** The Band [Name of piece not available]

**Announcer** The Salvation Army Territorial Staff Band of New York under the direction of Adjutant George Granger.

**Theme** The Band [Tune Book 189, "Aurelia" — "The Church's One Foundation"]

**Announcer** Today's program by the Staff Band marks the close of its third series over the Columbia system. The Salvation Army has felt proud to have been able to present this excellent combination and wishes to express to those who listen to this weekly presentation its appreciation for their interest. Bandmaster Granger and members of the Staff Band wish also to thank the many friends who have written to express their commendation of their efforts and it is hoped that when the Territorial Staff Band resumes its broadcasts in the fall, you will again be one of our audience.

**Announcer** Today's program opens with a march, the "New York Temple." This composition is by Adjutant William Slater, a member of the Staff Band and a prize winner in the 1930 music competition conducted by The Salvation Army.

**The Band** "New York Temple"

**Announcer** We now hear the much loved old hymn "Faith of Our Fathers."

**The Band** "Faith of Our Fathers" [*Tune Book* 216, "St. Catherine"]

**Announcer** In honor of the birthday of our republic which we celebrate on Saturday, the Staff Band now plays a medley of songs arranged by Major William Broughton of Pittsburgh. He has called the work "American Melodies."

**The Band** "American Melodies"

**Announcer** We continue the program with a march called "Banners Unfurled." This is the composition of the youngest member of the Staff Band, Richard E. Holz, and was written especially for the gradu-

| | |
|---|---|
| | ation exercises of the cadets of the Salvation Army Training College in Atlanta, Georgia. |
| **The Band** | "Banners Unfurled" |
| **Announcer** | How fitting it is that to close the program and its present season of broadcasts, the Band should play "America the Beautiful."<br>*America, America*<br>*God shed His grace on Thee,*<br>*And crown thy good with brotherhood*<br>*From sea to shining sea.* |
| **The Band** | "America the Beautiful" |
| **Announcer** | We have reached the end of this program, but although the Staff Band will not be heard over the air for some time, we want to again assure you that The Salvation Army is always at your service. |

## Comradeship: Canada, 1937

At Christmas 1937, former Staff Bandsman William Parkins, then divisional youth officer in Cincinnati, Ohio, sent an entertaining "Memories" booklet to all staff bandsmen who had made the great May 27-June 2 tour of Canada and New York State earlier that year. The booklet was complete with a 34-stanza "Tone Poem" which detailed funny incidents on the tour or unique personality traits of individual members, as well as a section entitled "Prophecy 1957—N.Y. Staff Band." Parkins' gift was symbolic of the shared camaraderie and friendships that developed in Granger's band at one of its peaks. While most of the humor is of the "in" kind ("you had to be there" variety), some of it gives us brief portraits of famous individuals in another light. Bill Bearchell's on-platform wit during John Allan's chairing of a program is captured kindly in stanza 16 of the "Tone Poem":

*The guy that had the humor*
*On the trip, we all could tell*
*Was a famous alto soloist,*
*Widely known as Bill Bearchell.*
*"He wants me for a Sunbeam—*
*Will be played," our leader cried,*
*"He can have you," spoke up Billy,*
*In that grand sweet bye and byed.*[22]

63

In his "Prophecy" projected 20 years ahead, Parkins had men strategically placed all over the Army world, mostly in somewhat absurd situations, including Leason Kington forming a new splinter group of the Army and Bill Slater ending up as a degenerate bum running the elevator at the Southern THQ. The opening section gives the flavor, as Bill Parkins arrives in Atlanta in his "Prophecy 1957":

*Twas a hot sultry day on the second of June as my train pulled into the old Peachtree station. I had...arrived in Atlanta for two reasons. First—the induction of the new territorial commander for the South, Lt.-Commissioner Charles Bearchell, and second, the commissioner and I were going to ride to New York together for the retirement service of Commissioner John Allan....Bearchell had made a brilliant record as chief secretary to Norway and as a reward had been promoted and been given the South.*

*Everybody was wishing him well. Poor old Chuck, I mused. He had a real task before him in setting the Territory right after the farewell of the field secretary—Brigadier Ken Ayres. The South had been given a terrific set back by Ayres' antics. Of course, he had done everything meaning well—but what a failure. He had never conducted an inspection, nor an Officers' Council, nor a series of meetings without his camera and he had put every field and staff officer in the territory on the spot with his photograph album. No matter what happened the brigadier had a permanent record and his little candid camera became the talk of the Army world. The entire territory became enraged. Finally, the General had sent orders that Ayres must dispose of his camera and farewell immediately to Tanganyika....* [23]

A "statistical summary" of that zany tour group was compiled by Richard Holz at the request of John Allan, who loved to cite these figures in festivals:[24]

| | |
|---|---|
| Average age—35.8 | Songster leaders—4 |
| Oldest member—58 | Single members—8 |
| Youngest member—18 | Married members—25 |
| Combined years of service—770 | Children (Two sets of twins)—54 |
| Average years of service—23.3 | First generation Salvationists—5 |
| Officers' sons—17 | Second generation—20 |
| Composers—5 | Third generation—7 |
| Bandmasters—7 | Fourth generation—1 |

The music of the touring Staff Band was excellent, with stellar soloists Ken Ayres (trombone), Harold Jackson (euphonium), Fred Farrar, William Wrieden, and guest soloist William Parkins (cornet). Frank Fowler was at the peak of his fame as the band's *basso profundo*. On the way to or from Toronto, the band played in Scranton, Pa.; Binghamton, Buffalo, Batavia, and Niagara Falls, N.Y.; and Hamilton, Ontario. In Binghamton, N.Y., the band was playing the march "Aberystwyth" to more than 1,000 persons jammed into Central High School when the lights went out due to a thunderstorm. The band and Granger continued as if nothing had happened, and when the lights came on precisely on the last note of the march, the audience ovation for this feat was deafening.[25]

In Toronto the band shared programs with the Dovercourt Citadel Band for capacity crowds during the weekend. The Male Chorus was featured in an emotional service of remembrance at Mt. Pleasant Cemetery commemorating the 23rd anniversary of the *Empress of Ireland* disaster.[26] Receptions at City Hall (Acting-Mayor H. Wadsworth) and the Royal Hotel (various members of Parliament) highlighted a busy and musically fruitful tour.

It had been 1909 since the band had last visited the Canadian capital but Bandmaster William Merritt and Colonel George Atwell, one of the survivors from the *Empress* sinking in 1914, affirmed their friendship for the NYSB and showed genuine high regard for the musical achievements of the group in recent years. They were a rightfully proud band, dressed in "crimson and black-sashed" high-collar tunics topped with white-braided epaulets. Fifty years old that June (though they were not aware of that milestone), they could honestly thank God and their leaders for a miraculous half-century of positive Christian service and fellowship.

### A Year in the Life of the Band—1938

This mid-point in the band's history seems a good time to reproduce one complete year's schedule in the life of the band. (Lack of space does not permit this for every year, but a summary of highlights for every year is provided in Appendix A.) The list of events for 1938 is typical of band schedules while still showing engagements particularly suited to this group.[27]

January:    On duty for two weddings:
            1) Faith Clifford to Fred Ladlow

2) Dorothy Welte to Philip Carney
Brooklyn S.A. Day; Band at Nostrand-Dekalb M.E. Church
F.E.T. duties (January-May; October-December)

| | |
|---|---|
| February: | Normal F.E.T. duties |
| March: | Prison Sunday at Bedford Hills Penitentiary for Women |

Engagements in Plainfield (12-13) and Arlington (20th), N.J.

March 18 F.E.T. musical with four bands, Temple Chorus, and Richardson Irwin, tenor soloist

April: Easter Weekend with Dovercourt (Toronto) Citadel Band (B/M William Merritt) 15-18:
    Festival with Temple Chorus (15th)
    United Churches Sunrise Service in Central Park, both bands (17th)

May: United Songster Festival, with B/M Thomas Giles (London, England) as guest cornetist
Weekend in Atlantic City, N.J. (21-22)
Cambridge Citadel Corps (Mass.) 50th Anniversary Weekend (28-29)

June: Commissioning Weekend (3-5)
Weekend in Southeast Pennsylvania (10-12)
Rochester, N.Y., Youth Councils (17-18) and area tour

August: Ocean Grove Weekend with General Edward Higgins (R)

September: Philadelphia (25th)

October: Elmira, N.Y., 46th Anniversary (8-9)
Northeast Pennsylvania (15-16)
Pen Argyl, Pa. (22-23)

November: Composer's Night at F.E.T. (9th)
Armistice Day Parade and 20th Anniversary Service of the Armistice, November 11, 1918 (11th)
Darby, Pa. (12-13)
Wedding of Evangeline Granger and William Parkins (14th)
Annual Thanksgiving Service (24th)

December: WABC Half-Hour Christmas Special (17th)
Women's Detention Home (18th)

Broad and Wall Street Caroling Service (22nd)
F.E.T. Christmas Carol Service, led by Darby
(23rd)

Like most "typical" years, this one was filled with many weekend trips for special anniversaries, F.E.T. programs, prison visitations, weddings, and parades. The visit of the Dovercourt Citadel Band from Toronto was probably the highlight, as these two bands renewed friendships made the previous spring. Each bandsman learned from the excellent music rendered by others across the border. Cross-cultural benefits of these exchanges would, within another decade, be recognized as one superb way of rallying Salvation Army bands to better achievements and musical standards. The band's prison visitations, too, gave evidence of a healthy, growing ministry. Begun as a regular event in 1916, when 24 prisons were visited on one day, Prison Sunday, by March 1939, when the band went to Rikers Island, included visits by Salvationists to 220 prisons and 33,000 inmates reached on one day alone.[28]

## World's Fair and the Year of Jubilee

May and June 1939 were particularly hectic but exciting months for the Staff Band. Aboard the excursion steamer *Belle Island* the band greeted Crown Prince Olav and Princess Martha of Norway at Quarantine Point, later escorting them to a mayoral reception at City Hall. The famed Westminster Choir under Dr. J. Finlay Williamson joined the TSB for the F.E.T. Finale, and the Montreal Citadel Band came to New Jersey in late May. Everyone was eager to attend the New York World's Fair, too. The Staff Band had several opportunities that year, presenting concerts at the Temple of Religion on May 13, June 17 and 24, returning there on September 27 for Salvation Army Day at the fair. During a six-day tour of Upstate New York in June, young soloists, particularly Edward Lowcock (cornet) and Pershing Flanders (piano), added to the band's fine line-up.[29]

Somehow former Staff Bandsman Commissioner Alexander M. Damon and his chief secretary, Colonel Donald McMillan, persuaded 1,500 Salvationists to attend the fair on Wednesday, September 27 (a work day). Following a grand reception at the

67

fair's New York City Building, when Mayor Fiorella LaGuardia addressed the entire delegation on the virtues of the Sermon on the Mount, a massive festival was held in the Temple of Religion:

> In the afternoon an inspiring service was held...before a crowd which jammed the auditorium of the imposing edifice. On this, the sixth visit of Salvationists to the Temple, the program largely consisted of musical items rendered by the Territorial Staff Band (G. Granger), the New England Provincial Band (H. Zealley) and the special World's Fair Chorus of 250 voices under the direction of Colonel George Darby. The aggregations rendered selections which "went over big," not a few of the attendants, particularly the more irrepressible, punctuating proceedings with such exclamations as "Hallelujah," "Glory to God," and "Amen," not forgetting the lone woman representative who rose to her feet after an especially stirring number and shouted "I like that." It was that kind of service. Every one was thrilled and did not mind telling the world about it.[30]

The Staff Band returned to the fair for a concert on June 26, 1940. Another Salvation Army Day was held September 25 of that year, with Granger's band on duty. During the fall of 1940, the band made two 78 rpm recordings on the Columbia label, the first since the 1922-23 Vocalion Series.

Interest in the band's past had been stirred by reflections shared at the F.E.T. Staff Band Night with Darby. Somehow the historical records at that time were incomplete, and calculations were made showing the band to be 50 years old in 1941, rather than 1937, based on what they thought was the beginning of the Staff Band, September 1891, a date that was actually only a reorganization after the dissolution of the National Guards Band. Plans were laid by Commissioner Alexander Damon, with the critical financial support of The Salvation Army Association of New York (Walter Hoving, president), for a grand celebration in December 1941. A tally of the events included:

—Christmas Carol Service at Wall Street (with Exchange Singers), followed by parade to City Hall and reception with Mayor LaGuardia.
—Golden Jubilee Festival, Dec. 19 at Temple; TSB, Temple Chorus; Guest Artists Albert Spalding, Larry Adler and Marian Anderson.

—A Jubilee Broadcast, Dec. 22, on local radio station WNYC, and a nationwide broadcast on Friday after Christmas.
—Reunion, January 3, 1942.

In the midst of it all, the band did not lose sight of its mission; it still went to the Women's Detention Home and Welfare Island.[31] The Jubilee Concert was a dazzler. The elite of New York social and business circles mingled with the typical F.E.T. crowd. Mayor LaGuardia got things moving when he led the band in Coles' march "Under Two Flags." Harmonica wizard Larry Adler, recently featured with the Philadelphia Orchestra and New York Philharmonic, was the first guest soloist. Violinist Albert Spalding followed, accompanied by Andre Benoist, playing excerpts from Chopin, Schubert and Paganini. Choral music was carried by the Male Chorus and the Temple Chorus.

Male Chorus:    "Charity" (I Corinithians 13, arr. C. W. Greene)
Temple Chorus:   "Onward Christian Soldiers"
            "Hail Smiling Morn" (led by Darby)

A cornet trio of Wrieden, Farrar and Orr lightened the program with "The Gabrielettes" (Holz). The Staff Band's "heavy" numbers were Ball's variations on "The Old Wells" and Coles' transcription of Tchaikovsky excerpts entitled "Moments." Soprano Marian Anderson (Franz Rupp, accompanist) sang Schubert's "Ave Maria" and the spiritual "Let Us Break Bread Together." The proceedings came to a triumphant conclusion with band, chorus, and congregation joining together in Irving Berlin's "God Bless America" as arranged by Erik Leidzen. Fittingly, Peggy Watson, a former Star Lake Musicamp student trained by these staff bandsmen, was the featured soloist.[32]

The more intimate banquet on January 3 allowed Commissioner Damon to thank the band personally for their outstanding support of the Army's work. J. J. Stimson was called upon to reminisce, as were Edgar Arkett and Robert Griffith. Three wives shared the "band widow" side of band history in a skit called "Sisters of the Skillet." Lt.-Commissioner John Allan paid tribute to the holding power of Army music in his life and accurately assessed the band's impact over the years:

*No matter where the band went it always excelled the greatest
expectations of the townspeople and has through the years lived
up to the highest traditions of Army bands all over the world.*[33]

Silent tribute was paid to deceased veterans of the band during
the program. A resolution was read by Colonel Norman Marshall
stating the current band's desire to rededicate their skills and
talents, asking former members to join them in prayer and faith.
Former "Spiritual Bandmaster" Walter F. Jenkins closed the happy
evening by asking God to bless the band for another victorious
fifty years.

**Another War**

The Jubilee Celebration was held at a difficult time in American
history. War had just been declared against the Nazi and Jap-
anese Empires. Although the band had survived the relatively
short American involvement in World War I, grave concerns were
now expressed, even in the midst of the Jubilee Celebration, as to
whether the Army and its Staff Band would ever be the same after
the new war had taken its toll.

Warning signs had been present earlier than Pearl Harbor. John
Allan had been called back into the U.S. chaplaincy as early as the
fall of 1940 as some American Army command officers began to
anticipate future needs if the nation should be drawn into the
conflict. The first staff bandsmen to enlist were William Perrett and
Pershing Flanders in March 1941. Soon the band was involved in
military morale events just as they had been from 1917-18: Fort
Dix, June 1940; launching of USO drive at the Waldorf-Astoria,
June 3, 1940, with Thomas E. Dewey as chairman; and a
"Spiritual Defense Parade" in Philadelphia, November 1940.

By early 1944, the band had only 22 members. Granger,
however, was adept at bringing in local bandsmen, military servicemen on leave in the area, and other recruits to swell the ranks of
his depleted band during this period so that the many engagements of the band could be met.[34] Before things got too lean,
however, there were some musical and spiritual highlights on the
band's itinerary. Moshe Paranov, conductor of the Hartford Symphony, after leading the band in several pieces during a spring
1941 visit of the TSB to Hartford, joined forces with the Male
Chorus and congregation in spontaneously improvising (at the
piano) background music to Lt.-Governor Odell Shepard's recita-

tion of Vachel Lindsay's poem, "General William Booth Enters into Heaven," at the close of a festival.[35] Several weeks later, the band heard the proper version, recited by Mrs. Dr. Olive Lindsay Wakefield, sister of poet Vachel Lindsay, when she was featured at the F.E.T. Finale for the 1940-41 season.[36]

Band visits in 1942 to military camps like Camp Upton, Long Island (which the band had also visited in 1918), and to patriotic rallies like the "Brooklyn Patriotic Song Fest" at Borough Hall were balanced by a trip to Pittsburgh (April 9-13) in support of retired General Evangeline Booth[37] and a Temple University Stadium Sunrise Service with 50,000 worshipers on Easter weekend that year. Auto travel restrictions and fuel rationing began to cut down on band activities except when government-sponsored programs were involved. The band's return trip to Philadelphia on Easter Weekend, 1943, included two USO concerts in Philadelphia, a visit to the Philadelphia Naval Hospital, two broadcasts designed for overseas transmission (WHAT and WFIL), and a visit to Fort Dix on the way home. Dr. Ross Stover and Walter Eddowes of Ocean Grove, friends of the band, again organized a massive ecumenical Sunrise Service, this one on North Broad Street not far from Philadelphia Divisional Headquarters.[38]

John "Jack" Wyrtzen called for the band's services twice in 1944 for help in his Youth for Christ rallies at Madison Square Garden, April 1 and September 30. The band at the F.E.T. finale that year could still manage Ball's "Triumph of Peace" and transcription of Schubert's "Unfinished" Symphony by B/M Theobald of Springfield (Mass.) Citadel. Ed Lowcock (cornet, "Memories") and Milton Kippax (euphonium, "The Warrior") were the work-horse end-chair men in this smaller ensemble. George Granger and his men were not "quitters." Their schedule and efforts in the remaining years of the war show but little letup. Even when his war injuries bothered him severely, Granger would not slow down when the band was required for service.[39] Only the most dramatic moment in Staff Band history would stop him, when during the Staff Band's annual concert in the Ocean Grove (N.J.) Auditorium, he received his heavenly summons and was "promoted to Glory."

## Ocean Grove

In the days of Ballington Booth and Frederick Booth-Tucker the Staff Band had made frequent appearances in Ocean Grove

71

during that community's camp meeting season. After 1903, the visits were halted until August 8-10, 1936, when The Salvation Army joined forces with the Ocean Grove Camp Meeting Association for a special weekend series of meetings. For the next 15 consecutive years, the New York Staff Band made its way to this quiet resort town to support famous Army leaders and acclaimed Christian speakers who preached there.

A happy friendship, which still exists today, was developed between the Staff Band and the regular musicians of the camp meetings. Walter D. Eddowes, director of music, and Clarence Kohlmann, organist, cooperated well with the band and an Ocean Grove Night at the F.E.T. even developed during the year when fellowship was renewed. A strong corps, with solid music forces under B/M Alfred Swenarton, developed in neighboring Asbury Park, N.J., which served an area where many Army officers and soldiers chose to retire. When the New York Staff Band was not called on by the Camp Meeting Association, frequently Swenarton's corps ensemble or New Jersey divisional musical groups occupied the Ocean Grove Auditorium platform with equal eagerness and efficiency. The connection therefore, between the Ocean Grove Auditorium and Salvation Army music-making is a strong one. On its stage the very finest in Army music and musicians are heard, and great spiritual awakenings have taken place in times of revival, renewal, and recommitment.

The 1936 partnership of The Salvation Army and the Camp Meeting Association brought immediate benefit to both parties. Attendance at the Sunday morning worship service increased by 5,000 that year, the largest since 1928. The concert attendance on Saturday evening was estimated at 3,000 and this figure would grow in succeeding years as the reputation of the Staff Band and Male Chorus grew.[40] The entire 1936 weekend included 18 engagements for the band, from the Saturday 2:30 p.m. march from the main gates of Ocean Grove to the Dr. Stokes' Monument, through to the Monday evening service in the smaller Temple. The band led beach meetings and youth rallies, and it supported various Army speakers, including retired General Edward Higgins, that year. They also offered music for worship, the outstanding feature being their Saturday evening Sacred Festival of Music.[41]

The repertoire for the 1936 festival set the pattern for many years to come, with the program divided into two parts separated by an intermission. Male Chorus and solo features balanced the heavier band items. Classics and patriotic items were always included. A combined number with Ocean Grove musicians was also a regular feature; for the first year, however, only the organ (Kohlmann) joined the band. The program, chaired by Commissioner Alexander Damon, looked like this:[42]

Preliminaries

**Part 1**

| | |
|---|---|
| March | "Torchbearers" (Eric Ball) |
| Vocal Solo | "Sea of Galilee" (Melody, "A Thousand Fathoms Deep," text by William F. Palmer; sung by Frank Fowler) |
| Cornet Solo | "Hallelujah" (William Parkins—Erik Leidzen), played by William Parkins |
| Male Chorus | "Comrades' Song of Hope" (Adolphe Adam) |
| Band | "Moments With Tchaikovsky" (arr. Bramwell Coles) |
| Trombone Solo | "Unfathomed Love" (arr. Frederick Hawkes), played by Kenneth Ayres |

**Part 2**

| | |
|---|---|
| March | "Banners Unfurled" (Richard E. Holz) |
| Euphonium Solo | "Lift Up the Banner" (James Merritt; played by Harold Jackson) |
| Male Chorus | "God's Voice" (arr. from Sibelius' "Finlandia") |
| Band Selection | "American Melodies" (William Broughton) |
| Cornet Duet | "Always Cheerful" (Albert Jakeway), played by William Parkins and Fred Farrar |
| Finale for Band and Organ | "Hallelujah Chorus" (G. F. Handel) |

In 1937 they also ended with the "Hallelujah Chorus" but added the attraction of turning on the huge electrically lighted American flag that was mounted on the stage wall. In later years they would switch the music for this most-awaited, climactic moment to pieces like Sousa's "Stars and Stripes Forever." William Bearchell had replaced William Slater as Male Chorus leader by the second annual event, and an old Male Chorus favorite, Kipling's "Hymn Before Action" (set by Davies) provided part of the patriotic segment. This "brilliant" festival also featured much of the band's Canadian tour repertoire plus a new piece by Clarence Kohlmann, "Hail to The Salvation Army." So popular was the band's music that the 1938 printed program carried the following underlined rubric: "Due to the length of the program, requests for encores cannot be granted."[43]

George Granger was in his element at these weekends. He loved the spirit in which his band participated, even though by 1939 it was routine. He sent personal letters of thanks to staff bandsmen following the weekend. Here is one received by Staff Bandsman Lawrence Castagna, dated August 11, 1939:

My dear Captain:

The Ocean Grove week-end is now an engagement of the past. *Just another town done!*

Everyone worked hard and I believe gave their very best, and from the reports I hear, the weekend as far as the Band's concerned was a success.

I want to thank you for your fine cooperation and look forward with great anticipation for an excellent Band this coming Fall.

Again please accept my thanks.

Sincerely yours,

George Granger, Major, Bandmaster[44]

The Ocean Grove Choir joined the band for several items during the 1940 festival, including a grand finale setting of "God Bless America," with Emil Nelson as tenor soloist. The previous year an "All Round the World" medley (not Soderstrom's piece) ending with "The Star-Spangled Banner" had also brought forth the rippling lights of Old Glory. The warhorse "Gems from Haydn" (Hawkes) showed up on the 1941 program, perhaps to please old Darby, as part of the "classics" section. During the war years, more and more patriotic items, such as salutes to the various branches of the armed forces, took on prominence. (See Chapter 12 for illustration of 1943 program.)

Great preachers added to the bandsmen's enjoyment of these weekends, particularly during the 10:30 Sunday morning service. They could sense the contribution they were making in preparing the hearts of the congregation before speakers like Dr. Harold Sloan would bring the morning sermon.[45] Their own Evangeline Booth joined them for an emotional Sunday evening presentation of "Christ on the Doorstep" in the great auditorium, August 4, 1940. Triumphs at "The Grove" for the band were always both musical and spiritual. The thousands taking their vacation at the shore had their spirits renewed and their hearts lightened by music designed to help lift burdens and to point people to a forgiving Saviour.

*Esprit de corps* is an important matter in a band, no matter how noble its intentions. A *Musician* article on Granger's last major trip with the band, to Syracuse, N.Y., in early 1945, included an upbeat report guaranteed to help the struggling war-year band gain confidence:

> *With plenty of life and lilt, the Eastern Territorial Staff Band and Male Chorus provided a musical festival par excellence at Syracuse, N.Y., on a recent trip.*
>
> *Rising to a brilliant crescendo of audience appreciation and instrumental mastery, the band delighted a great crowd of music lovers who taxed the capacity of the Indian Town's Mizpah Auditorium.*
>
> *From the first downbeat of Major G. Granger's baton through to the last double bar, the band performed with finesse and flourish, giving every note its maximum worth in tonal quality and easy execution. Ringing salvos of applause greeted classical arrangements and stirring marches alike.*[46]

With very few servicemen back in the band by the summer, the Pacific War still not resolved, the band needed that kind of boost. As they arrived in Ocean Grove, August 4, 1945, and held rehearsal for the evening concert, some of the men thought of it as "just another town," never realizing it would be their leader's last night with them.

George Granger's "promotion to Glory" on the auditorium stage that evening—in front of 5,000 people—has been told effectively in other books, most notably former Staff Bandsman William G. Harris' account in *Sagas of Salvationism*.[47] Untold features of this dramatic moment, however, have since come to light that can help give a new perspective to the remarkable behavior of the band, the audience, and the leaders on that occasion.

The regular part of the program began with the technically demanding festival march "The Canadian" (James Merritt). Canadian George Granger could not have been prouder as he led his band in front of that large crowd, among which sat his wife and children. Next was a setting of Beethoven's "The Heaven's Are Declaring" by the Male Chorus (under Bearchell) and a cornet solo "The Volunteer" (Hartmann, arr. Simons) by Edward Lowcock, accompanied by the band. During Frank Fowler's bass solo, "I Know a Voice" (Lillanes), Granger slumped over in his chair. When he did not respond to Colonel Norman S. Marshall's announcement of the next piece, euphonium solo "Song of the Brother" (Leidzen), two men carried their leader off-stage into one of the corridors where Dr. William Robinson and a first-aid attendant confirmed that he had already died of a heart attack.[48]

Back on stage, Deputy B/M Bearchell took over the baton for the solo accompaniment while Staff Bandsman Alfred Swenarton, on leave from the military and in the audience, took his place in the band. The program was being broadcast live on WCAP and no one, except Bandsman Swenarton, who in running down the side aisle and up on the stage had had to step over the body of Granger, yet knew the extent of the tragedy.

An emotionally-charged ovation greeted Milton Kippax, Bearchell, and the band following the Leidzen solo. Only then was it announced that the staff bandmaster had been "promoted to Glory." Now the true mettle of the band and its leaders was tested. The program continued in the most miraculous way. The audience, for the most part not Salvationists, sensed something special was happening and rallied behind these valiant men with an overwhelming affirmation of their musical efforts.

From the technical point of view, the actions of the band were understandable. Bearchell had "conducted nearly all of the pieces at one time or another at Brooklyn Citadel."[49] Swenarton had been sitting in with the band since he joined the armed forces whenever his C.O. at the nearby Raritan (N.J.) Arsenal allowed him leave to play with the band.[50] Even from the emotional side, it is understandable why the men could continue so effectively. As Swenarton put it, "It happened so fast, one couldn't react until afterward."[51] The men would deeply grieve for their leader though, just as they had rejoiced in his wonderful service as bandmaster. The great congregation, as it sang William Maltby's chorus "Christ Is the Answer to My Every Need," just two items after the announcement of Granger's death, could understand how the music of salvation should rightfully continue, celebrating a life lived victoriously and a soul's awakening to a warrior's rewards.

*Your friends, your comrades, play the songs of Zion*
*And knowing even then that you were there.*
*Yes, you were there when the final chord was played,*
*You went on wings of music—marching friend,*
*And left us with the determination to play our part to the end.*[52]

# 6

## "The Valiant Heart"
### (Philip Catelinet)

## Bandmasters William Bearchell
## and William Slater
## 1945-1954

In the decade following World War II, the Staff Band was fortunate to have two veteran musicians serve as bandmasters. Both men had served the band with distinction for many years before wielding the baton. Bearchell was a versatile staff bandsman, capable of switching with ease from cornet to solo alto, gifted as a consummate piano accompanist of both the Male Chorus and the band's vocal soloists, and talented as an arranger and composer. His compatriot, William Slater, was an articulate euphonium soloist and practically-minded band enthusiast skilled in the "nuts and bolts" aspect of band administration, equipment, and music. Both had had success as Male Chorus leader and as music leaders in local corps, particularly William Bearchell as bandmaster of Brooklyn No. 1 (Citadel).

Their bandmasterships would be marked by gradual improvement in the technical proficiency of the band and chorus and by remarkable strides in the overall health of the music forces within the Eastern Territory. Bearchell and Slater were willing participants in the new programs launched by territorial headquarters with the establishment of a Territorial Music Section under Richard E. Holz and his associate Alfred Swenarton in January 1946.[1] The Staff Band's role as model became more useful and demanding than at any previous period in its history. The continuity of leadership then available within the ranks of the band made for a prosperous and consistent period.

## Renaissance of Sacred Music in The Salvation Army

On May 13, 1949, the New York Staff Band (William Bearchell) and Temple Chorus (Richard E. Holz) presented their F.E.T. Finale Festival in cooperation with the Hymn Society of America (Rev. Deane Edwards, president).[2] Territorial Music Director Richard Holz presented a paper, "The Renaissance of Sacred Music in The Salvation Army," that summarized the recent achievements of Army musicians in the territory since the war. The program, as designed by both conductors, was a cross-section of the finest classics and new arrangements from the pens of Salvationist composers. Five hundred Hymn Society members joined the overflow crowd in praising the musicians who sang and played so splendidly that night.

Music by Bearchell, Holz, and Leidzen—the latter recently reinvolved in S.A. activities thanks to the efforts of the Territorial Music Section—represented America. Compositions by Eric Ball, Bramwell Coles, George Marshall, and Philip Catelinet stood for the finest of the current British generation of writers. The fathers of Salvation Army music, Richard Slater and Arthur Goldsmith, were not ignored either. In a marvelous way the program detailed the history of Salvation Army music, from early songs of Slater (Fowler singing "O Remember") and Goldsmith's trend-setting meditation, "Rockingham," to Bramwell Coles' tone poem/suite "The Divine Pursuit" and William Bearchell's festival march, "Marching to Zion."

Three years before this milestone event, Holz, Bearchell, and Swenarton had convinced various divisional and provincial commanders to launch regional music institutes as incentives in the rebuilding of the post-war band program. During 1946 these three men traveled to conferences in New England, Western New York, and their own metropolitan area. Soon a plan emerged to match the vision they held. A five-fold program was established to encourage this expected "Renaissance": [3]

1. Biennial music leaders' councils for the encouragement of existing and developing bandmasters and songster leaders [begun April 1947]

78

2. Biennial music congresses where corps groups could play for and learn from one another, besides hearing the very finest of S.A. music and musicians from both the NYSB and guest groups from outside the territory [begun May 1948].

3. Yearly bandmaster training courses under the tutelage of Erik Leidzen in various regional locations [first graduation in spring 1949].

4. Strengthening of the summer music camp program and curriculum, both on the divisional and territorial level, with special emphasis placed on the now Star Lake "Advanced" Musicamp [term used first in 1946], from which new leaders could be recruited.

5. A music publishing scheme, including the new, nine-part "Band Music for Evangelism" *American Band Journal,* launched by a composition contest judged and edited by Erik Leidzen in 1946-47.

What was the role of the Staff Band in all of this? Members continued to provide the basis of the staff at Star Lake and other music camps, trained as conductors in the courses offered, took on local corps positions, and performed the new music at all major events, providing definitive readings for corps ensembles. The band provided the work force from which the Territorial Music Department could begin to achieve the goals that Territorial Commanders Ernest Pugmire and Donald McMillan (both former staff bandsmen) had so wisely approved and encouraged.[4]

On February 22, 1946, the NYSB, joined by the Temple Chorus and the Northern New Jersey Songsters, honored George Granger in a Memorial Festival during which the Granger Memorial Scholarship to Star Lake Musicamp was launched.[5] Not only was Granger eulogized but this award would also stand for the finest in dedicated, selfless service that Granger had given year after year in the training of young musicians at Army music camps. Men like Frank Fowler, George Granger, John Allan, and a host of others from the band's ranks willingly gave of their time to "reproduce themselves" in the cause of sacred banding. Duplicated by countless soldiers, officers, and bandsmen across the nation, such efforts would lead to a genuine rebirth of bands and singing groups in the United States, leading by the late 1950s to the high-water mark in the history of Salvation Army music in the country.[6]

## In the Great Churches

> We thank God for the splendid Salvation Army Staff Band, and for the manner in which it presents the great music of the gospel. I have always felt it a shame that we allow the devil to capitalize on good music and have kept the church down to the solemn, the sad, and sometimes the unbeautiful in our musical programs. Why shouldn't Christians have the brightest and happiest music? The very essence of our faith and service demands snap, brightness!
>
> We congratulate the band upon its wisdom in having its music well-arranged for the instruments used so that the effects are comparable to that which the world attains in its music.
>
> As I listen to this Staff Band play their well-arranged music in such a delightful way, I thank God that kingdom service can be bright and attractive and equal to the world in its appeal, with the added blessings of the presence of the Spirit of Christ to make it effective.[7]

Noted preacher Dr. William Ward Ayer praised the NYSB in this manner on the occasion of their 3:00 p.m., December 19, 1947, concert in Manhattan's renowned Calvary Baptist Church. The yearly Christmas series at this church was to last into the present band's regular schedule. Playing in great churches had been a function of the band since its earliest days when it backed Ballington Booth, Frederick Booth-Tucker, and Evangeline Booth. Its musical impact had been more in the way of a novelty or curiosity, however. The gradual improvement in musical standards wrought by Darby, Broughton, and Granger, and the notable improvement in the quality of the Army's music made bands like the NYSB not only acceptable in the most sophisticated of congregations, but actually lauded as exceptional examples of a special kind of sacred music. This upper-crust acclamation would come to the band on the same day they would play at the Women's Detention Home in Greenwich Village![8]

By the 1940s, it was the band and its fine chorus that churches all over the country wanted, not just another evangelist with special music. The sight of 36 men (frequently introduced, to the amusement of the men of the band, as "all converted alcoholics or dissipated individuals") playing so sonorously the great hymns of the church in impressive, symphonic settings, or singing flawless four-part harmony, was a spiritual tonic for the typical "burned-out" parishioner.[9]

Other large churches soon asked the band for annual visits, Brookdale Baptist Church in Bloomfield, N.J., being an excellent example.[10] The Christian business community of Manhattan sought out the band for celebrations like their Corporate Communion Breakfast, first held March 20, 1949, at the Hotel Astor.[11] As early as December 1936, the band had played at the National Preaching Mission, Hudson County, N.J., with the clergy of hundreds of Protestant churches joining in ecumenical worship.[12] The ministry of the Staff Band and Male Chorus was effectively reaching all men regardless of their level of society.

## Now Let Us Praise Famous Men (and Women)

During 1948-49 Bearchell's band honored three key figures in its history: Erik Leidzen, Evangeline Booth, and John Allan. The unique relationship each had with the band was noted in a special festival wherein their compositions and friendship with the band (or, in the case of John Allan, sterling influence and leadership) were recognized and held in high esteem and admiration. Erik Leidzen, now effectively reconciled to the Army and its leadership, was recognized by Edwin Franko Goldman as "the greatest arranger for bands in America today."[13] Former General Evangeline Booth, retired in her beloved America, thus received one more bouquet for her contribution to The Salvation Army in the U.S.A. Commissioner John Allan, then Chief of the Staff in London, represented the host of excellent Army leading officers that had come through the band's ranks.[14]

Bearchell and Holz planned an "All-Leidzen" festival for April 24, 1948, at the Central Citadel Corps on East 52nd Street, where Leidzen had faithfully soldiered since his break with Evangeline in 1933. The program that night featured older works by Leidzen from his "First Period":[15]

Cornet Quartet
    "The Trumpeters" (MMS)
    (Soloists R. Schramm, W. Fox, L. Catlin, W. Orr)

March
    "Pressing Onward" (FS 24)

Cornet Solo
    "Happy All the Day" (FS 148)
    (William Perrett, soloist)

81

Male Chorus
"Onward" (*MS,* Vol. 43)
"A Charge to Keep" (*MS,* Vol. 43)

Selection
"On the Way Home" (*FS* 106)

Euphonium Solo
"Song of the Brother" (*FS* 136)
(Milton Kippax, soloist)

March
"On to the War" (*GS* 939)

Meditation
"The Savior's Name" (*FS* 98)

Trombone Solo
"A Never-Failing Friend" (*FS* 92)
(Arthur Craytor, soloist)

Horn Duet
"Only Jesus"
(Emil Nelson and Alfred Swenarton)

Meditation
"Home Sweet Home" (*FS* 47)

Festival March
"Fling Wide the Gates" (*FS* 64)

The program was repeated at the F.E.T. Finale that year, and by Star Lake Musicamp in August, Leidzen was providing challenging music like his new Meditation "Richmond."[16]

The April 1948 concert honoring Leidzen marked a change in the great composer's relationship with territorial leadership and the NYSB. From that time until his death in December 1962, Leidzen became the band's chief defender and principal composer, and he began working in close cooperation with Richard Holz, then territorial music secretary.[17] His output became even more productive than in earlier years, and his compositions were inescapably linked with the band, which premiered and featured nearly all his works, from solo features to the finest large-scale works.

Evangeline Booth's music was sounded forth at the November 19, 1948, F.E.T. All her famous "Songs of the Evangel" that had blessed millions were reviewed with heartfelt thanks. Leidzen provided a symbolic gesture of reconciliation by writing a new march, "E. C. B.," based on the notes of her initials, that carried sentimental but ironic carry-overs from the 1933 Ensemble Festival when Leidzen's Metropolitan Ensemble had premiered his "E.F.G." march in honor of Edwin Franko Goldman. Recalling the F.E.T. tribute to Evangeline Booth, Richard Holz said:

> Lt.-Colonel Bearchell and I prepared a complete program of the music of Evangeline Booth which proved to be a success, not only because of the excellent audience which received it enthusiastically, but because of the high quality of the presentations. The superb arrangements by Eric Ball, Erik Leidzen, William Broughton and others, of her compositions were in excellent taste. At the last minute, due to illness, General Evangeline Booth was unable to attend. Alfred Swenarton and I, with Colonel Maltby, then the Divisional Commander for Metro New York, visited the General at her Hartsdale home and presented the entire Festival via an excellent wire recording.[18]

## Congress Festival 1949

When John Allan chaired the Congress Music Festival of October 15, 1949, Eric Ball's music was prominently featured. Next to Leidzen, Ball was the Army composer most frequently associated with the band through the years. Bearchell had the band read through such classics as "Star Lake," "The Pilgrim Way" and "Sound Out the Proclamation." Two compositions written by students of Erik Leidzen were heard: Richard Holz's "Old Time Religion" for male chorus, and Howard Evan's cornet trio, "Sweetest Name," giving further evidence of growing talent among staff bandsmen. In a War Cry review, John Allan said the highlight of the festival was Fowler's bass solo "My Task" (Ashford). For 50 years Fowler had kept faithful to his appointed service and Allan had shared many of them knowing them to be genuinely fruitful years of singing God's praises.[19]

A glance at Appendix E, "Recordings," shows us that the Bearchell-Slater years were also noted for a resurgence of recording activity. We have been left a grand heritage of music-making from this period that gives us an aural glimpse of these resourceful men and their compatriot leaders and composers. Much of the material recorded reflects a healthy respect for native talent, both soloists and composers: Bearchell, Holz, Leidzen, Evans, Gustafson, etc., as arrangers; Lowcock, Craytor, Fowler, etc., as soloists.

## Gaining Respect

The front cover of *The Musician* (International) for November 15, 1947, showed a picture of the NYSB in the sunken garden of Radio City Plaza from which a series of programs was broadcast during United Nations Week.[20] All sections of the band were improving and their conductor had excellent taste in brass band repertoire. The yearly music leaders' councils or congresses placed special pressure on the band and its soloists to play at a high level indeed, if they were to remain true to one of their basic functions since 1887, that of setting the standard.

At the Music Congress Finale Festival, April 4, 1948, the band provided the last items at the close of a spectacularly successful weekend [1,500 delegates, 30 bands, 20 songster brigades; attendances averaging 3,000; guest soloists from Canada: Margaret McFarlane, soprano, and Ernest Parr, soprano cornet].[21] Two critiques, provided anonymously by selected judges survive to give us a picture of "Bill" Bearchell's band and one of his soloists:

*CAPTAIN EDWARD LOWCOCK—Cornet Solo "Happy All the Day"*

*Good opening—band well-balanced and playing in spirited style. Soloist gets away to a good start—clean—with plenty of spirit. Accompaniments well modulated. Melody coming through well at "A." Soloist giving nice interpretation—accomps well subdued and smooth, horns a little ragged in spots. Band interlude three bars before "B" performed well with excellent shading. Soloist doing varie at "B" in nice rubato style—well marked and pleasing. Accompaniments tastily done, horns slightly sharp on last note (top A). "C" generally well played. Main figure in lower part of band (bass solo) played well together—moving nicely—clean. Good robust style. Soloist coming through nicely on triplet varie at "D." Clean—nice tempo—not too rushed—very pleasing. Accompaniments a little choppy. Euphoniums moving smoothly—nice contrast. "E" much the same performance as in "C," except horns are rather boisterous—overblowing and thus untuneful. Modulation one measure before "F" very well executed—good molto rall. Soloist in good form at "F"—nice minor—well phrased—pleasing style. Accompaniments well played—good tone color—triplet figures well dovetailed—strict attention given to dynamics—nice performance. Tempo change at "G" not too well executed, rather ragged and takes two or three measures for* some parts to find correct tempo. Soloist brilliant at "H"—moving beautifully in nice easy style. Accomps well subdued but a bit ragged—seem to be having trouble keeping up with tempo. Better towards end of variation. Band good in Section "I." Cadenza very well done—good style. Presto nicely handled with band alert and moving well together. Ending rather unusual, but good. Have rarely heard Captain Ed Lowcock in better form. Excellent performance by both Soloist and Band.[22]

**THE STAFF BAND**—Suite "The Divine Pursuit"

After reviewing, for the first time, the full score of this remarkable tone poem, I see how inadequate my notes are. Obviously it is not fair to the Band or the reviewer to attempt to criticize such an outstanding and unusual piece of music without having the score for reference at the time of performance. I can only say that I have rarely heard the Staff Band in such top form. The playing was inspired. Only here and there throughout the entire number was the ensemble playing marred by an untuneful note or a late entry. The unusual 5/4 movement, "C" through "G," was exceptionally pleasing and very well done, showing hard work and strict application to the music. Section "H" also calls for special mention—this is a beautiful melody—expertly treated by Colonel Coles. The playing was ultra smooth with excellent balance—basses especially, solid. The last six measures were grand. Balance and tunefulness left nothing to be desired. The old melody, "O Love That Wilt Not Let Me Go," is placed in a beautiful setting—rather unusual, yet very pleasing. The horns did a grand job on this—well in tune and perfect blend. No one part could be distinguished above the others. Altogether, an excellent interpretation of a rather difficult piece of music such as would tax the ability of any brass band.[23]

Continuing the fine tradition of good repertoire, with some occasional attempts at Darby-style programming, William Slater kept right in stride with Bearchell when he took over the band in January 1951.[24] Within a few months they toured the Southwest Ohio and Northeast Kentucky Division with concerts at Asbury College (Wilmore, Ky.) and the Cincinnati Conservatory of Music. Dr. Luther A. Richman, director of the conservatory, said of the concert: "This has been a mountaintop experience, musically and spiritually....At this school the latchstring is always out to the New York Staff Band." Famed Cornet Soloist Frank Simon also expressed his appreciation, calling the band's presentations an excellent demonstration of "what can be done with an all-brass group."[25]

85

Radio appearances during the Bearchell/Slater years were frequent, perhaps best represented by a Mother's Day broadcast, May 1951, on NBC and Armed Forces Radio with Commissioner Pugmire and Rose Brampton of the Metropolitan Opera, and the Methodist Church's "The Circuit Rider" national broadcast, October 1951, with the band providing incidental and background music.

The television barrier was broken by a ten-piece ensemble of the Staff Band during the fall of 1951.[26] The first full-band broadcast was made Saturday, March 8, 1952, from the studio of WNBC on the eighth floor of Rockefeller Center. Ed Herlihy interviewed Commissioner McMillan during this half-hour program while the band played new pieces like Kippax's "Golden Jubilee" and Soderstrom's "Deep Passage," both items from the new *American Band Journal.*[27]

The previous month the band had visited Toronto, Canada, February 15-17, 1952; seven of their number had participated in the band's tour of Canada 15 years earlier, in 1937. On this latest tour, the band was received well by B/M Vic Kingston and the North Toronto Corps Band, celebrating the 70th anniversary of Salvation Army work in Canada and the 38th anniversary of the North Toronto Corps.[28] Major Arnold Brown (later General) arranged a fine regional festival that drew a large crowd, including critic Edward Wodson of the *Toronto Telegram,* whose review was quoted in a *War Cry* report:

> *Northern Vocational School Auditorium was filled to capacity on Saturday evening when the [NYSB] of The Salvation Army was heard in recital. The band has been called a "Symphony in Brass," and justly. The music it made on Saturday evening was symphonic in a most subtle sense. And the players were truest symphonists—meaning men whose musical genius is an attribute, individual and characteristic as the noses on their faces and the sparkle in their eyes.*
>
> *The instrumental soloists were virtuosi [E. Lowcock, M. Kippax, A. Anderson]. The quartet of cornets might have been organ music for clear, defined accent and faultless precision in the counterpoints....One of the bandsmen [F. Fowler] sang the one-time familiar "My Task"; his voice, a deep, searching basso that carried his faultlessly enunciated words to the farthest corner of the hall. In the band, he is first tuba [sic], the lowest-pitched instrument of the ensemble. He sang the beautiful ballad with a reverence deep as the tones of the cavernous tuba itself.[29]*

At the December 1951 Salvation Army Association of New York dinner honoring General Douglas MacArthur, William Slater's arrangement of "The Star-Spangled Banner" was hailed by the old warrior as the finest he had ever heard.[30] Alberta Powell Graham featured the NYSB in her 1952 book, *Great Bands of America.*[31] The band rubbed shoulders with musicians the caliber of Eric Ball (May 4, 1954), the Westminster College Choir (April 1951 Music Leaders' Councils), and with fine corps bands like Earlscourt Citadel, Canada (March 1953 Music Congress) and Tranas, Sweden (April 1954 Music Leaders' Councils). Each year the performance level of the band seemed to improve; each year new musical possibilities and challenges confronted them. When we reflect while listening to the many 78 rpm recordings made during the Bearchell/Slater years, it is noted that they had many miles to travel musically to reach today's standards, yet in that day they were among the best, and they could hold their heads high with dignity.[32]

## Banners and Bonnets

An unsolicited public-relations windfall came to the Army when noted Broadway composer Meredith Willson ("The Music Man") let it be known that he had written a song in honor of Salvationists' dedicated service to mankind. Struck by the challenge and beauty of a cadets' covenant service he witnessed during a commissioning in San Francisco, Willson was moved to write "Banners and Bonnets," which became one of the best-known songs about The Salvation Army. The New York Staff Band became the principal vehicle whereby this ballad became so popular.[33]

When Willson let Army headquarters in New York know what he had composed, Richard Holz rushed over to Willson's Rockefeller Center office so that a quick collaboration could begin. The hope was that a special arrangement could be made immediately so that the item could be included at a Waldorf-Astoria banquet scheduled in less than a week. Holz and Willson agreed on the haunting opening, with just the bass drum, tambourine and lone cornet player sounding the song as from afar. A leading Metropolitan soprano was designated as the soloist, with Staff Band and Male Chorus backup required. The meeting was a fast one, though friendly and cordial, with Willson entrusting all the details of the arrangement to the territorial music secretary.

Having finished the arrangement by "burning the midnight oil," Holz was then told that Christopher Lynch, tenor soloist at the Metropolitan, would be the featured singer. This meant substantial changes in the voicings of the arrangement and an entire shift of key level! Somehow, in the midst of a busy music weekend, with his department members feverishly assisting with the copying, another arrangement emerged, just in time for the March 11, 1952, premiere. Willson, a guest of honor at the dinner, praised the arrangement as "wonderful" and "excellent." Christopher Lynch sang the item again May 9 at the F.E.T. Finale to even more acclaim.[34]

The switch to tenor soloist was a happy one in the long run. The band had its own dramatic tenor in Olof Lundgren, and it would not have been long before this marvelous Swede would have been singing it with the band anyway. The inimitable Lundgren cheered the hearts of millions with his thrilling renditions of Holz's arrangement. The piece is the embodiment of the band's spirit and service, brass and voice welded together in a joyous celebration of the opportunities God gives to men who serve Him selflessly.

The Public Relations Department was most pleased by this kind of musical event! The Staff Band was its mobile public relations unit. Christmastime was always the busiest season, in this regard, as the band or its ensembles were sent scurrying around Manhattan in a schedule that turned department heads' hair gray.[35] Everyone connected in the least way with the Army wanted the band. Corporate presidents needed a quartet for a party celebration where employee donations would be handed over to the Army with some ceremony. Tree-lighting services, carol sings, radio spots, and full TV specials were by 1953, just part of the expected routine.[36]

Playing for famous men like Dwight Eisenhower (1950) or Douglas MacArthur (1951) and at Salvation Army Association of New York dinners may have had more direct appeal to the band, but trips to Welfare Island were no less important. Out of all this public-relations "hoopla," however, came an understanding of how modern media could be used in the proclamation of the gospel. The Army could remain faithful to its basic calling in the midst of tremendous fund-raising pressures. Proper use of its musical forces was one definite avenue to be explored.

The radio series "Christ Is the Answer," launched October 1952, was one initial experiment.[37] Public Relations Secretary Horace Weatherly and Richard Holz coordinated the programs using a small, ten-piece ensemble of the Staff Band plus a select songster group. The Army had always been in the forefront of Christian involvement in radio, and use of the television remained to be explored in a new era of media dissemination. Soon the TV series "The Living Word," to which the Staff Band would contribute music in later years, would be launched as a pioneer effort in television evangelism. Funding problems and administrative "haggling" have marred the ultimate success of these notable, visionary attempts.[38] Only recently has The Salvation Army begun to re-enter this arena in which they were, at one time, leaders. One of the most difficult tasks for Army fund-raisers during the second half of the 20th century has been maintaining the delicate balance between the Army's spiritual ministry and its social welfare work.

## A Band of Leaders

When Slater's band traveled to Chicago for the Central Territory's Music Congress, June 12-13, 1954, Central Territorial Music Secretary Bernard Smith noted in a *War Cry* report that the Central Territory at the time was governed by men who were all former New York Staff Bandsmen: Commissioner Claude Bates (former saxophonist), Colonel Edwin Clayton (former band executive officer), and Colonel Edgar Arkett (former French horn player).[39] The same was true at National Headquarters, and at both the Eastern and Western Territorial Headquarters; men like Commissioners Donald McMillan and Norman Marshall, and Colonels William Harris and Bertram Rodda. Even International Headquarters was infiltrated via John Allan, Llewellyn Cowan and Charles Bearchell, all men in the upper echelon of administration! The fact was (and is) that the New York Staff Band has through the years provided an extremely significant proportion of fine officers and leaders within the Army.

Since Edward J. Parker's appointment as national secretary (given title of national commander in 1943) succeeding Evangeline Booth in 1934 all but four U.S. National Commanders had been staff bandsmen:[40]

| | |
|---|---|
| Edward J. Parker | Edward Carey |
| Ernest I. Pugmire | Paul J. Carlson |
| Donald S. McMillan | William E. Chamberlain |
| Norman S. Marshall | Paul S. Kaiser |
| Holland French | |

Appendix D contains the names of 23 staff bandsmen that have achieved the rank of commissioner. A host of others have held important corps and administrative positions in the century of the band's existence. The present sessions at the Eastern Territory's School for Officers' Training contain several excellent former staff bandsmen destined for noble service as Salvation Army officers. During their first visit to Chicago in 1954, the NYSB presented some old Darby favorites, J. O. Hume's march "Conqueror" and Slater's vocal/brass arrangement of "The Stars and Stripes Forever," perhaps to please the veteran leaders present! New music included Stanley Ditmer's masterful suite "Triumphant Faith," Holz's "Banners and Bonnets," and Soderstrom's "Southland Memories." Fowler was still singing favorites like "The Wondrous Story," and Ed Lowcock displayed his gifted technical facility in "Heavenly Gales" and "Glory to His Name."

"Bill" Slater's final "tour of duty" as bandmaster came October 15-18, 1954, with a tour of northeast Ohio, including visits to Canton, Dover, Mount Vernon, Columbus, Mansfield, Akron, Cleveland, and Youngstown. In a replay of the old "motorcade" days, the band traveled 1,501 miles, 450 of which were by a fleet of station wagons.[41] Richard Holz was at the International College for Officers in England, but Vernon Post, who recently arrived in the Music Department, was serving as Slater's deputy during the fall.[42] Continuity and quality among its locals would again assure a smooth transition of leadership when Slater retired in December to assume further administrative responsibilities. He would remain a loyal supporter of the band, recording their programs on his new magnetic tape recorder and supporting Holz in the new, unprecedented series of professional long-play records produced by the cooperative efforts of the Music and Supplies and Purchasing departments.[43]

### Earlscourt and Tranas: First of Many

The goal of inspiring Eastern Territory musicians during the Bearchell/Slater years reached its first high plateau during 1953 and 1954 with the visit of the Earlscourt Citadel Band (Toronto, Canada) and Tranas (Sweden) Corps Band. These two bands represented real success stories for corps bands in the Eastern Territory.

Bandmaster Wallace Mason's Canadians made a significant

impression during the March 20-22, 1953 Third Biennial Music Congress, particularly in the realm of dynamic control. The NYSB tended to play rather loudly under Slater, who, if he could get it, preferred a large band. Demanding and subtle scores, like Steadman-Allen's "Young at Heart" or Skinner's "Heroes of the Faith," were read by Earlscourt with a definitive clarity and control. Sixteen corps bands were also featured at the congress; they could not but learn from this tight ensemble.[44]

The Staff Band was not outdone, however, and their scintillating performance of Dean Goffin's new "Symphony of Thanksgiving" was a particularly moving experience too, in the light of the death of Slater's wife but a few days before the congress. Arthur Anderson, solo trombonist of the Staff Band, was also a "smash hit" with his driving, exciting performance of another new, forward-looking solo, "The Eternal Quest."[45]

An even greater sensation was caused by B/M Gunnar Borg's Tranas Band when they toured the United States, April 3-27, 1954, and were featured at the Fourth Biennial Music Leaders' Councils in New York City. The reasons for the trip were simple ones—ones used to silence those critics who wished the money spent in other ways. The interchange of ideas and experiences between cultures is invaluable, particularly when the visiting group has something highly beneficial to offer. The first European band to visit The Salvation Army in the States since 1888, the Tranas Band was an outgrowth of a Chalk Farm (England) Corps Band Tour to Sweden! In the small Swedish town of Tranas, having a population of no more than 14,000, a marvelous brass band tradition developed by sheer hard work and study. The young enthusiasts, thrilled by the potential in sacred brass banding when they heard Chalk Farm, formed a band of their own, learning how to teach music and to conduct.[46]

These joyful Swedes could really play, too! E. F. Goldman, guest chairman at the Saturday evening concert by Tranas, the NYSB, and the Temple Chorus declared, "You are hearing tonight one of the greatest brass bands of nonprofessional musicians I have ever heard...Any of the brass players in any of the symphony orchestras could not play better than these men...."[47] A phenomenon, developed virtually in isolation by sheer hard work, Tranas thrilled American audiences and encouraged the struggling efforts of bandsmen in small bands across the United States. Commissioner Marshall summed it up well in his final challenge to the congress delegation at the Sunday finale: "Go away from this occasion with a new vision and a new consecration which will give new impetus to this task in which we are all engaged."[48]

Fellowship between the two featured bands stands high in many memories. At a dinner for both bands, "Olie" Lundgren, Vincent "Ben" Bulla and a young Tranas bandsman exchanged classic lines in a typically humorous "foul-up" in the translations necessary during the sharing time. The men did share the same music, even though the language barrier existed. Stig Uhner, solo cornetist of Tranas, featured in Steadman-Allen's transcription of the Haydn Concerto, could have dialogue with "Art" Anderson who gave the American premiere of Leidzen's "Concertino for Band and Trombone" at the congress. Emil Soderstrom and Erik Leidzen, both providing special music and encouragement over the years to Tranas, were also bridging the gap and beaming with Scandinavian pride.[49]

The men who may have received the greatest reward from these exchanges were the men who worked hardest to bring it off: Richard Holz, Alfred Swenarton, and Vernon Post. They and their small Music Department were consistently following through on their plan started back in 1946 and the dividends were coming in. Army banding in the Eastern Territory was entering its heyday and these men would see their vision realized in but a few more years in corps bands, divisional bands, and a Staff Band and Male Chorus equal to any in the Army world.

# 7

## "None Other Name"
(Erik Leidzen)

## Bandmaster Richard E. Holz
## 1955-1963

On January 4, 1955, at the Stockholm Restaurant in mid-Manhattan, a symbolic passing of the baton took place between William Slater and the new bandmaster Richard Holz, with Deputy Bandmaster Vernon Post looking on. The band had gathered to usher in the new season and to honor their retiring leader. Tributes by Vincent "Ben" Bulla and Llewellyn Cowan spoke of Bandmaster Slater's personal interest in every bandsman. An emotion-laden evening, it marked the end of one era and the start of a new, different adventure in the history of the band. The Bearchell/Slater years became the Holz/Post years in a smooth, efficient manner.[1]

The two new leaders came to their positions with excellent experience and training. Richard Holz had impressive academic and administrative skills, already demonstrated in his direction of the Territorial Music Section since 1946.[2] Incalculable insight into the compassionate but firm handling of men had been granted him during his chaplaincy in the South Pacific during World War II. His deputy, Vernon Post, was an honors graduate of the Cincinnati Conservatory of Music with laudable achievements as a corps music leader behind him. Both men shared a special vision for the

Staff Band and Male Chorus. They desired to build a music force marked by true musical and spiritual excellence.

Within the nine years that Richard Holz directed the Staff Band, the standard of personal and musical discipline among all the bandsmen was raised to a high level indeed. A disciplinarian— perhaps even "enforcer" is an apt description[3]—Holz demanded the very best by leading his men in a firm but understanding way. The achievements of that band are multifold: many effective spiritual campaigns, tours (including California and Great Britain), congresses, and an unprecedented series of long-play recordings. Their music-making was, for the first time in the band's history, equal to any in the Army world. Vernon Post was given considerable rehearsal time and flexibility in the development of the Male Chorus during this period, allowing him to achieve results with these "average" singers that astounded audiences from Royal Albert Hall to the Long Beach Municipal Auditorium.

These two fine musicians drew excellent performers into the ranks because of their "no nonsense" approach to Army music. Vocal and instrumental soloists of this era are among the finest in the band's history. Take the soloists for the British tour, for instance: Olof Lundgren, Albert Avery and Peter Hofman as vocalists; Derek Smith and Robert McNally as instrumentalists.[4] Yet the band, while not steeped in *virtuosi,* was a hard-working, serious band. Its executive officers, George Marshall and William Maltby, were particularly supportive administrators who recognized the special spirit that was being instilled in these men. All the right ingredients were present: musical and personal leadership, gradual acquisition of top-flight soloists and section leaders, administrative support, and a unity of purpose among the men of the band. This was not achieved overnight; some veterans did not appreciate the new methods, new music, and new instruments.[5] Yet the end result, best represented in the band's triumphant tour of Great Britain (1960), was worth all the struggle and commitment put forth by these conductors and their willing comrades.

## On the Mall

The pattern established during the Bearchell/Slater years of "setting the standard" for territorial music congresses was continued at the Diamond Jubilee Music Congress (April 29-May 1, 1955) at which 16 "solo" bands and 12 songster brigades participated.[6] At this initial test, the new band played well, accompanying

U.S. Navy Band Euphoniumist Harold Brasch, and assisting Edwin Franko Goldman and Erik Leidzen in special clinic demonstrations. Goldman was particularly impressed with the band and invited them to replace his band for an evening "On the Mall" in Central Park, an historic first for a Salvation Army band.[7] The mall concert was held on the evening of June 23 and billed as a salute to the 75th Anniversary of The Salvation Army in America.[8] Four new Besson basses were in evidence as part of Holz's plan to upgrade the equipment of the band. Both old and new repertoire were heard, from "Treasures from Tchaikovsky" to Heaton's "Praise," which was described as a "unique march in modern idiom."[9] A crowd of 3,000 was in attendance. Later that summer the band returned to Old Orchard Beach, Maine, for the first weekend of the camp meetings. A large grove audience of 2,200 heard a program similar to the Central Park concert but also special features like Lundgren's sensitive vocal solo, "He Took My Place," and former B/M Bearchell's "Marching to Zion," directed by him at special request of B/M Holz. In the week following, many staff bandsmen spent vacation time at Old Orchard Beach with their families, which included a "busman's holiday" for those who augmented B/M Eric Foster's Old Orchard Beach Camp Meeting Band.[10]

"Brass playing at its finest" was the way Frank J. Prindl, then director of bands at the University of Kentucky, described the NYSB's concert at Transylvania University, Lexington, Ky., during the band's tour of the Southwest Ohio and Northeast Kentucky Division, November 17-21, 1955. More than 2,000 in the audience, including hundreds of high school musicians, demanded several encores.[11] Arthur Anderson was among the heroes that evening, as he "brought down" the house with his "Count Your Blessings."[12] The band's music and playing was a revelation to these Bluegrass State band enthusiasts:

> The outstanding features of the concert were the beautiful, sweet singing tones produced by the players, as well as the interesting arrangements and original compositions presented. Bandmaster Holz revealed his sensitive musicianship through his conducting—his beat was clear at all times—the musicians responded to the slightest inflection of his baton.[13]

At nearby Asbury College in Wilmore, Ky., the band played for another enthusiastic crowd of 1,500 organized by Professor Lee

Fisher and Dean J. B. Kenyon in the stately Hughes Auditorium. The tour concluded with an appearance on WCPO-TV, Cincinnati, for an hour show with host personality Bill Baily and Divisional Commander William Chamberlain.[14]

## Mozart and the Metropolitan

The 69th season of the NYSB (1956) coincided with the 200th anniversary of Mozart's birth. The annual festival on February 10 was partially dedicated to this event.

Metropolitan Opera Basso Jerome Hines was the guest soloist in a program divided into two parts: Part I, Music of Mozart; Part II, Contemporary Music. Operatic arias from "Don Giovanni" and "The Marriage of Figaro" were flanked by brass transcriptions from "Exultate Jubilate," "Eine Kleine Nachtmusik," and the "Twelfth Mass" of Mozart in the first section. "Contemporary fare" in the second part included Leidzen's "Concertino for Band and Trombone" (Arthur Anderson, soloist) and Ralph Vaughan Williams' latest gift to Salvation Army bands, "Prelude on Three Welsh Hymn Tunes." Jerome Hines' final contributions were a series of gospel songs, such as he sang frequently to the men at the Bowery Corps since his rededication to a Christian ministry.[15]

Several days later Erik Leidzen wrote a note to B/M Holz about the evening that gave the new bandmaster an honest and encouraging review:

*Mon cher Coeur de Lion:*

*Just a line of sincere thanks for a most pleasant evening. I am, of course, referring to the Staff Band concert.*

*It is almost impossible to believe this is the same band we heard a year or two ago. But then, it isn't. A new and wholesome spirit pervades it.*

*When Anderson premiered the Concertino he was so far above the band as he could jolly well be and still play the same piece. This time—though he played far better than last time—the band gave the better performance. However, at times it was a sheer joy to listen. I saw Anderson afterward and congratulated him. In spots he was even better than Maisie.*

*Perhaps I was most surprised by the band's efforts on THE PRELUDE. It may yet become a standard on your repertoire when the boys find their respective levels.*

*As for the real music (and I mean Mozart) it was mostly a sheer delight. That you have forced or coaxed or guided that formerly so limited group into such playing commands my admira-*

*tion and respect.* MORE POWER TO YOU. *Please convey to the band my heartfelt thanks.*

*Yours for more and better* MUSIC.

EL[16]

Several weeks later, Jerome Hines had his opera *I Am the Way: Scenes from the Life of Christ* performed at the F.E.T. Good Friday service. Preliminary music was provided by the NYSB and the Temple Chorus/Male Chorus sang the Choral Prologue from St. John, "In the Beginning." The opera was done each Eastertide for several years running. Hines, the six-foot-six-inch Metropolitan Opera star, was a true friend of the Army and its evangelical efforts. He was just as "at home" on the small platform of the Bowery Corps giving his personal testimony in song as he was playing a contrasting role as the Mephistopheles of Gounod's *Faust* on the great Metropolitan stage.[17]

Hines graciously served as a clinician at the Fifth Biennial Music Leaders' Councils that brought the Chicago Staff Band to New York, March 10-11, 1956, under their able bandmaster Victor Danielson. The NYSB had its usual "demo" role, particularly with new *American Band Journal* and *Young People's Band Journal* music to be promoted. The two staff bands shared the platform Sunday afternoon, while on Saturday night the NYSB Male Chorus supported the Chicago Staff Band's solo concert. The "second-city" brass warriors proved their own worth, especially with noted soloists Ernest Miller (vocal), Howard Chesham (alto horn), and Ronald Rowland (cornet), the latter becoming a NYSB member in later years. On Sunday afternoon, both groups, as United Male Chorus and Staff Bands, were directed by Erik Leidzen and the staff bandmasters.[18]

The Toronto (Canada) Spring Festival, a tour of the Northeastern Ohio Division, Old Orchard Beach Camp Meetings, another Central Park Mall Concert, and corps weekends in Lynn, Mass., and Philadelphia (Pioneer), Pa., completed a busy year for the revitalized band. As the year began with "Mozart and the Metropolitan," it concluded with a WABC Christmas radio program featuring the band, narrated by Milton Cross, the voice of the Metropolitan Opera.[19]

Several months later Frank Fowler, the band's mainstay tuba player for many decades, was honored at the Staff Band's Annual Festival, January 25, 1957. Holz wrote a whimsical "Fantasia for Four Tubas and Band," in tribute to this dedicated bandsman.

Fowler was also a gifted "gospel singer" and his swan song on the Temple stage was "Rose of Sharon," accompanied by Bill Bearchell and with Male Chorus humming in the background. The deeply emotional evening provided a special means for the band to say "thank you" to a man who had served in its ranks with unprecedented years of service and devotion. One of its great warrior spirits would sing no more the song of Zion in this lifetime. It would not be long before the Male Chorus would sing by Fowler's grave on a New Jersey hillside.[20]

## From Sea to Shining Sea—"Long-Play" Records

"The Finest Band in the Army World," the International Staff Band (ISB) of The Salvation Army, arrived in New York for the April 5-7, 1957 Music Congress to the enthusiastic welcome of 1,671 delegates. On Saturday evening a Carnegie Hall crowd of 2,800 heard legendary soloists like Roland Cobb ("Wondrous Day"), Joshua Walford ("Ransomed") and Arthur Rolls ("Count Your Blessings") set new standards of excellence in brass band performance. Bandmaster Bernard Adams' fine-tuned ensemble provided dazzling displays of technique in pieces like "Treasures from Tchaikovsky" and Soderstrom's march "Fighting for the Lord." New music (Steadman-Allen's imaginative suite "Lord of the Sea" and Goffin's "Road to Emmaus") gave the delegates what they hoped for—renewal through exposure to new sounds and new styles of playing.[21]

The NYSB discreetly played a secondary musical role on the weekend, as well as serving as hosts to their British comrades in a special fellowship luncheon. There was no doubt that the New Yorkers had much to learn from these polished Londoners. They would absorb every possible detail of this excellent band's playing and learn from this exchange of cultures. The pattern established with Earlscourt and Tranas was now paying off its richest dividends for musicians across the continent. The NYSB was not intimidated. Bandsmen used it as a marvelous learning experience, with their bandmaster being the quickest learner. In discussions with Bernard Adams and Erik Leidzen, Holz became more and more convinced that the NYSB needed to secure the very best instruments along British brass band models, but he was also determined that the band must maintain its distinctly American sound and style. Within a year the plan, which had begun in 1955 with the purchase of four compensating-piston Besson basses, was complete. All bell-front instruments were now banished, short-model cornets were the order of the day, and even the baritones were large-bore and supplied with "compensating" valve systems. The band had a rich, warm sound; it looked and sounded impressive as all the sections "matched" in manufacture, timbre, and in appearance (golden lacquer finish).

Before that was accomplished the band began a trendsetting pattern, unequaled by any other Army band, in the release of a series of "long-play" (33 rpm) recordings, initiated in the June 1957 "Festival of Music" release on the Triumphonic label. The Male Chorus played an equal part in these productions, as a review of Appendix E will demonstrate. Long-play recordings allowed a marked improvement in the band's outreach ministry. The recordings had an evangelical purpose in addition to the financial help they would begin to supply. The band has continued to stay in the forefront of recording efforts, making these productions a decided and vital part of their yearly efforts. "Stereo," "cassettes," "digital" —in all these technological advances, the NYSB was a pioneer in terms of Salvation Army recording history. The initial efforts of Holz's band are particularly noteworthy for the quality of the music programs recorded and steadily improved quality of reproduction that came with each succeeding recording from 1957 to 1963. Final confirmation came with the "Record of the Year" award from Word Recordings, Inc., Waco, Texas, which produced the stereo "Symphony In Brass" recording in 1963. An earlier release on the Westminster label ("Christmas with The Salvation Army") was also a "hi-fi" award winner in its day.[22]

In the summer of 1958 (July 25-29) the band traveled "from sea to shining sea" to the Southern California Camp Meetings at Long Beach at the invitation of William Parkins, then divisional commander. Parkins was proud to be the one responsible for the band's first transcontinental trip. The Monday night festival followed Holz's new three-part scheme noted for a specific middle devotional section. In this concert challenging music like Leidzen's "The Cross," Coles' "Moments From Tchaikovsky," and Ray Steadman-Allen's "Lord of the Sea" were blended with Americana arrangements by Soderstrom, "Stephen Foster Fantasy" ("Southland Memories") and Leidzen's new solo for Robert McNally, "Home on the Range." "Banners and Bonnets," with Olof Lundgren as soloist, served as the grand finale. A syndicated Long Beach reviewer, whose remarks were reprinted in *The War Cry* wrote:

99

*This amazing aggregation of brass instrumentalists...*
*surpasses anything of its kind that I have heard...I had some*
*misgivings. But I was mistaken. The first mellow tones astonished*
*me with their caressing beauty. Instead of a blare the euphonious*
*blending of the different brass instruments gave a depth and*
*sonority to the music that I have never experienced....Putting*
*down their instruments they became a male chorus, singing as*
*beautifully as they played. It is really an astonishing group. They*
*perform for the love of their music and for the love of their God.*[23]

The long weekend had its lighter moments—a tour of Warner Bros. Studios, and later, Forest Lawn Cemetery/Memorial Park, where the band sang "Rock of Ages." This was a spiritual campaign, however, and the men worked hard in the meetings supporting Eastern Territorial Commander Commissioner Holland French, who was guest speaker. The total number of "seekers" for the weekend exceeded 360.[24]

The 1958-59 season was indeed a banner period for the band. Three nationwide television appearances placed the NYSB before a total viewing audience of 80 million. The band's West Coast tour was balanced by a visit to the Eastern Canadian Congress in Montreal. The Eastern territorial music program had featured an emphasis on youth recruitment with staff bandsmen leading the way as teachers and music leaders. The Music Leaders Councils of 1958 (642 registered music leaders) featured three outstanding red-jacketed young people's bands from Arlington, N.J., Niagara Falls, N.Y., and Troy, N.Y., as well as the Salvation Army Student Fellowship Band of Asbury College (the only Army band in the world at that time composed exclusively of college students) and the Metropolitan (N.Y.) Boys Band School (under Robert McNally).[25]

During the summer of 1958, in addition to their California trip, many staff bandsmen were busily engaged in music camps. Thirty-seven years after the establishment of the first Salvation Army band camp (by John Allan, Long Branch, N.J., 1921), there were ten divisional music camps plus Star Lake Advanced Musicamp, with a total student population of 1,300 (Eastern Territory figure only).

The following year's music congress saw another guest group, the spirited Netherlands National Band (B/M Bernard Verkaaik), display excellent Salvationist spirit and challenging, stirring music. The re-emergence of banding in war-torn Holland was a noble, uplifting story equal to "The Tranas Story" of several years before.

As these Dutch comrades campaigned in 20 Eastern cities, thousands heard their sacred ministry in leading festival halls, schools, universities and via television, radio, and recordings. Their principal rooters were members of the NYSB.[26] These men had been enriched by their visiting comrades: Earlscourt, Tranas, Chicago Staff, International Staff, and Netherlands National. Soon it would be the New Yorkers' turn to return the favor and bring their unique musical gifts and salvation songs to the motherland of Army music—Great Britain. By 1960 the NYSB was ready for such a demanding task.

## Great Britain 1960: "Sons Come Home"

The New York Staff Band's Tour of Great Britain, June 3-16, 1960, will stand in brass band annals as a remarkably daring and successful venture. At the Bon Voyage Festival, May 13, at the Centennial Memorial Temple, William Bearchell presented to the band a symbolic piece of anthracite coal for presentation in Newcastle, England. In the minds of many was the question, "Could our NYSB be carrying coals to Newcastle?" For an International Staff Band to tour America, where the brass band tradition was, relatively speaking, not strong or, at least not widespread, their presentations would naturally receive acclaim for excellence. Could a New York band really make it in a land filled with brass bands?

One answer came back quickly to folks at home via a telegram from General Wilfred Kitching during the band's first weekend: "The band has already made a great spiritual impact and been acclaimed as one of the Army's best."[27] The secrets of success had to do with being honestly American, not in trying to imitate British styles, although strongly acknowledging the cultural ties and debt. New, exciting *American* music, top-flight soloists, superb vocal music, and imaginative programming were those "secrets." An additional and vital aspect was the band's keen evangelical spirit, put in fine tune during the band's spiritual weekend just prior to the tour.[28]

The schedule was a demanding one; within an hour of their arrival at the Army's Denmark Hill complex, following a .12-hour trans-Atlantic flight, they "got down to business" rehearsing for their first big event, the Royal Albert Hall Bandmasters' Councils Festival the next evening. The overall schedule for the tour, graciously and efficiently handled by Dean Goffin, then National

101

Secretary for Bands and Songster Brigades in the British Territory, was as follows:

### NYSB Tour of Great Britain: General Itinerary
### Principal Events and Concert Sites[29]

| | |
|---|---|
| Friday, June 3: | Arrival in a.m.; Rehearsal and reception at Denmark Hill |
| Saturday, June 4: | British Councils Festival of Music in Royal Albert Hall (6:30 p.m.); preceded by rehearsals in hall |
| Sunday, June 5: | Bandmasters' Councils at International Training College, Denmark Hill (Sessions at 10:30, 2:30, and 6:30) |
| Monday, June 6: | Nottingham: Albert Hall |
| Tuesday, June 7: | Leeds: Town Hall |
| Wednesday, June 8: | Newcastle: City Hall (BBC North-TV program during the day) |
| Thursday, June 9: | Edinburgh: Open-Air Festival in Princess Street Gardens in afternoon; Usher Hall in evening |
| Friday, June 10: | Free day—Tours of Highland, Loch Lomond and City of Edinburgh |
| Saturday, June 11: | Manchester: Free Trade Hall (BBC Radio with Harry Mortimer in evening) |
| Sunday, June 12: | Manchester: Morning services in Openshaw Citadel; afternoon Festival and Salvation Meeting in Free Trade Hall |
| Monday, June 13: | Liverpool: Noontime luncheon program at Rotary Club; Philharmonic Hall in evening |
| Tuesday, June 14: | Birmingham: Central Hall |
| Wednesday, June 15: | Oxford: Town Hall |
| Thursday, June 16: | London: Morning recording session at BBC Studios (Maida Vale); Farewell Festival in evening, Clapton Congress Hall. |

The British/Scottish hospitality was marvelous—civic receptions with lord mayors, governors, consuls, and similar dignitaries; gracious tea/fellowships with corps groups or civic authorities;

special sightseeing arrangements and VIP tours of famous historic spots. Dean Goffin's role as efficient tour manager was augmented by the presence of ISB Bandmaster Bernard Adams June 6-10 of the tour, Charles Skinner (head of the International Music Editorial Department) June 12-16, and Brindley Boon (editor of *The Musician)* at various spots along the way. Bandsmen's needs were handled with ease and tact; the comradeship shared was genuine and warm. Beyond that, the generous response of British Salvationists, who opened their homes for "billets" to these Americans, will never be forgotten.

The band's premiere performance was an imposing one. The bandsmen found themselves seated in the cavernous Royal Albert Hall surrounded by the Kettering Corps Band (Cyril Manning), Sunderland Millfield Corps Band (Harry Woods), the International Staff Band (Bernard Adams) and a 700-voice British Congress Chorus (Dean Goffin). What an exciting evening for the New Yorkers! What a warm reception they received! Their soloist, Derek Smith, performed flawlessly on Leidzen's specially-composed *tour-de-force*, "Songs In the Heart"; the Male Chorus, with Soloist Albert Avery, hushed the great crowd with its legendary singing of "Rock of Ages" (Bearchell), and before the last chord of Leidzen's "None Other Name" was released, the great throng vociferously and excitedly approved of this challenging new music. The band drew the honor of playing the respective national anthems, the opening march, and accompanying the finale, Eric Ball's choral setting of "Psalm 150," sung by the united voices of the bandsmen and Congress Chorus.[30]

Eric Ball was asked to provide a review of the evening's concert. His objective report stands as testimony to Holz's band that evening:

*And now the question in so many minds—what of the New York Staff Band?*

*First-rate! Intonation, balance, blend, certainty of technique, control of dynamics and tone colour are all at high level and Major Richard Holz's economical conducting is to be highly commended. The tone is somewhat "different" from that of British bands: not so "deep" or organ-like (here I make comparisons only with the finest), but it is a flexible tone, never overborne, and there is fine clarity in the playing. I hope the band will never lose its own "personality."*

*We heard this band first in the U.S. and British National Anthems and Emil Soderstrom's "Army of God." Later came Erik*

*Leidzen's new cornet solo, "Songs In the Heart," music demand-
ing technical prowess and musicianship to a high degree. Our
good friend Bandsman Derek Smith was in wonderful form,
proving beyond doubt that he ranks amongst the greatest cornetists of today.*

*Toward the end of the programme the American visitors
presented another new work by Erik Leidzen— "None Other
Name." Played con amore, the wonderfully rich and varied
scoring of well-loved songs about our Lord captured the imagination, as does the earlier "The Saviour's Name." This is music for
the Salvationist par excellence.*

*As a choral group, under the direction of Captain Vernon Post,
the New York Staff Band sang the simplest arrangements (by Lt.-
Col. William Bearchell) of "Rock of Ages" (Tune: Wells). The
appeal was direct, with no "modern" harmonies, the words clear
(a few perhaps too-overstressed for purest taste), the solo voice of
Captain Albert Avery clear and expressive. One could have heard
the proverbial pin drop.*

*Our home bands will not begrudge this extra space devoted to
the visitors. They came, not as strangers, but as comrades in a
great tradition, seeking musical perfection and marked by
sincerity. The testimony of Senior-Captain Robert McNally, the
solo euphoniumist, left no doubt about that....*

*To the Chorus fell the final honour of bringing this great and
important festival to a close. For this Major Holz directed a fine
performance of "Psalm 150," the NYSB accompanying splendidly, and the rest of the bandsmen singing with the chorus. Here
was a great dignity and fervour (too many songster brigades
interpret the first and last sections of this work as a waltz!).*[31]

The New Yorkers were treated to superb new music by British
bands and composers, too! The ISB premiered Eric Ball's brilliantly demanding "Song of Courage" while Kettering Band offered
Ray Bowes' forward-looking suite "The King's Crusader." Sunderland Millfield read Dr. Thomas Rive's magnificent variations on
"I Know a Fount" and the ISB premiered Bramwell Coles' new
suite "The Living Word." For the hundreds of bandmasters present, it was a banquet of bountiful brass.[32]

On the following Sunday the NYSB received the honor of being
the first band, besides the ISB, to participate in the British
Territory's Bandmasters' Councils. Over 600 music leaders met
with General Wilfred Kitching for a spiritual and musical time of
renewal and recommitment. Both Holz and Post presented "tech-

nical talks," using their respective ensembles to illustrate their points in sound. Bandsman William Schofield and Executive Officer William Maltby testified during the day, joining several equally challenging witnesses by British band leaders. One highlight of the day was the NYSB's playing of Dean Goffin's "The Challenge of the Cross," this particular performance described by General Kitching as "a sacrament." Using various vocal soloists from the band on solo parts in the selection, Holz had the whole assembly join and sing the closing hymn, "When I Survey the Wondrous Cross" as a fitting corporate reaffirmation of faith and service.[33] Those hundreds of music leaders (whom Holz called "Christ's musical disciples") closed the magnificent day in a fitting manner, as described by Brindley Boon:

> Recovery of spiritual sight came to many in that meeting as the General listed the requirements of hallowed service and in the closing moments several confirmed their dedication at the Mercy Seat, men from New York and Great Britain mingling their prayers in glad surrender.
> The historic weekend concluded with the singing of "How Great Thou Art!" led by the British Commissioner [Edgar Grinsted] and accompanied by the International Staff Band conducted by Major Holz. With both hands held high above their heads and the light of holy joy shining in their eyes these leaders of men sang over and over again [the final refrain of "How Great Thou Art!"].[34]

The tour itself was filled with many blessings and victories, musical and spiritual. What follows is a series of excerpts from various British personalities who accompanied the band or who had responsibility for various programs. This summary can perhaps begin to underscore the band's impact:

**Brindley Boon** (editor, *The Musician)*:

> The band is making a tremendous impact upon Salvationists of the British Territory. Its clean, precise playing, well-rehearsed singing, programme presentation and hallowed mid-festival devotional periods are features which are making an impression upon the audiences. British bands have something to learn from these happy comrades.[35]

**Bandmaster Bramwell Williams** (Birmingham Citadel):

*You have given us a programme worth copying and raised the standards of listening.... You play with a great amount of enthusiasm but with control.... You have taught us a great deal.*[36]

**Ernest Rance** (Salvation Army officer and noted song composer):

*Band analysts have been amazed at the consistently high standard of performance by the New Yorkers after eleven days on the road. The Bandmaster [Holz] credits the "youngsters" for much of the sustaining ability, singling out Bandsmen Fred Jackson (soprano cornet), Bill Schofield (flugel horn), and Arthur Moulton (bass drum). Their performances in this festival were outstanding.*[37]

**Bandmaster Bernard Adams** (ISB):

*I enjoy this wonderful band...I have a great admiration for Major Holz; everything he conducts is well conducted....*
*[He goes on to credit Captain Post with]...having the touch of the artist in vocal music.*
*[In Yorkshire, Leeds Town Hall, he asked his countrymen what they thought of the band and writes that the audience]...jumped to their feet, applauding as if they would never stop.*[38]

**Bandmaster Alex Thain** (Edinburgh Corps and Councilman for the City of Edinburgh):

*Never in the history of this great hall [Usher] have we heard such uplifting and thrilling music.*[39]
*[Author's note: On this same occasion, Lt.-Commissioner William Leed led the audience in a tribute to the band, all the congregation singing to the band a most moving rendition of "Will Ye No Come Back." A similar experience in Manchester Free Trade Hall took place as over 2,000 Salvationists sang, pointing with affection to the band, "God Be With You Till We Meet Again."]*

**General Wilfred Kitching** (on the occasion of the Farewell Festival in Clapton Congress Hall):

*I want this written down in bold letters—this NYSB has in every way acquitted itself well. You have taught us some new ideas in new ways, and while Major Holz has said the Americans have learned a great deal from our bands, we, too, have gained from listening to the New York Staff Band and Male Chorus.*[40]

The tour ended at Clapton Congress Hall—a "standing-room only" occasion. In this emotion-charged atmosphere the band and its soloists (Derek Smith, Robert McNally, Olof Lundgren) received ovation after ovation:

*The historic occasion concluded with "The King of Kings" [Ball] and the echo of the majestic final chords had not died upon the air before this warm-hearted battalion of exemplary listeners had risen to its feet to display evidence of approbation scarcely seen in Army circles in this country. The British Commissioner [Edgar Grinsted] led the singing of "God Will Take Care of You" as a final token of affection and the great New York Staff Band tour was at an end.*[41]

Army music-historian Brindley Boon neatly summarized the trip's impact and meaning in a *Musician* editorial entitled "Sons Come Home":

*The tour of the New York Staff Band in Great Britain is at an end. As this issue goes to press the thirty-seven fine Salvationists comprising the party are scattering far and wide—on the Continent of Europe and in the British Isles—making the most of a few days' holiday before meeting in London to return home.*

*Those who had previously heard the band in New York became self-appointed ambassadors and began "banging the drum" on its behalf as soon as the visit was announced. Their confidence was not misplaced or their recommendation in vain. With sincere evangelism, natural charm, excellent playing and superb singing, these men from across the Atlantic came and conquered.*

*It will be a long time before the thousands who have attended festivals in nine cities stop talking about this band or forget the colourful platform scene of deep scarlet uniforms mingling with rich golden instruments. Here was deportment of the finest quality allied to excellent programme presentation to produce cultural satisfaction and spiritual stimulation.*

*One of the most hallowed memories of the tour will be the words of Sister Mrs. Marshall [widow of noted Army composer, B/M George Marshall] at Newcastle. "We welcome you as sons come home," she said, and the choice statement had deeper significance than a reference to the thirty-two bandsmen who*

107

*have British blood in their veins. These were sons of the Army returning to the land which gave William Booth to the world and in which the seed of an international movement was sown. In that sense these were indeed sons come home and with them they brought new ideas and novel methods from the New World.*

*There was much in our long-established tradition that impressed them: they spoke of introducing some of our trusted and tried ideas in America. In return there is much of what we saw and heard that could be retained over here.*[42]

## A Ministry of Musical Evangelism

The Staff Band's "test-piece" during the British tour, "None Other Name" (Leidzen), symbolically represented the highest motive behind the organization's service. If in their exuberant witnessing they relied on some "show-biz" techniques, like the famed standing sequences during the march "The Red Shield," they did not misplace the main purpose of their banding. The band's publicity brochure printed in the fall of 1960 declared that the band was "dedicated to a ministry of musical evangelism for Christ."[43]

The opportunities for expressing that zeal were plentiful in the years following the tour. Some events were along traditional lines, such as the Carolinas and Georgia tours in the spring of 1961 and 1962, respectively; large camp meetings or revivals, like the Billy Graham Crusades and the Ocean Grove Camp Meetings; or corps weekends, like that at Toronto Temple in November 1961. On the conclusion of the last-named event the Staff Band and Male Chorus recorded several excerpts for the Army's television feature "The Living Word." These more forward-looking uses of the band came fast and furious during the 1961 Christmas season, when in the space of but a few days the band made four national TV appearances.

Obviously some of these engagements were tied into public relations schemes as well. Their "Today Show" appearances on NBC that year included such gimmicks as "the world's largest kettle," designed by then Major Andrew Miller to capture the American public's attention. A gimmick used on "I've Got a Secret" (CBS) had the band appear from behind a curtain to accompany five-year old drumming marvel Sammy Deep from Macon, Ga. The band returned to NBC for a "Family Show" spot and a videotaped portion of the Christmas Day "Today Show" program, during which Robert McNally's son, virtuoso cornetist Bobby

McNally, played a fantasia on Jingle Bells (arr. Richard Holz), accompanied by the Staff Band. The appearances were "fun" and definitely good "PR," but they projected a Christian witness too, a witness that was clearly understood by men like Gary Moore, John Chancellor, and Frank Blair.[44]

Fifteen staff bandsmen had an historic evangelical role of a different nature when The Salvation Army officially opened up its ministry in Puerto Rico, February 1962. The ensemble, consisting of six cornets, three trombones, two alto horns, and one baritone, euphonium and $B^b$ Bass, worked hard for five days participating in festivals, open-air meetings, worship services, and ceremonial occasions for the launching of Army work on the island. The group was capable of playing and singing nearly all the standard literature the band and chorus had been featuring, including large works like "Themes from the Italian Symphony" (Goffin) or "All Round the World" (Soderstrom). Notable programs were enthusi-astically received at the University of Puerto Rico and the Colegio de Abogados de Puerto Rico.[45]

There was no musical "let-down" following the British tour. If anything, the band got better, adding good young players like Robert Bearchell and Laurie Robertson. Two English friends helped spur the band to new heights during 1961—Eric Ball and William Overton. Ball's "King of Kings" became the centerpiece of the band's repertoire and new record that year. His conducting of that work and "Constant Trust" during the blizzard-marked annual festival, February 3, 1961, is still remembered with awe by the men of that band. Will Overton, principal trumpet of the BBC, had shared the Royal Albert Hall stage with the NYSB in 1960 when he accompanied June Mingay in Handel's "Let the Bright Seraphim." In June 1961, he appeared as guest soloist with the New Yorkers in a now-familiar spot, the Central Park Mall, in works by Haydn, Purcell, Mozart and Eric Ball. In these he was accompanied by the band, while Goffin's Mendelssohn transcription and "None Other Name" headed the band's contributions.

During the band's Diamond Jubilee Year (1962, 75th anniver-sary) it seemed as if things could not get better for this interna-tionally-ranked brass ensemble. They made two feature albums just before the Puerto Rico tour in February that year: "Classics in Brass" featuring the Staff Band and "Songs of Victory" featuring the Male Chorus. Yale University opened Woolsey Hall to the NYSB in March and in April they were sharing the stage with a top-flight ISB during the Biennial Music Leaders' Councils. Two

109

Southern Territory trips, first to the Georgia Division and then to Washington, D.C. (the latter including a Watergate Amphitheatre concert), were followed by a Reunion Weekend in Ocean Grove with a grand 75th Anniversary Festival in the auditorium there on June 30.[46] General Kitching, who enjoyed the NYSB very much in 1960, heard the band again during a September 1962 territorial congress. Trips through Northeastern Pennsylvania and Western New York rounded out the busy fall season that year. The band had a special invitation to present a command performance at the prestigious Music Educators' National Conference Convention early in 1963.

The year 1962 ended tragically, however, for the band's dear friend and faithful contributor, Erik Leidzen, died suddenly on December 20. With great difficulty and emotion, the Staff Band and Male Chorus offered music to the many mourners who came to the memorial service several days later in Centennial Memorial Temple. For the moment, especially for men very close to Leidzen, such as Richard Holz and Vernon Post, it seemed as if their musical world was losing its main support pillar.

## On the Way Home

Almost three years before Leidzen's death, at the NYSB Annual Festival of February 5, 1960, a tape recording of Erik Leidzen introducing and then conducting his selection, "On the Way Home" had become an historic document for bandsmen not fortunate to have worked with this great man.[47] That entire festival had been dedicated to Leidzen, a man who had given Salvationists in America pride in their music and a mentor who motivated Holz, Post, and Swenarton to achieve the great milestones they did in this era. The band's repertoire was shaped around the gifted contributions which Richard Holz gently coaxed from this skilled and busy craftsman.

Somehow Leidzen had willingly given of his time to the Army in the midst of a demanding professional career. Part of his relationship with the Music Department was professional, particularly his editorial work on various projects and journals. As he made his living from music, he also received some compensation for his efforts in leadership training, both at music camps and in his Bandmasters' Training Courses.[48]

Hundreds of young people, many future staff bandsmen, had come under Leidzen's baton or influence at camps like Star Lake, where he challenged them to pursue excellence and integrity in their musical studies. He encouraged staff bandsmen to study with him and he would send personal notes of encouragement to various players in the band when he heard them play. His kindnesses were matched by a spiritual and philosophical sensitivity that was magnetic in its effect on Army musicians of that period. The music he arranged for Army brass so clearly communicated the gospel message of salvation. Leidzen himself embodied the best spirit of Salvationism.

No wonder then that some who survived Leidzen were guilty of nearly canonizing him as "St. Erik"! His loss was deeply felt, particularly by younger talented musicians who looked up to him. Initial eulogies were essential, of course, and both the NYSB and ISB gave superb "Memorial Festivals" in his honor several months later, the former also launching a very practical remembrance, the Erik Leidzen Memorial Scholarship, which to this day allows young people from around the world to attend Star Lake Musicamp.

In retrospect we can see Erik Leidzen as the first of what are now several superbly talented Salvationists in America who are ranked at the top in both their chosen musical profession and in the Army musical world. His vision, carried out with diligence by the combined efforts of the Music Department and men of the NYSB, is becoming reality. For Leidzen, the use of his professional skills for the furtherance of God's Kingdom was simply an expression of thanks to his Creator for gifts given. He called all Salvationist musicians to be responsible to their calling and to accept only the best in their struggle to make beautiful, God-honoring music. In this he imparted a priceless lesson to the New York Staff Band and Male Chorus, a gift that enabled it to offer sacrifices of praise in sound that were truly worthy of the label "sacred music."

### Incentive—Inventiveness—Insight

On March 2, 1963, the NYSB presented a demonstration and festival to a "standing-room" audience of high school and college band directors meeting at Haddon Hall, Atlantic City, N.J., during the joint conventions of the Music Educators' National Conference (MENC) and the College Band Directors' National Association. Erik Leidzen had been initially invited to present the demonstration. In his place, Holz presented a blueprint of the modern brass band to the attentive, musical audience with carefully selected illustrations provided by various sections or soloists in the band. Following the demonstration, the Staff Band, introduced by James W. Dunlap of Pennsylvania State University, presented a program of Salvation Army music, including "Steadily Onward" (Leidzen), "Come Sweet Death" (Bach/Leidzen), cornet solo "Glorious Fountain" (Bernard Smith) with Derek Smith as soloist, choral song "Rock of Ages," and the "Finale from The New World Symphony" (Dvorak/Steadman-Allen). At the conclusion of the final march "The Red Shield" (Goffin), the audience "rose in unison to give the band a thunderous ovation."[49]

MENC President Dr. Francis Andrews declared the concert the "highlight of the entire conference, a truly memorable experience that will be remembered for a long time to come."[50] These veteran musicians could now play before the most critical of audiences with confidence. Their leader was honored several months later by an invitation from Dr. Richard Franko Goldman to conduct the famed Goldman Band during its July 1, 1963, "Leidzen Memorial Concert." Salvation Army music and musicians were becoming respected across the nation by professionals at the highest levels without any loss of spiritual impact. Nothing could have vindicated Leidzen's efforts more, and nothing could have made him justifiably prouder, than these two signal honors.

Holz brought his 1963 Music Congress (March 29-31) "uptown" to Philharmonic Hall, Lincoln Center for the Performing Arts, for the Saturday evening spectacular. Products of the Army's successful training program were on display: Star Lakers like Trumpeter Carole Reinhart, Soprano Keitha Holz, and Pianists Robert Richardson and David Appleby, B/M Alfred Swenarton's Northern New Jersey Youth Band, and the United Congress Chorus, led by Vernon Post. Captain and Mrs. Ernest Miller, stars of the Army's TV show "The Living Word" were also featured. Center stage, however, was the New York Staff Band and Male Chorus. The music these two groups presented, including Eric Ball's "Song of Courage" and Vernon Post's taxing vocal setting "Joshua Fit the Battle," seemed to compliment very well the gracious but modern concert hall. The entire weekend came to a triumphant high peak on Sunday afternoon with two Leidzen gems (played by the NYSB), the manuscript march "Danish Festival" and the now-classic "None Other Name." More than 2,000 Salvationist musicians had registered as delegates for the weekend.[51]

During the next few months, the "Manhattan Melody Makers," as William "Bill" MacLean had dubbed them, visited Pittsburgh for

Armed Forces Weekend; Kingston, Ontario; and several New England corps. Word Records that spring commissioned a disc entitled "Symphony in Brass" and the band even played at Yankee Stadium May 21 when New York Yankee and outspoken Christian Bobby Richardson received a special Citation of Merit from The Salvation Army. In August, Richard Holz received his "farewell orders" appointing him as divisional commander of the Southern New England Division after 18 consecutive years in the Territorial Music Department. With mixed emotions he traveled to his last engagements—"Holz's last stand" as one *War Cry* writer from the band put it—to Portland, Maine, September 21-22, and Western New York, October 26-29. Appropriately, the new staff bandmaster, Vernon Post, had the privilege of taking the band on his first weekend trip to Bristol, Conn., November 9-10, during which Holz was installed in his new position.

At a farewell dinner for B/M Holz, Robert McNally presented a tribute that stressed what he thought Holz had imparted to the band in addition to great trips, tours and triumphs. He said Holz had imparted an experience of banding with "Incentive, Inventiveness, and Insight." McNally concluded with these remarks:

> You have always been astute enough to refrain from wholesale preachments and wise enough to bring up important matters in personal conversations. Many of us have been helped by the counsel and concern offered by you at the right time and in the right manner.
>
> So every time we play a composition particularly well, every time we use music to bring people closer to God, every time we are able to inspire some young musician, every time we show evidence of the highest banding standards—you will know that that is our way of telling you over and over again, "Thank you, Bandmaster."[52]

# 8

## "Take Salvation"
### (Emil Soderstrom)

## Bandmaster Vernon Post
## 1963-1972

The succession of Vernon Post to the Staff Band podium went smoothly. With this particular change of leadership there was optimistic projection that the organization would continue in the excellent achievements of the Holz period. In fact, in some ways it is easy to view the two periods as one. These two men shared the same dreams and plans; they had worked hard together for a decade. Post held to that shared vision for nearly ten more years. These men were different personalities, however, and they faced different challenges. While Holz faced initial indifference or hostility among the old guard, Post would face major upheavals in American social life that would profoundly affect the band's development. The perseverance and patience Vernon Post learned under Richard Holz's guidance would stand him in good stead when things became difficult.

The achievements of Post's band are notable. In musical proficiency it would surpass the previous generation as more and more excellent players swelled its ranks. A European tour and another triumph in Royal Albert Hall would allow this band equal status with the 1960 band. The continued program of music congresses and councils, guest bands from other countries and, above all, a wealth of talented young musicians, ably encouraged by Post, would help stem the growing loss of momentum in American banding as Americans became less interested in such demanding pursuits and more self-involved in leisure activities.

Vernon Post had a gift, like his predecessor, for getting excellent music for his band. With Leidzen gone, he relied on men like Soderstrom, Steadman-Allen, and a whole new generation of American writers. In this way he would maintain NYSB pace-setting standards and also establish some new milestones in daring programming and repertoire.

Both Holz and Post were "sons of the regiment," from families with deep Salvation Army heritage and notable achievements. They respected that heritage and built upon it. Vernon Post's earliest recollections of the band were from radio broadcasts and an occasional contact in his native southwest Ohio with "Billie" Parkins. How he became influenced by the band is told in his own words in an amazing document praising the ingenuity and initiative on the part of men like Granger and Holz:

> *In 1940 a pivotal event for my life took place. My family was vacationing in Elizabeth, N.J., and following the Sunday morning meeting, the corps officer, Captain Richard Holz, asked if I wanted to attend Star Lake Musicamp, beginning in about a week. Since we lived in Ohio, my father hesitated, but soon agreed.... The Monday camp opened I was at the C.O.'s quarters early. He very kindly played a number of recordings, including some by the NYSB. This was the first opportunity I had of talking with a staff bandsman on a one to one basis. At Star Lake I played solo cornet in the Star Lake Band conducted by Staff Bandmaster Granger, and sang in the Star Lake Chorus conducted by R. E. Holz. Along with such students as Ethylwyn Whittmore, Vincent Bulla, and Donald Seiler, I was fortunate enough to win my section on the soloist contest. Near the end of the camp, B/M Granger talked with me at length, asked if I would move to New York, invited me to live in his home and play in the NYSB. My parents thought otherwise. Fourteen years later I joined the NYSB [1954].*[1]

In between came military service, undergraduate study at the Cincinnati Conservatory, corps music responsibilities and Officers' Training College. Meeting up with Holz after that, Post was to find himself destined to follow Holz not only in the Staff Band but also as director of Star Lake Musicamp.

## Salvation Army Centenary

When Post assumed command of the NYSB in November 1963, he had a busy schedule already at hand. A National Composers' Contest was launched in January 1964, a Territorial Music Leaders' Councils, with Tottenham Citadel of Enfield, England as the guest band, was on the agenda, and the great Centenary Year of The Salvation Army (1965) was fast approaching. Wise enough to know his band needed an incentive, especially with a new leader and many personnel changes, Post was also able to get a tour of Louisiana scheduled for the fall of 1964, just in time to get the band in fighting trim.

Other "tests" came earlier in 1964. The Annual Festival for that year, held in February, included the premiere of Ray Steadman-Allen's new "Fantasia for Band and Piano," with the composer as guest soloist and guest conductor.[2] Al Swenarton, having left the Music Department several years before to direct the New Jersey Division's music program, also helped arrange a special clinic by the band at the New Jersey All-State Band gathering in February.[3]

In the summer of 1964 the band returned to Ocean Grove for the July 4th weekend where five staff bandmasters joined hands at the reunion table. With David Swyers, a southerner, serving as cornet soloist, the band eagerly traveled south to Louisiana that autumn, participating in concerts at Grambling College, Louisiana Tech., Tulane University, and the First Baptist Church of New Orleans.[4] With a new executive officer, Herbert T. Martin, and many new faces, the band still maintained a high standard. As a band report of the tour which was published in *The War Cry* put it, "Despite changing personnel, the NYSB is still capable of rising to the occasion to provide the finest in musical experience."[5]

The repertoire of the Louisiana tour included a mixture of old standards ( "Treasures," "Banners and Bonnets," "Steadily Onward," and "Home on the Range") and new manuscripts ( "Do Your Best," one of Leidzen's last compositions; a festival selection "American Rhapsody" by Emil Soderstrom, and "The Call of the Righteous," by Leslie Condon, first heard in America the previous April when Tottenham Citadel's rendition was the smash hit of the Music Leaders' Councils).[6]

The Centenary Year began with the band playing its dutiful role in a media-blitz, including a spot on WABC-TV's "New York, New York" show. The band's Annual Festival, or Centenary Festival,

117

featured Soderstrom's daring new work "Take Salvation," "Call of the Righteous," and several section showcases— "Never Give Up" (Ball) for cornets and trombones, "Alpine Fantasy" (Leidzen) for altos, and "Old Soldiers Fantasia" (Holz) for the basses. Traditional fare was not ingored on this historic evening. Old-time items were included like the euphonium solo "Ransomed" (Marshall) with McNally as soloist, the tenor solo "The Door Sergeant" (Marshall) with Lundgren as soloist, and the full band on Leidzen's "The Call." Particularly sensitive presentations were given by the Male Chorus in Post's arrangement of "Balm in Gilead" and by Al Avery as flugelhorn soloist in Grieg's "Solveig Song."[7]

Trips to Sunbury, Pa. (April 3-4), Pittsburgh, Pa. (May 15-16), Indianapolis, Ind. (May 29-30) and Toronto, the latter as part of the 1965 Spring Festival in Massey Hall, further prepared the band for the climactic fall celebration. The band and chorus recorded again for "The Living Word," this time in color, and also had the distinction of marching in the Indianapolis 500 Festival Parade.[8]

The Eastern Territory's Centennial Congress, October 22-25, 1965, was marked by much "pomp and circumstance" and, of course, impressive music. A music congress ran concurrent with the overall celebrations. Sharing center stage were the Staff Band and Maisie Wiggins, guest trombonist from the Halle Orchestra. (Wiggins was a Salvationist, but professional musician in this fine British orchestra from Liverpool.) The Saturday evening festival in Philharmonic Hall, Lincoln Center, will always be remembered for a breathtaking performance of "Victorious" by Derek Smith, accompanied by the Staff Band. Other accompanying duties brought them under the baton of their former leader, Richard Holz, as he directed a hearty and enthusiastic Congress Male Chorus of 300 voices.

Most impressive of all the wonderful events of the weekend was the Sunday afternoon Service of Dedication held at the Cathedral Church of St. John the Divine. Though a recording exists of this event, nothing can capture the majesty of 300 Salvationist leaders and leading robed clergy of all faiths processing through the grand edifice to the stirring sounds of the NYSB playing stately "Sagina" ("And Can It Be") and "I've Found the Pearl of Greatest Price."[9] Of all the festive strains heard that day, what stands out is a sharply contrasting item, Vernon Post's choral introit "Let Thy Holy Presence," sung so expressively by the Male Chorus. This prayer seemed intimately linked to the articulate, dignified and challenging words spoken by General Frederick Coutts on that occasion.

In his closing remarks he reminded all participants not to become complacent and self-satisfied in the midst of this great celebration. Every bandsman could sense how personal these words were and how important the lesson they contained at this critical time in Army history and Army music:

*In all our thanksgiving, we must never forget why we who were not a people have been made a people—certainly, let me say, not to share only and solely congenial fellowship the one with the other with our music and song, increasingly competent though we are to do that, and greatly as that is a personal delight to me and to all of us who are lovers of music dedicated to the service of God. To do that, to fall for that temptation, to yield to that error, would be to repeat the mistake of Israel when they supposed that God had chosen them as His own for their private pleasure, and not for the sacrificial fulfillment of His redeeming purpose.*[10]

## The New Music

Finding and choosing acceptable repertoire can be a difficult, time-consuming task for any bandmaster. For a staff bandmaster the search is critical. From thoughts supplied by Vernon Post we can understand the philosophy and motivation behind his thoughtful programming:

What does the band and the bandmaster want the listener to receive? *GOOD MUSIC*—a must!

1. Acceptable by the best standards of the type of music performed
2. In the idiom of the performing group
3. Suitability to the skill and musicianship of the performing group
4. Structure (including form and sense of humor or proportion)
5. Content
6. Artistry
7. Directness and clarity
8. Sincerity (Does it say what it pretends to say?)
9. Dramatic impact
10. Suitability to audience, occasion, location of program, location of item in program (Is there variety?), etc.

*Having said all of the above, one of the joys is to rehearse and perform NEW MUSIC that is attractive, appealing and useful. The proven gifted composers must have their latest creations brought to life, but so must the struggling young writers, who, for whatever reason, want to be heard and are willing to pay the price of study, industry, and perseverance. In addition, the band, the audience, the Army and musicians everywhere benefit if the music—and our performance—is worthy. This is how we grow.*

*Many are disturbed by the "forward-looking" idiom, style or content of a composition. In most instances, the "new sound" is often time-worn in some circles outside of the Army but not yet fully accepted by the average Salvationist-listener.*

*As staff bandmaster (as well as corps bandmaster) I felt compelled to prepare and perform "new music"—not to ignore [however] our rich heritage in the "tried and true." Not that all new music presented to me was performed—there had to be substantial reason for the performance, and, if desirable, a second, third, or fourth performance. It was my privilege to present American or even world premieres of works of many Army composers...*[11]

Post's repertoire would bear the marks of the earlier Holz/Leidzen collaboration but on the whole, Post branched out—of necessity—to a whole new range of composers. Emil Soderstrom became a close friend of Post, serving as editor for the winning entries in the National Composers' Contest of 1964. Very imaginative pieces came from Soderstrom's pen at this time, including some still unpublished: Meditation— "Come Thou Fount," Tone Poem— "Take Salvation," Study in Stereo— "Marching to Zion," and Elegy— "Low in the Grave."[12] Established British writers received American premieres as well: Eric Ball's "The Eternal Presence;" Steadman-Allen's "Fantasia," "King's Minstrel," and "The Holy War;" Leslie Condon's "The Present Age" and Heaton's "Victory for Me."

North American writers received special attention including a host of contributors to the *American Band Journal,* headed by such self-taught talents as Lloyd Scott and Lloyd Reslow. Stanley Ditmer continued to supply well-crafted marches, selections and solos. Philip Catelinet, then in Pittsburgh, sent forth some lovely items, including his arrangement of Capuzzi's bass concerto, which he played on tuba with the band. Morley Calvert's "Canadian Folk-Song Suite" served as one main staple for the 1968 European tour. Special encouragement was given to developing young American, professionally trained composers like Bruce

Broughton, James Curnow, and William Himes, whose music showed up more and more frequently in later Post programs. The first-named Broughton, grandson of the former staff bandmaster, made a tremendous impact with his original approach to Army band writing, particularly in "The Good Old Way" and "Covenant," works given special preparation and dazzling performances by Post's band in the early 1970s.

The bandmaster, a composer himself, was not idle either. His lovely Male Chorus arrangements still flowed forth, like "It Took A Miracle" and "Must Jesus Bear the Cross Alone?" For the European tour Post made a fine transcription of the last two movements of Hummel's "Trumpet Concerto" for Derek Smith. Heavy administrative responsibilities in the Music Section* with continuing staff shortages probably curtailed more prolific output at this time.[13]

As a young bandmaster I looked forward to the playing of new music by the NYSB. I remember notable readings by the band of works like Soderstrom's "Elegy," Broughton's "Covenant," and Curnow's transcription of "Procession of the Nobles" at music leaders' councils and congresses in 1971 and 1972 that stirred my musical imagination and encouraged my hopes for the future of Army music and banding.

### The European Tour—1968

After the smashing success of the 1960 Great Britain Tour, staff bandsmen had mused among themselves about a possible European tour. When their executive officer, Paul Kaiser, was transferred as territorial commander to Germany, the band jokingly asked him for the promise of a tour there. Once installed in his new position, however, Kaiser did, in consultation with other European commanders, send an invitation. After considerable "red tape" and good perseverance by band board members like T. Herbert Martin (executive officer), Peter Hofman (secretary), and Vincent Bulla (finance), the trip was set. In addition, the NYSB received a special invitation from General Frederick Coutts to participate in the 90th Anniversary Bandmasters' Councils in London at the end of the trip.[14]

The itinerary included the Netherlands, Germany, Switzerland and England. Statistics recorded include 16 festivals (30,100

*The name was periodically changed from "department" to "section." At the time of the writing of this book, it is called "Music Bureau."

121

attendance), eight open-air engagements (3,650 attendance), two parades, six civic receptions (1090 attendance), seven Salvation Army meetings (4,700 attendance), and 12 performances taped for TV and radio.[15]

## NYSB European Tour Itinerary:
## Principal Engagements/Locations[16]

| | |
|---|---|
| Thursday, May 16: | Depart Kennedy Airport on KLM, DC-8 Jet |
| Friday, May 17: | Arrive Schipol Airport, Netherlands. No engagement this day. |
| Saturday, May 18: | Hilversum, Netherlands: Festival in Grand Hotel "Gooiland" |
| Sunday, May 19: | Three services in Rotterdam Congress Hall Corps, Netherlands |
| Monday, May 20: | Civic reception in Bremen, West Germany; Concert in Bremenhaven, West Germany |
| Tuesday, May 21: | Town Hall Festival in Bremenhaven; Concert in Hamburg (Both filmed and recorded by German National TV) |
| Wednesday, May 22: | Flight, via Hanover, to Berlin, with evening concert |
| Thursday, May 23: | Flight back to Hanover; bus to Wuppertal, West Germany (cities of Barmen and Elberfeld) for evening concert |
| Friday, May 24: | Siegen, West Germany |
| Saturday, May 25: | Freudenstadt, West Germany |
| Sunday, May 26: | Stuttgart, West Germany: two programs in government building |
| Monday, May 27: | Zurich, Switzerland |
| Tuesday, May 28: | Sightseeing trip through the Alps; evening festival in Bern, Switzerland |
| Wednesday, May 29: | Parade in Bern; evening festival in Cathedral of Lausanne |
| Thursday, May 30: | Basel, Switzerland, followed by train ride, on a "sleeper," back to Holland |
| Friday, May 31: | Leiden, Netherlands |

| | |
|---|---|
| Saturday, June 1: | London, England; B/M Councils Festivals (2) in Royal Albert Hall |
| Sunday, June 2: | Bandmasters' Councils at International Training College, Denmark Hill |

While the band faced language barriers, Salvationist fellowship bridged the gap. Corps music sections, large and small, from Rotterdam and Basel to Stuttgart and Freudenstadt, made the New Yorkers feel that their contributions were deeply appreciated, even if only by a handshake and a smile. Staff Bandsman Jacob Hohn could function well as he spoke German; years later he would be made a divisional commander in West Germany. Notable Salvationists were met along the route, including Commissioner Charles Péan, who accompanied the band in Bern and Lausanne, at the latter place arranging for the band to play in the 13th-century cathedral where only the International Staff Band had been allowed to play before.[17]

Arthur Boritzki, special efforts secretary for the Army in Germany, while diligent in his duties and a hard worker, provided some bright, humorous incidents for the band. Post explained it as follows:

*...having served in Hitler's military forces as a lieutenant, [Boritzki] carried over some of his military preciseness, the trait of being able to order anything—even ordering the timpani trunks placed under the buses when they were two inches too large...He chartered our German tour bus from a company that did not have the latest (although comfortable and safe) equipment. It was not unusual in city driving, when the bus had to ascend a steep hill, for the men to disembark and walk up the hill, with a few lending a push![18]*

Pim van der Spoel, former cornet soloist of the Netherlands National Band, helped the bandsmen get their records from Holland to Germany without losing their "shirts" in duty fees.[19]

Billet stories abound, but among the best are William "Wiggy" Simons and Eric Sampson's run-ins with German widowed *Hausfrauen* who spoke no English. One night they found themselves locked in their rooms with no way to get out till morning. On another occasion their efficient hostess burst in on Sampson to test the warmth of the bath water while he was already about his evening ablutions![20]

The Europeans were wonderful hosts, however, and the band marvelled at the kind receptions they received. In Switzerland, and in other spots along the tour, there was a tradition of not allowing applause in church. To get around this "ban" the congregations would enthusiastically wave their programs after each number to convey appreciation. The sightseeing was terrific—particularly in Switzerland, where *War Cry* correspondent Charles West noted that "it is rumored that Eastman stock went up a point due to the film consumed by staff bandsmen" during the trip through the Alps.[21]

Not every stop was "Sound of Music"-perfect, however! In Hamburg the band received a reminder of student unrest, though not overt, during their concert at the university there. Anti-American feeling did exist, but did not hinder the band's ministry. The cruelest reminder of the "real world" came in West Berlin:

> *Our visit to the Berlin wall left us grateful for our own freedoms and a void in our hearts for those entrapped. The wall at times incorporated the facade of apartment houses which had been obviously vacant for some time, in vacant disrepair, including large broken windows whose middle had been smashed as if some human form had crashed through seeking freedom. The epitaphs scribbled on the wall where loved ones had fallen victims.... We climbed the wooden platforms erected to help sight-seers view the depth of the barricades and peer into East Germany.... For this activity we wore our travel blazers, and at the request of the TV cameramen, wore our Salvation Army caps. While we gazed in horror at this physical barricade of steel, concrete, and space that divides one world from another, we also photographed the East German Guards in a high wooden tower type of sentry post.... Finally, as more staff-bandsmen mounted the several platforms, we saw a guard reach out of the open window and fire a signal pistol into the air several times. Nearby, startled roosting pigeons filled the air, sirens were heard in the distance and a number of armed armored vehicles took their places with automatic weapons and cannon on the Eastern side of the wall. The hundreds of blank staring windows facing us from the east were soon filled, each with a citizen brandishing a rifle or automatic weapon. We really didn't know we would get this much reaction![22]*

Safely out of Berlin, the group experienced one of the tour highlights in a 17th-century church in Freudenstadt. Among the most revealing reviews during the tour was one from the daily

Freudenstadt paper, here offered in translation as a sample of how the band was received during the tour:

*The visit of the New York Staff Band of The Salvation Army to Freudenstadt on Saturday was part of a musical tour of the continent. Only a few states of the Bundesrepublik had the privilege of receiving the New York Staff Band, and among these was Freudenstadt, a place where The Salvation Army is particularly active.*

*The planning for this musical trip was done by personnel of the National Headquarters of The Salvation Army in Cologne. A local television station carried a report of the band's arrival on Saturday in Freudenstadt, and after a concert in the Kurgarten, the band was welcomed by Major Wolf and several members of the City Council in the Great Council Chamber.*

*The religious concert during the evening in the State Church was like a musical folk festival, and it opened with a march "A Call to Arms." The musical discipline and tonal substance were thrilling. They aroused enthusiasm and stirred the hearts of the more than one thousand listeners. Spontaneous applause broke out on several occasions.*

*In accordance with American customs a short procession with flags took place. To the accompaniment of the two national anthems, the American flag and that of the Bundesrepublik were carried in by Salvation Army soldiers while the audience stood and rendered honor to both countries.*

*Colonel Boritzki from the headquarters at Cologne greeted the friends of The Salvation Army and promised them a joyous concert. To bring joy is one of the primary goals of The Salvation Army. The Colonel thanked the church congregation, particularly Deacon Keller, for their kind permission to use the beautiful church. Deacon Keller responded with heartfelt words of appreciation, and spoke of the destruction and subsequent rebuilding of the State Church.*

*Colonel Clausen from Cologne was responsible for the announcements and comments during the concert, and the brilliant musical program was soon under way. The band, under the direction of Captain Vernon Post, played marches, typical folk pieces, suites and songs from America, all of which were invested with religious words and significance. During these numbers, several staff bandsmen played solos and revealed the high quality of their craft.*

*The spirit and verve of the New York Staff Band showed that they held to one ideal: the ideal of musical competence and artistic perfection.*

*The Male Chorus, accompanied by a few brass instruments, sang with expressiveness and occasionally used jazz rhythms. Soloists with fine voices took part in these numbers as well. The melodies of the Bach song "Come Sweet Death" filled the wide expanses of the church with exquisite sound and beautiful intonation. This choral rendered by brass instruments represented a high point in religious music which was complemented by the Bible lesson of Staff Bandsman Ivor Rich.*

*Colonel C. Emil Nelson, the leader of the band, brought some amusing words to the audience and expressed his joy (Freude) at being in Freudenstadt, even though for only a short time.*

*The many people of Freudenstadt who attended the concert were undoubtedly in agreement that they had heard in the New York Staff Band one of the finest American bands. Indeed, one might rightly speak of them as the finest.*[23]

The tour band was in good shape musically, spiritually, mentally, and physically, and Post said this of his men:

*Each member of the band board seemed especially gifted for his particular responsibility and pulled more than his share of the load. Among the bandsmen were no evident* prima donnas *but all worked as a team. All were helpful beyond their responsibilities indicating their tremendous commitment to the NYSB and the tour. Add to this* esprit de corps *the week's vacation following the tour's schedule and you know why we felt a privileged people.*[24]

Two veteran soloists from 1960, Derek Smith and Olof Lundgren, were joined by Euphoniumist Lawrence Robertson, Trombonist Allister Stickland, and Flugelhornist Albert Avery. The band had excellent music, good soloists, depth in every section and valiant leaders, Post and Nelson. By the time they left their final continental site, Leiden (Netherlands), they shared the same wonder of God's grace for blessings received as the Pilgrim fathers felt when they set out from Leiden centuries before. For the last leg of the tour, they then headed for London.

### Bandmasters' Councils 1968

Four excellent bands, two staff bands and two corps bands, graced the stage for the two festivals in Royal Albert Hall, June 1: The International Staff Band (Bernard Adams), New York Staff Band (Vernon Post), Wellington Citadel Band (Herbert Nieve), and Portsmouth Citadel Band (Harold Nobes). Some items were played at both festivals, especially the large, "test-piece" types, while some exchanges took place, for instance, by having the New Zealander's cornetist (Les Harford) play in the afternoon and the American soloist (Derek Smith) in the evening. While by now all the bands were in standard concert pitch and thus able to join together in some thrilling massed items, there were remarkable contrasts in these four excellent bands. The three "Commonwealth" bands played rather heavy items: "My Strength, My Tower" (Goffin), "Triumph of Peace" (Ball), and "The Present Age" (Condon). The NYSB offered Calvert's new classic "Canadian Folk Song Suite."

British composer Edward Gregson, writing for *The British Bandsman,* singled out the NYSB's performance, although he was also delighted in the other bands:

> *My personal highlight was the performance by the New York Staff Band of a new composition by the Canadian composer Morley Calvert, "Canadian Folk Song Suite."*
> *The writing was always interesting, from the high chromatic harmonies of the second movement, to the variations in the third movement, in which at one point, some of the band downed instruments and clapped, a novel effect which fleetingly reminded one of the music of Aaron Copland.*
> *The performance was good. The sound of this band, with its general lack of vibrato and mellow tone, is most appealing, at least to this writer's ear.[25]*

If Gregson's perspective emphasized the symphonic brass world's endorsement of the "New York" sound, brass band dean Eric Ball would still call the "different" sound not mellow but brighter and lighter than British concepts:

> *The NYSB produced a quite different sound—lighter, brighter in texture, but still valid musically. This was particularly suited to Morley Calvert's "Canadian Folk Song Suite" —a refreshing, colourful work, affording welcome contrast to the mainly "serious" nature of the programme (we have little enough good music of this kind). Captain Vernon Post directed a performance which evoked the Gallic spirit of much of the music, which also makes considerable technical demands. Here was gaiety and grace.[26]*

Of course, Army bands do not contest, so the arguments, for those so inclined, can continue concerning who was best, which sound was best suited to the pieces played, and so on. For the bandsmen on the stage, it was a celebration of praise.

Other participation by the American group included their famed chorus, extolled by B/M Henning Schon-Larsen of Copenhagen, Denmark:

> For a male voice performance with perfect as well as soulful singing listen to the NYSB's Male Chorus. Their "Must Jesus Bear the Cross Alone?" brought the message right home to our hearts. Thank you, Captain Vernon Post, and the soloists, both for the arrangement as well as for the performance.[27]

A weary Derek Smith presented the Hummel Concerto on Saturday evening; if not as flawless a performance as his 1960 debut, it still received a 99.5 from Brother Ball.[28] The band's final contribution came near the close of the evening festival, in an "In Memoriam" section which Ball reviewed as follows:

> ...our thoughts were directed to Salvationist composers for whom "the trumpets sounded on the other side," and for this purpose music by Erik Leidzen had been chosen. Major Brindley Boon directed the chorus, ISB ensemble and organ in "The Pilgrims." Colonel Emil Nelson read effectively an excerpt from John's Gospel and the NYSB then played "On the Way Home" with an intimacy and delicacy of touch that hushed the large audience. We will not soon forget the closing phrases—sung by the band's fine male chorus—"He will keep you from falling."[29]

On the next day the bandsmen learned of further evidence of God's leading through their music. Charles West relates that one bandmaster from an English corps who had decided to give up his commission prior to the weekend, rededicated his life and service as a result of the playing of "On the Way Home." His testimony at the Bandmasters' Councils was one example of the many results of rededication and transformation wrought via the ministry of the band in such "music with a message."[30]

Seven hundred British bandmasters met in councils with General Frederick Coutts that day with, as in 1960, the ISB and NYSB sharing musical responsibilities. The band "never felt so exposed as a musical group as we did this day, realizing the quality of musicians present...." Post put them "through their paces" in clinic and devotional functions. Their comrades in Britain were particularly complimentary of the New Yorkers' willling spirit during the hectic but marvelous weekend. The feelings were reciprocal:

*How we enjoyed the fellowship with the men of the ISB who pitched in and carried instruments, chairs, and stands for us. They took us into their homes at night. The warm bond of friendship that exists between bandsmen of all nations is something that we will remember for years to come.[31]*

## Let No One Despise Thy Youth

During Post's tenure, Eastern Territory musicians heard internationally-renowned bands on their own soil, too. The pattern established back in the early 1950s was kept up as much as possible—guest groups stirred local musicians to better efforts! England's Tottenham Citadel Band (James Williams) was a revelation of what a top-flight corps band could achieve during their smash-hit tour of 1964. Two years later a Scottish band, Govan Citadel (George Brown) delighted music leaders gathered for councils in October 1966. Continental bands came through, too, including Hamilton, Ontario's Argyl Citadel (William Burditt), spring of 1965, and Hollywood Tabernacle (Ronald Smart) two years later.

Stockholm VII Band (Erland Beijer) made a fine impact during the 1970 Music Leaders' Councils in New York and subsequent tour. The Chicago Staff Band (Ernest Miller) came a year later to renew banding camaraderie with their Eastern friends. Guest soloists were also drawn from far and wide during the Post years: Ken Smith, cornet, from Australia; Phil Catelinet, piano and tuba, from Pittsburgh. Even young talent, like Star Lakers Arnold Burton and Charles Baker, were given the limelight.

Vernon Post's later years as bandmaster were, in fact, marked by sensitive nurturing of many young Army musicians, both in the band and in other parts of the territory. In a time when some American leaders did not understand people of the younger generation with their long hair and unorthodox ideas, Vernon Post encouraged them, pushed them, challenged them, even when they thought they were not worthy. His band in the early 1970s was beginning to fill with bright, young talent.

The establishment of an educational scholarship program for young college students who wanted to play with the band was a major achievement. The initial grants, starting in 1972, were for

$1,000, paid in segments, plus usual engagement expenses. The difficult problem of finding competent replacements in the continually shifting personnel of the band was greatly eased by this decision. Margaret Hale, territorial education secretary, and the band leaders (Post and his executive officers, like R. E. Holz and William Harvey, among others) knew such a plan would "utilize our natural resources, continually improve the caliber of the band, and provide first-hand indigenous leadership in the future." The results of the past 15 years, in so many cases, have proven them right.[32]

A young band, with budding stars Philip Smith, Philip Ditmer, Charles Baker, Vernon Post Jr., Phillip and Stephen Bulla, to name a few, can be a real tonic. The NYSB that played at Temple University in the fall of 1971 was declared by Dr. David L. Stone and Dr. Allen M. Garrett as "the finest non-professional group ever to visit the college (of music)."

Problems with young bandsmen could abound, too, especially with regulations on hair length and facial hair. The reaction of a conservative administration to the current styles among "rebellious" American youth caused no small amount of petty harassment, resentment, and, if one did not become too personally involved, jokes and ribbing. One temporary solution was for the "boys" to wear wigs into which they could tuck their flowing locks! (Older men in the band were beginning to call the offenders by feminine names.)

Every band faces tensions of this sort. Post's band experienced it more intensely because of the rapid social changes and political ferment happening in America during the late 60s and early 70s. Just as America would emerge somewhat shaken from Vietnam—hurt but not mortally wounded—the NYSB, in a less monumental way, came out of these minor scuffles in good shape, better organized than ever, and ready for a promising future. The band at the 85th Reunion Festival, held concurrently with the April 1972 Twelfth Biennial Music Leaders' Councils, was one of the finest in recent memory. Approximately 100 former staff bandsmen joined to form a Reunion Male Chorus that weekend. Spirits were high. Les Condon proved an inspiring guest. Future events would include an historic participation in a sacred service at St. Paul's Cathedral (Catholic) in Pittsburgh, Pa., and Post's band was anxiously awaiting a West Coast tour, including participation in the famed Tournament of Roses Parade.

## A Tragedy

There is no other way to describe Vernon and Katie Post's dismissal from Salvation Army officership than as a tragedy. To delve too deeply into the matter would cause more and unnecessary pain. It is enough to state that the organization lost two wonderful, gifted individuals who had given selflessly in the cause of Christian music and in the furtherance of God's Kingdom.

The problem was not one of misconduct but one of theological doctrine. Mrs. Post was confronted with accusations dealing with deviation from Salvation Army doctrine. In the final analysis, the Posts were asked to leave, despite an impressive record of service. Vernon Post, though not charged himself with any heresy, chose to support his wife at this time, in much the same way as the territorial commander, Commissioner Bramwell Tripp, sadly felt that there could be no other solution for him to make than the one decided upon.

The Posts keep in contact with The Salvation Army and their Army friends. They have returned several times as guests at various musical events, including Star Lake Musicamp and the Central Music Institute (Central Terrritory, U.S.A.). In recent years Vernon has contributed to Salvation Army music journals and has assisted the Army in publication projects. Both he and his wife pursue successful professional careers: Vernon serves as a music teacher in the Summit, N.J., Public School System, and Katie holds a responsible position as a psychiatric social worker for the State of New Jersey.

A concern for the individual bandsman and interest in developing young music leaders were special marks of Vernon Post's character that must be highlighted in addition to his achievements as a conductor and territorial music secretary. He remained faithful to his vision he shared with Leidzen and Holz. For his loving, caring and fostering leadership, a whole generation of Army musicians in the Eastern Territory, and beyond its borders, are gratefully in his debt.

# 9

## "Ambassadors"
(Peter Graham)

## Bandmaster Derek Smith
### 1972-1986

A mbassadors" most adequately identifies the NYSB of the Smith era. A world tour, national and international congresses, a Great Britain tour, Western U.S. tour and outstanding Canadian visits highlight a traveling ministry unequaled by any other period in the band's history. At the same time the band reached a level of musical excellence that was a natural consequence of the impetus given during the precedent-setting Holz and Post eras.

Derek Smith's initial appointment as conductor came at a difficult time. Appointed to the podium in September 1972 (though initially as deputy bandmaster), he carefully and thoughtfully guided the band back from a real morale low. Smith's close contact with his two predecessors had taught him the musical and spiritual integrity required of the staff bandmaster.

Smith became the first non-officer conductor since Robert Griffith. His tenure, in length of service, is surpassed only by George Darby. The overall achievements of the band in his 14 years of service must be reckoned as perhaps the band's finest.

The closer the historian comes to the present, the more difficult it is to be objective, to have a sense of perspective that the lapse of time allows. Equally so, it is more difficult to be selective in

133

highlighting for a summarized history the many wonderful events in the Smith era. If this review stresses the tours, the "musical ambassador" aspect of that band, it does not imply a lessening of the band's commitment to the normal week-in, week-out duties it still faced and continues to carry out to this day with loyalty and devotion.

Smith grew up in England where he first learned music from his father, a cornet and euphonium player who was junior band leader at the Hendon Corps in North London. From 1944-1951, Smith was a member of the Rosehill Band connected with the Salvation Army Assurance Company at International Headquarters. Like the ISB, Rosehill functioned as a type of staff band, and Smith was its cornet soloist. When Smith joined the military in 1946, he became cornet soloist also for Her Majesty's Royal Horse Guards Band. Ten years later, his family immigrated to Canada, and Smith became bandmaster of Toronto's Earlscourt Citadel Band (now called Yorkminster Citadel). At the prompting of Richard Holz, Smith moved to New York City in 1959 to become cornet soloist with the NYSB and to hold various administrative positions in data processing at Eastern Territorial headquarters.[1]

Except for an 18-month leave of absence in the mid-60s, Smith's service with the band had been continuous. Directing other area corps bands during this time, he has been called upon to travel extensively as soloist/conductor in Australia, New Zealand, Canada, Great Britain, Europe, and the United States.[2]

As one of the most gifted cornetists in brass history, Derek Smith brought a renewed lyricism and beauty of tone to a nearly lost art that has inspired thousands of young musicians. *Expressive* playing was Derek's delight. If the band under his baton has excelled in this area at times, it is because he sought, to put it in his own words, "to reproduce myself, my concept of playing, to 35 other men."[3]

Smith did not seek the bandmastership. Initially, because he loved playing so much, he worried that he lacked the communication skills necessary to achieve the desired results he knew he wanted. Through diligent work, with the help of a marvelously supportive band board throughout his tenure, he achieved that result, most notably in the World Tour band of 1982. To his delight, the live recordings of that band matched "studio polish."[4] The "Ambassadors" were worthy emissaries of the best in Christian banding.

## Tournaments, Conferences, Retreats, Recordings

The schedule set for the 1972-73 season—Smith's first as bandmaster—was an ideal if demanding one for pushing a band out of a mood marked by confusion and frustration. In late fall, they were in Northern Illinois for various festivals and clinics. New soloists like Thomas Mack (euphonium), Philip Smith (Derek's son on cornet) and Philip Ditmer (soprano cornet), were joining veterans like Olof Lundgren in the limelight.[5] Over the Christmas/ New Year holiday the band traveled west to participate in the Tournament of Roses Parade. Along the route, they visited many cities not visited by a New York Salvation Army band since the "Continental Campaign Band" under Anderson had supported Booth-Tucker on his great cross-country trek: Denver, Phoenix, Los Angeles, San Diego, San Francisco, Oakland, Salt Lake City, and Detroit.[6]

In March 1973, the Canadian Staff Band (Norman Bearcroft) returned to New York for the first time since the Consul's funeral in 1904. Re-formed in 1969, 55 years after the May 29, 1914, *Empress of Ireland* tragedy, this spirited band made a great hit with many "sparkling" program features from the pen of its bandmaster. Soloists like Bob Merritt (trombone), Deryck Diffey (cornet), and William Brown (euphonium) made fine presentations. One special surprise of the weekend, verified by the congress recording, was the marvelous playing, too, by the revitalized NYSB under Smith. Both bands shared excellent fellowship and played beautifully together in massed items.[7]

Band retreats had been part of the group's schedule in the past, particularly spiritual periods during recording sessions or prior to special tours. A new style of band retreat was introduced in the winter of 1974 with that held at the Hillcrest Conference Center in Sharon, Mass., with Commissioner Bramwell Tripp as speaker.[8] While retreats could not be held every year, they became special times of reflection, times of musical and spiritual refreshment and renewal. Wives would be invited to attend the retreats and fellowship/recreation activities would be stressed, though some retreats included busy performance schedules on the closing day. A "standout" retreat of the past decade or so was the International Retreat for the NYSB and Canadian Staff Band held at Woodlands Conference Center in Speculator, N.Y., in March 1984. These two bands still talk about the relaxing, fun-filled weekend in which banding camaraderie and Christian sharing proved to be the tonic needed to finish the year's hectic season. Two years later, at Ladore Conference Center, Waymart, Pa., the NYSB and their wives met, *without instruments* (no rehearsals allowed!), at the beginning of their 99th year, to examine the motivations, purposes, and functions at work in 100 years of staff-banding.[9]

When a band plays at F.E.T. meetings, building dedications, welcome meetings, fund-raisers, and other routine events, or when it receives feedback only from Army audiences, the group can become complacent in its approach to music-making. A regular series of appearances at professional conferences during Smith's era, similar to the Music Educators' National Conference (MENC) triumph under Holz, went a long way to restore confidence in the band's personal sense of achievement. On January 11, 1975, the NYSB played at the now-famous New York Brass Conference for Scholarships. The acclaim received from a host of brass professionals and developing players from all over America went a long way in boosting band morale and pride.[10]

Philip Smith, completing his master's degree at Juilliard and having received a NYSB scholarship for several years, was a star attraction that day. Band "display" pieces, like Bowen's Rimsky-Korsakov transcription "Kaleidescope" were also enthusiastically received. Many and long standing ovations greeted these presentations. Other appearances at this yearly conference followed in 1976, 1977 and 1980. MENC East Regional Convention (Philadelphia, April 1975), American School Band Directors' Association Convention (December 1976), Temple University Brass Conference (March 1981), Southwest Ohio Brass Conference (April 1977), and clinic/concerts at Manhattan School of Music, Kent State University, and other schools of music rounded out an impressive series of concerts for the professional community.[11]

Appendix A cites all the superb guest soloists that joined the band for their annual festivals from 1974-1986. Local Salvation Army and outside professional talent were involved. During the 90th season (1977) there were two special celebrations, the first in February, under the guest baton of Bernard Adams, and a second, featuring euphonium virtuoso (and Chicago Staff Bandmaster) William Himes, at Alice Tully Hall, Lincoln Center in October.

When Terry Camsey joined the band in the mid-70s he instituted, from his Greater New York Divisional Music Director's office a series of "Profile" concerts honoring gifted Army composers. The first was Eric Ball, with the Cambridge Citadel Silver Band (Mass.) as the guest unit at a concert given in early 1979.

"Profiles" featuring the NYSB and Male Chorus have been as follows:

1980   Albert Jakeway
1981   Brindley Boon
1983   Richard E. Holz
1984   Ray Steadman-Allen
1985   Leslie Condon (Posthumous)
1986   Stanley Ditmer*

Honoring great men in Army music is a noble idea. For Derek Smith, featuring the music of his former Rosehill bandmaster, Albert Jakeway, was a natural way of expressing his appreciation to his brass band mentor.

Smith's repertoire would be marked by a decided balance between old Army classics, which he felt needed new, definitive readings to keep them alive, and adventuresome new literature from the pens of America's best young writers: Stephen Bulla, James Curnow, Bruce Broughton, William Himes, and, eventually Scottish "transplant" Peter Graham.

When he could have his way, Smith preferred descriptive, programmatic music, particularly that music which did not entirely abandon its brass band heritage stylistically. Though he was willing to program the new American works, marked as they were with many modern idiomatic figures from jazz, popular TV and movie scores, and contemporary art music, he would rather have pieces that successfully "wed the old style to the new." Most representative of this category for Smith were works like Condon's "Thy King Cometh," featured at the 1978 International Congress, and the signature march by Peter Graham of the World Tour entitled "Ambassadors."[12]

The recordings of the NYSB under Smith are an impressive achievement. During Post's tenure the pace of production seen during the Holz era had slowed down considerably for any number of reasons, mainly beyond the band's control, but under Smith, production increased. The 1974 release, "New Frontier," set a pattern for imaginative promulgation of new Salvation Army music, balanced with fine readings of old "chestnuts" from the standard repertoire. Bicentennial music on "Sounds of Our Heritage" (1975), great Army classics on "Ninety Years" (1977), superb Army

*In 1982, Philip Catelinet was honored, with the Montclair (N.J.) Corps Band as duty unit.

137

solos by Philip Smith on "Bravo" (1981), and commissioned works especially written for the two tour recordings (1982, 1985) are ample proofs of this claim and will last for years as irrefutable documents in assessing the gradual improvement of musicianship in the NYSB.

## International Congress, 1978

At the June 9, 1978, "Bon Voyage" Festival "NYSB, London, 1978" T-shirts were hot items. Representative of the spirited enthusiasm with which the band faced their first trans-Atlantic trip in ten years, these T-shirts would become not only good advertisements for the band, but also symbolic gestures of international goodwill. When Cornetist Kim Yong Bok of the Seoul, Korea, Boys Home Band presented Terry Camsey's solo "Life's Pageant" to the accompaniment of the NYSB in the Wembley Sports Complex Empire Pool, his rousingly-received performance was capped by a handshake from the composer, at that time solo cornetist of the NYSB, and with a complimentary NYSB T-shirt presented by Derek Smith.

Those wonderfully pleasant days in London during late June and early July saw thousands of Salvationist delegates join in great spirited meetings and festivals, held primarily at either the Wembley Sports Complex or at Royal Albert Hall. Superb bands from many nations had gathered for the congress, among the American groups being the Chicago Mont Clare Corps Band (John Jones) and the NYSB. As in other past international congresses, staff bands shared the major musical duties: International Staff Band (Ray Bowes), Melbourne Staff Band (Colin Woods) and the NYSB (Derek Smith).

For the New Yorkers it was a whirlwind series of programs spread out over a ten-day period. Among the most memorable engagements, three stand out in my memory, as an observer, for special mention: Tribute Service at Westminster Abbey, concert on the steps of St. Paul's Cathedral, and the Symphony of Praise, featuring the three staff bands. I was among an honored group of international delegates that processed through the streets of London and then into the magnificent Westminster Abbey on Sunday, July 2, at 10:00 a.m., for "Morning Service: A Tribute to The Salvation Army on the Occasion of the International Congress." We walked solemnly to the rich sound of the NYSB, tightly seated in the organ loft above the choir. Their music before the service included masterworks by Mozart, Bach and Elgar as well as equally lovely Salvation Army hymn arrangements by Donald Osgood, Eric Ball and Dr. Thomas Rive. Great hymns of the Church were movingly sung by the great congregation but none more so than Booth's "O Boundless Salvation," accompanied by the band. Contrasting choral works accented the international aspect of the service: the NYSB Male Chorus (Thomas Mack) singing "Rock of Ages" (arr. Bearchell); the Westminster Abbey Choir, "O Clap Your Hands" (Vaughan Williams); and the Central Division Songsters from Soweto, South Africa, "A Song of Heaven." The Dean of Westminster, the Very Reverend E. F. Carpenter, challenged all present to uphold the standards of humble, sacred service rendered by Salvationists of the past. As the band played the tune "Helmsley" from Eric Ball's "Kingdom Triumphant" at the conclusion of the service, the dean's words came back to me, reminding me of the faithfulness of Christian musicians who proclaim Christ's gospel throughout the world: "Their sound is gone out into all lands: and their words into the ends of the world."[13]

Less solemn was the tight gathering of Salvationists, sightseers, and the generally curious who surrounded the band during their St. Paul's Cathedral outdoor concert. The band and chorus sounded forth spirited American-style music to the delight of the festive and informal audience. At other times in the congress, I would hear the band in more serious fare, like the Chopin "Polonaise" transcription by Leidzen or an extended contemporary item like Bruce Broughton's overture to the musical "Hosea." The spirit of the band seemed best captured, however, in this remarkable outdoor setting. New York staff bandsmen have always been a fun-loving, genuinely warm and engaging group, and there was no exception that noontime in either their music or words of witness.

For banding fans, the three staff band "Symphony of Praise," July 6, 1978, in Royal Albert Hall made the congress complete. The ISB played host in processing the two guest bands to their respective locations. After the ceremonies were over, the musical feast, filled with new manuscripts, began with a rousing, golden-oldie, Goldsmith's "Banner of Liberty" (GS 863). Here is a rundown on this twice-offered "battle of the bands":

## ISB

"The Holy War" (Steadman-Allen)
"Better World" (Bearcroft), Euphonium Soloist Derick Kane

### MELBOURNE

"Quintessence" (Redhead)
"New Horizons" (Redhead), Trombone Soloist Ken McClimont

### NEW YORK

"Thy King Cometh" (Condon)
"To Set the People Free" (Broughton), cornet duet—
   Lambert Bittinger, Ronald Waiksnoris

There were even two united male chorus items, a tripled double-quartet of trombones and cornets, and a grand finale showstopper, Ray Steadman-Allen's effective symphonic treatment of the hymn "Fairest Lord Jesus," called "Daystar." Three distinct band styles were heard, each band having something about its playing, soloists, and new music to commend it. No one group excelled beyond the other two. The programs were a marvelous confirmation of the album title, "With One Accord," produced for the congress, featuring the three bands.

### National Centennial Congress, 1980

Kansas City, Missouri, offered a particularly warm, windy welcome to the thousands of national congress delegates gathered for a five-day extravaganza under the Blood and Fire flag, June 13-17, 1980, at Convention Center. In comparison to the 1930 congress, where the NYSB or, in Evangeline Booth's mind, the *National* Staff Band, played the central band role, the 1980 American congress saw the musical assignments divided equally among five bands, one for each territory and one for National Headquarters:

| | |
|---|---|
| Chicago Staff Band (William Himes) | Central |
| National Capitol Area Band (Campbell Robinson) | South |
| New York Staff Band (Derek Smith) | East |
| Santa Ana Corps Band (Ed Freeman) | West |
| S.A.S.F. Band, Asbury College (James Curnow) | NHQ |

Each band had various outdoor events and parades, the NYSB on City Hall Plaza, Friday, June 13, and as escort for the cadets' parade Sunday morning. Each band also drew a spot on the large

Heritage Hall stage (NYSB, Sunday afternoon), and each drew a rally for a special solo spot (NYSB, Men's Rally, Saturday morning).[14] All five groups were united for the Monday evening "Festival of Praise."

The outstanding contribution from the New York band came during the Saturday evening "Marching to Glory" pageant. Staff Bandsman Stephen Bulla had been commissioned for the arrangement of short "overtures" or "linking music" for this production that would serve as introduction to the successive tableaus presented by each of the territories. Bulla used the chorus "Will You Go" from the hymn "The Eden Above" (which George Scott Railton and his seven Army Lassies first sang on American shores in March 1880) as the thematic link between each regional "overture," and shaped a witty, humorous and crowd-pleasing potpourri of American sounds that delighted the huge crowd. His "Central" overture takes a kind "shot" at compatriot composer Bill Himes through quotes from Bill's music, and each locale was "evoked" by appropriate musical references, from the "Gone With the Wind" movie score for the South to similar Hollywood quodlibets for the West ("Star Wars," "Bonanza," etc.). So popular did the music prove that the four sections were combined in later years, with added slideshow, to form a "Suite of American Overtures," one of the most innovative program features in Staff Band history.

On the "Festival of Praise" the NYSB drew the unglamorous but rewarding duty of presenting some of the competition winners in the 1980 Composers' Contest. Two first-prize ribbons went to Stephen Bulla for his well-crafted selection, "A Soldier's Proclamation" and an equally well-written 6/8 march. The night will probably not be remembered by the bandsmen as one of notable achievement, but they had as solace the fact that they had given yeoman service during the congress and, in the little "free time" available, had succeeded in beating the Chicago Staff Band in softball, the score alleged to be something like 13-5.[15]

No spirit of competition entered into the "Sounds Inspiring" concert in Massey Hall, Toronto, just a year after the congress. Three Canadian songster brigades and the Canadian Staff Band (Robert Redhead) joined the NYSB in a program made special by the presence of Eric Ball. The New York Staff Band was given the lion's share of the brass spots, and they magnificently demonstrated some new, exciting repertoire:[16]

March— "Assignment" (Dudley Bright)
Festival Air— "Promises of God" (Erik Silferberg)
"Suite of American Overtures" (Stephen Bulla)
"Fantasia on Lobe Den Herren" (Eric Ball)

Each item was specially commissioned by the band for use on its upcoming world tour. Thomas Mack's Male Chorus was also in fine form, offering two manuscript settings, "Canaan's Land" (Stephen Bulla) and "Just As I Am" (arr. Thomas Mack).

Eric Ball praised the NYSB that night for their inspired music: "The artistic playing of the New York Staff Band under the direction of Derek Smith has really pleased me!" This vote of confidence rang clearly in the bandsmen's ears. Such approbation gave them the courage and stamina to complete hard work the following year as they prepared for their most significant campaign to date—a world tour.

## World Tour, 1982

Derek Smith told me that he relies heavily upon the band board as an active agent in running the Staff Band. When the board is strong the bandmaster is able to concentrate on musical concerns. The band board headed by Executive Officer Stanley Ditmer that planned the 1982 World Tour functioned with peak efficiency. Such a costly, difficult venture needed superb administration of fund-raising efforts, personnel, equipment and the details of travel and engagements. The complete band board, with other subcommittees supporting it, was as follows:

| | |
|---|---|
| Executive Officer | Stanley Ditmer |
| Deputy Bandmaster | Ronald Waiksnoris |
| Male Chorus Leader | Thomas Mack |
| Band Secretary | Sidney Langford |
| Finance Secretary | Vincent Bulla |
| Property Secretary | Charles Rowe |
| Librarian | Andrew Kelly |
| P.R. Secretary | Charles Olsen |
| Band Sergeant | Harold Banta |

Each man was particularly well suited to his task. Ron Waiksnoris deserves notable credit for his many imaginative ideas in programming music and for his general encouragement and support of the staff bandmaster in the workings of band details. Veterans like Bulla, Mack and Olsen were "professionals" at this sort of venture. Youngbloods, like Rowe and Kelly, would carry heavy burdens effectively and energetically. Over it all, Stanley Ditmer, backed by meticulous "Sid" Langford, would preside graciously and firmly. To Ditmer's credit, the band was able, in addition to raising huge sums for their travel, to completely re-outfit its instruments, music cases, uniforms—all the way down to its Florsheim, "uniform-issue", toe-cap shoes.

A new look came to the NYSB on the eve of its tour. Silver replaced its traditional lacquer in brass finish, the bright-red laydown tunic was switched to a high-collar festival tunic of similar hue, and even the old maroon travel blazers were gratefully exchanged for a new matching travel outfit. These changes would have been inevitable; their realization before the tour was a special delight!

Careful planning in repertoire choices for the tour led to the commissioning of several works by noted Army writers, including Eric Ball, Stephen Bulla, William Broughton, Dudley Bright, Erik Silferberg and Peter Graham. Brass soloists for the tour were led by veteran Euphoniumist Tom Mack, Principal Trombonist Charles Baker, and Cornetists Ron Waiksnoris and Gordon Ward. Personnel was as strong as any in recent years:

Soprano Cornet
Arnold Hulteen

Cornets
Ronald Waiksnoris
Kenneth Kirby
Gordon Ward
Ian Anderson
Stephen Ditmer
Ronald Rowland
Carl Avery
Ronald Foreman
James Kisser Jr.

Flugelhorn
Mark Tillsley

Trombones
Charles Baker
Andrew Kelly
Charles Rowe

Bass Trombone
George Banta

Euphoniums
Thomas Mack
Roger Rischawy

E♭ Bass
Jeffrey Schultz
William Francis
Charles Olsen

B♭ Bass
Harold Banta
Vincent Bulla

| Percussion | Baritones |
|---|---|
| Brent Norton | Thomas Scheibner |
| Eric Sampson | Harold Anderson |
| | Frank Psaute |
| Alto Horns | |
| William Hood | Color Sergeant |
| Peter Hofman | Charles F. Olsen Jr. |
| Charles Schramm | |
| Daniel Moore | |

Why a world tour in the first place? Could not the money be better spent on other more humanitarian efforts? Do bands always need tours to maintain their fitness and personnel? These questions are old ones that get batted around every time a group begins planning a trip. For a band the caliber of the New York Staff Band, tours take shape because people *want to hear* the band and share in the band's musical ministry. In short, people ask for the band. Stanley Ditmer cited the principal focal points of the tour in his jacket notes on the band's tour album:

> ...the members of the [New York Staff] band come as emissaries of salvation engaged in an extensive and ambitious world tour. In response to many invitations, they will participate in Norwegian and Swedish Salvation Army Congress events, and they will be featured as the guest band for the centenary celebrations of the Sydney (Australia) Congress Hall Corps. To reach these distant places the band will completely circle the globe....
>
> The main purpose of the band's world tour is that members might be...ambassadors for Christ...and that people who hear them might be "...reconciled to God" (2 Corinthians 5:20).[17]

The complete "Musical Cavalcade Itinerary" was as follows:

| June 23 | Depart New York |
|---|---|
| 24 | Oslo, Norway |
| 25-27 | Norwegian Congress |
| 28 | Open Day |
| 29 | Oslo, Norway (a.m.) |
| | Gothenburg, Sweden (p.m.) |
| 30 | Jonkoping, Sweden |
| July 1 | Orebro, Sweden |

144

| | |
|---|---|
| 2 | Stockholm, Sweden |
| 3-5 | Swedish Congress |
| 6 | Copenhagen, Denmark |
| 7 | Bangkok, Thailand |
| 8-9 | Adelaide, Australia |
| 10-12 | Melbourne, Australia |
| 13 | Canberra, Australia |
| 14, 16 | Brisbane, Australia |
| 15 | Gold Coast, Australia |
| 17 | Open Day |
| 18 | Sydney, Australia |
| 19-20 | Wellington, New Zealand |
| 21 | Auckland, New Zealand |
| 22 | Travel Day |
| 22-23 | Honolulu, U.S.A. |
| 24 | Los Angeles, U.S.A. |
| 25 | Arrive in New York |

The intricate flight and travel plans were neatly handled by Salvationist Sven Ljungholm, who traveled with the group as general tour guide, translator, trouble-shooter, and procurer.

If a review of the band's tour brief reveals the usual tour engagements—festivals in fine concert halls, civic receptions with local and national dignitaries, open-air concerts and parades, holiness and salvation meetings—it also reveals a task of unprecedented proportion for the maintaining of stamina, health, and good spirits. Most men I have talked to speak freely about how comfortably the whole schedule was followed and how little tension there was within the band during the 32-day tour. After the tour a booklet called "Reflections" was put together to preserve the lovely memories of this outstanding venture. Even that 40-page booklet is inadequate in covering the responses of 32 men or in recording the monumental achievements logged on route.

Rather than provide an engagement-by-engagement summary (the old "three yards and a cloud of dust" approach), I have included capsule summaries, often with responses from leading musicians from the countries visited. Each bandsman, each audience member along the great trek, will have their special musical, spiritual, or fellowship highlight to treasure. "Reflections" and Ron Rowland's fine summary printed in the September 1982 *Musician* (American) are particularly valuable documents for more detailed study.[18]

**Bon Voyage Festival:** *A packed house in the Temple enthusi-astically cheered the New Yorkers as they previewed some of the tour music. A four-part program, colorfully introduced by cos-tumed representatives from each country visited, contained much new music, including Dudley Bright's "Confrontations," based on Executive Officer Stanley Ditmer's song, "I'm In His Hands." BB$^b$ bass wonder Harold Banta was honored during his last festival on the CMT stage, after twenty-six years as a staff bandsman. "Appropriately, the festival was concluded by a prayer of dedication and commitment of the bandsmen on behalf of the tour by Commissioner W. R. Goodier...."*[19]

**Norway:** *The first major festival of the tour was held in Oslo's 2,000 seat Concert Hall on the Saturday night of the Norwegian Congress, for which the band served as the principal musical force. Major Paul Marti, Territorial Music Secretary for Norway, sent his own "reflections" on this weekend to the band after the tour:*

My personal reflection is that I was very much impressed by the NYSB's deportment and discipline. Everything seemed to go smoothly and the many internal functions were well-cared for. It was a good atmosphere over the band which I was very grateful to recognize. A feature which I won't forget was the open-air meeting in the center of Oslo and the selection of music you played there and the warmhearted testimonies, all with a personal experience and a very human touch...Highlight of your visit in Oslo was, of course, the festival...where we really heard the NYSB at its best! When I visited the Concert House early in December for another festival, the staff of the Concert House was still talking about the outstanding quality of playing by the NYSB...[20]

**Sweden:** *More great crowds, music groups (a real treat on this tour to hear many fine sections), great Salvation Army "hoopla" were in evidence in this section of the trip. 3,200 delegates had gathered for Sweden's 100th Anniversary of the founding of Army work there. Alusjo, Stockholm, was the center for the multifarious activities the band participated in. Their presentation of the multi-media piece "Suite of American Overtures" was appropriately linked to a Swedish centenary celebration because the cyclic theme, "Will you go?" was also the first song used by Swedish Salvationist pioneer Hanna Ouchterlony. Bill Himes' "quasi-hip" setting of "This Little Light of Mine," sung by the Male Chorus in Swedish, was a real crowd pleaser. Perhaps most memorable for music enthusiasts was the late-night spontaneous festival by Stockholm VII, Tranas and New York Staff Bands at Stockholm VII*

Corps where many delightful, informal things happened, including seven-man rendition of the cornet variation solo, "A Happy Day." The mountain-top experience of the congress was the great march up into Skansen Park overlooking the harbor and city of Stockholm. Bill Francis writes in his diary: "We have been to the mountain! It was indeed the thrill of a lifetime, not only to march through downtown Stockholm with the thousands of on-lookers, but to climb the mountain and be part of the march to Skansen Park and see the [10] brass bands follow our lead with their string band members, their delegates, and, of course, their flags coming up the mountain first as they all gathered for what the park official said was about 12,000 people...At the conclusion of this great congress as the last bands climbed...to Skansen Park there was a great rainbow that captured our attention; it seemed that God had intervened and was giving his sign...for another 100 years."[21]

**Australia:** After a brief, and culture-shocking visit to Bangkok, Thailand, en route to the lands "down under," the band arrived in Adelaide for another 100th—this for the Norwood Corps. So many Army music friends shared fellowship with the band in Australia: Staff Bandmaster Colin Woods and his men, Ray Steadman-Allen, Bob Beasy, Ian Hankey, Barrie Gott, and Max Nixon, the latter accepting much responsibility in setting up the band's visit. Here are some Australian reflections:

**Ray Steadman-Allen:** The comments which reached me about the high quality programmes have not diminished. A tribute to the band's influence has been seen in emulation of some features by at least one of our bands. Naturally one looks to a Staff Band for something beyond performances and in spiritual outreach, deportment and public dignity all events set a world-class example. To encounter so much new music was of course a personal joy and I would record my gratification in finding some of my work in your repertoire. [Author's note: particularly the Tone Poem, "Logos"] The privilege of conducting the band is a precious memory. Lastly to meet old friends and make new ones. This is the essence of Salvation comradeship—the friendships formed at the battlefront.[22]

**Colin Woods:** Two things in particular stand out in my own mind. Firstly, the friendliness of the members of the band; and secondly, the musicianly approach to both the playing and singing of the band. We of the Melbourne Staff Band shall always remember the very relaxed and friendly approach of the men of the New York Staff. We have not experienced anything quite like it before. They were not aloof—all appeared humble and sincere Christians. It was greatly appreciated. This feeling was not peculiar to the MSB but was a general feeling amongst all who came in contact with the band. The musicianly approach applied to both the playing and singing. The band didn't blow, it played and played in a most sensitive and sympathetic manner. Nothing overdone. Everything controlled. The playing was clean, tight, and articulate. The NYSB has always been recognized for its extremely fine vocal work and we in Australia were not at all disappointed. The singing lived up to its fine reputation. We would have loved to have heard more.[23]

**Max Nixon:** The final reflection would be that whilst the time and effort spent by so many people and so many centres in order to bring about such a most successful tour could never be accounted for in dollars and cents, for our part, whatever the cost, it was more than offset by the joy at having had the opportunity of the internationalism of Salvation Army banding.[24]

**New Zealand:** While only two cities could host the band, they were intensely responsive hosts—Wellington and Auckland:

**Commissioner Dean Goffin:** The visit of the NYSB was very well received and the only regret we have is that the band was able to visit only two centres in our country. In both Wellington and Auckland capacity crowds gathered to welcome the band and to warm to the Christian atmosphere, good fellowship, and splendid music. There is maturity of sound in this band which received favourable comment. The slide presentation to the music of Stephen Bulla proved interesting, entertaining, and inspiring. The singing of "Rock of Ages" at the conclusion of the festivals was effective and spiritually challenging....[25]

**Grant Reay:** After years of rumors that the NYSB was to visit Auckland, N.Z.'s largest city, the band's visit became a reality on the final leg of the round the world journey....The sight of hundreds of Auckland Salvationists in line, blocking the sidewalk, waiting to get into a NYSB Concert, will probably stay with the bandsmen for some time. The sights and sounds that the NYSB left with the Aucklanders earned the band a standing ovation, and a memory of a night well worth the years of expectation.[26]

**Trevor Davis:** *I would obviously wish to add a particular word of greeting to the bandsmen since I was privileged to spend the whole time with you in New Zealand. The level of fellowship was something unforgettable and the comradeship most valued. I don't suppose you can print such memories as rather frightening takeoffs and landings at sundry New Zealand airports, nor on the indisposition of one of the BB$^b$ bass players upon arrival in Auckland, after a rather bumpy approach! However, the very serious intent with which the band approached the job, together with the fun we had in between will remain personal memories for me for a long time.*[27]

"Outside" reviews were not always available on a tour that centered around Army congresses and "in-house" gatherings. A notable exception was one in Sydney, Australia, entitled "A Nice One From the Salvos." The reviewer was obviously delighted and surprised by the band's effective programming, playing, singing—in fact, all those characteristics that make it a first-class ensemble. An excerpt follows:

*On Friday evening, July 16, a very large attendance at the Sydney Opera House witnessed a fine concert by New York's Staff Band of The Salvation Army. We all know that Salvo music is "different," but this concert demonstrated once and for all, that the differences are in detailed repertoire only, and certainly not in quality. I suspect that on the North American continent, the Salvation Army just about carries the entire torch for the all-brass concept of banding, which is spread pretty thin otherwise; and if that's true, then this concert provided ample proof that the torch is carried high and proud indeed. The band's repertoire was completely new to me, non-Salvo that I am, and for that probably was the more entertaining. If one can make comparisons, the programme was somewhat lighter than that we heard from the Grimethorpe Colliery Band a couple of months ago; and I think the better for it. This band is not above ripping off a good foot-tapping march, Opera House notwithstanding; in fact the soprano player Arnold Hulteen gave us a good demonstration of what can be done about that awkward obligato in Sousa's "Stars and Stripes Forever," if you haven't got a piccolo....probaby the very finest [brass band] the United States of America has to offer. Well done, New York Salvos.*[28]

With grateful hearts, the band saw the "Stars and Stripes" flying high over Honolulu, Hawaii, during the last official stop on the tour.

Band statistics cited a 32-day trip, 14 cities, 44 playing/singing engagements, 6 Salvation Army territories, 6 airlines used, 16 flights, and a staggering 26,000 miles traveled.[29] While two "normal" programs remained to be done by these happy but weary travelers, the opportunity to sing "Rock of Ages" in the memorial hall at Pearl Harbor, near the *U.S.S. Arizona,* was one that all bandsmen speak of with reverence. While tourists silently read the names of honored dead, the band sang their spirit-filled alma mater "Rock of Ages" and Stanely Ditmer offered a prayer of remembrance, thanksgiving, and hope that properly served as the tour's benediction.

## Return to England, 1985

The NYSB returned to England for a sixth time in May 1985. No other American brass band can approach that record. International congresses drew the band overseas in 1904, 1914, and 1978. The band's 1960 Great Britain Tour and 1968 European Tour were climaxed by acclaimed performances at the British Territory's Bandmasters' Councils. In 1985 the Songster Leaders' Councils served as tour centerpiece.

The years between the World Tour and the 1985 British Tour were marked by the challenge of rebuilding personnel, with 14 changes immediately after their World Tour, including the entire trombone section![30]

There were other challenges and rewards, particularly in the area of new repertoire and festival opportunities. A Profile V Concert, February 1983, allowed the band to pay tribute to their former bandmaster, Commissioner Richard E. Holz, particularly through William Himes' imaginative festival suite "To the Chief Musician," written in Holz's honor. Several months later the New Yorkers repaid Swedish hospitality by hosting the Stockholm VII Band (Per Ohlsson) in a spectacular two-band "Superfest."

Anniversaries marking 100 years were being celebrated in many corps, and the NYSB was in demand for these festive events. Camp meetings and congresses continued, including the "Camp Meeting Congress" in the Eastern Territory in June 1984, in which the NYSB shared the stage of the famed Ocean Grove Auditorium with the youthful Salvation Army Student Fellowship Band (Ronald Holz) of Asbury College.

The annual festival just prior to the 1985 tour included a tribute to Walter Orr, long-standing mainstay of the band's front cornet bench. Virtuoso Euphoniumist Derick Kane, who as a young bandsmen attended Star Lake Musicamp on the Erik Leidzen Memorial Scholarship, was the featured guest, proving his amazing worth as a soloist, just as he had done during the ISB's wonderfully successful tour of the United States in October 1980.[31] Preparations for the 1985 NYSB tour demanded another search for good new music. Several brass works were commissioned:

Sinfonietta— "The Dawning" (Peter Graham)
"Gowans and Larsson Overture" (William Broughton)
Cornet Solo: "The Amazing Mr. Leidzen" (Spowart, arr. Graham)
Euphonium Solo: "Tell the World" (Thomas Mack)
"Rondeau" (Mouret, tr. Peter Graham)
Soprano Cornet Solo: "Pastorale" (Peter Graham)

Some pieces were drawn from other Army bands that had shared fellowship and music with the band in recent years:

Chicago Staff Band:
Festival March— "Able" (Turkington, arr. Himes)
"Elsa's Procession to the Cathedral" (Wagner, tr. Himes)

S.A.S.F. Band:
Cornet Ensemble: "Faithful Forever" (Richard E. Holz)

Melbourne Staff Band:
Soprano Cornet Solo: "Cavalleria Rusticana" (Mascagni, arr. Baxter)

Vocal literature was given a boost in new, contemporary settings by Thomas Mack, Stephen Bulla, and Peter Graham. The return of tenor soloist Albert Avery to the band greatly enhanced that part of the repertoire. Some World Tour music was maintained, particularly the impressive "Suite of American Overtures," as well as the famous "Rock of Ages."

The band board geared up for this next trip. In good entrepreneurial spirit, they produced T-shirts, ties and cassettes for sale on tour. They even planned videotape coverage of events! They decided that another memories booklet would be produced after the conclusion of the trip, Harold Anderson serving, as he had with *Reflections,* as general editor. Robert Watson was given the responsibility of writing the various reports.

151

The tour brochure's festival contained a program somewhat similar to the 1960 model, opening as it did with a cornet ensemble and including a middle devotional section. The overall style was distinctly 1980s, however, as much modern-idiom music for brass and voice was featured, though Derek Smith always wanted both old Army gems ("Heroes of the Faith" or "The Divine Pursuit") and classic transcriptions (like Himes' Wagner adaptation or James Curnow's transcription of a Frescobaldi organ toccata). Where possible, each program concluded with the "Grand Finale—Multimedia Spectacular," the Bulla overtures. The back page of the brochure contained a brief historical summary of the band's contact with and indebtedness to Great Britain (provided by this author for the tour recording as well, which featured historic photos of the band). As in the world tour, congregational songs were incorporated in every program.

Other than Royal Albert Hall, all the other locations on the tour itinerary were different than the tour of 25 years before:

### 1985 Great Britain Tour—General Itinerary[32]

| May | 17 | Hendon Citadel Corps |
|---|---|---|
| | 18-19 | Ipswich Citadel |
| | 20 | Cambridge/St. Andrews St. Baptist Church |
| | 21 | Derby Central Corps |
| | 22 | Hull East Corps |
| | 23 | Darlington |
| | 24 | Burnley Citadel |
| | 25-26 | Gloucester Corps/St. Catherine's Church |
| | 27 | Hereford |
| | 28 | Exeter, including recording session for BBC, "Listen to the Band" program |
| | 29 | Bournemouth International Centre (Boscombe, Christchurch, Pokesdown, and Winton Corps) |
| | 30 | Leigh-on-Sea/Crowstone St. George's Church |
| June | 1 | London/Royal Albert Hall—"Happiness and Harmony Festival" as part of Songster Leaders' Councils |
| | 2 | Regent Hall Corps (Three meetings, three open-airs, and "afterglow" festival) |
| | 3 | Buckingham Palace/Concert in Forecourt |

The band played and sang with controlled enthusiasm throughout the tour. British *Musician* reports were glowing in their affirmative response to the band's delightful music and their serious message. Executive Officer Edward Fritz led the men with his virile, energetic personality through many a concert and reception with a lord mayor, and he stirred the hearts of audiences with his forceful, evangelical appeals.

For men like Derek Smith, Gordon Ward, Peter Graham, and Ian Anderson, it was a true homecoming. Corps large and small shared in accepting these talented British transplants (Scottish for Peter) and their hearty American comrades. At the conclusion of each festival, as the band sang "Rock of Ages" as a benediction, many hearts and minds turned heavenward in thanksgiving for the gift of music that allows humans to praise their Creator in so many rich and beautiful ways.

The band had much to thank God for on this tour. Their bandmaster, who had suffered a heart attack a few months prior to the tour, gradually became stronger as the tour lengthened. Band board members, headed by Executive Officer Edward Fritz and Deputy Bandmaster Ronald Waiksnoris, made the burden all the lighter for their beloved conductor. Robert Watson, solo cornetist, whose well-written tour summary appeared in the American *Musician* later that year, provided us with a capsule statement of what the tour meant to the band on a deeply personal level:

> ... all that had taken place over the preceding eighteen days had been a testimony to the Lordship of Jesus Christ. God's gifts were overflowing throughout the tour—fellow Salvationist drivers who leant new meaning to the term "servanthood," new friendships, an increasingly healthy bandmaster and a very capable deputy bandmaster, a broader view of The Salvation Army, supportive families at home, meaningful and redemptive times in communion with the Holy Spirit—it is all a treasure we have buried deep within our humble hearts and minds. May Jesus Christ be praised![33]

The final weekend in London was as near an apotheosis of Salvation Army brass banding as could be expected. What a marvelous experience for Derek Smith to lead his men triumphantly on the stage of Royal Albert Hall, on the streets of London, and in the forecourt of Buckingham Palace! We conclude this all-too-brief survey of the tour by citing three British reports to their *Musician*. In the context of these writers addressing a British audience, their acclamation and support of the band's ministry justly needs to be preserved:

**Ray Steadman-Allen** (in reviewing the Royal Albert Hall contributions of the band):

*The New York Staff Band, at the organizers' request, included "Marching to Glory." This is a sequence of music put together by Stephen Bulla for the centenary of the Army in the USA. Composed of popular Broadway hits, TV themes and the occasional folk song (plus "God Bless America") the music is really intended to accompany a slide presentation. It is lively and the crowd as one might expect, loved the "guns" and hoedown/cowboy cries. What were the yelps? Apocryphally "Let's eat" was heard on another occasion! This music is a wonderful piece of arranging craft and its playing was full of character and, a word I once heard Terry Camsey use, pizzazz.*

*The band put its corporate hair back for a major work in serious vein by its Scottish member Peter Graham. Peter is making his mark as a composer and many were keen to hear his composition. Having the title "Dawning," the music considers man's bitterness and strife and his need for God. The thinking is "cosmic," borrowing imagery from one of the songs "There will be God" (Joy Webb), together with "Morning has Broken" and "My Lord, what a Morning." The composer reveals a refreshing modesty about his work, but it has style, live content, sound technique, and a sense of design which augurs well for the future. A splendid contribution which was readily recognized.*

*Deputy Staff Bandmaster Ronald Waiksnoris will have a paragraph to himself. Not only did he play brilliantly but he also deserves special acknowledgement of the share of responsibility he has taken during the recent band tour, a responsibility which has helped to ease pressure for Staff Bandmaster Derek Smith, still mending from a period of ill health. Ron's cornet solo was the fascinatingly titled "The Amazing Mr. Leidzen" (arr. Peter Graham)....Ron's presentation aroused the crowd to rapturous applause. Ron is, by the way, the quietly-competent director of the New York Territorial Music Bureau.*[34]

**George Wilson** (in reporting the Sunday at Regent Hall Corps):

*What were the highlights? For some people, no doubt, the impassioned address in the holiness meeting by Lt.-Colonel*

154

Edward Fritz when three seekers knelt at the mercy seat. For others, the delightful, ever youthful-sounding singing of Lt.-Colonel Albert Avery. For some, the near perfect blend and balance of vocal sound as the male chorus melted our hearts and enthused our spirits with its ministry. Yet again for others the expertise of the presentation of "Toccata," a tour de force for any band. Maybe for others the "new brass" sound in the "Gowans and Larsson Overture." For some, the breathtaking entry of the trombone section near the end of "Elsa's Procession to the Cathedral," to add a wondrous aura of sound and lift the music to a stunning conclusion.

There was so much to remember and for which to thank God. There were the snap-happy hordes of bystanders lining the route to the open-air march, with the patrolling policemen allowing a car to park in the middle of Regent Street so that the driver could "snap" away to his heart's content. Then there was the Sunday evening open-air congregation which was "riveted" by the heart-stirring testimony of Staff Bandsman Paul Cranford.

The fact that the New York Staff Band gave almost an hour's programme in the wind-up at the end of the day gave an indication of the stamina of these men after a long arduous tour.

We of the "Rink" fellowship would simply say "Thank You" to the NYSB for "a day to remember." It will remain in our hearts and minds for many years to come.[35]

### Front page report from the British *Musician* "NYSB Plays in Palace Forecourt":

A mounted police escort led the way as the New York Staff Band (Derek Smith), headed by the Army flag and the Stars and Stripes of America, made its way from Admiralty Arch, along The Mall, past the Victoria Memorial and through the gates of Buckingham Palace where, in the forecourt, it presented an hour-long programme.

Representing the royal household was Footman Ray Wheaton, an Upper Norwood bandsman, who greeted the band.

Cameras clicked as Salvationists and tourists crowded around the palace railings in brilliant sunshine and recorded the event. Among them was Colonel Albert Jakeway (R) who heard the band give a splendid performance of his march "Rosehill."

Among other pieces presented were "Jerusalem," Leidzen's "What a Friend," the suite "Day of Rejoicing" and "Kentucky"...

The Queen's Lady-in-waiting (Lady Susan Hussey) and the Controller General (Lt.-Colonel Sir John Johnston), who had listened to the programme in the palace, were introduced to the bandmaster and the bandsmen by the Public Relations Secretary (Lt.-Colonel Arthur Thompson).[36]

The video of the band's entrance into the Palace Courtyard is a stirring experience. America's national hymn "God of Our Fathers" sounded forth in joyous praise as these men proudly marched to their honored concert site. As prestigious as the signal honor was, it was only a part of a full tour of ministry, of musical evangelism. Staff bandsmen are rewarded more deeply when their music does more than delight—they are rewarded when it reaches the hearts of listeners and, as a result, lives are changed and redirected. Commissioner Orval Taylor, then territorial commander of the Eastern Territory, U.S.A., addressed that balanced functioning in his official recognition of the band's achievements on their tour:

> The New York Staff Band has returned from its history making Return to Britain tour having received the applause and appreciation of Salvationists and other brass music lovers across the length and breadth of Great Britain. Ordinary listeners and critics alike were high in their praise of the musical presentations of the Staff Band who rose to every occasion with top rated presentations. New music, mostly the product of America and new American composers and arrangers, captured the interest and attention of the listeners in England.
>
> Of even greater significance have been reports received by letter in the territorial commander's office concerning the Salvationism, the Christian witness and the outstanding fellowship and friendliness exhibited by the bandsmen at corps meetings as well as at their several billets. A number of outstanding witnesses to the spiritual impact of the band have been received, and for this we are grateful to God for His blessing upon the band's ministry.[37]

## Only One Intention

After a strenuous weekend in Puerto Rico in March 1986, Derek Smith began to wonder if his days of leading the Staff Band should come to a close. Increasing concern for his health made him reluctantly announce his retirement in April with the official retirement service being conducted in June.[38] Fourteen years of pursuing the ideal in Salvation Army banding came to an end, leaving behind a marvelous record of achievement. The band had been richly rewarded during his era.

Derek Smith is a musical perfectionist. He admits that, but not in the way most people understand such a designation: "I am a perfectionist," he says, "but not for myself. The pursuit of excellence is what is demanded of us all, yet there is a balance needed in this pursuit—the balance between the perfecting of motive and the perfecting of musical performance." He had learned this lesson when going through an earlier difficult period, while on tour of Australia as a cornet soloist, when he doubted his abilities and his calling as a musician. A chief secretary there challenged a musical gathering to first examine the reasons why they were involved in sacred music. He claimed that "the perfecting of motive is as important as, or more important (higher) than the perfection of musical performance."

This thought renewed Smith's spirit, allowing him to make the difficult transition from performing soloist to a leader of men. He asked his friend Ray Steadman-Allen to arrange a cornet solo for him based on an old Army chorus, "Only One Intention" *(Salvation Army Song Book,* Chorus Section #93). When played, it became the embodiment of Staff Bandmaster Smith's approach to sacred music-making:

*Only one intention, only one intention,*
*Lord, at the Cross I claim it mine.*
*Every treasure spending in Thy cause contending,*
*Held by the power of a love like Thine.*

# PART II

# 10

## "Thy King Cometh"
### (Leslie Condon)

### Instrumentation and Instruments

The current New York Staff Band follows standard British brass band instrumentation, established as "official" for Salvation Army bands by 1902.[1] While the number of players per part varies slightly from year to year, the following listing by part accurately reflects the size of the band since the days of William Broughton:[2]

### The New York Staff Band, as of March 1986

E♭ Soprano Cornet
Gordon Ward

B♭ Solo Cornet
Ronald Waiksnoris, Dep. B/M
Kenneth Kirby
Michael McDonald
Peter Graham

B♭ First Cornet
Ronald Foreman
Lawrence J. Beadle

B♭ Second Cornet
Warren Smith
Peter Vaughan

B♭ Second Trombone
Carl Carvill
Victor Gilder

Bass Trombone
Darren Mudge

B♭ Solo Euphonium
Thomas Mack, Male Chorus
Leader
Frank Psaute

EE♭ Bass
Jeff Schultz
Charles Olsen
Paul Cranford

B♭ Flugelhorn
Donald Spencer

E♭ Solo Horn
Albert E. Avery
Norman Voisey

E♭ First Horn
Colin DeVault

E♭ Second Horn
William LaMarr

B♭ First Baritone
Harold Anderson
Craig Evans

B♭ Second Baritone
David Childs

B♭ First Trombone
William Riley
Thomas Scheibner

BB♭ Bass
Philip Ferreira
Vincent Bulla

Percussion
Albert Avery Jr.
Robert Coles

Flag Bearer
Charles Olsen Jr.

Bandmaster
Derek Smith

Executive Officer
Edward Fritz

All parts are written in treble clef, with the exception of bass trombone, in much the same way as that for the clarinet and saxophone families.[3] This practice has made the switching of instrument assignments an easy matter from the viewpoint of reading and fingering. Salvation Army bandsmen are still aware that they can be moved to other sections at the discretion of the bandmaster.

Acceptance of the internationally imposed, all-brass instrumentation (1902) was not fully achieved by the NYSB until the mid-1930s. By 1959 the last remnants of American-style brass instruments had been removed in favor of British brass band models. The history of this gradual compliance can be divided into five periods:

1887-1897 Formative years; no stable leadership; group resembles American brass bands of the period with some woodwinds.
1897-1912 First standard seating, by Anderson, following British models; some woodwinds remain.

1912-1932 American reaction; George Darby established a band more like Sousa's, including trumpets, saxophones, clarinets, and French horns; he uses much non-Army music.

1932-1959 All woodwinds and French horns removed; American-style cornets, altos, baritones, and basses mixed with British manufactured instruments.

1959-1986 Complete alignment with British models in instrumentation and instruments.

Factors contributing to this particular "evolution" included the personality/background of bandmasters, strength of local administrative control, varying quality/price/availability of instruments, and the slow change to standard "concert pitch" among brass band instrument makers. Continued administrative control over music (most of it published in Great Britain) further intensified the link between London and New York. The reasons for the lack of a distinct or separate American brass band or wind band tradition within the denomination has as much with autocratic, ecclesiastical authority as it does with musical considerations in regard to literature, equipment and personnel.

The earliest document of NYSB instrumentation is derived from a *War Cry* cover sketch of February 1888 showing four cornets, one euphonium/baritone, one helicon-style bass, and one valve trombone.[4] In the following year, the band grew from seven to 13 members, but detailed listing is not available. By 1890 the group was 18 strong, including two clarinets and two percussionists. From another *War Cry* sketch, the first identified band, a fuller scoring can be seen:[5]

| | |
|---|---|
| 1 E♭ Cornet (Trumble) | 1 B♭ Euphonium |
| 4 B♭ Cornets | 1 E♭ Bass |
| 1 B♭ Clarinet | 1 B♭ Helicon Bass |
| 3 E♭ Alto Horns | 1 Trombone (valve?) |
| 2 B♭ Baritones—Tenors | 2 Percussionists |

The National Guards Band of 1891-92 was of approximately the same size and instrumentation (average of 17 players). No usable records survive for Trumble's band, 1893-96, but starting in 1897 the *Disposition of Forces* began listing the band by assignment of parts:

163

## National Staff Band, 1897:[6]

| | |
|---|---|
| 5 B♭ Cornets (3, 1, 1) | 2 B♭ Euphoniums |
| 3 E♭ Altos (1, 1, 1) | 1 E♭ Bass |
| 2 B♭ Baritones (1, 1) | 1 B♭ Bass |
| 2 B♭ Trombones (1, 1) | 2 Percussionists |

In 1898 Anderson added a flugelhorn. An E♭ soprano cornet returned in 1902, as did clarinets (2), including an E♭ clarinet by 1903.[7] In July 1903, the band had four basses. The NSB at the International Congress in 1904 numbered 29 members, including a "picolo" [sic] played by George Lock:[8]

## National Staff Band, July 1904

E♭ Cornet
Edward Trumble

B♭ Solo Cornet
Charles Anderson, B/M
Samson Hodges
Daniel Black
John Allan

B♭ First Cornet
Bert Wright
Ed Higgins

B♭ Second Cornet
Albert Norris
Kris Booth-Tucker

E♭ Solo Alto
Frank Fowler

E♭ First Alto
W. Gooding

E♭ Second Alto
Henry Burlew

E♭ Third Alto
Adj. Kraft

B♭ Second Baritone
George Polhemus
*(Note: no first baritone cited)*

B♭ Clarinet
John W. Lock (Solo)
Adj. Hansen

E♭ Clarinet
Tom Narraway

Picolo [sic]
George Lock

B♭ First Trombone
Gustave Reinhardsen, ExO

B♭ Second Trombone
E. Gerberich
Hubert Roberts

B♭ Solo Euphonium
Alfred J. Pike

E♭ Bass
Edgar Irvine
Karl Bergh

B♭ Bass
Charles Van Leusen, B. Sec.
Edward Nuber

Percussion
J. J. Stimson (Bass Drum)
B. Hillman (Cymbals)
Lt. Emerson (Snare Drum)

The War Cry of January 2, 1886, contained an advertisement about instruments for sale, including a "full brass band complete" for $130.00 (cash!): Four varieties of B♭ cornet ($9.50-$27.00), valve trombone ($22.50), B♭ Tenor ($16.50), B♭ Baritone ($19.00), and "Bass B♭" ($23.00). Several types of snare and bass drums were also available.[9] The instrument manufacturers were not announced! An October 1893, Trade Headquarters (London) price list pamphlet listed an extensive inventory of brass instruments. Their "top line" horns were called OUR OWN MAKE, including Besson and Courtois model cornets. Sopranos, cornets, pocket cornets, tenor horns (E♭ altos), B♭ baritones, euponiums, E♭ bass "Bombardons," E♭ and B♭ Circular helicons, valve and slide trombones, including a G bass trombone, were all available as well as lyres, mouthpieces, shanks, cases, mutes, and an assortment of percussion instruments—even "improved shoulder lamps," or "band lamps" for evening open-air meetings.[10] Not all of these were available in New York, however, and the Salvation Army Price List released from the NHQ Trade Department (111 Reade Street) in the early 1890s was not nearly so well-stocked, though most brass instruments were listed, including the rare E♭ solo alto that was played like a flugelhorn, and a valve alto trombone. Both European and American manufacturers' instruments were sold.[11] By 1903, French "Belleville" brass instruments were on sale in the New York Trade.[12]

Frank Fowler, at first an alto player in the band, was shifted to the first modern BB♭ bass in 1906. In that same year the first saxophone appeared in the band, played by James Bovill. The band of 1907 had 32 members, including a flugelhorn, six alto horns and two BB♭ basses. A bass trombone was introduced in 1909, just in time for the band's trip to Toronto.[13]

Procuring good equipment must have been particularly difficult, at least through official Army suppliers. Early band minutes cite heavy reliance on Carl Fisher's corporation in New York City for quality instruments and repair. Very little "official" promotion was given for musical instruments, although one zany experiment from 1901 gives us an idea of the conditions back then. In the November 1901 War Crys, and for several years afterwards, ads appeared for a whole line of fake brass instruments, called "zobophones," that were essentially fancy kazoos. The ad read: "There is nothing to learn or study, no practicing; just a couple of rehearsals and you can play with as much confidence as a professional cornetist." Salvationists were encouraged to form these "instant" humming bands, described as sounding like "something between a brass band and a string orchestra, leaning to the latter!" Instrumentation of "zobos" ranged as follows: cornetto, cornet, alto cornet, saxaphone [sic], slide trombone, and bass horn.[14] What a setback this must have been to the establishment of a quality music program!

There were serious musicians active in the early Army, of course, and George Darby was very earnest in his approach to band instrumentation. When he assumed the bandmastership in 1912, he printed a list of his ideal band, even positions not yet filled, in the June 1912 *Dispo* list of the band, his idea being, perhaps, to encourage men to try out for these positions:

### Darby's Ideal Band, 1912[15]

| | |
|---|---|
| E$^b$ Soprano Cornet (1)* | B$^b$ Tenor Saxophone (1)* |
| E$^b$ Soprano Saxophone (1)* | B$^b$ Solo Baritone (1) |
| E$^b$ Clarinet (1) | B$^b$ Second Baritone (1) |
| B$^b$ Solo Cornet (3) | B$^b$ Solo Trombone (1) |
| B$^b$ Solo Trumpet (1) | B$^b$ Second Trombone(1) |
| B$^b$ Solo Clarinet (1) | G Bass Trombone (1)* |
| B$^b$ Repiano Trumpet (1) | BB$^b$ Bass Trombone (1) |
| B$^b$ Repiano Cornet (1) | (double slide)* |
| B$^b$ First Clarinet (1) | B$^b$ Solo Euphonium (2) |
| B$^b$ Second Cornet (1) | E$^b$ Baritone Saxophone (1)* |
| B$^b$ Flugelhorn (1) | E$^b$ Bass, medium (1) |
| E$^b$ Solo French Horn (1) | E$^b$ Bass, monster (1) |
| E$^b$ Alto Saxophone (1) | BB$^b$ Bass, medium (1)* |
| E$^b$ First Horn (1) | BB$^b$ Bass, monster (1) |
| E$^b$ First French Horn (1) | Side Drum and Traps (1) |
| E$^b$ Second Horn (1) | Bass Drum (1) |
| E$^b$ Second French Horn (1) | |

*Positions not filled in July 1912

Darby purchased Fowler's famous Conn BB$^b$ bass in 1912 plus excellent Besson baritones. In 1913 he had a BB$^b$ bass trombonist (H. Stanyon), tenor sax (K. McIntyre), E$^b$ soprano (H. Miller), and baritone saxophone (J. Jackson). A true French horn (not an E$^b$ mellophone) was purchased in 1914. The band at the International Congress of 1914, however, contained only two woodwinds. A balanced saxophone section was achieved briefly in 1916.[16]

## National Staff Band at the 1914 International Congress[17]
### B/M George Darby; ExO Walter Jenkins

B♭ Solo Cornet
John Allan
Robert Griffith
Stanley Sheppard

B♭ Solo Trumpet
W. H. Barrett

B♭ Solo Clarinet
J. W. Lock

B♭ First Clarinet
Charles Anderson

B♭ Repiano Trumpet
Howard Margetts

B♭ Repiano Cornet
Bertram Rodda

B♭ Second Cornet
William Hammond

B♭ Flugelhorn
George Nicholls

E♭ Solo Horn
Ort Mitson

E♭ First Horn
Albert Norris

E♭ First French Horn
Leslie Arkett

E♭ Second Horn
Charles Van Leusen

B♭ Solo Baritone
William Palmer

B♭ Second Baritone
Karl Bergh

B♭ Solo Trombone
Samson Hodges

B♭ Second Trombone
E. R. Miller

G Bass Trombone
Walter Harvey

BB♭ Bass Trombone
Harold Stanyon

B♭ Solo Euphonium
Robert Young
Alfred J. Pike

E♭ Bass
William Gilks
H. Ernest (monster)

B♭ Bass
Frank Fowler

Side Drum and Traps
Richard Von Calio

Bass Drum
J. J. Stimson

Other "firsts" under Darby include the use of chimes and a xylophone by at least 1920 and a pair of timpani by 1924. The clarinet section was at its largest in 1928, with four. There were six trombones in the band in 1922, and seven horns in 1928 (three French horns, four altos). Darby usually had three basses, though he preferred four and he used a sousaphone in 1921 (see *War Cry* photo, September 24, 1921). The saxophone section reached its peak just after World War I, with two altos, one tenor and one baritone.

George Darby and John T. Flynn (B/M of the Chicago Staff Band) were mainly responsible for shifting Salvation Army bands in America to "low pitch," or A = 440, just after World War I. By 1919 the stock of band instruments in U.S. trade departments was entirely low pitch. British Salvation Army bands were still in high pitch (approx. A = 450). Edgar Arkett summarized the reasons behind this change in an article from 1929:

> The U.S. Government had previously adopted low pitch [A = 440], and the musical unions, federations, orchestras, and bands had been employing it for many years. Salvation Army bands were possibly the only bands in the country using high pitch, and as a result found it extremely difficult to obtain instruments which could be properly tuned. Instrument makers turned their attention to the exclusive manufacture of low pitch instruments, and when one of our bands needed replacements, the makers would merely cut down the tuning slide regardless of what effect this had on the rest of the instruments, especially the valve slides.[18]

American manufacturers most often used during the 1920s and 1930s were as follows: Millard, Conn, Buescher, White, Martin, and York. Most frequently, the trade departments ordered those instruments used by the bands of the U.S. military, especially the U.S. Navy Band.[19] Some foreign manufacturers, like the "Courturier Conical Bore Cornet" (available in high or low pitch) were used, as confirmed in William Broughton's endorsement statement of 1921:

> The Courturier Cornets are excellent. I was agreeably surprised at their quality and perfectness of tone. Also the easiness in reaching high or low notes. You are representing an instrument of high grade.[20]

William Broughton removed all woodwinds from the Staff Band by 1933, when the band stood at "prize" size—24. Granger introduced American-manufactured "bell-front" variety alto horns and euphoniums in 1936, with his 31-piece band. By the early 1940s Granger was also using some bell-front basses. As a result, the alto, euphonium and bass sections were featured in Conn Company ads of this period.[21]

The basic problems faced with these bell-front instruments were intonation and the direction of the sound. The band from Darby to Bearchell had a rather unBritish sound anyway; the bell-front instruments accentuated that difference.[22] The alto horn players of the 1940s complained about the Conn altos; Emil Nelson insisted on using an upright Besson. By 1948 Bearchell purchased a set of upright altos from the Reynolds Company, which had volunteered to make them. William Slater secured a set of good Salvation Army-made Triumphonic altos while on a trip to London in 1951, and had Ray Steadman-Allen test them before shipping. He asked for "low pitch—but now *too* low"; they came in *very sharp!*

While the *Dispos* from the early 1930s to 1940s did not list membership in the band, giving only total numbers instead, the band still maintained an all-brass (plus percussion) format. William Bearchell's 1948 band was properly in line with official international Salvation Army band instrumentation:

### The New York Staff Band, November 1948[23]
B/M William Bearchell, ExO Holland French

Eᵇ Soprano Cornet
Roland Schramm

Bᵇ Solo Cornet
Edward Lowcock
James Henderson
William Perrett
Walter Orr

Bᵇ First Cornet
William Fox
Robert Barton

Bᵇ Second Cornet
Wilbur Range
Leslie Catlin

Bᵇ Flugelhorn
Richard E. Holz, Dep B/M,
 Male Chorus Leader

Bᵇ First Baritone
George Harvey
Floyd Hooper

Bᵇ Second Baritone
Thomas Craig

Bᵇ First Trombone
Arthur Craytor

Bᵇ Second Trombone
Arthur L. Fox
Charles Mehling

Bass Trombone and Chimes
John Sarer

Eᵇ Bass
Gordon Rodda

Bᵇ Bass
Vincent Bulla

| | |
|---|---|
| E♭ Solo Horn | BB♭ Bass |
| Afred Swenarton | Frank Fowler |
| E♭ First Horn | Percussion |
| J. Fletcher Agnew | Edwin Gooden |
| Ralph Miller | Rowland Hughes |
| E♭ Second Horn | Color Sergeants |
| Thomas Gorman | William Rombey |
| Walter Porter | Sidney Shields |
| B♭ Solo Euphonium | |
| Milton Kippax | |

The band has essentially maintained this seating, with the addition of a bass or two, and an extra cornet or trombone, right up to the present day. The great changes came with the instruments used. Richard Holz began the move towards total brass-band instrumentation with the purchase of four Besson, compensating-valve system basses early in his tenure. Frank Fowler would attempt to sabotage the new Bessons from time to time. Other opposition came from Milton Kippax who did not wish to give up his bell-front euphonium. The greatest change for the band, however, came with the switch to all Besson short model cornets with slide triggers by 1959. These "classic" style horns finally allowed the cornet section to achieve a cohesive, unified sound. Soon Besson euphoniums and baritones and a new set of Triumphonic altos—all lacquer—transformed the band's sound and image.[24] The trombones were medium-bore Conns except the G bass trombone (the band used an F Bass Trombone in 1936-37, switched back to the G, then again to the F in 1962).[25] The flugelhorn was a Boosey and Hawkes and the soprano cornet was a Besson.[26]

The sound and appearance of the NYSB on its 1960 Great Britain tour had an interesting impact on British brass band aficionados. To some, the low pitch seemed lighter; others called it "warmer." The middle and bass section of the band were particularly appreciated by Bernard Adams, and this has remained a trademark of the band ever since—a rich alto and baritone texture and full bass sound. The differences one encountered in British reactions to this American lacquered band (Ball— "brighter"; Gregson— "mellow, darker") were also influenced by the much less pronounced use of vibrato in the band. As the NYSB sat on the Royal Albert Hall stage, June 1960, it finally *looked* like a British brass band, even if its "unique" sound was different enough to keep discussions lively for several years. Within recent years the American's more "symphonic" sound has taken over most British bands. (Of course, this change is a very complex one and relates to British brass symphonic traditions, too.) A review of recordings over the period 1961-1981 confirms this—less vibrato, switch to "low" pitch, and many stylistic changes, particularly in articulations, are evident.

Further changes in Staff Band instrumentation were minor until 1981.[27] In the year prior to the tour, the entire inventory was replaced, the finish changed from its "traditional" lacquer finish back to silver. All the instruments were of Boosey and Hawkes manufacture, except for the Bach trombones. The cornet soloist, Ronald Waiksnoris, was allowed, as was Smith two decades before, to keep his own "Signature" D. E. G. model. Some argue that the switch back to silver has added a bright luster to the band's sound; others feel it has detracted from the band's mellow tone of "bygone" days. Like the old 1960s illusion of "bright versus mellow," much of this is in the "ear" of the listener. What has been maintained is a fine tradition of symphonic brass sound first nurtured in the late 1950s.

In comparing the following three band lists—from tours in 1960, 1968 and 1985, respectively—one finds little deviation from the all-brass pattern fixed for the band from the days of Broughton. These three bands did share uniform manufacturers and British brass band-style instruments, something not true of the earlier bands.

### NYSB Great Britain Tour, June 1960[28]
B/M Richard Holz; ExO William Maltby

E♭ Soprano Cornet
Fred Jackson

B♭ Solo Cornet
Vernon Post, Dep B/M, Male
    Chorus Leader
Derek Smith
James Abram
Walter Orr
Olof Lundgren

B♭ Second Baritone
John Dockendorff

B♭ First Trombone
Arthur Anderson
Fred Elliott

B♭ Second Trombone
Allister Stickland
Fred Clarke

B♭ First Cornet
Albert E. Avery
Peter Hofman

B♭ Second Cornet
Harold Anderson

B♭ Flugelhorn
William Schofield

E♭ Solo Horn
Alfred Swenarton
George Harvey

E♭ First Horn
Frank Moody
Eric Lundsten

E♭ Second Horn
Chris Robinson-Cooke
Thomas Craig

B♭ First Baritone
William MacLean
Harry Hartjes

Bass Trombone
William North

B♭ Solo Euphonium
Robert McNally
Donald Ross

E♭ Bass
Charles Olsen
Ivor Rich
Mark Freeh

B♭ Bass
Wilfred Cooper
Harold Banta

Percussion
Arthur Moulton
David Robinson-Cooke

Publicity
Ralph Miller

## NYSB European Tour, May 1968[29]
B/M Vernon Post; ExO Emil Nelson

E♭ Soprano Cornet
Kenneth Davis

B♭ Solo Cornet
Derek Smith
Peter Hofman
Walter Orr
Olof Lundgren
Lawrence Beadle

B♭ First Cornet
William Scarlett
Lambert Bittinger Jr.

B♭ Second Cornet
Roland Schramm
William Simons

B♭ Second Baritone
John Phelan

B♭ First Trombone
Allister Stickland
Charles West

B♭ Second Trombone
Jacob Hohn
Wilbur Smith

Bass Trombone
Howard Hastings

B♭ Solo Euphonium
Lawrence Robertson
Russell Prince

*Earliest picture (sketch) of National Staff Band, 1890; B/M Walter Duncan (second from left, bottom row). Members from left to right: BOTTOM ROW—Capt. Hall, Capt. Duncan, Maj. Bryant, Capt. Straubel, Cadet Miller; MIDDLE ROW—Staff-Capt. Glen, Lieut. Flory, Capt. Trumble, Bro. Bale, Bro. Wright, Capt. Cook, Cadet Mantz; TOP ROW—Lieut. Taylor, Capt. Reinhardsen, Cadet Mills, Bro. Gooding, Capt. Hartwright. [Source: WC, December 20, 1920, p. 1, courtesy of S.A. Archives.]*

*"Trumpeter" Edward Trumble with E♭ soprano cornet, 1888, Elyria, Ohio (before joining National Staff Band). [Source: Seiler Collection.]*

*National Staff Band, c. 1899 (B/M Charles Anderson and 'The Lady Cornetist,' Felicia Gircopazzi, first two from left). [Source: Holz Collection (photo), Nelson Collection (slide).]*

*National Staff Band (B/M Charles Anderson) of 1904, with Commander Booth-Tucker (directly behind bass drum), dressed in International Congress "Cowboy" uniforms. [Source: WC, July 16, 1904, p. 5.]*

*National Staff Band, 1909 (B/M Robert Griffith) that visited Toronto, Canada; made into postcard photo. [Source: WC, July 10, 1909, p. 1; or S.A. Archives, 35-1887 (postcard).]*

*National Staff Band at Lake George, N.Y. (part of Adirondacks Tour), July 1913 (B/M George Darby, to left of megaphone, front row). [Source: Nelson Collection.]*

*National Staff Band, 1914, headed for International Congress (B/M George Darby). [Source: S.A. Archives; or NYSB Photo Collection.]*

*Eastern Territorial Staff Band begins August 1921 motorcade to Old Orchard Beach, Maine. [Source: S.A. Archives, 35-224.]*

*Staff Band of 1924 about to board "modern superbus." [Source: Nelson Collection.]*

*Composers featured at the 1930 National Congress. From left to right: FRONT ROW—K. M. Fristrup, William Broughton; BACK ROW—Emil Soderstrom, Bramwell Coles, Erik Leidzen. [Source: Holz Collection.]*

"Top brass" at the 1930 National Congress 'Mammoth' Music Festival. Left to right: Commander Evangeline Booth, John Philip Sousa, Commissioner Richard Holz. [Source: Holz Collection; photo by Paul Parker.]

B/M J. Stanley "Red" Sheppard. [Source: NYSB Photo Collection; photo by John Sarer.]

Richard Von Calio (accordion, chimes, etc.) and "Billie" Parkins (cornet) warm up the crowd on the Commander's motorcade (with Staff Band) of 1931. [Source: Nelson Collection.]

*Commander Evangeline Booth in "rags" or "slummer" outfit. [Source: Holz Collection.]*

*John Allan as commissioner and chief of the staff. [Source: Holz Collection; photo by Henry Chapman, Swansee, England.]*

*New York Staff Band (B/M George Granger, and Executive Officer John Allan, front row center) at CBS studio, 1936. [Source: Holz Collection; photo by Paul Parker.]*

*The New York Staff Band, 1949, under B/M William Bearchell and Executive Officer Holland French (flanking flags at back). [Source: Bearchell Collection.]*

*The 1937 band (B/M George Granger) that toured New York State and Canada. [Source: NYSB Photo Collection.]*

*The Staff Band of January 1952 (B/M William Slater). [Source: NYSB Photo Collection.]*

*Male Chorus Leader Vernon Post and B/M Richard E. Holz, c. 1962—a unique team! [Source: Holz Collection.]*

*The band that toured Great Britain, June 1960 (B/M Richard E. Holz). [Source: NYSB Photo Collection; photo by Paul Parker.]*

*E. F. Goldman Memorial Festival, February 1959. Left to right: B/M Richard Holz, Dr. Richard Franko Goldman, Erik Leidzen, Commissioner Norman Marshall. [Source: Holz Collection; photo by John Sarer.]*

*"Old Timers" Vocal Quartet, 1957, in dignified pose. Left to right: Al Avery, Vincent Bulla, Vernon Post, Roland Schramm. [Source: NYSB Photo Collection; photo by John Sarer.]*

*Leaders at the 75th Anniversary Dinner, 1962. Left to right: Executive Officer William Maltby, former B/M William Bearchell, B/M Richard Holz, former B/M George Darby and former B/M William Slater. [Source: NYSB Photo Collection; photo by John Sarer.]*

*European Tour 1968.*

*[Souce: NYSB Photo Collection]*

**World Tour (1982) picture.** *[Source: Charles Olsen]*

**The "Ambassadors" of the 1982 World Tour (B/M Derek Smith). [Source: Eastern Territorial Music Bureau.]**

*Staff Bandsmen Philip Smith, Derek Smith, William Hood, and Thomas Mack serenade a bemused General Frederick Coutts (R). [Source: Eastern Territorial Music Bureau.]*

*Male Chorus Leader and Euphonium Soloist Thomas Mack. [Source: Eastern Territorial Music Bureau]*

*Staff Bandmaster Derek Smith. [Source: Eastern Territorial Music Bureau.]*

*Philip Smith, co-principal trumpet of the New York Philharmonic and former soloist with the NYSB. [Source: Eastern Territorial Music Bureau]*

*Deputy B/M and Cornet Soloist Ronald Waiksnoris. [Source: Eastern Territorial Music Bureau]*

*The NYSB at Buckingham Palace, June 1985.*

*The National Staff Band Male Chorus, 1914 (B/M George Darby), just prior to the International Congress. [Source: S.A. Archives.]*

*Male Chorus sings graveside of Willia and Catherine Boo during 1914 Intern tional Congres [Source: WC, D cember 19, 1914, p. 1 courtesy of S. Archives.]*

...e Male Chorus, c. 1956, under Vernon Post. [Source: NYSB Photo Collection.]

...e Male Chorus of 1968, led by Vernon Post and Executive Officer Emil Nelson. [Source: NYSB Photo Collection.]

...famous fellowship festival: the NYSB (B/M Richard Holz), left, with the ISB (B/M Bernard ...lams), right, on the CMT stage, April 1962. [Source: NYSB Photo Collection.]

Staff Band Reunion Male Chorus at the 1972 Music Leaders' Councils. [Source: NYSB Phot Collection.]

The TSB Sextet fro the early 1920s. Left right: Charle Bearchell, Herbe Bartlett, Charle Williams, Edg Arkett, Willia Bearchell, J. Stanl Sheppard. [Sourc Bearchell Collectio

The TSB Sextet from the late 1930s. Left to right: Frank Fowler, Kenneth Ayres, Harold Jackson, William Bearchell, William Wrieden, Fred Farrar. [Source: NYSB Photo Collection; photo by John Sarer.]

Frank Fowler, vocal soloist, accompanied by William Bearchell, at the 1957 Annual Festival, he in Fowler's honor. [Source: NYSB Photo Collection; photo by John Sarer.]

The TSB Sextet of the 1940s. Seated, left to right: Milton Kippax, Frank Fowler; standing left to right: James Henderson, Arthur Craytor, William Bearchell, Edward Lowcock. [Source: NYSB Photo Collection.]

Albert E. Avery, vocal soloist, with Male Chorus (Thomas Mack) at Bon Voyage Festival prior to the 1978 International Congress. [Source: NYSB Photo Collection.]

Olof Lundgren, vocal soloist, with the NYSB at the 1968 Bandmasters' Councils. [Source: NYSB Photo Collection.]

The
New
York
Staff
Band
and
Bandmaster
Sept. 1986

*Brian A. Bowen.*
*Appointed B/M Sept., 1, 1986.*
*[Source: NYSB Photo Collection]*

*The New York Staff Band–1986 [Source: NSYB Photo Collection]*

B♭ Flugelhorn
Albert E. Avery

E♭ Solo Horn
Myron Sharp
Norman Voisey

E♭ First Horn
Frank Moody
Eric Eliasen

E♭ Second Horn
Chris Robinson-Cooke
James Scott

B♭ First Baritone
John Dockendorff
Lloyd Scott

E♭ Bass
Vincent Bulla
Ivor Rich
Richard Baker

B♭ Bass
Harold Banta
Wilfred Cooper

Percussion
Edward Lowcock
Eric Sampson

## NYSB "Return to England"Tour, May 1985[30]
B/M Derek Smith; ExO Edward Fritz

E♭ Soprano Cornet
Gordon Ward

B♭ Solo Cornet
Ronald Waiksnoris, Dep B/M
Kenneth Kirby
Ian Anderson
Michael McDonald
Robert Watson
Lambert Bittinger Jr.

B♭ First Cornet
Ronald Foreman
Peter Graham

B♭ Second Cornet
Warren Smith
Peter C. Vaughan

B♭ Flugelhorn
Mark Tillsley

B♭ Second Baritone
David Childs

B♭ First Trombone
William Riley
Thomas Scheibner

B♭ Second Trombone
Carl Carvill

Bass Trombone
Darren Mudge

B♭ Solo Euphonium
Thomas Mack, Male Chorus
  Leader
Frank Psaute

E♭ Bass
Jeffrey Schultz
Charles F. Olsen
Paul Cranford

173

| E♭ Solo Horn | B♭ Bass |
|---|---|
| Peter Hofman | Vincent Bulla |
| Albert E. Avery | A. Philip Ferreira |
| E♭ First Horn | Percussion |
| James Kisser Jr. | William DeMoranville |
| Norman Voisey | Albert Avery Jr. |
| E♭ Second Horn | Color Sergeant |
| Donald G. Spencer | Charles Olsen Jr. |
| B♭ First Baritone | Band Secretary |
| Harold Anderson | Sidney Langford |
| Arthur Carlson | |

The instrumentation and part doublings cited for these three tour bands line up properly with current performance practice in Salvation Army banding. British "prize" bands (non-sacred) do not double the alto or baritone parts, use only three trombones and four basses, and have no more than four solo cornets plus a special repiano cornet part, but Salvation Army bands generally follow the part distribution found in the NYSB.[31] For comparison, note the ISB's instrumentation during their 1980 Tour of America:

**The International Staff Band, U.S.A. Tour, October 1980[32]**
B/M Ray Bowes; ExO Ronald Cox

| | |
|---|---|
| 1 Soprano | 2 Second Baritones |
| 6 Solo Cornets | 2 First Trombones |
| 2 First Cornets | 2 Second Trombones |
| 2 Second Cornets | 1 Bass Trombone |
| 1 Flugelhorn | 2 Euphoniums |
| 2 Solo Horns | 3 E♭ Basses |
| 2 First Horns | 2 B♭ Basses |
| 2 Second Horns | 2 Percussionists |
| 2 First Baritones | |

Does a staff band have to be this size? Couldn't they do with smaller forces? Temporary small ensembles have been formed in the past, of course, like the one for Puerto Rico in 1962.[33] However, if the band is to sustain major campaigns and perform music like this chapter's title piece, "Thy King Cometh," full personnel is essential. Derek Smith, William Bearchell, and Richard Holz agreed, in their response to what they considered to be an ideal

174

seating arrangement, that a rich middle was essential, usually calling for doublings in the horn and baritone parts.[34] Salvation Army bands, in contrast to contesting bands, call for at least four trombones, with usually the second part doubled as well. Demanding solo horn and first baritone parts also call for an assistant player in the most challenging scores. The trimmest the NYSB could be, based on average personnel over the past 30 years, without making substantial changes in repertoire, would be something like the seating of the Cambridge (Mass.) Citadel Silver Band in 1981 (with the addition of one other percussionist):

## The Cambridge Citadel Silver Band, 1981 Great Britain Tour[35]
B/M John Appleby; Captain Randall Davis, C.O.

| | |
|---|---|
| 1 Soprano | 1 Second Baritone |
| 5 Solo Cornets | 2 First Trombones |
| 2 First Cornets | 2 SecondTrombones |
| 2 Second Cornets | 1 Bass Trombone |
| 1 Flugelhorn | 2 Euphoniums |
| 2 Solo Horns | 2 E♭ Basses |
| 1 First Horn | 2 B♭ Basses |
| 1 Second Horn | 1 Percussionist |
| 2 First Baritones | |

The NYSB has had lean periods as well as times with an abundance of fine players. They have toured with short sections and been very successful. Now that there is harmonious accord between NYSB instrumentation and the denomination's regulations and traditions, the question still facing bands of this specialized nature have more to do with personnel, finance, function, and mission than they have to do with instruments and instrumentation.[36] That is, of course, if the NYSB is to remain a *brass band* and male chorus.

175

# 11

## "Rock of Ages"
### (William Bearchell)

## The Male Chorus

The name "New York Staff Band and Male Chorus" has justly given credit to the invaluable role of vocal music in that organization. In fact, the unique success of this band's male chorus is unsurpassed by any other similar venture within Salvation Army banding. Vocal soloists of the group are among the finest in the denomination's history, and the music written for them and the Male Chorus has enriched the musical ministry of male choirs throughout the Army world.

While the Male Chorus plays a secondary role in most NYSB programs (in other words, it is not the main attraction), its function has been taken very seriously since the days of George Darby. Many times in the band's history the greatest musical and spiritual impact has come through the sensitive singing of the Male Chorus. The chorus is not used as "program filler" nor as "a lip rest." The primary function of the group is to directly communicate, through musical means, words about the gospel of Christ which might not be as clearly understood through the instrumental music offered.

When you consider that brass proficiency, not vocal skill, is a prerequisite of Staff Band membership, the Male Chorus' achievements are even more remarkable. Vernon Post shares an objective overview of the Male Chorus:

> ...its membership is rarely chosen for its individual voices; the balance of the number of voices in each section has to be built from those that are chosen for their brass playing; the rehearsals are limited to 20-30 minutes per week (except for rare occasions); the musical range is limited to two and one-half octaves at the extremes, generally two octaves; most members have not studied voice or singing; a goodly portion of the arrangements sung come from the writings of someone in the NYSB; items are sung from almost any type of formation when the occasion demands; the choral group seldom has the opportunity to "try out" the "sound" of the auditorium before the vocal presentation; the vocal demands vary from hymns, spirituals, to fugues and complex arrangements of the masters.[1]

In the spring of 1889, the National Staff Band first sang as a choir, just two years after its founding.[2] That 15-piece band received the inspiration to form a "Singing Brigade" from the exuberant vocal presentations of the Household Troops Band under Harry Appleby. In early April of that year, both bands had joined together in New York City for the final weekend of the Household Troops Band tour. No record survives of what the band sang while in America or what their vocal soloists presented other than the compliments received in various *War Cry* reports of the tour.[3] Yet within weeks the New Yorkers were trying out one of several lessons learned from this notable group.

The National Guards Band, formed in imitation of the Household Troops Band, featured an extensive vocal repertoire, much of it contained in the booklet "We Are Building Up the Temple: Salvation Songs Sung by the National Guards Band," which was sold to help raise funds for the new National Headquarters. During this group's extensive travels, the singing brigade most frequently sang hymns like "The Blast of the Trumpet" and "Nearer My God to Thee."[4]

Not until 1907 do reports appear that take particular notice of the band's choir beyond the occasional offering of a hymn:

> It has long been an axiom that the staff bandsmen not only know how to play but to pray, but we must add a third qualification which is by no means least—for they can also sing! That their singing is as much above the average as their playing will be

178

*sworn to by anyone who heard them in their songs, "Crown Him,"*
*and "At the Great Review," which spoke of careful training.*[5]

During Griffith's and Anderson's tenures, the "male chorus" still was treated as more of a novelty. The simple four-part hymn provided the extent of the vocal repertoire.[6] Programs in Plainfield, N.J. (1908), and the NHQ Memorial Hall (1909) both included a popular setting of "that tender, old song by Pastor Monot, 'None of Self and All of Thee.'"[7]

The appointment of George Darby as vocal coordinator for Evangeline Booth's "Living Tableau" extravaganza of 1911 marks the beginning of the true New York Staff Band Male Chorus.[8] By the June 1912 Staff Band Festival, Darby had the Male Chorus singing rather sophisticated literature. His own mini-cantata, a *Bible Picture,* "Wonderful," was premiered on this occasion. It became the center of the vocal repertoire for years, producing a sensational response at the 1914 International Congress. Donald McMillan (then adjutant) provided a review of this item when it was sung at the fall 1919 Territorial Congress; since the music has not survived, his description is particularly enlightening:

> *The Staff Band Male Chorus' interpretation of Adjutant Darby's "Bible Picture" was a hit of the evening. This is an old favorite with those who have been privileged to hear the Staff Band. It will be recalled that this number was a specially pleasing one on the occasion of the International Congress in 1914. The story told is that of Isaiah's prophecy concerning the Christ. During the midnight of Israel's apostasy and sin Isaiah has a vision. The future is revealed: 750 years hence the angels should sing, "For unto us a Child is born....His name shall be called Wonderful, Counselor, the Mighty God, the Prince of Peace." Under inspiration the prophet foretells the rejection of Christ and His Passion. This passage is given splendid interpretation by Envoy Frank Fowler in his bass solo, "Who hath believed our report?" and also by the recitative by Adjutant John Allan, "Surely He hath borne our griefs"—"He was wounded for our transgressions." The weird accompaniment in F minor to this recitative is appealing and leads to the hopeful message of salvation, "With His stripes we are healed." The finale strikes a note of triumphant praise. A well-rendered number in every sense of the word.*[9]

On that same program the Male Chorus presented the simple chorus "On Calvary." Other items from the early Darby years included Sullivan's "The Lost Chord," "The Christian Martyrs" (L. de Rillè), and the spiritual "I Got Shoes." During the winter of 1914, Darby composed a piece called "Sleigh Ride" that included barking of dogs and the thudding of hoofs, no doubt lustily provided by certain gifted members of the choir. One "low point" for the Male Chorus came during their 1914 trip to Scranton, Pa. Descending a mine shaft in the Hyde Park district there, they sang "All Hail the Power" (tune "Diadem") to the appreciative miners of predominantly Welsh background.[10]

In a booklet, "Songs Used by the American Delegation to the International Congress, London, 1914," one category contained 12 songs "to be sung by the National Male Chorus."[11] Sixteen songs by Thomas Ferguson of the "Colored Songsters" were also included. Used effectively by Evangeline Booth during her appearances at the congress, the Male Chorus attracted much attention. At the graveside of William and Catherine Booth, Abney Park, these men sang with great dignity and emotion. The picture of the scene confirms the group's practice of singing *"a cappella"* at this time, albeit with music![12]

Much of the choir's activity during the Darby years was linked to Evangeline Booth's presentations, already discussed at some length in previous chapters. Among the more notable pieces presented during these occasions were popular hymn settings like "When I Survey the Wondrous Cross," "Nearer My God to Thee" and "Rock of Ages," the latter first reportedly sung in March 1925.[13] William Bearchell was in the band at this time, and while this may not be his original four-part setting of "Rock of Ages," it may have provided the initial inspiration. Darby not only favored outside band compositions but outside vocal compositions as well. Victorian classics, like Barron's "The Trumpeter" (music by Dix), and Kipling's "Hymn Before Action" (music by Davies) graced many a program in the 1920s.

The simpler arrangements from this period were sung without accompaniment. Pianists like Samson Hodges and William Bearchell provided both vocal soloists and the Male Chorus an added dimension and flexibility in their choice of music. The frequent use of brass accompaniments for the Male Chorus was not common until the Holz/Post era. Vernon Post relates several practical reasons why the contemporary Male Chorus has tended to use almost exclusively brass accompaniments or to sing *a cappella.*

*After the first year or so of leading the Male Chorus, it became apparent that piano accompaniment could mean intonation problems between the chorus and the piano. When we sang, it was not unusual for the accompanying piano to be much too far away—too far for the chorus to hear at higher volume. [Author's note: These pianos would also be dreadfully out of tune themselves!] The singers would then drift to the brass instrument pitch, generally a bit higher than 440. Wow! Mostly for this reason we sang without accompaniment or with brass and voices.*[14]

The Staff Band Board Minutes for September 12, 1933, contained the following lament:

*It is felt that the value of the band would be greatly enhanced if the Male Chorus could again be a feature of our regular engagements. All agreed that this is so, but the difficulty at this moment seems to be as to who should conduct this combination. Further thought is to be given the matter....*[15]

The four-year hiatus ended with William Slater's appointment as Male Chorus leader, early in 1935. Continuing in the Darby tradition, he and his successor, William Bearchell, programmed "outside" items like Romberg's "Stout-Hearted Men" and C. W. Green's setting of I Corinthians 13 entitled "Charity." Salvationist music for the Male Chorus was much more readily available at that point and settings by Leidzen (Vocal March "Onward!"), Holz ("Praise Ye the Father," after Gounod), and Slater ("The Christ of Calvary," to the tune "Annie Laurie") became standard items.

The Male Chorus, under the leadership of Richard Holz, sang even more Salvation Army music. Some of the more frequently heard items were:

"Love Stands the Test" (Eric Ball)
"The Battle Is the Lord's" (Brand/William Bearchell)
"Goodbye, Egypt" (Holland T. French)
"O Save Me, Dear Lord" (Evangeline Booth)
"The Old-Time Religion" (Richard E. Holz)

A novelty item heard in the late 1940s was the fanciful spiritual "Dry Bones" as arranged by Gearhart. Slater added "pizzazz" by arranging Sousa's march "Stars and Stripes Forever" for male chorus and brass ensemble—used with particular effect in the F.E.T. Finale Festival, May 9, 1952.[16]

Most of the literature of the Male Chorus has come from the pens of band members. This has been especially true since the Bearchell years. Allowing Erik Leidzen the status of "band arranger," we can cite a marvelously productive output of music for the Male Chorus since 1950; this selective list cites the year in which a confirmed "first mention" or "premiere" has been established:

1954 "Never Quit the Field"* (Saunders—Leidzen)
1956 "He Lives"* (arr. Post)
     "Peace, Perfect Peace" (Leidzen)
     "Praise Ye the Lord"* (Leidzen)
1957 "How Great Thou Art"* (arr. Post)
1959 "Were You There?" (arr. Post)
1961 "He Leadeth Me" (arr. Leidzen)
1962 "Immanuel's Tide" (arr. Post)
1963 "Will Your Anchor Hold?" (arr. Leidzen)
1964 "Joshua Fit the Battle" (arr. Post)
     "It Took a Miracle" (arr. Post)
1968 "Must Jesus Bear the Cross Alone?" (arr. Post)
1972 "The Solid Rock" (Mozart—Lloyd Scott)
1975 "He Giveth More Grace" (Thomas Mack)
1976 "Bound for Glory"* (Terry Camsey)
1977 "Lift Up Your Voices"* (Thomas Mack)
1978 "Confident Follower"* (Terry Camsey)
1980 "My Hope"* (Thomas Mack)
1983 "Through Eternity" (Thomas Mack)
1985 "A Joyful Song" (Thomas Mack)

*with brass accompaniment

The "Songs of Victory" recording of 1962, which features just the Male Chorus, represents one of the peaks in this group's development. Blessed with excellent soloists and a finely balanced repertoire of both American and British arrangements, Post's group has been unsurpassed by any Salvation Army band male chorus. The sheer hard work put into learning demanding items like Eric Ball's two classics, "O Fire of the Spirit" and "Contrition," or Charles Skinner's "Lord, See Me Kneeling at Thy Feet," paid off—the results are standard-setting to this day.[17]

The current Male Chorus leader, Thomas Mack, came to his position in 1975, after Derek Smith had led the group for a few years. Richard Holz maintains that a separation of leadership in the band and Male Chorus is a wise arrangement. When one man does both groups, the vocal part tends to suffer. Allowing another person to develop the choir and its repertoire has led to the two peaks in the group's history, one under Post's tenure and another under Mack's leadership.

The chorus leader is at the mercy of the brass personnel in the group. The old description of a male quartet as "one good tenor and three other guys" holds more truth for a male choir. Fortunately, the band's solid tradition of singing has helped it through lean times. Thomas Mack states it well:

> It amazes me that the Male Chorus continues through the years as a proficient and viable expression of the band's ministry. This is due, I feel, in part to the aural concept that is handed down from one bandsman to the next and the careful emphasis and nurturing given to the Male Chorus. To have a few solid first tenors and second basses at all times is also helpful! The future of the Male Chorus is open to new and exciting repertoires as well as the old standards. We can also use any and all good voices as they come along.[18]

Mack's current 11-year appointment is third in length of service to the Male Chorus. His tenure is marked by excellent adaptability, both in the kind of repertoire and the style of presentation. When this group was thin, flattering items like Dean Goffin's setting of "The Pilgrim's Song" for predominantly unison chorus and trombones made perfect sense. In his own arrangements, Mack has vigorously tried to incorporate more contemporary styles (rock and jazz idioms). He has not abandoned the traditional part-song approach, however. This is best represented in Stephen Bulla's setting of "He Walks With God," featured on the 1985 Great Britain tour. The Male Chorus music featured on that trip exemplifies the balance Thomas Mack has struck between the old and the new:

"A Joyful Song" (Thomas Mack)
"Redeemed" (Stephen Bulla)
"He Walks With God" (Stephen Bulla)
"He Leadeth Me" (Erik Leidzen)
"The Upward Road" (Leslie Condon)

"Poor Man Laz'rus" (Jester Hairston)
"Rock of Ages" (William Bearchell)
"Song of Happiness" (Michael Kenyon)
"Thy Will Be Done" (Darren Mudge)

## The Soloists

The vocal soloists of the NYSB have played an enormously important role in the band's sacred ministry. Initially, one thinks of a Frank Fowler, Olof Lundgren, or Albert Avery. Certainly these men, and their accompanists, represent the highest achievements in this category of band service. Other bandsmen have contributed valiantly as vocal soloists throughout the band's history as well.

The earliest recorded soloists for the band were self-styled humorist J. J. Stimson and bass-baritone Harry C. Taylor, both featured prominently in the 1890s. The band's one female vocalist, Norma Thompson (later Mrs. Captain James Durand), was a stellar attraction at the turn of the century and a "National Singing Brigade," first listed in the *Dispo,* December 1899, was formed around her talent.[19] Frank Fowler made his solo singing debut in typical early-Staff Band style. Having just joined the band officially in 1902, he was called upon spontaneously by Charles Miles. Fowler initially refused, to which Miles responded, "I shall call on you in any case."[20] That is how a great vocal ministry was launched!

A Staff Band male quartet functioned during the early years of this century. In 1905 the group consisted of Gerberich, Bergh, Griffith, and Sylvester.[21] A more recent quartet of Roland Schramm, Vernon Post, Albert Avery, and Vincent Bulla used to "ham it up" portraying the old days of the Army through their "The Salvation Soldier of 1896" (Catelinet) presentations of the late 1950s. During the 1960 tour, "Ezekiel Saw the Wheel" (Post) was effectively sung in good American "barbershop" style by Albert Avery, Vernon Post, Robert McNally, and Donald Ross.

While Fowler reigned in the lower range of vocal soloing from 1902 to 1955, several other men had excellent opportunities to solo. In the 1920s William C. Arnold and Clifford Brindley, and in the 1940s Emil Nelson and Thomas Gorman held up the higher-range work. Brindley was noted for his rendition of "The Lost Sheep"; Nelson was heard on several special arrangements, including "God Bless America." Later tenors who shared the limelight with Olof Lundgren and Al Avery included Peter Hofman ("Were You There?" and "There's Still Time Brother"), John Marshall, and Eric Sampson.

Frank Fowler, the "Gospel Singer," best exemplifies the spirit of NYSB singing:

> You must feel what you sing....It is necessary to place yourself in the position of the listeners. If you want to bless the sinner, then put yourself in his place in your interpretation of the song...I try to get blessed myself as I sing, and I find that if that happens the "blessing" is generally passed on to the listener.[22]

His repertoire was simple, mainly serious gospel songs, with an occasional novelty like "The Big Bass Viol" (which he could play, along with *bass* saxophone) and also included:

"Asleep In the Deep"
"Stranger of Galilee"
"I Will Sing the Wondrous Story"
"I Love to Tell the Story"
"This World Is Not My Own"
"The Sea of Galilee"
"The Ninety and Nine"

If Fowler needed accompaniment, he used either the humming Male Chorus or the gifted pianists Samson Hodges and William Bearchell. While the recordings we have are of Fowler beyond his prime, one can tell that it was a remarkable bass voice. In a tribute to Fowler, entitled "My Favorite Bandsman," Richard Holz provided a vivid portrait of this legendary soloist:

> No doubt he is best remembered for his evangelical bass vocal solos delivered with warm expression and intuitively sound musical taste. The voice itself was massive. Colonel George Darby, former bandmaster and sacred music champion, called it "a magnificent instrument." Among those who acclaimed his vocal music were the renowned George Beverly Shea and Edwin MacHugh, even crediting Frank for inspiring and encouraging their vocal ministries.
>
> A highlight of the Staff Band festivals would be Frank's solo, with Lt.-Colonel William Bearchell providing sympathetic accompaniments of rare originality at the piano. The crowds would always clamor for an encore.

> *Despite the hundreds of times we heard him, Frank's solos, immediately preceding the sermon, would never fail to move us deeply. Standing quietly before the band, he would begin to sing with the barely audible humming of the male voices as the only accompaniment. "The Stranger of Galilee" and "I Will Sing the Wondrous Story" were used the most, but he had a large repertoire, including choice settings of sacred words to popular melodies.*
>
> *Great freedom with tempo and notation enhanced the emphasis on the text. Every word was crystal clear. The word "found" in the line "I was lost, but Jesus FOUND me!" would cascade from the heights to the depths in loving adoration for this miracle of grace. At the conclusion of the song, he would sing an appeal for decision, gesturing toward the penitent-form or communion rail— "Here bring your wounded hearts, here tell your anguish, earth has no sorrow that Heaven cannot heal." Few there were, including the staff bandsmen, who did not experience moved hearts and moist eyes.*[23]

Fowler maintained that he "foist played in this band when Admiral Dewey came back from Manila in 1898." In each succeeding interview over the years his date of service became earlier! Actually, he did play as an "extra" before his official membership in 1902. At first an officer (lieutenant), he did not maintain that calling, but held the non-commissioned rank "envoy" that was so frequently given to staff bandsmen prior to the 1950s. Though his service at Star Lake Musicamp was continuous from 1935-1954, his Staff Band record is marked by short "leave-of-absence" breaks. Despite these minor problems, his service record is unmatched by any other bandsman in the group's history.

One final story about Fowler can stand for a hundred more. One day in 1935, while loading *War Crys* for dispatch at THQ, Fowler was approached by a man from Catskill, N.Y. The man told him:

> *I heard you sing in Catskill... My wife and daughter had prevailed upon me to go to church. Your message in song stirred my heart. I turned to Christ, and for twenty years I have not missed a Sunday at church....*[24]

That was a true reward for the Army's great gospel singer.[25]

"Dramatic Tenor" Olof Lundgren would be known more widely in The Salvation Army as an NYSB soloist than Frank Fowler. Serving officially in the band for 30 years (1946-76), his unofficial involvement goes back to 1939, and includes a 1941 recording of "Rock of Ages" with the Male Chorus. The list of special feature items produced for "Olie" is impressive. Memorable among them (with their premiere dates) were:

"Song of the Soul Set Free" (1951, Emil Soderstrom, for band and tenor solo)

"Banners and Bonnets" (1952, Richard Holz, for tenor, band, and male chorus)

"Down From His Glory" (1960, Emil Soderstrom for tenor, band, and male chorus)

"A Man May Be Down" (1960, Erik Leidzen, for tenor and band)

"He Took My Place" (1939—1959, an arrangement by Vernon Post for tenor and male chorus)

In addition, Lundgren was frequently heard in middle verse solos in several of the band's part-songs. With an inherent sense of the dramatic and fine stage presence, Lundgren could magnificently "put across" a song:

*Many male chorus arrangements were conceived for a particular occasion. Good Friday's "Three Hours At the Cross" and the subsequent Good "Friday Evening at the Temple" spawned many of them. "Were You There?" "Immanuel's Tide," "It Took a Miracle," "There Is a Balm in Gilead," "Are Ye Able," and "Must Jesus Bear the Cross Alone?" are a few of the titles. Olof Lundgren often requested one or more of these. One day he brought me several tunes that he had received "from an old Sergeant-Major." The tunes and the texts were scribbled on some old manuscript paper—but they were not only beautiful, but moving. One of these, "He Took My Place" was arranged for humming male chorus accompaniment and became in a sense, Olof's theme song. On our tour of Britain in 1960, the NYSB was conducting the Sunday morning holiness meeting for the Manchester Division in the mammoth Manchester Free Trade Hall. The International Staff Band was seated in the first three rows. The crowd was so great even part of the platform behind us was filled with worshipers. Before the morning message Olof stood to sing for the first time in Britain, "He Took My Place." Some of the ISB seemed quite disturbed. Where was the piano—overlooked in the plans? Olof stepped forward and began to sing. Soon the NYSB joined in the humming background. We could sense the movement of the Holy Spirit throughout. The ISB asked for a copy and soon included it on every tour for a season with Leslie Condon as soloist.[26]*

The men of the band could tease their vocal star by suddenly blocking his path for the "grand entrance" on "Banners and Bonnets" or by unmercifully mimicking his Swedish accent. An excellent improviser, he always overcame these hurdles, with one exception. The story is told of his beautiful rendition of the Swedish carol "Nar Juldagsmorgen Glimmar" ("When Christmas Morning Brightens") at the famous Calvary Baptist Church in the late 1950s. Normally he would first sing it in Swedish, then English. One weary Sunday in December, Executive Officer William Maltby missed his cue to ask for the translation by standing up late, after Lundgren had sung both versions, and announced, "We will now hear this lovely song in English" —to which an indignant "Olie" replied, "I 'yust' did!"[27]

Lt.-Colonel Lundgren has received many accolades for his excellent service to the Army's Scandinavian work in America and to Army music in general. He has received one of the highest civilian citations from the Swedish government—Order of VASA— and he even arranged for the NYSB to play for the King of Sweden, Carl Gustaf XVI, on April 24, 1976, in his last year of service in the band. The happy union of Staff Band music and great Scandinavian pomp and color at the F.E.T. "Scandinavian Nights" are cherished memories among regular attenders of the series.

In contrast to Lundgren's "dramatic" voice, Albert Avery's tenor quality is lighter, more lyric. Avery is recognized worldwide for his solo "Rock of Ages" as Lundgren is for "Banners and Bonnets." He has sung the band's main anthem, "Rock of Ages," all over the world. Joining the band in 1956, Avery was usually featured in middle verse solos, most notably on "Lord, See Me Kneeling at Thy Feet," "Immanuel's Tide," and, of course, "Rock of Ages."

Four times (1960, 1968, 1978, 1985), Avery has received international acclaim, particularly in Great Britain, for his solo singing with the band. His solo on "Must Jesus Bear the Cross Alone?" in the June 1968 Bandmasters' Councils Festival received as much notice as his "debut" there eight years before. On the most recent British tour his solos were quite different, including Peter Graham's "pop" setting "It's a Wonderful Day." Two solo albums (one with the NYSB Male Chorus) and many recent solo trips show a forward-looking, contemporary style for this famous soloist.

William Simons related one of the strangest performances and yet, most representative of the Male Chorus' ministry—the time the singing stopped a riot in a Newburgh, N.Y., high school during the late 1960s:

> ... our trip to Newburgh, N.Y., when there were trying times in the schools. A riot was scheduled to take place just as Al Avery started singing "Rock of Ages"! The student body melted—and the riot with it. Later in the day at a civic welcome, the Mayor of Newburgh commended the band for their part in "melting" the riot, and many of the young people brought their parents to the evening festival to hear "this band that stopped the riot from taking place." That's what happens when you have a leader like we do—Jesus!—The Rock of Ages![28]

This chapter of the NYSB's first hundred years would not be complete without recognizing the piano accompanists/soloists of this fine band. While the band cannot always depend on a setting where a good piano is available, at least six individuals have been used effectively over the years for both vocal accompaniments and solos: Samson Hodges, John Allan, William Bearchell, Douglas Bethune, Robert Barton, Stephen Bulla, and, most recently, Peter Graham.

# The Salvation Army.

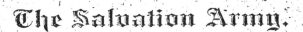

## "WE ARE BUILDING UP THE TEMPLE."

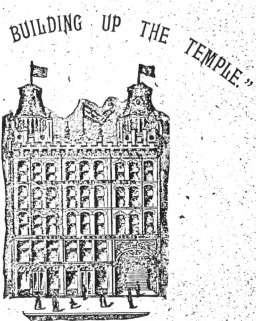

## Salvation Songs

SUNG BY THE

# National Guards' Band.

PRICE **5** CENTS.

N. B.—The proceeds of the sale of these Songs to go towards the
**MEMORIAL HEADQUARTERS BUILDING FUND.**

SALVATION ARMY PRINT, 111 READE ST., N. Y.

11-1.  *Front cover of National Guards Band "Salvation Songs," 1892. (Source: S.A. Archives)*

# 12

## "Christ Is the Answer"
### (Ray Steadman-Allen)

## The Music and the Festivals

The relationship between the music played by the NYSB and its conductors has been addressed to some degree in the previous chapters. The story of the band's brass repertoire and the development of the musical "festival" (the Army's name for a sacred musical concert), provides rich material for this complete historical review. Individual initiative on the part of staff band-masters and the increasingly productive Territorial Music Department has been neatly balanced with the denomination's carefully-controlled "evolution" of its music.

### The Music

When the National Staff Band first attempted "salvation" music they had two band books in hand:

Salvation Army Band Music (88 congregational song accom-
        paniments, first released November 1884)
The Salvation Army Brass Band Journal (Now called General
        Series (GS); first issues released in 1884)

From a *War Cry* report of the band's visit to Rockville, Conn., October 1887, we learn that the first recorded items by the band were "Roll On Dark Streams" (the first tune of *GS* 31), and "My Heart Is Now Whiter Than Snow" (#30 in *Salvation Army Band Music*).

For the first decade of the band's existence these short songs and hymns were their main musical diet, with an occasional popular ditty or patriotic song thrown in to keep things lively ("Home, Sweet Home," "Hail to the Chief," "Wachet am Rhine," etc.). The musical department at 98-100 Clerkenwell Road, London, tried to keep things interesting by the release of special issues, in spite of severe restrictions, such as the 1890 "Special Funeral Number," *(GS* 139-142, including Herbert Booth's "Promoted to Glory," #139) and the 1891 "Special Anniversary Number—National Anthems of the World" *(GS* 159-164. America's Anthem, #159 [2] was not the "Star-Spangled Banner" but "Hail Columbia"). The latter issue would have been particularly useful in the teaming melting-pots of lower Manhattan and Brooklyn where this early band saw so much action.[1]

Evidently British efforts did not always meet American needs. By March 1898, Booth-Tucker appointed Staff Bandmaster Charles Straubel to head a "Music Publishing Section" that was to be:

> ...a fully established branch of the Trade Department. It is presided over by Ensign Straubel, who, by his vast experience, knows so fully requirements of our bandsmen. The American Band Journals *will be arranged under his personal supervision.*[2]

Vast experience or not, Straubel's experiment was short-lived and publishing ceased by July of that year. The "journals," a sample first cornet part of which appeared in the June 25, 1898 *War Cry,* consisted of a 15-part arrangement (all brass parts except E$^b$ cornet) of two journals per hard cardboard sheet, printed both sides. (See Illustration 12-1). Eight journals, incorporating 17 tunes, were printed.

By the turn of the century, music published by London for Army brass bands numbered almost 400 separate items in the *Brass Band Journal* and a nearly equal number of tunes for the accompaniment of congregational singing.[3] All Army band music at this time had to be specifically related either to a text written by a Salvationist or to a text previously approved for Army use, even in the case of classical transcriptions. General William Booth had insisted that the music published for his bands be associated with an evangelical message. This music was drawn from the following sources:

1. Simple, one-strophe settings of well-known hymn tunes;
2. Popular songs or classical airs to which Salvationists had written new texts;
3. Transcriptions of new songs printed in *The Musical Salvationist* (vocal periodical).

In the score notes to *GS* 383-386 (1900), Richard Slater, then editor-in-chief of the International Music Editorial Department, provided a summary of this band music which illustrates the specific functions for which it was intended:

> *Music for Army bands is such as to form three classes of pieces, viz, 1) tunes intended for congregational singing, 2) marches, and 3) pieces for stationary playing, as for use when the collection is being taken, or when the band is called upon to exercise its power of musical attraction.*[4]

In the above-mentioned issue (*GS* 383-386), there were 11 pieces contained within the four journal entries. These were grouped into units of songs which could be played together as medleys. Each group of tunes was comprised of items related in subject matter to the associated text as well as in key area and tempo. *GS* 383, for example, could be played as a "march," as Slater referred to it, by repeating the first tune after the others were played successively:

*GS* 383 (All in 4/4 meter)[5]

| 1. "Hampshire" | Tonic |
| 2. "Our King" | Tonic |
| 3. "We March to Victory" | Dominant |
| 4. Repeat of "Hampshire" | Tonic |

Each of these tunes was, of course, associated with an appropriate text. Music specifically written for band without reference to an approved text was strictly forbidden. Only the "outside" brass bands had access to original works and large-scale transcriptions. The Army moved cautiously in the expansion of its band music.

The cautious, controlled evolution of this band music, given a great boost in September 1901, via an interview with William Booth granted Richard Slater, was not sufficient for American bands.[6] They felt certainly uncomfortable, in any event, with stringent British control of their Army, a source of contention in the Army's overall history in America. American publishers did have some brass band pieces in their inventories. One typical item, probably featured by the NYSB, was Andrew Herman's "Salvation Army Patrol," published by Carl Fisher, in New York, in 1892 with brass band scoring.[7] Though Charles Anderson was "loyal" to Army procedures, he was not above using a good, rousing secular march, like A. Bergh's "American Guard" at a December 5, 1903, festival.[8]

The new, experimental forms Booth was now allowing his music editors to release (original marches, selections, early variation forms, meditations, etc.) would slowly reach American shores. Anderson's 1904 International Congress band would mostly feature American popular tunes, with new texts supplied. The reader will recall Booth-Tucker's use of popular tunes like "In the Good Old Summer Time," and "Down Where the Wurzburger Flows" in his September 1904 tent meetings.

By 1906, however, the early experimental pieces like "The Morning Hymn March" (GS 411) or "The Festival March" (GS 442) were in NYSB pouches. That same year the "Cadets March" was essayed at commissioning. Richard Slater's innovative programmatic piece, "Stilling the Storm," was performed in London, May 1911, soon to be a favorite of George Darby and the NYSB.[9]

George Darby, however, was particular about what his band would play. If Salvation Army band journals were not of sufficient quality, he would turn to outside publishers without a second thought. London was still very far away! In the course of his tenure, however, Darby gradually added more and more of the best Salvation Army works. Fancying himself a gifted arranger (a judgment evidently not shared in London *if* he submitted his works, for very little was published), he filled in the gaps of the band's repertoire, as he saw it, from his own pen or from outside brass publications. The following selective list cites the contrasting aspects of the band's music, 1912-1931, showing an Army number and an outside composition for various years:

### The Darby Band Repertoire: Selective List

| Year | S.A. Literature | "Outside" Arrangements |
|------|----------------|------------------------|
| 1913 | "My Guide" (Goldsmith) | Arrangements by J. Ord Hume ("Gems of Song," "Conqueror," etc.) |
| 1916 | "The Cleansing Current" (*GS* 782) | "Stars and Stripes Forever" (Sousa) |
| 1920 | "Atonement" (Coles) | "Mill in the Forest" (arr. Darby) |
| 1923 | "Olivet and Calvary" (Marshall) | "Excerpts from Verdi" |
| 1924 | "Man of Sorrows" (Coles) | "Eugene Onègin" (Tchaikovsky) |
| 1928 | "Adoration" (Ball) | "Rosamunde Overture" (Schubert) |
| 1929 | "Home Sweet Home" (Leidzen) "Wareham" (Coles) | "Eroica" Symphony (Beethoven) |
| 1930 | "The Red Shield" (Goffin) | "Andante Cantabile" (Tchaikovsky) |

Darby's band had a distinctively different sound. His mixture of cornets and trumpets, alto and French horns, and an assortment of woodwinds, allied with the improvised melody percussion of Richard Von Calio, can be heard to good effect on the 1922-23 Vocalion recordings. In the early Darby band, the woodwinds merely doubled the brass parts, sometimes at the octave, as verified by former clarinetist Albert Lock:

> *At a commissioning in June 1916, I got a phone call—"Do you have a uniform? Would you like to sit in with the band tonight? We are a bit short-handed." So I sat next to William Barrett playing a B♭ clarinet and reading 1st cornet music, but playing the part an octave higher....*[10]

Later, Darby used military and/or brass band journals (Wright and Rounds, Boosey and Hawkes, R. Smith) that allowed him more instrumental color, or he re-scored pieces on his own, such as the march medley on the 1922 recording. A few of the outside publications have survived in the band's library, but none of the Darby manuscripts are extant.[11]

With American composers the caliber of William Broughton, Erik Leidzen, and K. M. Fristrup winning international competitions, and a host of other developing writers like R. H. Keeler, Walter Swyers, H. E. Brewer, A. C. Laurie, F. M. Crewdson, and Edgar Arkett, the establishment of a musical department under Edgar Arkett in 1928 was not surprising. *The Salvation Army Brass Band Journal (U.S.A.)* was launched with the release in mid-1928 of the march "Our Leader" (William Broughton) as an appropriate salute to Commander Evangeline Booth (The solo cornet/conductor part identified the publisher as National Headquarters). Nearly two dozen separate items were printed before the Depression shut down the presses. In addition to this "ordinary" series, Arkett and his successor, Broughton, produced the short-lived *American Festival Series,* which contained the winning items of the 1930 National Composers Contest ("Army of God" by Soderstrom, "Homeward Bound" by Turkington, "Our Redeemer" by William Slater, etc.).

Broughton restored the NYSB to an exclusively Army brass repertoire. By now there was no real excuse to continue the rather cavalier approach of Darby since many works were flowing off the Army band presses, soon establishing an international sacred brass literature second to none in Protestant Christendom. The literature of the Granger/Bearchell/Slater years is evidence of this new, superior music the NYSB proudly performed.

## Selective Repertoire of the NYSB, 1935-54

| Title | Composer | Year first performed |
|---|---|---|
| "Moments With Tchaikovsky" | arr. Bramwell Coles | 1935 |
| "A Soul's Awakening" | Eric Ball | 1935 |
| "The Savior's Name" | Erik Leidzen | 1936 |
| "The Sunbeam" | Philip Catelinet | 1937 |
| "The Cross" | Erik Leidzen | 1937 |
| "The Triumph of Peace" | Eric Ball | 1939 |

| Title (continued) | Composer | Year first performed |
|---|---|---|
| "The Old Wells" | Eric Ball | 1941 |
| "The Divine Pursuit" | Bramwell Coles | 1947 |
| "When They Cru- cified My Lord" | Ray Steadman-Allen | 1948 |
| "The Valiant Heart" | Philip Catelinet | 1949 |
| "Praise" | Wilfred Heaton | 1950 |
| "Heroes of the Faith" | Charles Skinner | 1951 |
| "Symphony of Thanksgiving" | Dean Goffin | 1952 |
| "Crusaders" | Dean Goffin | 1953 |

The above classics were supplemented by works by new American composers during this same period:

| | | |
|---|---|---|
| "Dovercourt"; "Onward America" | William Wrieden | |
| "Brooklyn Citadel" | William Bearchell | |
| "What A Friend"; "The Carollers" | Richard E. Holz | |
| "Triumphant Faith" | Stanley Ditmer | |

The development of the Eastern Territory's Music Department under Richard E. Holz, and the subsequent reinvolvement of Erik Leidzen, has previously been discussed. The host of new compositions and new composers launched in the 1948 "Band Music for Evangelism" became standards in the NYSB repertoire. Composers like Bernard Ditmer, Lloyd Reslow, Harold Gustafson, Harold Zealley, and Vernon Post, all received debuts in the early issues of the journals.

A cooperative spirit was established between the Eastern Territory's and IHQ's Music Departments that allowed for positive growth and indigenous repertoire while opening channels for greater international sharing of fine music. From the early 1950s to the present day, the NYSB has played a major role in premiering, commissioning, and demonstrating for the first time on American shores the greatly improved brass literature of The Salvation Army:

## Selective Repertoire of the NYSB, 1955-1985

| Title | Composer | Year first performed |
|---|---|---|
| "Southland Memories" | Emil Soderstrom | 1955 |
| "Prelude on Three Welsh Hymn Tunes" | Ralph Vaughan Williams | 1956 |
| "Lord of the Sea" | Ray Steadman-Allen | 1957 |
| "Ode to Freedom" | Philip Catelinet | 1958 |
| "Post Bellum Rhapsody" | Erik Leidzen | 1959 |
| "None Other Name" | Erik Leidzen | 1960 |
| "March of the Hours" | Emil Soderstrom | 1961 |
| "Themes from the Italian Symphony" | Mendelssohn—Goffin | 1962 |
| "Song of Courage" | Eric Ball | 1963 |
| Fantasia— "Christ Is the Answer" | Ray Steadman-Allen | 1964 |
| "Take Salvation" | Emil Soderstrom | 1965 |
| "The Holy War" | Ray Steadman-Allen | 1966 |
| "A Pilgrim's Song" | Thomas Rive | 1966-67 |
| "Canadian Folk Song Suite" | Morley Calvert | 1968 |
| "The Good Old Way" | Bruce Broughton | 1969 |
| "The Eternal Presence" | Eric Ball | 1969-70 |
| "Victory For Me" | Wilfred Heaton | 1971 |
| "The Present Age" | Leslie Condon | 1972 |
| "New Frontier" | William Himes | 1973 |
| "Kaleidoscope" | Rimsky-Korsakov | 1974-75 |
| "Heritage of Freedom" | James Curnow | 1976 |
| "New York 90" | Stephen Bulla | 1977 |
| "Thy King Cometh" | Leslie Condon | 1978 |
| "Psalm 100" | James Curnow | 1979 |
| "Nicely Saved" | Bruce Broughton | 1980 |
| "Assignment" | Dudley Bright | 1981 |

| Title (continued) | Composer | Year first performed |
|---|---|---|
| Fantasia on "Lobe den Herren" | Eric Ball | 1982 |
| "To the Chief Musician" | William Himes | 1983 |
| "Faithful Forever" | Richard Holz | 1984 |
| "The Dawning" | Peter Graham | 1985 |

Imagine the feelings of John Allan as he experienced the gradual and miraculous transformation of Army brass music over 50 years. While he was Chief-of-the-Staff of the international Salvation Army, Allan presided as chairman of the International Music Board. Writing to Richard Holz during this experience (early 1950s) he said:

> When I joined the New York Staff Band in 1902, the first music I noticed on my stand was "Champagne Charlie Is My Name" and "The Man Who Broke the Bank at Monte Carlo." Now the music being written and arranged by our own composers is second to none. And think of this, Dick, I have this wonderful privilege in this appointment, to uphold the highest standards of music-making for the service of our Lord.[12]

Men of the NYSB have intimately participated in the development of Army music. They aided in the consistent publishing of instrumental music for Army bands, music that remains true to the simple functions required of this music in worship services and musical festivals. That one denomination could publish all its own vocal, instrumental and congregational music throughout its history is a remarkable achievement, unique in the 20th century. However, the administrative and ecclesiastical controls placed on the development of this repertoire have kept the Army's music in basic isolation for the majority of its existence. Nevertheless, the Army continues to receive contributions from both amateur and professional musicians without any payment fee for such contributions. This is a testament to the vitality and integrity of an apparently little-known musical culture.

If, in recent years, some new NYSB pieces have challenged the average listener's aural skills with new and daring sounds, with festival literature that seems to become more complicated, more demanding, the practical worship music this band offers remains simple, always relaying straightforward messages, based on familiar melodies and texts. This is as it should be, as General Albert Orsborn once put it:

> We have no wish to be outcasts of the musical world but our music is, and must continue to be functional as distinct from the merely artistic, aesthetic, or impressionistic. Our message, our praise, our mission, our worship embody our function.[13]

## A Chronological Listing of Salvation Army Territorial Music Departments in New York City, 1890-1986

1890—A "Music Section," headed by May Agnew, established in August 1890. Primarily concerned with arrangements of songs for *The War Cry* and other magazines, compilation of song collections by Ballington Booth, etc. Short-lived enterprise.

1893—Staff Bandmaster Edward Trumble coordinates music forces at several large congresses, 1893-1896. No publishing duties.

1898—A "Musical Department" under Staff Bandmaster Charles Straubel exists for five months, March-July 1898. Straubel publishes first SA "American Band Journal"—eight "journals" produced, two journals per music sheet.

1928—Edgar Arkett appointed Territorial Secretary for Bands and Songsters for the Eastern Territory, January 1928. He releases a national band journal and *American Festival Series.*
Replaced by William Broughton in January 1933. Broughton farewelled September 1935, without replacement.

1946—Richard E. Holz, territorial music secretary, January 1946-October 1963. Establishment of modern music department charged with publishing music and promoting musical forces throughout the Eastern Territory. Sometimes called a Department, sometimes a Bureau or Section, it has maintained the primary music publishing role within The Salvation Army in the U.S.

1963-present: **Succeeding Territorial Music Secretaries:**
Vernon Post, November 1963-August 1972
William Simons, Fall 1972-1975
Thomas Mack, 1975-1981
Charles Baker, 1981-1983
Ronald Waiksnoris, January 1984-present

## The Festivals

Musical festivals were designed to challenge music sections in the development of their musical skills and to add another dimension to Salvation Army evangelical outreach. When early Army bands drew in the large crowds by stirring street marches, their function inside the hall remained, at best, supportive, usually providing a hymn accompaniment and, where necessary, an offertory. Only in recent years has the careful planning of all parts of a service or praise meeting also included the judicious use of the music forces at hand, particularly where the choice of music and its appropriateness to the whole worship experience was concerned. Former ISB Staff Bandmaster Bernard Adams wrote to Erik Leidzen about the early dilemma faced when the band was used primarily as a "filler":

> As recently as the days when Eric Ball was staff bandmaster we would play during meetings conducted by the top "brass" over here and the main function would be to fill in times. I can even remember during the playing of a lovely hymn tune arrangement as the collection was being taken that the "all-highest" had Eric's coat pulled and he was told "that's enough."[14]

No wonder that the Army wisely nurtured the musical festival! The contributions of the NYSB to this unique cultural phenomenon have been notable with regard to form, content and style.

The first regular use of the designation "music festival" was attached to the work of Staff-Captain Blandy and his musical minstreling in the mid-1880s.[15] These "potpourri" reviews were mostly unorganized successions of stunts and songs. Charles Anderson's music festivals of the late 1890s ushered in the modern NYSB festival, albeit in primitive form (see Chapter 2). His December 15, 1903, festival was more structured and included the NSB, the National Singing Brigade, vocal and instrumental solos, and a vocal quartet. Tickets were sold and even a souvenir songsheet was printed for the event. Robert Griffith placed ads in *The Morning Telegram* and *Evening Post* promoting his February 13-14, 1909, Staff Band festivals held in New York City at the Warner Hall YMCA.[16] The program was hailed on the flier produced as: "Grand Musical Festival (15¢ admission, 25¢ reserved)—25 Trained Musicians"!

The earliest festival we find complete record of, described in George Darby's "National Staff Band and Male Chorus" program of May 31, 1913, took place in the Memorial Hall, 120 West 14th Street (see Illustration 12-2).[17] Divided into two parts separated by an intermission, the concert lists a varied fare—monologues, vocal solos, instrumental solos, Male Chorus, instrumental selections—and, as necessary by *Orders and Regulations,* a Bible reading and a congregational song (listed on the back of the program). Only one official Salvation Army band work was heard, Goldsmith's "My Guide." John Allan sparkled on a technical "outside" cornet solo, Hodges worked overtime as trombone soloist and piano accompanist, and Darby displayed his arranging talents on two vocal works, "Southern Melodies" and "Boundless Salvation." The former piece received the following program note:

> A collection of old favorites from the plantation and cotton field:
> A. "Steal Away to Jesus"
> B. "Hear Dem Bells" (Bell Accomp.)—Tenor Solo
> C. "I Got Shoes"
> D. "De Old Folks at Home"—Tenor Duet, with Banjo and Humming Effects.

Indeed, the program resembles the "something for everyone" type so common in America vaudeville, with perhaps a bit more dignity, especially in the closing portion of the program. The music was attractive and entertaining—and progressively more serious, one wise approach in balancing entertainment with evangelism.

Within a year, the band gave a similar festival, March 4, 1914, that demonstrated some of their International Congress repertoire. Notice that Executive Officer Jenkins served as "chairman" or general announcer:

# National Staff Band Concert

## Good Crowd Hears Excellent Program

The National Staff Band and chorus gave to about 800 New Yorkers the musical treat of the season, when, on Wednesday evening, March 4th, they gave a program which was, at least to the ears of the writer, superb. Our first word must be one of congratulation to the band and the bandmaster, Captain Darby, on the quality of the music, instrumental and especially vocal....

Lt.-Colonel Jenkins, as leader of the band and by virtue of that fact chairman of the concert, opened the program with a brief, sententious prayer. A grand march, entitled "Happy Soldier," was the first number, a full band piece, of a martial order. A monologue by Staff-Captain Palmer followed, in which he told in wondrous rhyme how the water came "sheeting, beating, meeting, delaying, straying" (and so on, ad infinitum) over "the cataract of Ladore." As an encore he recited "The House that Jack Built."

The third number, a part song by the chorus, entitled "Comrades," was one of the "star" pieces of the evening and a difficult number, with a note in harmony with the character of and fact expressed by each word. It was good to see Ensign Allan once more in his place with the band, and his cornet solo, "Air Varie," with all its double and multiple-tongueing, was a marvelous and sweet display of great skill. Now followed an overture by the band in which all the moods of music found expression, and a part song by the chorus, entitled "Sleigh Ride," with the barking of dogs, the thudding of hoofs, the shouting of the party, the jingling of the bells as variations. A little negro strain, "I Got Shoes," was sung as an encore.

"The Mill in the Forest," a descriptive band selection, closed the first part of the entertainment. The piece is described something like this:

*With the approach of dawn comes the murmur of the breeze among the trees, which wakes the sleeping birds, who break forth into their morning song of praise, accompanied by the ripple of running water. The mill-wheel next comes into action, and the song of the millers continues until the close of day.*

Envoy Von Calio, at the traps, did some great work on this number. During the intermission a generous collection was taken.

The first band number following the intermission told the story musically of the Prodigal Son—the Oriental background, the demand of the younger son, the parent's sorrow, the scenes of revelry in the far country, the famine days, the pull of the old home, the father's welcome, the homecoming feast, all told as only music can tell it.

In full, rich, resonant voice Envoy Fowler sang "Thy Will Be Done," and the audience demanded an encore. Captain Young also had to return after he had recited "The Last Hymn," with musical interludes by the band chorus. The chorus sang "Hark! the Trumpet Calleth"; then followed a cornet quartet by Ensign Allan and Envoys Sheppard, Griffith and Margetts. The old favorite, "The Palms," was rendered with great feeling and good taste.

Lt.-Colonel Jenkins, after reading a short passage of Scripture, made a warm appeal, and the concert was closed with the playing of the American National Hymn.[18]

During the International Congress of 1914, the band and Darby heard much Army music and participated in several grand festivals, both of which had influence on future NYSB programs. Here, at a glance, are some of the programs in which the band participated:

June 16  7:30 p.m. (Central Hall) U.S.A. Demonstration
     18  7:00 p.m. (Strand Hall) Massed Musical Meeting
     19  7:00 p.m. (Strand Hall) "Western Music" Festival
     23  Crystal Palace Day
             10:40  Reception—ISB, NSB, Regent Hall, and St. Albans bands
             1:30  U.S. Bands at Canada Bldg.
             5:00  Grand March Past
             7:00  Gigantic Brass Band Festival in Central Transept, including the ISB, NSB, and Chicago Staff
             8:45  NSB on Central Band Stand

In the years following the congress, Darby kept up a solid series of concerts, including noontime concerts for evangelical outreach, benefit concerts for various groups (Life Saving Scouts in 1916), and memorial festivals (such as that for "Gus" Hillstrom in 1922). His programs continued to follow the two-part formula from 1913, concluding with a Bible reading just prior to the grand finale.

Festivals under Sheppard and Broughton were scarcer. George Granger followed in Darby's footsteps as to format, but not in content or style. His three programs, marked A, B, and C, for the 1937 New York State/Canada tour (see Illustration 12-3) demonstrated a two-part division, but with almost exclusively Army music of a more serious nature. Heavy band items were followed by vocal solos or chorus items, and instrumental solos and features were similarly interspersed throughout the program.

Granger's famous Ocean Grove festivals were usually shaped around patriotic themes, especially during the war years. A sample program (shown in Illustration 12-4) is from the festival held July 31, 1943. Again a two-part structure prevailed, with the usual and fitting alteration of music types. In this concert, the Ocean Grove choir (director Walter D. Eddowes), and organist (Clarence Kohlmann) joined the band for several special items. Bearchell and Slater programs continued this same approach to the music festival—a balanced variety package with a spiritual message (if the latter was not always clearly discernable in the "flow" of items).

Richard Holz began to experiment with program design as soon as he became staff bandmaster. His famous three-part format, which placed a devotional section earlier in the program— a section during which applause was discouraged—transformed the way bands structured their concerts. Like any other format, it could become routine, without meaning, but the initial efforts, especially during the 1960 Great Britain tour, were most successful. Vernon Post, a co-contributor to this program style, maintained the format during his directorship.

The 71st Anniversary Festival, February 14, 1958, best exemplifies this new format (see Illustration 12-5). The festival had an overall scriptural theme, "Not by might, nor by power, but by my Spirit, saith the Lord of hosts" (Zechariah 4:6). Each of the three parts had its own scripture verse and heading:

I. Spirit of Proclamation
II. Spirit of Contemplation
III. Spirit of Exultation

Guest Cornetist James Burke of the Goldman Band was the added attraction. He had served recently at the Star Lake Musicamp. Even with a secular artist, the program was unmistakably sacred in orientation.

This form of program gave even greater flexibility to the music festival. One did not always need to juxtapose items of marked difference in such a startling way. In the 1958 program, the Male Chorus was used only in the last two sections, but used most efficiently! The contemplative section was set off with great classics on either side, the final third of the program being the least demanding on the listener, when he/she would be most "sound-weary"!

Not every festival is on a grand scale. Many times a more compact, lighter sequence is needed. A program presented in Puerto Rico by the NYSB Ensemble in February 1962, was structured very well for the intended audience and situation: students and faculty at a university, most of whom would have had no contact previously with the Army. The package devised included a bright march, a virtuoso solo, a "novelty" male quartet, a classical excerpt, two short choral items, a witty "travelogue" variation set, and a final "show-stopper" (see Illustration 12-6). In this case Holz and Post definitely followed the dictum of letting the audience demand *more* rather than forcing them to cry "uncle" because of saturation!

Not every NYSB musical program takes the shape of a concert or festival. The NYSB Nights at F.E.T. provide special opportunities for the band to share their unique ministry in a different manner. The November 21, 1969 F.E.T. (see Illustration 12-7) is a superb example of a well-balanced worship service that uses music as a channel, a vehicle for spiritual renewal. After brief preliminaries Executive Officer Emil Nelson got the people of the congregation participating in joyous songs of praise. All other program items, even the "greetings" and the offering, tied into the main idea of the meeting—communion with God. A wide sample of bandsmen participated and the guest speaker/conductor had opportunity to address the audience twice, both before he conducted his haunting tone poem "The Eternal Presence," and directly following. Even the final song, led by Staff Band veteran Frank Moody, was carefully chosen to restate the spiritual appeal presented during the music and sermon of the evening. Not every night at an F.E.T. proves to be as memorable as this one was; those backed with equal planning and prayer, however, would see similar results and responses.[19]

Derek Smith's programs have been an interesting balance between the old two-part "something for everyone" concept and the Holz-Post, more carefully structured three-part scheme. He and his energetic advisor, Deputy Bandmaster Ronald Waiksnoris, have devised some exciting, innovative programs. Outstanding guest soloists and toe-tapping, upbeat music have been hallmarks of more recent NYSB festivals. The programs rarely bog down with too many "heavy" brass band pieces. The

NYSB's 98th Annual Festival, March 29, 1985, with ISB Euphoniumist Derick Kane, is a representative sample of this new approach. While the program (see Illustration 12-8) is divided by an intermission, there is a devotional section just prior to that interlude. Two large-scale works, one in each section, is heard— "Heroes of the Faith," an "oldie but goodie," and "The Dawning," a manuscript sinfonietta. The soloist is heard on four items so that the audience feels that they have "gotten their money's worth." The Male Chorus sings once in each section, two modern items and one more traditional part-song (the Bulla arrangement). The concert begins with a flourish, reminiscent of the 1960 "Heralds of Victory" opening, and the congregational song receives a special accompaniment, courtesy of Thomas Mack.

For the more serious listener an early baroque toccata is included, along with a Saint-Saens transcription. The young at heart can "get into" the more "hip" rhythms of Bill Broughton's new overture while nostalgia is evoked by the honoring of former Staff Bandsman Walter Orr. The whole festival evening comes to a marvelous climax in a feast for ear and eye, the multi-media setting of Bulla's "Suite of American Overtures."[20]

This kind of program is entertaining, no doubt! But it also does not abandon the basic premise of a music festival—the gospel is proclaimed and an appeal is given. God's Name is acknowledged in joy and praise through the gifts of music He has given to His children. If the NYSB continues to energetically present festivals of this nature, they will not lose their vision, their mission, *or their audience.*

# Sheet Music for Bands.

## Published at National Headquarters.

Two Journals on each sheet. Published for all brass instruments except E' flat Cornet.

## SPECIAL REDUCED PRICE, ·5c. PER SHEET,

### Post Paid.

The following is a list of the tunes on each Journal:

### JOURNALS No. 1 and 2.

"I Was a Guilty Sinner."
"Auld Lang Syne."
"Jesus Saves."
"Morn, Noon, Night."

### JOURNALS No. 3 AND 4.

"Fighting On."
"Stick to the Army."
"Come to the Saviour."
"Ever On."

### JOURNALS No. 5 AND 6.

"God Bless Our Army."
"My Country 'Tis of Thee."
"Arise, My Soul, Arise."
"I Feel Like Singing All the Time."
"I Have Anchored My Soul."

### JOURNALS No. 7 AND 8.

"Christ is All in All,"
"Cheer Boys, Cheer."
"Salvation is the Best Thing In the World."

12-1    *Advertisement for 1898* American Band Journal, *edited by Staff Bandmaster Charles Straubel; AWC, March 10, 1900, p. 15.*

---

12-2.    *National Staff Band and Male Chorus Festival Program, May 31, 1913.*

 Program "A"

FANFARE

OPENING SONG

PRAYER

**MARCH** "Aberystwyth"<br>PERCY MERRITT

*A concert march published in the American Band Journal, which takes as its theme the old Welsh hymn tune whose name it bears.*

**VOCAL SOLO** <div align="center">"Sea of Galilee"</div> **Envoy Frank Fowler**

*New words in an old setting—the favorite old bass solo, "A Thousand Fathoms Deep," with lyric by Colonel William F. Palmer.*

**TROMBONE SOLO** <div align="center">"A Never-Failing Friend"<br>ERIK W. G. LEIDZEN</div> **Captain Kenneth R. Ayres**

*An arrangement of theme and variations, offering an exceptional opportunity for a display of technique and interpretation on the part of the soloist.*

**MALE CHORUS** "Charity"

*A musical setting by C. W. Greene, of the Thirteenth Chapter of First Corinthians.*

**CORNET SOLO** <div align="center">"Happy Day"<br>ERIK W. G. LEIDZEN</div> **Adjutant William Parkins**

*Variations on an old Scandinavian melody.*

**SELECTION** "We Shall Win"<br>MAJOR WM. J. SLATER

*A fantasie on a well-known Army melody, depicting the early day struggles in the attempt to form bands, the gradual forward march of Army music and bands, evolving into a symphonic climax, which is introduced by a few strains from Wagner's "Pilgrim's Chorus."*

### INTERMISSION

**SELECTION** "Moments With Tschaikowsky"<br>BRIGADIER BRAMWELL COLES

*The opening excerpt is from the Fifth Symphony (Op. 64.) Throughout this work runs a sad motto theme which, in the Finale, from which the excerpt is taken, becomes transfigured, and shines forth in ravishing splendor. The delightful "Chant sans Paroles" follows, and then, as a cornet solo, comes "Chanson Triste." The concluding excerpt is the brilliant Finale of the Fourth Symphony (Op. 36).*

**CORNET TRIO** <div align="center">"What a Friend We Have in Jesus!"<br>BANDSMAN RICHARD E. HOLZ</div> **Envoy F. Farrar<br>Envoy W. Wrieden<br>Envoy R. Holz**

*A delightful, lilting arrangement of an old melody.*

**MALE CHORUS** "The Christ of Calvary"

*A male voice arrangement by Major Wm. Slater of the familiar tune, "Annie Laurie."*

**EUPHONIUM SOLO** <div align="center">"Song of the Brother"<br>ERIK W. G. LEIDZEN</div> **Captain Harold W. Jackson**

*A new arrangement of the old English folk song, "When You and I Were Young, Maggie," giving the soloist an excellent opportunity to display his interpretive and technical abilities.*

**SELECTION** Air Varie—"A Sunbeam"<br>CAPTAIN P. CATELINET

*A capriccio on the children's song, "Jesus Wants Me For a Sunbeam." The various moods illustrate: (a) Dawn. (b) Play-time. (c) School-time, with its problems and griefs. (d) Release from school and the gay laughter of the happy children as they wend their way homewards.*

**MARCH** "Under Two Flags"<br>BRIGADIER BRAMWELL COLES

### BENEDICTION

12-3. *New York Staff Band and Male Chorus,* New York State/Canadian Tour Brochure, *1937, Program A.*

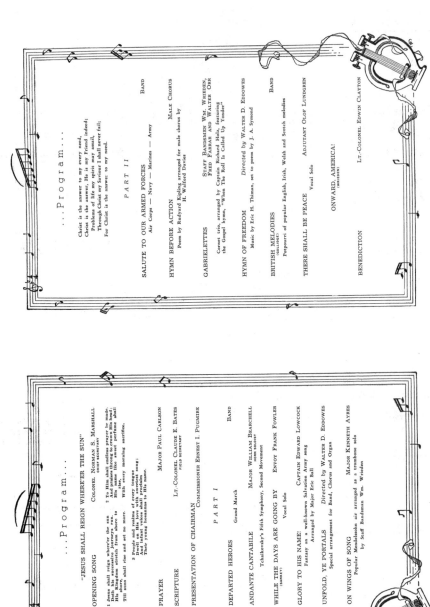

...Program...

OPENING SONG
"JESUS SHALL REIGN WHERE'ER THE SUN"
COLONEL NORMAN S. MARSHALL.
CHIEF SECRETARY

1 Jesus shall reign where'er the sun
  Doth his successive journeys run,
  His Kingdom stretch from shore to shore,
  Till suns shall rise and set no more.

2 To Him shall endless prayer be made,
  And praises throng to crown His head;
  His name like sweet perfume shall rise,
  With every morning sacrifice.

3 People and realms of every tongue
  Dwell on His love with sweetest song;
  And infant voices shall proclaim
  Their young hosannas to His name.

PRAYER                          MAJOR PAUL CARLSON

SCRIPTURE          LT.-COLONEL CLAUDE E. BATES
                                  FIELD SECRETARY

PRESENTATION OF CHAIRMAN
                COMMISSIONER ERNEST I. PUGMIRE

PART I

DEPARTED HEROES          Grand March          BAND

ANDANTE CANTABILE     MAJOR WILLIAM BEARCHELL.
                                       HORN SOLOIST
Tchaikovsky's Fifth Symphony, Second Movement

WHILE THE DAYS ARE GOING BY   ENVOY FRANK FOWLER
                                       Vocal Solo
(JANCY')

GLORY TO HIS NAME:       CAPTAIN EDWARD LOWCOCK
Fantasy on a well-known Salvation Army song
          Arranged by Major Eric Ball

UNFOLD, YE PORTALS     Directed by WALTER D. EDDOWES
Special arrangement for Band, Chorus and Organ

ON WINGS OF SONG          MAJOR KENNETH AYRES
Popular Mendelssohn air arranged as a trombone solo
          by Staff Bandsman Wm. Wrieden

...Program...

Christ is the answer to my every need,
Christ is the answer, He is my Friend indeed;
Problems of life my spirit may assail,
Through Christ my Saviour I shall never fail;
For Christ is the answer to my need.

PART II

SALUTE TO OUR ARMED FORCES          BAND
Air Corps — Navy — Marines — Army

HYMN BEFORE ACTION          MALE CHORUS
Poem by Rudyard Kipling arranged for male chorus by
          H. Walford Davies

GABRIELETTES     STAFF BANDSMEN WM. WRIEDEN,
                 FRED FARRAR AND WALTER ORR
Cornet trio, arranged by Captain Richard Holz, featuring
  the Gospel hymn, "When The Roll Is Called Up Yonder"

HYMN OF FREEDOM     Directed by WALTER D. EDDOWES
Music by Eric H. Thiman, set to poem by J. A. Symond

BRITISH MELODIES          BAND
(SOLLIGE)
Potpourri of popular English, Irish, Welsh and Scotch melodies

THERE SHALL BE PEACE     ADJUTANT OLOF LUNDGREN
                             Vocal Solo

ONWARD, AMERICA!
(WRIEDEN)

BENEDICTION          LT.-COLONEL EDWIN CLAYTON

# 71st Anniversary Music Festival

## The New York Staff Band and Male Chorus

FESTIVAL THEME: *"Not by might, nor by power, but by My Spirit, saith the Lord of hosts."*—ZECHARIAH 4: 6.

LT.-COLONEL WILLIAM MALTBY
*Executive Officer*

FIRST LIEUTENANT VERNON POST
*Deputy Bandmaster and Male Chorus Director*

### COMMISSIONER HOLLAND FRENCH, *Presiding*

MAJOR RICHARD E. HOLZ
*Bandmaster*

CORONATION—FESTIVAL FANFARE VERNON POST
(Audience will stand at conclusion of fanfare and prepare to sing
the opening song without announcement)

CONGREGATIONAL SONG LT.-COLONEL WILLIAM MALTBY
1 All hail the power of Jesus' name!
 Let angels prostrate fall;
 Bring forth the royal diadem
 And crown Him Lord of all!

2 O that with yonder sacred throng
 We at His feet may fall!
 Join in the everlasting song,
 And crown Him Lord of all!

INVOCATION COLONEL WILLIAM G. HARRIS
*Chief Secretary*

CHAIRMAN'S REMARKS COMMISSIONER HOLLAND FRENCH

### Part I—SPIRIT OF PROCLAMATION

*"The Spirit of the Lord is upon me . . . to preach good tiding . . .
to proclaim liberty. . . ."*—ISAIAH 61: 1.

MIGHTY TO SAVE—March GEORGE MARSHALL

LORD OF THE SEA—*A Suite in Three Movements* RAY ALLEN
This epic work for brass band is by one of Britain's most talented composers of the post-World War II era. Captain Ray Allen is on the staff of the London Music Editorial Department of The Salvation Army. The first two movements are based on the composer's own settings of poems by Major Miriam Richards. The third movement introduces a broad hymn-like melody, unassociated with words, but in the spirit of exultation and praise. The composer has supplied a scriptural quotation for each of the three movements.

 I. *Water's Edge*
  *"And Jesus went forth . . . by the seaside . . ."*—MARK 2: 13
 II. *Seascapes*
  *"His dominion shall be from sea to sea."*—ZECHARIAH 9: 10
 III. *Seafarer's Song*
  *"Sing unto the Lord . . . ye that go down to the sea."*—ISAIAH 52: 10

Presenting JAMES F. BURKE
*America's Premier Cornet Soloist, with* JOLENE MITCHELL *at the Piano*

SOLILOQUY JAMES MORRISSEY

TRUMPET CONCERTO FRANZ JOSEF HAYDN
 I. *Andante* *Arranged for Brass Band and Trumpet by Kay Allen*
 II. *Allegro*

### Part II—SPIRIT OF CONTEMPLATION

*". . . for, behold, the Kingdom of God is within you."*—LUKE 17: 21.

(Audience is requested to refrain from applauding during PART II)

LOST IN THE NIGHT FINNISH FOLK SONG
Tenor Solo by STAFF BANDSMAN OLOF LUNDGREN, *Arranged by Christiansen-Holz*
with the Male Chorus and Brass Ensemble.

THE SCRIPTURES *Read by* LT.-COLONEL WILLIAM MALTBY

BY THE WAY OF THE CROSS TOM FERGUSON
 *Arranged for Male Chorus by Vernon Post*

ON THE WAY HOME ERIK LEIDZEN
A selection of well-known songs describing the Christian pilgrimage to the heavenly goal.

### Part III—SPIRIT OF EXULTATION

*". . . in whom . . . ye rejoice with joy unspeakable and full of glory . . ."*—I PETER 1: 8.

MOMENTS WITH TCHAIKOVSKY *Arranged by* BRAMWELL COLES
 1. Finale from the 5th Symphony
 2. Chanson Paroles
 3. Chanson Triste
 4. Finale from the 4th Symphony

JAMES F. BURKE
JOLENE MITCHELL *at the Piano*

SCHERZO EDWIN FRANKO GOLDMAN

MAGIC TRUMPET JAMES F. BURKE

TRUMPETER'S LULLABY LEROY ANDERSON

POOR MAN LAZARUS A NEGRO SPIRITUAL
 *Arranged for Male Chorus by Jester Hairston*

HOW GREAT THOU ART SWEDISH GOSPEL SONG
 *Arranged for Male Chorus and Brass Ensemble by Vernon Post*

MANHATTAN—March ERIK LEIDZEN

BENEDICTION LT.-COLONEL WILLIAM SLATER

12-5.  **NYSB and Male Chorus 71st Anniversary Music Festival, February 14, 1958.**

# University of Puerto Rico

(CENTRO UNIVERSITARIO)

## MONDAY FEBRUARY 26TH. 1962.

6:00 P. M. TO 7:00 P. M.

353 TETUAN STREET
SAN JUAN, PUERTO RICO

(FESTIVAL OF MUSIC - DEDICATED TO FACULTY AND STUDENTS)

## BY THE SALVATION ARMY NEW YORK STAFF BAND AND MALE CHORUS

SPONSORED BY SPONSOR CORPS R.O.T.C.

University of Puerto Rico

NATIONAL ANTHEM

INTRODUCTION: Brigadier Richard Holz, Bandmaster,
        By: Miss Carmen Ongay – Sponsor Corps U. P. R.

(1) STAR LAKE        March Brilliante        Eric Ball

(2) A HAPPY DAY        Cornet Solo        Erik Leidzen
        Soloist: Staff Bandsman Derek Smith

(3) MALE QUARTET
    EZEKIEL SAW de WHEEL        Arr. Vernon Post

(4) EXCERPTS FROM THE SIXTH SYMPHONY
               TCHAIKOVSKY   Arr. B. Coles

(5) MALE CHORUS
        (A) ROCK OF AGES
        (B) THE OLD TIME RELIGION

(6) ALL AROUND THE WORLD     NOVELTY    Emil Soderstrom

(7) REMARKS: Commissioner Holland French, Territorial Commander

(8) BANNERS & BONNETS        Meredith Willson
        Soloist: Staff Bandsman Olof Lundgren    Arr. R. E. Holz

PRAYER             Colonel Albert Pepper

## TODOS BIENVENIDOS

12-6.    *NYSB Mini-Concert in San Juan, Puerto Rico, February 26, 1962.*

# FRIDAY EVENING AT THE TEMPLE

For the Salvation of the Lost
The Santification of the Believer
The Strengthening of the Spiritual Life

**1932** • **38th SERIES** • **1969-70**

(Brigadier Charles J. Southwood, Executive Officer)

NOVEMBER 21, 1969   -:-   7:35 P. M.

## *New York Staff Band Night*

### Speaker: **Eric Ball**

### Leader: **Colonel C. Emil Nelson**

| | |
|---|---|
| SALVATIONISTS' SALUTE—*"In the Ranks"* (Eric Ball) | **Staff Band** *(Major Vernon Post)* |
| FANFARE AND THEME—*"Christ Is the Answer"* (Maltby-Leidzen) | **Temple Chorus** and **Brass Ensemble** *(Major Lloyd Scott)* |

— *SING FOR JOY* —
Colonel C. Emil Nelson, *Song Leader*

| | |
|---|---|
| MEDITATION FOR PRAYER—*"Contrition"* (T. B. Pollock-Eric Ball) | **Staff Band Male Chorus** Staff Bandsman Albert Avery, *Soloist* |
| SPOKEN PRAYER | Staff Bandsman Kenneth Davis |
| CHORAL PRAYER—*"O Fire of the Spirit"* (E. Stone-Eric Ball) | **Staff Band Male Chorus** |
| GREETINGS | Lt.-Commissioner Paul S. Kaiser International Secretary and former N. Y. S. B. Executive Officer |
| SONG—*"Begin the Day With God"* (M. Pike-Eric Ball) | **Temple Chorus** Conducted by the Composer |
| ANNOUNCEMENTS AND OFFERING | Brigadier B. Barton McIntyre |
| OFFERTORY | Major Shirley Sipley |
| SCRIPTURE READING | Eric Ball |
| TONE POEM—*"The Eternal Presence"* (Psalm 139) (Eric Ball) | **Staff Band** Conducted by the Composer |
| MESSAGE | Eric Ball |

PRAYER AND MEDITATION

| | |
|---|---|
| SONG—*"Still, Still With Thee"* | Staff Bandsman Frank Moody |
| BENEDICTION | Deputy-Bandmaster Roland Schramm |

*(Continued on other side)*

---

**The Salvation Army** • **Centennial Memorial Temple** • **120 West 14th St., New York, N. Y.**

---

# PROGRAM

## Lt.-Colonel Edward Fritz, Presiding

*Cornet Ensemble  FAITHFUL FOREVER ....................... Richard Holz

WELCOME ............................. Lt.-Colonel WALLACE C. CONRATH

Song—"Redeemer's Praise" ................................... Thomas Mack

1. O for a thousand tongues to sing
   My great Redeemer's praise;
   The glories of my God and King,
   The triumphs of His grace!

3. Jesus the name that charms our fears
   That bids our sorrows cease;
   'Tis music in the sinner's ears;
   'Tis life and health and peace.

2. My gracious Master and my God,
   Assist me to proclaim,
   To spread through all the earth abroad
   The honors of Thy name.

4. He breaks the power of canceled sin.
   He sets the prisoner free;
   His blood can make the foulest clean.
   His blood avails for me.

PRAYER

*Festival March  ABLE ................................ Turkington/Himes

Tone Poem  HEROES OF THE FAITH ....................... Charles Skinner

A musical portrayal of the heroism of the early day Christians in the face of Roman Persecution. Six sections without break.

    I.  Rome
    II.  The Early Christians
    III.  The Arena Spectacle

    IV.  The Seeming Triumph of Paganism
    V.  The Romans Pass from the Scene
    VI.  The Spirit of the Faithful Lives On—
      "Faith of our Fathers"

*Male Chorus  A JOYFUL SONG ........................... Thomas Mack

### INTRODUCING INTERNATIONAL STAFF BANDSMAN
### DERICK KANE
### Euphonium Soloist

Euphonium Solo  THE BETTER WORLD ................... Norman Bearcroft

This solo was written for the International Congress of 1978 and first played by Staff Bandsman Derick Kane. The theme is the much-loved song "There is a Better World," which speaks of "music," "angels," "harps of gold," and "mansions fair." The central movement features the song, "There's A Crown Laid Up In Glory." Other references to the Homeland include "I Shall See Him Face to Face" and "The Homeward Trail."

*Selection  GOWANS & LARSSON OVERTURE ............ William Broughton

Euphonium Solo  THE SWAN ...................... Saint-Saens; arr. RSA

*Transcription  TOCCATA ...................... Frescobaldi; arr. Curnow

---

*Male Chorus  HE WALKS WITH GOD ..................... Stephen Bulla

SCRIPTURE & COMMENTS ............. COMMISSIONER ORVAL TAYLOR

*Euphonium Solo  JESUS I COME TO THEE ............. Norman Bearcroft

Derick Kane performs this devotional solo for the first time this evening. Lt.-Colonel Norman Bearcroft arranged this well known song, "Out Of My Bondage" especially for Staff Bandsman Kane's visit to the Eastern Territory.

### INTERMISSION

*March  THE PIONEERS ............................... James Anderson

*Sinfonietta  THE DAWNING ............................. Peter Graham

In this work, the composer attempts to capture the moods and events suggested in the text of Joy Webb's song, "There will be God":

"Ten thousand years may pass away and bring the dawning of a cosmic day, age after age, time after time hold its sway. Man walks alone amidst uncertainty, only one thing can still make him strong, in the pain...doubt...and loneliness...amidst the confusion...there will be hope...there will be God."

The initial ideas of timelessness, of the eternal, which are evoked in the opening measures of the music, at once lead us to "the dawning of a cosmic day." The realization of this new age of despair and doubt of the existence of God is unfolded in a series of themes contradictory in nature, at once cold, aggressive, harsh, reflective and dancelike.

"Like the first morning" morning has broken, but we are reminded we exist now in the "new age" of man's song, "There will be God."

The solo cornet soliloquy which begins the second movement depicts the solitary journey of man "on a life unknown," eventually leading to a statement of hope and the absolute that despite all the fear and despair, "there will be God."

This declaration of faith and mood of optimism pervades the third movement—the spiritual "My Lord, what a morning, when the stars begin to fall!" forms the climax of the work, when the combined senses of urgency, anxiety, anticipation and excitement prevail, finally being dispersed by the majestic final chords symbolic of the sovereign power and the realization, the dawning, of the absolute truth of God the eternal.

This is the world premiere performance of The Dawning.

### SPECIAL PRESENTATION to
### STAFF BANDSMAN WALTER ORR (R)
### by COMMISSIONER ORVAL TAYLOR

Euphonium Solo  THE SONG OF THE BROTHER ............... Erik Leidzen

This set of variations on the traditional melody "When you and I were Young" was originally written as a cornet solo by the young Erik Leidzen in 1916. Sixteen years later Leidzen revised the solo, scoring it for euphonium and band. Since its publication in 1939, "The Song Of The Brother" (the new title being Arch. Wiggins song wedded to the traditional tune) has become, and remained a classic in the Army's solo repertoire.

Male Chorus  THE UPWARD ROAD ...................... Leslie Condon

COURTESIES

*Multi-Media Presentation  SUITE OF AMERICAN OVERTURES ....... Stephen Bulla

BENEDICTION ......................... MAJOR SIDNEY LANGFORD

*Played by permission of the Eastern Territorial Music Council

---

**12-8.  NYSB and Male Chorus, 98th Annual Festival, March 29, 1985**

# 13

## "Songs in the Heart"
### (Erik Leidzen)

## The Instrumental Soloists and Ensembles

B rass soloists and ensembles have always been a notable feature of NYSB programming. Salvation Army music literature has been greatly enriched by the special solos written for these musicians. In the lists that follow only the most notable and outstanding soloists/ensembles are listed, with the compositions most frequently associated with them. The dates chosen reflect the year in which the piece was premiered with the Staff Band or a year in which we have a confirmed performance on a band program. The cornet soloists have been chosen to receive a more complete survey, because the principal cornetist serves as the model player, or the concertmaster, of the brass band.

### The Cornet Soloists

The array of truly outstanding cornetists within the band's first hundred years dazzles the brass band enthusiast. As the solo cornet bench thrives, so thrives a band. From native-trained to self-taught imports from the "homeland" (Great Britain), to conservatory-polished professionals—we see the entire range just within the cornet list:

## Cornet Soloists of the New York Staff Band

"Trumpeter" Edward Trumble (E$^b$ and B$^b$ cornet)
  Improvised solos based on hymns and songs
  "My Soul by Christ Is Saved, Hallelujah" (1890)

Felicia Gircopazzi
  No titles available (1897-1900)

John Allan (featured soloist by 1904)
  "The Star" (1913)
  "Memories" (by 1921)

Charles Mattheson
  "Columbia" (1924)

George Wilmer
  "Happy Day" (1927)
  "Grand Fantasia on a Theme by Weber" (1928)

William Parkins
  "Hallelujah" (1931)
  "Lover of the Lord" (1931)
  "Tucker" (1932)
  "Happy All the Day" (1932)

Fred Farrar
  "Maoriland" (1938)
  "Wondrous Love" (1938)

Edward Lowcock
  "Silver Threads" (1939)
  "Glory to His Name" (1943)
  "Happy All the Day" (1947)
  "Wondrous Day" (1957)

William Wrieden (E$^b$ Soprano)
  "Deep Harmony" (1940s)

William Perrett
  "Happy Day" (1946)

Derek Smith
  "Glorious Fountain" (1959)
  "Songs in the Heart" (1960)
  "Speak My Lord" (1961)
  "Beautiful Christ" (1961)
  "Haydn Concerto" (1961)

"Rhapsody on Negro Spirituals" (1963)
"Victorious" (1965)
"The Challenge" (1967)
"Hummel Concerto" (1968)
"Someone Cares" (1971)

David Swyers
"Happy Day" (1964)

Peter Hofman
"Cheerful Voices" (1965)

Philip Smith
"Rhapsody on Negro Spirituals" (1972)
"Hummel Concerto" (1973)
"What A Friend" (1974)

Terry Camsey
"Life's Pageant" (1976)
"Rhapsody for Cornet and Band" (1976)
"Sing Glory Hallelujah" (1978)

Ronald Waiksnoris
"Sunshine and Shadow" (1981)
"Longings" (1982)
"Jubilate" (1983)
"The Amazing Mr. Leidzen" (1985)

Gordon Ward (E♭ Soprano)
"Pastorale" (1985)
"Cavalleria Rusticana" (1985)

The earliest cornet soloists, Trumble and Allan, were products of American professional bands that flourished in the last two decades of the 19th century. The term "Trumpeter" was applied to Trumble in the early 1890s in much the same manner as that for "Trumpeter Sheard," the cornetist who accompanied William Booth in his travels. Trumble was Ballington Booth's find and he used his expert improvisatory gifts to good advantage. John Allan was a "show-stopper" from the moment he sat in with the Staff Band at the tender age of twelve.

No recordings exist of Trumble or the Italian "lady-cornetist" Gircopazzi, but we can hear Allan's confident technical facility and well-controlled tone on the 1923 recording of his own variation solo, "Memories." As the Army was slow in officially sanctioning "technique" solos, it is not surprising to see the cornetists of the first 50 years or so using outside solos by Hartmann, Clarke, Levy, or Arban. Not until the Leidzen solos of the 1920s, written for the stars of the New England Staff Band, did a comparable repertoire begin to emerge.

J. Stanley Sheppard was a student of the cornet, amassing a large library of solo music (now in this writer's possession) and developing a series of well-written articles for young players that appeared in *The War Cry* and the *Local Officer's Counselor* during the 1920s. While not a flashy soloist, Sheppard had a beautiful tone and served as a solid principal-chair player in the band for decades. His training, like so many others in the band, was self-motivated.

Provinicial Commander William McIntyre served as music patron for several young talented musicians in New England during the 1920s. William Parkins was given seven years' private instruction with Louis Kloepfel, principal trumpet of the Boston Symphony Orchestra. Later NYSB cornet soloists who also studied with Kloepfel, ostensibly at New England Conservatory, were "Chet" Mattheson, George Wilmer, and Fred Farrar. While Leidzen was New England staff bandmaster he developed and featured a number of fine young players, writing solos for them (particularly Parkins) and giving them personal coaching.

Many of these fine players followed Leidzen's lead and also moved to New York in the late 1920s, and early '30s. They became a solid part of the 1930s Staff Band: Stanley ("Spud") Parkins, William Parkins, Harold Jackson, Walter Squibb, Kenneth Ayres, and several others. William Parkins was the standout among them. His self-assured, polished presentations thrilled audiences across America. Here was a cornetist Evangeline Booth could put up any time and never fear that a disaster might occur. She was a demanding critic—"If you made a mistake, Eva wouldn't use you for awhile—she'd put you in the refrigerator."[1] Parkins usually featured the tailor-made Leidzen solos, "Tucker," "Happy Day," or "Happy All the Day" (the latter first titled "At the Cross Where I First Saw the Light") and then followed with shorter encores which he had written, with Leidzen's editorial help—"Lover of the Lord," "Hallelujah," and "Far Beyond Jordan."

Another home-grown talent, noted for his fast, bravura-style technique, was Edward Lowcock. Receiving two years training at the Eastman School of Music, preparatory level, he won national honors at the National Cornet Competition, Madison, Wisc.,

1936-37.[2] His comrades from that same period had studied also at leading music centers, Fred Farrar with Kloepfel and William Perrett with famed New York Trumpeter Ernest Williams (as well as William Vacchiano).

Derek Smith, whose "Songs in the Heart" still remains among the most challenging cornet solos ever written, was the first real "transplant soloist," coming to the band from Canada in 1959. His earlier career in the Rosehill Band and the Horse Guards was already quite substantial. His achievements with the NYSB, however, are legendary. The ovation he received on the stage of Royal Albert Hall in 1960 confirmed his position among the highest "constellations" in the "cornet heavens." What young cornet player of that era did not try to match Derek's beautiful sound and delicate vibrato, and try to mimic Smith's inimitable rubato in lyric passages. The music written for Smith, just as that written for Parkins, speaks eloquently of his gifts. His son, Philip, also became an outstanding NYSB cornet soloist.

Several other fine, American-trained cornetists had a chance in front of the band. Peter Hofman, always a solid solo cornet-row player, briefly soloed while Derek was out of the band. David Swyers, whose professional career as a trumpeter has included the Baltimore Symphony Orchestra, was also among some of the fine cornetists in the band that came up through the Star Lake Musicamp training program.[3]

Philip Smith now serves as the co-principal trumpet of the New York Philharmonic Orchestra, and is frequently a featured soloist on that orchestra's programs and tours. Receiving the best of two worlds, his father's disciplined home training on the cornet and an equally rigorous professional schooling at the Juilliard School of Music (receiving both the B.A. and M.M. degrees there), Smith is at ease with the most demanding, modern trumpet sonata or the most charming of 19th-century style cornet work. Prior to his current position, Smith played for three years in the Chicago Symphony Orchestra, during which time he was also solo cornetist in the Mont Clare (Chicago) Corps Band.* Before that, besides serving as soloist with the NYSB, he traveled with the International Staff Band as a soloist during one of their tours of Switzerland. In the Smith family, from Derek's father (who not only trained his son but other stars like James Williams and Roland Cobb) right through to the present, the entire history of Salvation

*The name of this corps was changed to Norridge Citadel in 1983.

Army banding is manifest. When Derek was eight years old, at his home corps in Hendon, England, he played a duet with 80-year-old "Trumpeter" Sheard. This symbolizes a tradition that cannot be manufactured and which must be preserved if the NYSB is to maintain quality soloists.

At age 11, Terry Camsey began teaching himself cornet in Cheltenham, England. Soon he played solos in the divisional band of that Gloucestershire region. Military service, as principal cornet in the H.M. Irish Guards, and then 13 years as solo cornetist in the International Staff Band, were preludes to his brief but successful stint as principal cornet with the NYSB. His American compatriots of this same period, Lambert Bittinger (B.S. in Music Education at Montclair (N.J.) State College) and Ronald Waiksnoris (Hartt College of Music and private study with Edward Treutel) lent contrasting styles to Camsey's lyrical cornet during their brilliant duet work, "To Set the People Free" being an example.

In the current band, the home-grown and transplanted players are still in evidence. Waiksnoris continues to perform in a bravura style reminiscent of Edward Lowcock, having several notable works written for him by Stephen Bulla and Peter Graham. Gordon Ward, recently arrived in New York as that area's divisional music director, received several undergraduate and graduate degrees and diplomas from the Royal Northern College of Music (student of Cecil Kidd and Philip Jones). His lyrical, tasteful tone solos on the soprano cornet were treasures remembered from the 1985 Great Britain tour. Waiksnoris and Ward are quite a combination—one needs only to listen to them blaze forth on Graham's scintillating duet "Quicksilver" to know that the most recent cornet soloists of the band are holding high the great legacy of excellent cornet playing.

### Other Brass Soloists

An equally interesting story could be told about the trombonists, euphoniumists, alto hornists and other brass soloists of the band. Here, too, much new music appeared specifically for these men. A similar pattern—a mixture of Army-trained, college-taught, and self-instructed players also emerges after a detailed review of these other soloists. Some soloists were extremely versatile. When Kenneth Ayres and Harold Jackson first arrived in New York, Darby placed them on saxophone. Soon both were switched to trombone. Leidzen had written "A Never Failing Friend" for Jackson, one of the few men who could play the last variation as intended with a flawless, light triple-tonguing on the devilish triplets. Jackson was next moved to euphonium (with the newly revised "Song of the Brother" soon in his possession) and Kenneth Ayres became principal trombone.[4]

## Alto Horn/Flugelhorn Soloists

Edgar Arkett (French horn)
No specific titles available (1920s)

William Bearchell
Tchaikovsky's "Andante Cantabile" from "Symphony #5" (1943)

Emil Nelson
"Mendelssohn's Nocturne" (1944)

William Schofield (Flugelhorn)
"The Old Rustic Bridge" (1962)

Paul Thompson (Flugelhorn)
"Jesu, Joy of Man's Desiring" (1958)

Albert E. Avery (Flugelhorn)
"Solveig's Song" (1965)

## Trombone Soloists

Samson Hodges
"Ora Pro Nobis" (1912)

Charles Williams
"The Southern Cross" (1923)

Kenneth Ayres
"Unfathomed Love" (1936)
"A Never-Failing Friend" (1937)

Arthur Craytor
"The Palms" (1947)
"The Old Rugged Cross" (1955)

Arthur Anderson
"The Eternal Quest" (1952)
"Count Your Blessings" (1953)
"Concertino for Band and Trombone" (1954)

Allister Stickland
"The Eternal Quest" (1967)
"A Never-Failing Friend" (1968)

Charles Baker
"Song of Exuberance" (1972)
"Journey Into Peace" (1982)
"The Guardian" (1983)

Lindsay Evans
"Now I Belong to Jesus" (1974)
"Lights Along the Shore" (1977)
"A Never-Failing Friend" (1977)


**Euphonium Soloists**

William Slater
"Beautiful Colorado" (1928)

Harold Jackson
"Lift Up the Banner" (1935)
"Land Beyond the Blue" (1937)
"Song of the Brother" (1937)

Milton Kippax
"The Warrior" (1944)
"We'll All Shout Hallelujah" (1947)

Robert McNally
"Home on the Range" (1958)
"Ransomed Host" (1959)
"Neath Starry Skies" (1961)
"Call of the Seasons" (1962)

Lawrence Robertson
"The Conqueror" (1967)
"Song of Triumph" (1969)

Thomas Mack
"Youthful Pilgrimage" (1971)
"The Pathway" (1974)
"Allegro Spiritoso" (1982)
"Tell the World" (1985)

## Duets, Trios, and Ensemble Features

### Cornet Duets

J. Stanley Sheppard and Edgar Arkett (1917)
No titles available

William and Stanley Parkins
"Always Cheerful" (1933)

Fred Farrar and William Wrieden
"Always Cheerful" (1937)

Derek Smith and Philip Smith
"Wonderful Words" (1971)

Lambert Bittinger and Ronald Waiksnoris
"To Set the People Free" (1977)

Ronald Waiksnoris and Gordon Ward
"Quicksilver" (1982)

### Cornet Trios

J. Stanley Sheppard, Edgar Arkett, and Leslie Arkett (1920)
No titles available

William Parkins, Fred Farrar, William Wrieden
"The Gabrielettes" (1937)

Fred Farrar, William Wrieden, Richard Holz
"What A Friend" (1937)

Edward Lowcock, Albert Olley, Walter Orr
"Sweetest Name" (1951)

### Cornet Quartets

William Parkins, Paul Carlson, Fred Farrar, William Wrieden
"The Trumpeters" (1939)

### Cornet Ensembles (entire cornet section)

"Heralds of Victory" (1960)
"The Ash Grove" (1982)
"Faithful Forever" (1985)

## Alto Horn Features

Duet: Alfred Swenarton and Emil Nelson
"Only Jesus" (1947)

Trios: Alfred Swenarton, George Harvey, Robert Lundsten
"Alpine Fantasy" (1953)
"What A Friend" (1958)

## Tuba Features

Quartet: Vincent Bulla, Charles Olsen, Harold Banta, Wilf
Cooper
"The Old Soldier" (1957)

Duet: Philip Bulla, Harold Banta
"Radiant Pathway" (1971)

## Unusual Instrumental Features

The early NYSB featured some exotic characters. Richard Von Calio,* converted soldier of fortune, was among the most notorious. Claiming service in the armies of the Czar, Kaiser, King Edward VII of England, and the French Republic (if we are able to believe these reports), his appearance in the NYSB was more than colorful. Darby let him improvise extensively on mallet percussion during regular band items. As a soloist he was a real crowd-pleaser, with anything from accordion to drum-set and xylophone. In the band room he always had a strange story to relate from his "Black Hand" society experiences. He also presented a challenge to band administration in finding him a job to hold for any length of time![5]

Less "wacky" but equally unique were the pyrotechnical displays of "Gus" Hillstrom delivered on the "sweet potato" or ocarina, with Von Calio supplying appropriate, and usually improvised accompaniment. More regular fare came from other unusual instruments for an Army band, such as violin, clarinet, tuba, and saxophone. The British tradition of the elocutionist has died out in American Salvation Army circles, but at one time William F. Palmer was in much demand for his monologues.

---

*A fanciful description of Richard Von Calio's playing with the NYSB is contained in Ford C. Ottman's Herbert Booth: A Biography (Doubleday, NY, 1928) pp. 99-100.

Similarly, the concertina, a constant part of NYSB programs when William Halpin was in the band, has all but disappeared.

## Additional Featured Soloists
**Violin Solos:** Dr. Fritz Nice (1900-1914)
**Concertina Solos:** William Halpin (1896-1898)
**Clarinet Solos:** John Lock (1904 International Congress)
**Tuba Solos:** Frank Fowler (1906-1912)
**Ocarina Solos:** "Gus" Hillstrom
   "Songs of the Forest" (1914-1922)
**One-Man Band and Xylophone:** Richard Von Calio
   "The Water Falls" (1923)
   "Grand Russian Fantasia" (1930)
**Xylophone Solos:** Andrew Laurie
   "America Melodies" (1928)
**Saxophone Solos:** Kenneth Ayres (1920s)
**Monologues:**
William F. Palmer
   "Extreme Unction" (1913)
   "The House that Jack Built" (1916)
   "Memories" (1919)
Fletcher Agnew
   "The Veteran's Soliloquy" (1940s)

## Brass Ensembles

In times when the band was not in top form, or when the exigencies of war cut personnel, small brass ensembles were formed from the membership of the band to provide service when the full band could not meet an engagement. The small group also was most practical in supporting long tours by Army dignitaries when the large group would be too expensive.

The initial efforts were four-part, the Naval and Military League Quartet of 1918 and the Silver Quartet of 1923. The first sextet, with its standard two cornets, alto, trombone, euphonium, and bass instrumentation, saw active service starting in the mid-1920s, when Commissioner Estill took the sextet on long trips. A unique quartet of 1929 was short-lived, but the sextets of the 1930s and 1940s have an interesting history.

With the formation of Leidzen's special nine-piece Metropolitan Ensemble of 1930 (see Chapters 3 and 4) a move toward elite groups was ever under the surface of band board talk. William Bearchell confided to me that he had to be very careful with the scheduling of the sextet lest too often the full band see the elite group as a threat. Indeed, these special musical groups were very proficient with a distinct repertoire of rearranged Army band music, classical transcriptions, and a few outside pieces. So problematic did they become that by Slater's tenure, these "special" ensembles were discouraged, never to emerge as "official" units again except for very specific program duties of a limited nature.

One positive by-product has been the recent development of a sextet journal, published by the Eastern Territory, that features both some of the old NYSB and Hyde Park Sextet literature and much new music for this interesting combination.

These special ensembles were often the essence of staff banding. Harold Anderson has shared a brief glimpse of one of these, the sextet from the 1940s:

> *The Staff Band spirit was projected very clearly with a visit every year of the Staff Band Sextet to Hazelton, Pa., and as a youngster they captured my imagination with their artistry, abundance of levity and their down-to-earth Salvationism that took them out to the Open Air with our own corps band, but also saw them in the high Presbyterian Church. I believe that Bearchell, Fowler, Lowcock, Henderson, Kippax, or Craytor could have run for mayor of that city.[6]*

## NYSB Brass Ensembles

1918 Naval and Military League Quartet
Sheppard, Griffith, Campbell, Fowler

1923 Silver Quartet
John Allan, Herbert Bartlett, Harold Wellman, Charles Bearchell

1925 Territorial Staff Band Sextet
J.S. Sheppard, H. Bartlett, E. Arkett, C. Bearchell, W. Bearchell, C. Williams

1929 Staff Band Quartet
C. Brindley, flugelhorn; K. Ayres, saxophone; H. Jackson, trombone; W. Slater, euphonium

1931 Staff Band Radio Quintet (later, with W. Bearchell, a Sextet)
W. and S. Parkins, W. Slater, H. Jackson, F. Fowler

1938 Territorial Staff Band Sextet
F. Farrar, W. Wrieden, W. Bearchell, K. Ayres, H. Jackson, F. Fowler

1944 Territorial Staff Band Sextet
E. Lowcock, J. Henderson, W. Bearchell, A. Craytor, M. Kippax, F. Fowler

# 14

## "Triumphant Faith"
### (Stanley Ditmer)

## Personal Glimpses

The New York Staff Band involves more than just music, festivals, instruments, and engagements. The band has been a shaping force in the development of men's lives. Whatever a bandsman's initial reaction to the NYSB, ultimately the vast majority of members have treasured their days in the group. Valiant contributor to the band Frank Moody put it this way:

> There is a great tradition associated with membership in the band, and while some have griped and complained while they were members because of certain personal circumstances, I have yet to meet a former bandsman who was sorry he ever wore the insignia of the NYSB on his uniform epaulets.[1]

For The Salvation Army, the NYSB has been a pivotal experience in the directing of young men towards full-time Christian service. Hundreds of officers are in the ranks in no small way due to the influence of NYSB fellowship. Frederick Clarke's experience is a perfect example of what has happened and continues to happen in each generation:

> My association with the Staff Band played an important part in my decision to dedicate my life to God and the Army as an officer.

*It was at the urging of a fellow staff bandsman, Doug Seaver, that
I decided to enter Training College (SFOT) in 1941.*[2]

The success stories are many. Charles F. Olsen and Vincent
"Ben" Bulla joined the band while they were employees at
territorial headquarters, then left to be trained as officers. Now
both are stationed at THQ and are staff bandsmen once again.
Notable music leaders, now in far-flung places, like Arthur Anderson as divisional music director in Texas, or Al Stickland as
songster leader at the Santa Ana (Calif.) Corps, first caught the
true spirit of excellence in sacred music via the Staff Band and its
leaders. We see men like William MacLean or Thomas Mack
groomed for special skill tasks in publications, administration,
music, and legal services while serving in the NYSB. Don Ross
became a classical and romance language scholar as a result of
incentives brought his way from band leadership; catching the
spirit of excellence and the pursuit of God-given talents to the
fullest, he then became a lawyer and corporate executive for a
major U.S. firm.

Not every bandsman is transformed while in the group. Many
times the impact of the group's corporate ministry only "strikes
home" much later. In a letter to Richard Holz, November 30, 1956,
Chaplain/Major Wreford Devoto, former staff bandsman, responded to a tape the Male Chorus and Staff Band sent him while
he was on service in Korea:

*I remember that when I played in the band I didn't give too
much thought to the far-reaching influence of our music. Rather it
was more a transient thing—just putting the best in the playing at
the time for pure personal enjoyment. Perhaps some of you feel
the same. So I would remind you of the great advantage of our
music. It not only pleases the musical ear but it blesses the soul.
This you have done for me this Christmas...your music will also
bless the officers and men of this area....*[3]

Bandmaster Fred Jackson of Newburgh, N.Y., former E$^b$ soprano
cornetist of the 1960 tour band, tells a similar tale in a letter to
Charles Olsen:

*I hope you don't mind a personal testimony from me right here,
Charlie. You asked our thoughts about the band and the use of
young people in the band. I think the young fellas are great.
(Somebody has to help you and Ben Bulla carry your horns and*

*help you up and down the stairs.) But, as I look back now and see myself as a young man in the New York Staff Band, I realize that I rationalized my playing in the band as being my service to God. I loved God, but I hadn't turned everything over to Him. I thought God would be satisfied with me playing "His music" in an organization that was inspired by "Him," and I would still be able to go my own way without making any real commitment to "Him." As it turned out, the pride that I developed from playing in the Staff Band overshadowed the Lord in the music we played. Maybe that's why my time in the Staff Band ended when it did. Unfortunately my spiritual condition stayed the same way for quite a few years after that and resulted in some problems in my life. But, God is good and He didn't give up on me. A few years ago, I was playing in the Old Orchard Camp Band, still hiding behind my cornet and still letting that horn be my commitment. Well, the Holy Spirit let me know that night that it was time for a full and definite change in my life. I fought it right down to the last song, but when they sang "Take my life and let it be consecrated Lord, to Thee...take my will and make it thine...," I put my horn down, and got up out of my seat and went and knelt at the altar and asked Jesus to be Lord of my life....*

*Down deep in my heart, I would love to be playing in the Staff Band again, but I am being required to "march to the beat of a different drummer," and the Lord is using me right where I am....*

*...I believe that the time that I spent in the New York Staff Band was one of the greatest experiences of my life and that God was planting seeds in my heart that were to come to fruition at a later date.[4]*

Staff bandsmen are easy targets for the cynical or the self-righteous. Because they don a special tunic, many feel staff bandsmen need be near sainthood before being granted membership. Needless to say, that was fortunately not a criteria for membership. Early members were newly converted saloon-keepers, like Major Wray, or office boys with musical talent, like "Brother Gale," or, they were men whose sense of adventure had recently been channeled from the physical to the spiritual. Take "Comrade" Charles Van Leusen, one-time band secretary and finance officer in the Anderson band:

*It requires some dexterity to handle such an assortment of names as Charles Meindert Rodolf Johan Van Leusen. If our brother was rather slow about coming into the ark of God's salvation, he certainly has extenuations. In beautiful, quaint old Holland he was reared to a formal allegiance to the State Church, his parents being connected with it, and his father being in fact a dignitary of the congregation; but he had no depth of spiritual knowledge or experience, and when in his early manhood he left home "to dig gold in the United States," he brought little of the restraint of godliness with him.*

*Incidentally he found little gold also, whereupon he took to roving, was a sailor, a farmer, any old thing. In one of his seafaring trips he attended a meeting led by the Commander and Consul in Calcutta, little imagining he was subsequently to serve under them in America. He roamed wildly for a few years, but seven years ago—about a year after he had heard the Commanders in India—at a holiness meeting held in the old hall of No. 1 New York, he was saved. After serving here as a soldier for two years he took transfer to No. 4, in Harlem, where he has done good service both as a soldier and as corps secretary and a member of the band.*

*Comrade Van Leusen is also a member of the National Staff Band, being employed in the financial department at headquarters.*[5]

## Bandsmen Witness

Ballington Booth, Frederick Booth-Tucker, and Evangeline Booth all expected their boys to speak a gallant word of Christian witness. Reports of the band up to World War I tend to stress the band's evangelical efforts as much as their musical exploits. After the Great War, the testimonies were not as glib, not as easily spoken, as some men had had difficult war experiences. Many good, loyal, and competent bandsmen could not testify without great difficulty or embarrassment. Even the faithful Frank Fowler, when called on by the band leader one night in the 1920s, responded to the question, "Frank, are you well saved?" with a quick, "Yes," as he immediately sat down.[6] Bandsmen's testimonies were fair game, of course, for band "pot shots" as the membership became more "sophisticated."

Take Charles Bearchell, for instance. As one of the few staff bandsmen besides "Old Lock" (John William Lock) willing to give a testimony extemporaneously during the mid-1920s, "Chuck" Bearchell was frequently "on call." Always ready with a polished, rather glib "answer to every occasion," his most infamous testimony has been retold by his brother. The Territorial Staff Band Sextet was travelling in Florida with Commissioner Estill and was in front of a huge crowd in Jacksonville, Fla., where a "new-fangled" public address system was in use. As Bearchell reached the climax of his eloquent sharing, he concluded with "and in the words of Jesus..." followed by a sudden silence. Turning to his fellow musicians, he simply asked, "What did Jesus say?" all the while being broadcast clearly to the thousands awaiting the conclusion of his remarks. The bandsmen, of course, were quick to "help out" by supplying suggestions. Bearchell must not have been able to get a clear answer, however, so he turned back to the throng and replied, "Never mind what Jesus said...."[7]

The band has certainly made progress in this area since then! Take Jacob A. Hohn's remembrance as a balance to the less serious aspect of band activity:

*Ah, yes, there are many, many memories, but the best are when the band concerned itself first with the Kingdom of God, not only in its music but in the way the bandsmen conducted themselves. For instance—the time we were in Cincinnati, Ohio, and many people came to the mercy seat for prayer. There was a ready, quick response from the bandsmen as many came to kneel with the seekers and to pray with them; or the time we were in Montreal, Canada, and Derek Smith tried to give his testimony, but ended up simply saying, "I can't adequately put into words what I want to say—let me play it for you:" then turning to us he said, "Put up 'Beautiful Christ.'" That morning, in the holiness meeting, his rendition of "Beautiful Christ" became a breathtaking confirmation of his own commitment, as well as ours, and left us all completely awed, soundless, and daring not nor wishing to stir as we too contemplated the magnitude of the Beautiful Christ. Then there was the time during our 1968 European trip. We were in Holland and had a little bit of time before a concert so Chuck West, Ken Davis, and myself decided to take a short walk. A young Dutch sailor approached us in quite a drunken condition. He recognized us as Americans and decided to try to practice his English on us. Soon he discovered Ken could speak Spanish. Rather than let it be simply a chance meeting, then and there, Ken, between Spanish and English proceeded to point this young man to God.[8]*

## A Family Affair

At least 22 families have had two generations represented in the band. The figure may be higher, but early records are not clear about certain family connections. At least 14 pairs of brothers have served side by side. Two families, Riley and Holz, have had three generations on the membership roles. A quick review of the roster in Appendix D confirms the close ties that many share.

There has been remarkable consistency in the band's membership over 100 years despite the initial response to dub the band as one plagued by frequent turnover. Actually, the roster is small for an organization 100 years old. Many members served several "tours of duty," their experience helping to lend maturity and sound judgment to the running of the band.

A proper balance between the experienced veteran and the enthusiastic rookie was given a boost with the Staff Band Scholarship program, realized in the early 1970s. This program alone has been not only an excellent source for band personnel but also a channel for the directing of young lives as explained by Bandsman William "Wiggy" Simons:

> I was in the band when the first students were brought in. While there were many pros and cons to this project, I feel it was well worthwhile. It is also very important to continue the use of young people in the New York Staff Band—providing, as the majority have, they continue to live up to the principles not only of the NYSB and The Salvation Army, but of those set forth for us by the Lord Jesus Christ. Naturally, this would also go for all members of the band—but the question asked was to share thoughts regarding the use of young people. We must always remember, young people attract young people! Follow through with a list of some of the young people who were in the NYSB through the scholarship fund—look where they are today! (without naming names!) I am sure the NYSB had a very important part in each of their lives...and they in countless lives where the NYSB ministered.[9]

Agreeing with Simons' assessment is Tom Scheibner of the Territorial Music Bureau:

> I am currently in my eighth year of service as a member of the New York Staff Band. I was appointed to the band in 1973 as a university student receiving a Staff Band scholarship, and remained in the band until 1977. I rejoined the band in 1981 and have had continuous service through the present date.
>
> This unique fellowship has greatly enhanced my spiritual growth and total overall musicianship. The latter is undoutedly due to the influence of Bandmaster Derek Smith, while the former is due to the influence of the bandmaster and many other officers and laymen that I have been privileged to come in contact with during my years in the band.[10]

Band friendships go beyond the fulfilling of band engagements. The men care for each other and their families. The support system is a genuine and warm one that few ever forget.

## Faithful In Small Things

During the mid-1950s, Richard Holz's NYSB played one Sunday morning in New Haven's First Congregational Church. To the bandsmen it seemed like just another church, but they faithfully and dutifully proclaimed the gospel through music. After the program, Miss Martha Curtis Miles spoke to the bandmaster about the band and its ministry. Soon she was a fan of the band, bringing her Milford, Conn., Ladies' Music Club to the band's annual festivals.

Whenever possible she submitted music to Holz for criticism and also heard the band when she could. Then, for several years Holz did not hear from Miss Miles. When he became the divisional commander for the Southern New England Division in 1963, Holz soon had contact with her again, this time via her will, that left nearly half a million dollars to the Army "to be used for alleviation of human suffering in the Southern New England area."[11]

As far as Holz knew, she was an older woman who had become interested in Salvation Army social service work through the music of the NYSB. The band's faithful service and its kindness, with no idea of the lady's financial background, had brought much-needed funds into the social service and welfare program in that region.[12]

Stories like these are not uncommon, even if the amounts of money differ, or if the effect of service brought about a different kind of reaction than a financial one. A bandsman's life is filled with moments of eternal significance. His "sacrifice of praise" is a daily offering that brings back rewards, if not directly to him, then to many in need. George Harvey referred to this in his *Book of Memories* letter:

> Let me hasten to say it was not only at the big events...that God used the band to bless. It was always exciting to visit the small corps and take part in their Sunday services. What a joy to meet and encourage the faithful soldiers who take their stand week after week, year after year.[13]

While many other men of "triumphant faith" could share further on a bandsman's service, I chose two men with equally notable careers in the band: Roland Schramm, who served 27 years, holding a variety of band officer positions, including executive officer, and Harold Banta, 26 years a staff bandsman and a keen member, as well, of several band boards. Each highlights a special aspect of banding that further supports the personal ministry each bandsman shares. Schramm has stated:

> Never in my wildest dreams did I ever think that I would be a member of such a distinguished group and for such a long period of time. I have served with many individuals, some of whom have long since gone to their eternal reward, but I can remember their enthusiasm, their dedication and the spirit in which they served and it still is an inspiration to me as I think back over the years....
>
> I have always been proud to be a member of the greatest fellowship of musicians in the Army world, and I continue to be interested in the personnel and the activities of the current group that makes up this unique organization. It is very satisfying to note the number of members through the years who have gone in to the School for Officers' Training to become officers.[14]

Banta evaluates his experience as follows:

> It would be impossible for me to describe the spiritual highlights of 26 years as a staff bandsman. Needless to say, they were the happiest years of an officership which was filled with happiness. The joys of fellowship with other bandsmen all around the world can never be described in words. The opportunities to witness for Christ in the multitude of billets over the years would never have been possible in any other situation and I praise and thank the Lord for those opportunities.[15]

# 15

## "Endless Day"
### (Lloyd Scott)

## A Second Century?

W est 14th Street, between Sixth and Seventh Avenues, colorfully portrays the ever-changing life of Manhattan. In 1986, as you walk towards the Army landmark, art-deco headquarters of the Eastern Territory, you are confronted with a bazaar of bargain goods, sidewalk hucksters, and a babel of voices in several languages, English being in the minority. In the center of the block, a Protestant evangelical mission, made up primarily of white, middle-class Salvationists, holds forth its spiritual warfare, "19th century brass bands" included! To the average passerby the contrast might seem severe; the term "anachronism" might readily be applied to the uniformed workforce that commutes to and from New Jersey and Long Island each day.[1]

NYSB Executive Officer Edward Fritz knows that the band, as the headquarters' mobile ministry unit, faces a problem of "relevance" daily in its activities and programs. How many of its members, for instance, can converse with the masses on 14th Street in Spanish? Is the band destined to play merely ceremonial roles or to continue just an entertainment function at "in-house" gatherings of "Sallies"?[2]

Certainly recent efforts in the band's musical repertoire have begun to bridge the gap. Contemporary styles can be adapted to a

237

brass and percussion ensemble with excellent results. Men like Stephen Bulla and William Broughton have readily contributed music of this nature. Peter Graham's recent selection, "Las Lluvias Grandes," which received such enthusiastic response from young people in Puerto Rico, March 1986, begins to address a repertoire need of significant proportion. Most traditional "Army" music, though relying as it does on a rich 19th-century hymn heritage, becomes useless in certain contexts without adequate explanation. Bruce Broughton, when asked about the difficult challenges facing Army composers who arrange "typical" hymn and song settings, stated the problem bluntly:

> The most difficult challenge will be that no one will want to sit long enough to hear this kind of introspective music. This music is too grounded in 19th-century style and practice to be very effective to any but the old and very conservative. For a generation raised on "Styx" and Dolly Parton, or even on Bartok or Stravinsky, this type of music is doomed.[3]

Doomed or not, this music still reaches many with the gospel, and the NYSB wisely balances its offerings! In present-day programs or open-air meetings, you can hear rock and jazz styles ("Gowans and Larsson Overture"), American Broadway and vaudeville ("It's Been a Wonderful Day"), television and movie sounds ("Suite of American Overtures"), and good old flag-waving Americana ("Stars and Stripes Forever"). Yet the band and its leaders cannot be complacent with these noble efforts; everyday they recognize the need to be more and more flexible in their musical ministry if they are to reach those they claim to serve.

In some ways, however, things never change, and on May 10, 1986, the NYSB repeated an historic function they used to fulfill many times in days gone by: they played for a wedding. Staff Bandsmen Peter Vaughan (son of former member Robert Vaughan) married Lorinda West (daughter of former member Charles West) at the Hempstead (N.Y.) Citadel Corps to the majestic sounds of "Elsa's Procession to the Cathedral" (Wagner/ Himes). During the "receiving line" formalities, the band furnished a sparkling mini-festival. In this instance the band provided for its own "family" in a fitting manner, in a way it had done for scores of couples through the years.

Striking a balance between routine "Army" functions and true, dynamic evangelism will be the test for the future NYSB. More aggressive pursuit of media presentations, both on television and radio—areas in which the band once had a prominent role—should help. This presents considerable, but not insurmountable, difficulties, both financially and administratively, particularly if the events are of "special nature." Edward Fritz proclaims the band's willingness to take on a host of exciting media offers, all within the time constraints that must be observed with such a diverse band filled with men holding considerable responsibilities in wide-ranging aspects of the Army's work.

## Administration and Personnel: Vision and Challenge

The NYSB of today is an efficiently administered organization. Each member applies for band membership either through an official application or by officer appointment. Upon acceptance to the band, which includes an audition with the bandmaster, the new member is issued a copy of the *New York Staff Band Manual* and told by the executive officer to carefully review its wealth of information and exhortation.

There are other forms—NYSB Scholarship Grant Application, Proposed Engagement Questionnaire (seating charts and menu suggestions)—and "Procedure of Acceptance of Engagements" (procedural guidelines) that make for a smooth operation.

The band now rehearses in its own band room, on the mezzanine level of THQ, complete with library, instrument-uniform lockers, and memorabilia showcases. The band board consists of officers and laymen who work at THQ.

The most difficult problem facing administration is staffing the band with capable, competent personnel via officer appointments and lay employees. The executive officer must be sensitive to the overall career of an officer when a Staff Band appointment is contemplated. Fortunately, in recent years morale has been excellent in the group and only people who *want* to serve need be involved. The executive officer receives letters from officers and laymen who request consideration for membership.[4]

Good communication exists currently between upper administration—the territorial commander and the chief secretary—and the band board. How fortunate the band has been throughout its history to have almost unanimous support from succeeding national and territorial commanders. This open dialogue, much more balanced now than perhaps it used to be, is essential for an efficiently and humanely run band. A territorial commander's genuine interest in the Staff Band is treasured!

With this support in hand, the excellent position that the NYSB finds itself in as it enters its centenary year is in large part due to the hard work of its executive officers, bandmasters, and band board officers within the past 30 years. The modern, internationally recognized NYSB has made steady progress in each area of band activity since the mid-1950s. Each succeeding triumph has been of a higher caliber than the one preceding it. Peek years of 1960, 1968, and 1982 saw a band becoming more and more refined and polished in its musical presentations. Recordings reviewed over this same period provide objective data on this gradual improvement. From today's perspective the future of the band appears to be a happy one.

The band is not without its critics, however. From as early as its first few years, complaints were lodged that men were given jobs merely because they were musicians. In 1888, *The War Cry* noted that some NHQ "people tell them [NYSB] they do not work."[5] Many criticize the band's spiritual state; by this they mean certain individuals of whom they disapprove. The band's history is filled with these discontented responses to a genuinely positive activity. Personnel has always been the major difficulty for the band, and, if in its haste to fill the ensemble, the band board has occasionally appointed less than angelic, wholly-sanctified saints, the Kingdom of God was advanced despite these "hangers on."[6]

Other, more legitimate criticism has been leveled at the band when its members have not always taken leadership positions in local corps, a task considered fundamental in the design of the band's founder, Ballington Booth. An auxiliary/captain, former Staff Bandsman Terry Camsey has neatly summarized the best expectations of a staff bandsman's role as a local soldier:

> For me staff banding has always been something that I felt to be in addition to corps band membership and I still feel that membership should be an "addition to" not "instead of" corps bandsmanship.
>
> I have also felt that it is easy to be very selfish and enjoy the membership entirely for oneself. My conviction is that it is something that, once learned and experienced, should be shared with others who might be inspired. This was my reason for leaving the ISB and coming to this country.
>
> Banding has, in my life, been one of the influences that has gradually led me to being what I am today, an officer totally

*committed to the work of the Army and to extending its efficiency and influence in reaching and saving lost souls. Music is a vital aid in achieving this end.*[7]

When the band was filled exclusively with officers, and was small, problems of this type were scarce. Early in its history, however, personnel/staffing problems, plus a desire to increase the size of the band, had Ballington Booth advertising in *The War Cry* for Salvationist brass musicians to fill employee positions at headquarters. With it came the usual pressures of job versus band.

Department heads have always complained about lost work time. The men have always been overscheduled, and band leaders always feel that upper administration does not do enough to defend the band's position and health. We cannot ignore the serious plight of band wives and children, who have always been abandoned during Staff Band duty. Our modern, anxiety-ridden age has nothing on the old days in that last category. In a June 5, 1897, *War Cry,* a reporter, when asking a toddler to identify or describe his staff bandsman-father, received the reply "...the man who comes here Sunday."

These are criticisms and problems that need to be addressed. Sentimental waving of the Army flag won't dispel these real issues. Army leadership does try to deal with these questions. When I spoke to the Staff Band and their spouses at their 1986 retreat, I sensed a genuine desire to enter into the second century with both forward-looking vision and down-to-earth pragmatism. One thing was certain: their spiritual commitment, despite the complexities of the lifestyle these men and women share in metropolitan New York, was solid. Their music-making keeps them united. As Ron Waiksnoris told a *New York Times* reporter, "There is holding power to the music; there are many of us who have gone through questioning times and wondered about our commitment, but you get the music in your blood, and often it carries you through."[8]

## The Future

In planning for its 100th Anniversary, the Staff Band Board has projected many fine events and projects. Many composers, for instance, have been approached about submitting a specific type of composition for the band's centenary. James Curnow is completing rhapsodic variations on "Lobe Den Herren"; Terry Camsey is submitting a cornet ensemble; Ronald Holz is providing a postlude on "Lead On, O King Eternal." Other composers range from Bruce and Bill Broughton to Brenton Broadstock of Australia.[9] The return of territorial music events, such as the June 1986 Music Ministries Weekend, portend well for the reinvolvement of the NYSB as musical standard-setter within the Eastern Territory.

A U.S.A. tour heads the billing for the band's centenary year, along with the March 1987 anniversary festival and reunion. Already the next several years' calendar is filling up with corps visits across the territory and "outside" invitations, like the March 1987 (tentative) Music Teachers' National Association Convention. The second century seems to bring a continued, active ministry for the band.

Hopeful signs of spiritual and musical leadership renewal are evident in the current band. The "Messengers of Peace" Session of Cadets (1985-1987) includes two former staff bandsmen, James Kisser and Mark Tillsley, men of professional training (masters degree level) which the "new" Army desperately needs. Bass Trombonist Darren Mudge is a member of the "Messengers of Joy" Session of Cadets (1986-88) and Flugelhornist Donald Spencer has begun filing his preliminary application for training. Two staff bandsmen head up the divisional music departments in Greater New York (Gordon Ward) and New Jersey (Jeffrey Schultz) while several of the fine corps music ensembles in the area are conducted by staff bandsmen, including, besides the above-named, B/M Thomas Mack, Hempstead Citadel; and B/M Vic Gilder, New York Central Citadel.

The men of the band are not complacent about their heritage. They, and alumni of the band across America, realize their critical responsibility for reproducing themselves, developing a whole new generation of sacred musicians. Harold Burgmayer, a product of the NYSB scholarship program and now music director for the Eastern Pennsylvania and Delaware Division sounded a challenge to his comrades in his *Book of Memories* letter that rings true in the context of this speculative chapter:

FROM: Harold Burgmayer

RE: Staff Band Tenure

I served in the New York Staff Band from January of 1974 to June of 1977.

242

*I served in the New York Staff Band while engaged in a grueling academic schedule at the Cooper Union studying architecture. The Wednesday afternoon rehearsals, only a 15-minute walk from my architecture studio, served as an exciting and fulfilling departure from my studies, if only for a few hours.*

*Looking back, the Staff Band provided me with an important overview into the old and new brass repertoire of a standard and variety I had not known at my home corps in Levittown, Pennsylvania, or as a member of the PENDEL Brass. Bandmaster Derek Smith's band training concepts remain with me as basic to developing an ensemble sound and technique. While in the Staff Band, I began to consider the future of Army banding, especially whether our programs are relevant to attracting folks to the gospel. Weakly attended open-airs, clinics and concerts continued to bear out my suspicions that we should be considering new venues of expression. This question still looms unsettled and even in my present position as music director of the PENDEL Brass and Singers, I still wonder about new program ideas and formats. Nevertheless, despite the questions, my Staff Band experience resides in my memory as rich and meaningful musical memory.*

*Since my departure from the New York scene, I believe the Staff Band has developed and matured musically and spiritually for which many of us struggling to start new musicians are grateful. Looking to the future, I would encourage the leadership of the territory and the Staff Band to consider, not only the past and the noble tradition of this important musical aggregation, but also a far-reaching vision of the future.*[10]

When the band and their wives gathered for the band retreat in January 1986, I perceived throughout that weekend an open desire and fervor among the entire group to make the band's ministry meaningful in this present age. They openly responded with genuine enthusiasm to challenges Commissioner Orval Taylor and I presented. There was no lack of fellowship and humor, so long-standing a part of this band's experience. Surveying this particular band, and a hundred before it, I marvel at the consistent leadership it has provided The Salvation Army both in its officers and its laymen. These men have been a large part of the shaping force that gives the Army in this part of the world such a positive role in society. This is not an overstatement, either; if anything, a case could be made that the personal, musical, and spiritual disciplines many have received within the ranks of the band have been of incalculable value in the overall development of The Salvation Army in the United States.

243

While the Male Chorus sang Stephen Bulla's "He Walks With God" during the retreat holiness meeting, my own spirit was renewed as I remembered, even within my own family, four generations that were connected with the gospel mission of this band. When the board honored that mission and its leaders provided the necessary vision, the Kingdom of God was advanced. The closing song of the weekend, by Elton Trueblood, contains a verse that struck me as a most appropriate one for this time-honored ensemble:

> *Thou, who still a sword delivers,*
> *Rather than a placid peace;*
> *With Thy sharpened word disturb us*
> *From complacency release!*
> *Save us now from satisfaction,*
> *When we privately are free*
> *Yet are undisturbed in spirit,*
> *By our brother's misery.*

In 1887 Ballington Booth had sound reasons for forming a "staff band." The humble, seven-strong ensemble that first blared salvation music on the streets of Brooklyn has become a globe-encircling brass phenomenon hailed from Sydney to Stockholm. Yet how remarkably similar are the functions of the 1987 band to that of a century ago. Styles change, cultural fashions shift, but this band has maintained and is maintaining a flexible posture, as flexible as its brass and vocal medium allow, to meet the needs that confront it. Fortunate in musical, spiritual, and ecclesiastical leadership, this band of musicians, this fraternity, now numbering over 500, have been loyal, faithful stewards of Ballington's vision. They have been the heralds of Christ's victory over sin, hate and want wherever they were sent to combat these with their music. God grant them the strength, the wisdom, and the courage to continue that noble task. Praise God that the New York Staff Band and Male Chorus still strives to play and sing, as their old banner proclaimed, "For God and America's Salvation"; for the current band, we change the motto to read, "For God and the World's Salvation!" How faithful each bandsman is to that challenge is what will count in the final analysis.

15-1.    *Holz attempting to control band dynamics.*

15-2.    *"Art" Moulton, who was a "star" on the Great Britain Tour (Kitching wanted to keep him!), from behind his bass drum.*

# EPILOGUE

## "Hope Variations"
(Brian Bowen)

## Bandmaster Brian A. Bowen
## 1986-

At the conclusion of his breath-taking performance of "Song of Exultation" (Bearcroft), Philip Smith walked across the stage to embrace his father, Staff Bandmaster Derek Smith, while an enthralled audience attending the climax festival of the June 13-15, 1986 Music Ministries Weekend of the Eastern Territory greeted soloist, bandmaster, and Staff Band with thunderous acclaim. One of Derek's last triumphs with his band, it was also a tender, personal moment. Family, friends, and staff bandsmen also paid tribute to his 14 years of outstanding leadership during a breakfast held in his honor the next morning. Among the guests attending the informal gathering was B/M Brian Bowen, the appointed successor to Staff Bandmaster Smith.

Since 1961, Brian Bowen has directed the corps band in Staines, England, a town on the Thames River just outside central London. His excellent brass and vocal compositions are played throughout the Army world; he was for years a member of the International Music Editorial Department of The Salvation Army. At the time of his appointment to the NYSB, Bowen was a music editor for Eulenburg Edition, a music publishing firm. His consistent success with the Staines Band over a period of 25 years portends well for the NYSB. (During May 1986, Bowen led his corps band on a 10-day tour of the Netherlands, West Germany, and Denmark.) His solid, practical experience and his professional expertise, backed up by his accomplishments as a Fellow of Trinity College of Music, will be most welcome on this side of the Atlantic.

If B/M Smith's retirement and B/M Bowen's appointment seemed sudden and unexpected to some, the decision to allow women in the New York Staff Band starting with the fall 1986 season was marvelled at by many who considered the band one of the last bastions of all-male comradeship. The experiment has proved successful in the Chicago Staff Band, however, and very few brass bands in North America still maintain a sex barrier. Since the decision would not be precedent-setting in any event (Remember Felicia Gircopazzi annd Norma Thompson from the 1890s?) the band board has quietly begun the work necessary to implement this decision, including a separate locker area off the present band room, and new uniforms for the proposed new members, Lori Jackson (daughter of former Staff Bandsman Fred Jackson Jr.) and Captain Lauren Garell.

Steadfastness coupled with adaptability—this combination has been a hallmark of the NYSB for 100 years. There should be no doubts as to the prospects for success in the next century.

# APPENDIX A

## A Chronology of Major Events and Engagements of The New York Staff Band and Male Chorus

| Abbreviations used: | |
|---|---|
| Anniv. | Anniversary |
| CMT | Centennial Memorial Temple |
| DHQ | Divisional Headquarters |
| Div. | Division, Divisional |
| F.E.T. | Friday Evening at the Temple |
| MC | Male Chorus |
| M.E.N.C. | Music Educators National Conference |
| NGB | National Guards Band |
| NHQ | National Headquarters |
| NSB | National Staff Band |
| N.Y. | New York |
| NYC | New York City |
| NYSB | New York Staff Band |
| S.A. | Salvation Army |
| S/L | Songster Leader |
| Terr. | Territory, Territorial |
| TSB | Territorial Staff Band |

**1887** **June 18:** First appearance of Staff Band, Brooklyn Lyceum, 7th Anniv. Congress

**July 9-10:** With Marshal Ballington Booth, Scranton, Pa.

**Aug. 13-14:** Asbury Park and Ocean Grove, N.J., with Marshal Booth

**Oct. 1-2:** With Major Keates (chief of staff) and B/M Keep, Rockville, Conn.

**Dec. 8-12:** National Staff Councils at Brooklyn Lyceum; band of 7, B/M Wray

**1888**    Many local corps engagements and rallies including Harlem, Brooklyn, Paterson, Men's Training Home, New York No. 1, and New York No. 4

**May:** With Marshal Booth in Albany, N.Y.; band under Wray

**July 21-22:** Cohoes, N.Y.

**Aug. 11-12:** Asbury Park, N.J. (also June 30-July 1)

**Oct.:** Three-day campaign in New Brunswick, N.J.

**Nov.:** Trumble and Duncan join NHQ staff; recruited by Ballington Booth

**1889**    **Apr. 3-4:** Household Troops Band (from London, England; B/M Appleby) visit to NYC; HTB 27 members, NSB 13 members

**May:** Volunteer Brigade Band (#2 at NHQ) formed under Major Aspinall and B/M Duncan

**June:** First of many weddings that band participates in— Captains Faulkner and Wylie

**July 20-22:** Old Orchard Beach, Maine, Camp Meetings, with Ballington Booth

**Sept. 2-27:** Volunteer Brigade Band on extensive tour

**Oct.:** Mr. Montigani of Brooklyn presents National Staff Band with parade banner

**1890**    **Feb.:** "Rehearsals under tutelage of Secretary Miles"

**May 17-19:** Boston, Mass., and Fall River, Mass., trip with Ballington Booth; B/M Miles

**Aug. 9-10:** With "Hindoo Party," New Brunswick, N.J.

**Sept.:** Miles exhausted, gets extended furlough; band led by B/M Duncan

**Oct. 3-13:** Tour with Ballington Booth including Wilmington, Del., Baltimore, Md., and Harrisburg, Pa.

**Nov. 9:** Asbury Park Methodist Church (also in Summer 1890)

**Nov.:** Interstate Congress in Association Hall, 23rd St., NYC (17 members)

**1891** **Mar. 14-Apr. 27:** Extensive tour through states of Del., Pa., N.J., Md., and N.Y.

**Aug. 22:** National Guards Band is formed, B/M Duncan, for National Bldg. Fund

**Sept.-Dec.:** Guards Band on tour throughout eastern seaboard

**Dec. (late):** Duncan and Trumble transfered to Chicago

**1892** **Jan.-May:** Guards Band continues tour, directed by B/M Bridgen

**May 17-18:** Congress in NYC; NSB and NGB combined

**July-Aug.:** Guards Band has several engagements with Ballington (Asbury Park, N.J., etc.)

**Sept.:** National Staff Band reorganized under B/M Trumble

**Nov. 21-23:** Continental Congress, NYC; Trumble leads massed band of 150, representing bands from six cities

**1893** Not many engagements; band poorly staffed—only 8 members in May

**July 27, 31:** Prohibition Park Camp Meetings on Staten Island, N.Y.

**Nov. 12-18:** Columbian Congress, NYC; band at 13 members

**Dec. 15:** At Cooper Union Hall with Ballington Booth

**1894** **Jan.-Apr.:** Many local engagements, primarily for Self-Denial and bldg. funds

**May 15-17:** Congress in NYC

**Oct. 20-27:** American Jubilee Congress, NYC, with General William Booth

**Oct.-Nov.:** Tour with General Booth as far as Baltimore

**1895** **Feb. 24-25:** Farewell meetings for General Booth, NYC

**Apr.:** NHQ moves from Reade St. to 14th St.

**June:** Dedication of new Memorial Bldg. NHQ during Thanksgiving Congress

**July 24:** "Concert" at Harlem Corps

**1896 Jan.:** Ballington Booth resigns

**Mar.:** NSB plays for Evangeline Booth's welcome but B/M Trumble resigns

**Apr. 7:** NSB plays in Carnegie Hall for Commander Booth-Tucker's welcome

**May:** Local engagements with Booth-Tucker

**June-Aug.:** "Victory Boys Brigade" fulfills NSB functions

**Nov.-Dec.:** Major Halpin leads a NHQ "Officers Band"

**1897 Feb. 22:** Washington's Birthday program at Memorial Hall, NHQ; NSB reorganized, in new uniforms, directed by B/M Charles Anderson

**Mar.:** "Festival" at New York No. 9 Corps (Bowery)

**Apr.-June:** Band busy in local engagements and festivals

**Summer:** Band under Halpin while Anderson is in Europe; band participates in several "boat excursions" including one to Long Branch and Asbury Park, N.J.

**Sept.:** Prohibition Park Campaign and Central Division's Congress

**Oct.:** "Foreign-Speaking" Congress, NYC

**1898 Mar.:** Musical Department established under Ensign Charles Straubel; first band publications available by Apr.

**Apr. 23-25:** Meetings in NYC with General Booth; Straubel is B/M till Aug.

**Oct.:** Commissioning at Memorial Hall, NSB on duty (not first for band; at this time there were two commissionings for new officers each year)

**Dec. 13:** Great Salvationist Rally in Carnegie Hall; "Famed" Staff Band gives half-hour concert in pre-program

**1899 Feb. 4-5:** Band in New Haven, Conn., as part of "Red Crusade" Spiritual Campaign

**May 27-28:** Campaign to Poughkeepsie, N.Y., with S. L. Brengle

**Aug.:** Asbury Park weekend with Booth-Tuckers

**Oct.-Nov.:** Wed. evening holiness meetings (continues for many years)

**Dec. 25:** Feeding of 20,000 at Madison Square Garden; NSB and NHQ Staff Orchestra (Dr. Nice) provide music—becomes a regular function for band

**1900 Feb. 9-15:** 20th Anniv Congress, NYC; NSB and NHQ Orchestra on duty

**Apr.:** Junior Brass Band formed at NHQ

**July:** Dedication of "Salvation Navy" Ship *The Salvationist*

**Aug.:** "Asbury Park" auditorium with Booth-Tucker

**Sept.:** Memorial services and fund drive related to Galveston, Texas, disaster and Cincinnati Slum Nursery fire

**1901 May 4-5:** Eastern N.Y. trip

**Sept. 28-29:** Newburgh, N.Y., trip

**Nov.:** Continental Campaign Band ("Special Staff Band") formed from NSB; small NSB still to function in NYC area under Gooding

**Nov.'01-Jan.'02:** Continental Campaign Band tours with Commander Booth-Tucker across the country

**1902 May 21-28:** Pan-American Congress, NYC; Mayor Seth Low has band play on City Hall steps

**June:** Brooklyn Sunday School Association Parade (a regular event for many years)

**Aug.:** Asbury Park weekend

**Oct. 4-9:** Meetings in NYC, with General William Booth

**1903 Feb. 25-Mar. 3:** Congress in NYC with General William Booth

**May 16-17:** Catskill, N.Y.

**June 27-28:** Dover, N.J.

**July 11-12:** Asbury Park, N.J. (also Aug. 22-23)

**Nov.:** Service, funeral, and interment of Consul Emma Booth-Tucker (with Canadian Staff Band)

**Dec. 15:** Festival of Music at New York No. 1 Corps

**1904** **June 13:** Pre-Congress Musical Festival in Carnegie Hall

**June 14-22:** Ocean voyage on *Carpathia*

**June-July:** International Congress, London, England

**Nov. 15:** Farewell meetings for Commander Booth-Tucker

**Dec. 6:** Welcome meeting for Commander Evangeline Booth

**1905** **Jan.:** NSB in Philadelphia with Evangeline Booth

**Mar. 25-28:** 25th Anniv. Congress, NYC; band accompanies Evangeline Booth in her dramatic presentation "The Shepherd"

Band involved throughout the year in "Siege" spiritual campaign, including weekends at Easton, Pa.; Jersey City, N.J.; and Schenectady, N.Y.

**1906** **Jan.:** Band given new crimson and black uniforms for Evangeline's lecture/demonstration series at Carnegie Hall

**Apr.:** Binghamton, N.Y., weekend and Union Square (NYC) Fund-Raiser for San Francisco earthquake relief

**May 11-13:** Congress in the NYC Hippodrome

**July:** Elmira and Binghamton, N.Y.

**Nov.:** Dedication of Mount Vernon, N.Y., Corps

**1907** **May:** Robert Griffith as B/M

**June:** Dover, N.J.

**Nov. 2-9:** NYC Congress with General William Booth

**1908** **Mar.:** Dedication of Dover, N.J., Corps bldg.

**Apr.:** Festival of Music at the Cherry Street Settlement

**May:** Camden, N.J.

**Nov.:** Plainfield, N.J.

**1909 Feb. 13-14:** Bridgeport/Ansonia, Conn.

**Aug. 21-Sept. 6:** New York State and Canada (Toronto) Tour

**Nov.:** "Popular (POPS) Tuesday Night" series begins at Memorial Hall; NSB largely responsible for program

**Nov.:** Dedication of Arlington, N.J., Corps bldg.

**1910 Apr. 16-17:** Perth Amboy, N.J.

**Apr. 23-24:** Scranton, Pa.

**Sept.:** Tent Rally Evangelistic Services in Union Square, NYC

**Nov.:** "Water-Wagon Day" Parade and "Ex-Boozers" Demonstrations, NYC

**Dec.:** NSB plays at the "Tombs" NYC Prison for 600 inmates

**Dec. 31:** Great "Watchnight" Parade with NSB, New York No. 3, New York No. 4, and Newark No. 1 Bands

**1911 Feb.:** Band featured in Chapman-Alexander Revival Meetings in Brooklyn

**Mar. 6-13:** Commander E. Booth's Sale, at NHQ; opened by John Wanamaker, band provides music for four evenings

**Nov. 14:** Carnegie Hall spectacular, "The Living Tableau"

**Dec.:** Noon-time open-airs on Wall Street and Tombs Prison again

**Dec. 14:** NSB has "Thanksgiving Social" dinner with wives

**1912 Mar.:** B/M Griffith resigns

**June 5:** First "Annual" Concert, under B/M Darby

**Sept.:** Memorial services for General William Booth in NYC and Ocean Grove, N.J.

**Oct.:** "Tag Day" for raising money for Training College (first of many)

**Dec. 28:** NSB is first band of any sort allowed to play for inmates of Sing Sing Prison (becomes an annual event)

**1913** **Jan. 30:** Montclair, N.J.

**May 31-June 3:** Central Congress and "Second" Annual Festival of NSB, dressed in red and white tunics

**June 14:** Sing Sing Prison

**July:** Tour of Adirondacks area

**Nov. 19-25:** New York Congress with General Bramwell Booth

**1914** **Jan. 17-18:** Waterbury, Conn.

**Feb. 19:** NYC "Slums" Concert

**Mar. 4:** "Annual" Concert at Memorial Hall

**May 2-3:** Scranton, Pa.; band sings in a coal mine

**June-July:** International Congress, London, England, including concert at Buckingham Palace

**1915** **June:** Central Province Bandsmen's Councils, NYC

**June 26-27:** Easton, Pa., weekend

**Sept.:** Billy Sunday Campaign, Paterson, N.J.

**Oct.:** Friday noon concerts at NHQ for "working people in the area" (till Dec. 17)

**1916** **Feb.:** Concert in Weehawken, N.J., Hamilton #3 School

**Apr.:** National Staff Songsters formed under Darby's leadership, making their debut in May congress (5/9-14). (Group exists until 1932)

**June 19:** Benefit concert for Life-Saving Scout Encampment Fund; six bands participate; Commander Booth plays her harp in public; New York No. 2 Band under the direction of "Brother Erik Leidzen"

**Dec. 4:** Annual concert raises $2,250, enough to clear band's debts still held from International Congress

**1917** **Apr. 19-24:** Tour of upstate N.Y. and Canada

**May 11-16:** Eastern Congress in Philadelphia

**June:** Many engagements, including patriotic rallies, Billy Sunday Tabernacle, etc.

**Sept.-Dec.:** Band greatly reduced in size due to military enlistments

**1918 Apr. 5:** Liberty Loan Campaign launched in NYC from Times Square at midnight; NSB is featured band

Frequent appearances in Liberty Loan parades and related functions throughout 1918

**Nov. 11:** Spontaneous NYC "Thanksgiving" Procession led by Evangeline Booth and NSB

**1919 Mar.:** Band featured in Washington, D.C., at parade for President Wilson and war heroes; also engagements in Newport News, Va.

**May:** Visit to Richmond, Va., and Washington, D.C., with Commander Booth

**Sept. 17:** Pershing Parade in Washington, D.C.

**Oct. 15-19:** Eastern Territorial Congress, NYC

**Nov.:** Carbondale, Pa.

**1920 Mar. 20-21:** 40th Anniv. Weekend in Philadelphia, Pa.

**Oct. 9-10:** With Commander Booth in Southern New England

**Nov. 6:** Concert at Ellis Island for 6,000

**Nov. 11:** NYC's Armistice Day Parade

**1921 Feb. 15-20:** NSB takes over New York No. 5 (Bronx) Corps for a week

**Apr. 6-10:** Territorial Social Congress, Washington, D.C., (band is now frequently called the Territorial Staff Band [TSB] but also called National Staff Band [NSB] up till 1927)

**Aug.:** Grand motorcade through New England en route to Old Orchard Beach Camp Meetings, Maine

**Nov. 30-Dec. 4:** Eastern Territorial Congress, in Washington, D.C.

**1922**  **Mar. 11-12:** Wilmington, Del.

**May 20-22:** Western Pennsylvania tour; first radio broadcast for band from Emory M.E. Church and Pittsburgh Theater, Pittsburgh

**May 27-30:** Eastern Ohio tour

**June 16-18:** New England tour

**Nov. 4-8:** Territorial Congress, NYC, with Memorial Festival for "Gus" Hillstrom

**Fall:** First recording (permanent) made by band by request of the Aeolian Co. of NYC, on the Vocalion label

**1923**  **Jan. 27-31:** Philadelphia Congress; TSB broadcasts from Wanamaker Store

**Feb. 16:** Annual Festival broadcast on WOR (Newark)

**Mar.:** Part of band with Evangeline Booth at Princeton Univ.; TSB Quartet travels with her to Florida; second record for Aeolian is made

**Sept.:** Band on duty for Labor Day at Star Lake Camp, Bloomingdale, N.J.; earlier in summer TSB ensemble had played at camp's official dedication

**Nov. 19:** New York Area Music Festival (part of Regional Congress)

**1924**  **Jan. 5-7:** North and South Carolina tour, including concert at Billy Sunday Tabernacle in Charlotte for 7,000

Tours in spring through Western N.Y., Eastern Ohio, and Eastern N.Y.

**Oct. 18-19:** Weekend in Washington, D.C., which includes playing for President and Mrs. Calvin Coolidge

**Nov. 21-26:** Territorial Congress, NYC, including large music festivals

**1925**  **Jan.-Feb.:** TSB Sextet with Commissioner Estill in Florida

**Mar.-Apr.:** Several engagements with Commander Booth; she presents "Rags" with band back-up in Brooklyn (Academy of Music), Trenton, N.J., and Baltimore, Md.

**May 9-11:** Trip to Pittsburgh, Pa., for dedication of new DHQ

**Dec.:** TSB on WEAF Radio with Dr. S. Parkes Cadman, Brooklyn Bedford Ave. YMCA; estimated listening audience of two million

**1926 Apr. 24-29:** General Bramwell Booth's visit to NYC

**May 28-31:** Eastern N.Y. tour under DB/M Sheppard; Darby in England for funeral

**June 5-6:** Scranton, Pa., dedication of DHQ bldg.

**Sept. 25:** TSB plays at Herbert Booth's funeral; one month later at Commissioner Estill's funeral

**1927 Jan.:** 22 officers from NYC are farewelled to new Southern THQ in Atlanta

**Feb. 19-22:** Tour through Southeast Pa., Delaware, Baltimore, Md., and Washington, D.C.

Continued active service in local engagements, broadcasts, and programs supporting Commander Evangeline Booth

**Nov. 12-17:** Territorial Congress in NYC, including massive music festival, 11/13

**1928 Jan.:** Edgar Arkett appointed territorial secretary for bands and songsters (he releases national band journal and first *American Festival Series* issue by July)

**Feb. 6:** Concert in Memorial Hall (Arkett's official inauguration)

**Apr. 19-23:** Western N.Y. tour

**Apr. 28-29:** Bandsmen's Councils in Central Province (NYC)

**July 14-17:** Eastern N.Y. tour

**Oct. 11-14:** Centennial Motor Campaign (Pa., Del., N.J.)

**Nov. 12, 23:** Final festivals in the old Memorial Hall, 122 W. 14th St., NYC

**1929** New THQ under construction

**May 10-12:** Three-day motorcade through Western Pa. with Commissioner Richard Holz

**June 3:** NYC Town Hall Festival of Music by TSB and Male Chorus, Staff Songsters, Cadets Band and Chorus

**Oct. 12-13:** Philadelphia's 50th Anniv. weekend

**1930** **Jan.:** The "Metropolitan Ensemble," a group of nine staff bandsmen, is formed under Erik Leidzen's direction

**Mar.:** Battery Park, 50th Anniv. Reenactment of Railton's Landing

**May 16-22:** National Salvation Army Congress, NYC, including National Festival of Praise and Song at the Metropolitan Opera House and Festival of Bands and Songster Brigades in the 71st Regiment Armoury (estimated musicians for the congress, 4,000; largest attendance, over 8,000)

**1931** **Apr.:** Darby resigns; Sheppard appointed B/M

**May 1-5:** Congress in NYC with General Edward Higgins

**June 3-15:** Commander Evangeline Booth and TSB on Grand Motorcade Campaign throughout Eastern Territory

**July 2-5:** "Mini" Motorcade through Eastern N.Y.

**1932** **Apr.:** Visit of Montreal Citadel (Canada) Band to NYC for Easter Weekend; shared programs with TSB

First of many programs at the Gold Dust Lodge, 40 Corlears St., NYC

**May:** Launching of United Appeal at Metropolitan Opera House; E. F. Goldman leads Army bands

**Nov. 4:** Friday Evening at the Temple (F.E.T.) begins (Staff Band not on duty)

**Nov.:** William Broughton replaces Sheppard as B/M

**Dec.:** Radio broadcast series begins on WRNY, featuring TSB

**1933** **Jan.:** Arkett farewelled; Broughton assumes duties as territorial music secretary

**Feb. 3:** "Grand Soiree de Repertoire" Festival at F.E.T. includes TSB

**Mar.:** John Allan appointed "spiritual leader" of TSB

**May 26:** F.E.T. Finale "Ensemble" Festival, with E. F. Goldman and Evangeline Booth; confrontation between Evangeline Booth and Erik Leidzen takes place on stage at close of concert

**June 1:** Leidzen removed from payroll of the Central Province as divisional bandmaster

**Nov.:** Portion of F.E.T. now broadcast on WRNY instead of Tuesday night program

**1934** **Jan.:** WRNY series dicontinued

**May:** TSB begins broadcasting on WABC, part of CBS network; regular series begins in July

**Nov. 1:** Farewell extravaganza for General Evangeline Booth at Madison Square Garden

**1935** **Feb.:** Male Chorus reactivated under William Slater

**FEb.:** TSB Sextet in Montreal (also in Washington, D.C., in June)

**Mar. 10:** Prison Sunday visits (radio programs now on Thursday)

**Sept.:** Broughton farewells; George Granger now B/M

**Nov. 1:** F.E.T. launched for third year, with TSB as duty band for first time

**Dec.:** Christmas broadcasts on WOR, WABC, and WMCA

**1936** **Feb. 14:** Annual Festival, part of F.E.T.

**May:** F.E.T. Finale Festival with Olin Downes, *New York Times*

**Aug. 8-10:** Ocean Grove, N.J., weekend, with Saturday night concert in the auditorium, first of a long annual series

**Aug.:** Star Lake Musicamp, with staff bandsmen serving as basis for instruction staff (Note: in 1935 a "Bands men's Camp and Councils" was held Aug. 28 to Sept. 2 also with staff bandsmen involved)

**Dec.:** Broadcasts on WABC, WNYC; Ellis Island Concert; New York Stock Exchange Carol Sing

**1937** **Jan. 18:** United Songsters Festival at Brooklyn Citadel; Male Chorus featured

**Feb. 26:** Annual Festival

**May 27-June 2:** Canadian tour

**Aug.7-9:** Ocean Grove weekend, band in red tunics again

**Nov. 6-10:** Eastern Territorial Congress, NYC, with General Evangeline Booth, Eric Ball; music festival at Brooklyn Academy of Music

**Dec.:** WABC-CBS radio series discontinued

**1938** **Apr. 15-18:** Dovercourt Citadel Band (Toronto, Canada) visits NYC for Easter weekend; joint programs with TSB

**May 20:** United Songsters Festival with TSB accompanying B/M Thomas Giles, cornet soloist from England

**May 28-29:** Cambridge Citadel, Mass., 50th Anniversary

**June 10-12:** Southeast Pa. tour

**June 18-20:** Upstate N.Y. tour

**Aug. 8-10:** Ocean Grove weekend, with General Edward Higgins (R)

**1939** **Apr.:** Greater N.Y. Federation of Churches sponsors Sunrise Service in Central Park; John Allan serves as song leader and TSB provides music

**May 4:** F.E.T. Finale Festival with Westminster College Choir

**May-June:** Concerts at the New York World's Fair—5/13, 6/17, 6/24; S.A. Day at the Fair is held on Sept. 27

**Aug. 5-7:** Ocean Grove weekend with Commissioner William McIntyre

**1940** **Mar. 31:** Festival in Arlington, N.J.

**May:** F.E.T. Staff Band Night, with Darby as guest speaker

**June 26:** N.Y. World's Fair Concert; S.A. Day was held Sept. 25

**Aug. 3-4:** Ocean Grove weekend with General Evangeline Booth

**Fall:** Two 78 rpm recordings made, Columbia 501-502; John Allan to U.S. Chaplain Service; as in other years, normal F.E.T. involvement and Christmas activities

**1941** **Mar.:** First staff bandsmen now in U.S. Army—William Perrett and Pershing Flanders

**Mar.:** Southern New England tour

**Apr.:** Concert at Fort Dix, N.J.

**June:** USO Drive launched at Waldorf-Astoria Hotel (TSB prominent role)

**Aug. 2-3:** Ocean Grove weekend

**Dec. 18-22:** Territorial Staff Band Jubilee Celebration, including Christmas service at Women's Detention Home, Carol Service at Wall Street, parade to City Hall and reception with Mayor Fiorello H. LaGuardia, Jubilee broadcast on WNYC, and Grand Festival 12/19, sponsored by The Salvation Army Association of New York

**1942** **Jan. 3:** Jubilee Reunion Dinner

**Apr. 4-6:** Easter weekend in Philadelphia and Atlantic City, N.J.

**June:** "Patriotic Community Song Fest" at Brooklyn Borough Hall

**Aug. 1-2:** Ocean Grove weekend

**Oct. 30-Nov. 3:** Officers' Councils with General George Carpenter

**1943** **Jan.:** Hudson River Division tour

**Apr. 24-25:** Easter weekend in Philadelphia

**July 31-Aug. 1:** Ocean Grove weekend

**1944** **Mar.:** Prison Sunday at Rikers Island

**Apr. 1:** "Word of Life Hour," part of "Youth for Christ" rally at Madison Square Garden (band asked again for Sept. 30)

**Aug. 5-6:** Ocean Grove weekend

**Sept. 17:** At "Welcome to the Cadets" services; TSB is down to 22 members

**1945** **Jan. 13-15:** Syracuse, N.Y., weekend

**Feb.:** Annual Festival, with Carl Lindstrom of the Chicago Staff Band as guest soloist

**May:** V.E. Day Celebration at CMT

**June 24:** First program at Calvary Baptist Church, NYC

**Aug. 4-5:** Ocean Grove Weekend; George Granger suffers heart attack on stage during Saturday festival, dies moments later; festival continued under DB/M William Bearchell; (B/M Charles Miles and B/M Charles Anderson also die during the year); William Bearchell becomes B/M

**1946:** **Jan.:** Richard E. Holz appointed territorial music secretary (also DB/M)

**Feb. 22:** Granger Memorial Festival of Music

**Apr. 15-18:** Wall Street open-air meetings during Holy Week becomes a regular Staff Band activity

**Apr. 19-20:** Visit of Montreal Citadel (Canada) Band to NYC

Regional music institutes are held in N.Y. metropolitan area, New England Province, and Western N.Y. as part of rebuilding program

**1947** **Feb.:** Annual Festival, salute to Salvationist chaplains

**Apr.:** Radio broadcasts during United Nations Week from Rockefeller Center Plaza

**Apr. 19-20:** First Territorial Music Leaders' Councils, in NYC, featuring winning compositions of "Band Music for Evangelism" Contest

264

**Aug. 2-3:** Ocean Grove weekend

**Dec. 12:** WNBC nationwide Christmas radio broadcast

**Dec. 21:** First of yearly 3:00 p.m. Christmas concerts at Calvary Baptist Church

**1948 Feb. 27:** Annual Festival, with Temple Chorus, S/L C. Peter Carlson

**Apr. 2-4:** First Territorial Music Congress ("Fighting Faith"); Ernest Parr, soprano cornet, and Margaret Mac-Farlane (both of Canada) guest soloists

**May:** All-Leidzen program at F.E.T. (first given at N.Y. Central Citadel, 4/24)

**Aug. 7-8:** Ocean Grove weekend, with Bramwell Coles

**Oct.:** Recording of Christmas records, 78 rpm

**Nov. 19.:** Festival featuring the music of Evangeline Booth

**1949 April. 16:** Brookdale Baptist Church, Bloomfield, N.J.

**Aug. 6-7:** Ocean Grove weekend

**Oct. 13-17:** Territorial Congress with Chief of the Staff Commissioner John Allan, including Music Festival, 10/15

**1950 Feb. 25-27:** Western Pa. tour

**Apr. 21-23:** 70th Anniv. (Second Biennial) Terr. Music Congress, NYC and Brooklyn; special guests Erik Leidzen and Euphoniumist William Brown (Earlscourt, Canada)

**May 12:** Staff Band Reunion and F.E.T. Finale Festival

**Aug. 5-6:** 15th Annual Ocean Grove Weekend

**Dec.:** A typical line up—N.Y. Association Dinner (Dwight Eisenhower honored), Detention Home, Calvary Baptist concert, etc.

**1951 Jan.:** William Slater appointed B/M as Bearchell transferred to Boston

**Apr. 5-8:** Southwest Ohio and Northeast Kentucky tour, including concerts at Cincinnati Conservatory and Asbury College

**Apr. 21-22:** Third Biennial Terr. Music Leaders' Councils, NYC; TSB and Westminster College Choir featured

**Fall:** First recordings pressed during B/M Slater's tenure

**Oct.:** NYSB involved in Methodist Church's "Circuit Rider" Nationwide radio broadcast (band now referred to regularly as The New York Staff Band)

**Oct.:** Ensemble from NYSB (10 players) on TV for the first time

**Dec.:** General Douglas MacArthur hails NYSB's rendition of "The Star Spangled Banner" (arr. Slater) as the finest he has ever heard (at N.Y. Association Dinner at which he was honored)

**1952** **Feb. 15-17:** Toronto, Canada, weekend

**Mar.:** Half-hour TV show on WNBC-TV (Rockefeller Center)

**Apr. 11:** Premiere of "Banners and Bonnets" (Willson, arr. Holz) at Waldorf-Astoria, sung first by Christopher Lynch of the Metropolitan Opera

**Sept. 27-28:** Pen Argyl, Pa.

**Nov. 8-9:** Pittsburgh, Pa., weekend, including several TV appearances

**1953** **Jan.:** Paterson, N.J., Corps 65th Anniversary

**Mar.:** Third Biennial Terr. Music Congress, with Earlscourt Citadel (Canada) Band as guests

**May 23-24:** Newark, N.J., and dedication of new DHQ

**Aug. 15-16:** Return to Ocean Grove for weekend

**Dec.:** Featured on the Margaret Arlen Show, WCBS-TV, during S.A. Week

**1954** **Apr. 3-4:** Fourth Biennial Music Leaders' Councils, NYC, with the Tranas (Sweden) Corps Band as guests

**May 7:** Eric Ball Night at F.E.T.

**June 12-13:** NYSB in Chicago for Central Terr. Music Congress

**Oct. 15-18:** Northeast Ohio tour

**Oct. 29-Nov. 2:** Territorial Congress with General Wilfred Kitching

1955 **Jan.:** Richard Holz appointed B/M and Vernon Post DB/M and Male Chorus Leader

**Apr. 29-May 1:** "Diamond Jubilee" Terr. Music Congress in NYC; guests are E.F. Goldman, conductor, and Harold Brasch, euphonium

**June 23:** NYSB and MC "On the Mall" Festival, Central Park, NYC (full title of band is now consistently the New York Staff Band and Male Chorus)

**Aug. 12-14:** Old Orchard Beach, Maine, Camp Meetings

**Nov. 17-21:** Southwest Ohio and Northeast Kentucky tour, with concerts at Transylvania University, Asbury College, and WCPO-TV, Cincinnati

**Dec.:** NYSB featured on "The Today Show" with Dave Garroway (WRCA-TV)

1956 **Feb. 10:** Annual Festival with Jerome Hines, basso at the Metropolitan Opera, as guest soloist

**Mar. 10-11:** Fifth Biennial Music Leaders' Councils, NYC, with Chicago Staff Band as guests

**Mar. 30:** Jerome Hines' opera, "I am the Way," premiered at CMT; NYSB and MC perform

**Apr. 28-29:** Toronto, Canada, for Spring Festival

**May 18-21:** Northeast Ohio tour

**June 18:** Central Park Mall concert

**Aug. 10-12:** Old Orchard Beach Camp Meetings

1957 **Jan. 25:** Annual Festival, tribute to Frank Fowler

**Apr. 5-7:** Territorial Music Congress, with International Staff Band (London) as guests

**May 21-28:** Ohio-Kentucky tour

**June:** First official LP recordings taped: "Festival of Music," and "Carolers' Favorites"

**Aug. 8-11:** Old Orchard Beach Camp Meetings

**Oct.:** Final Billy Graham Crusade Meeting, Polo Grounds, NYC

1958　**Jan. 25-26:** N.J. Divisional Music Councils with Derek Smith of Toronto, Canada, guest cornet soloist

**Feb. 14:** Annual Festival, with James Burke (Goldman Band) guest cornet soloist

**Apr. 19-20:** Terr. Music Leaders' Councils, NYC, with B/M Harry Stillwell (Los Angeles, Calif.) cornet soloist, and featuring various youth bands

**May 15:** Billy Graham Crusade, Madison Square Garden

**July 25-29:** Long Beach, Calif. Camp Meetings

1959　**Feb.:** Annual Festival, Goldman Memorial Program (E. F. Goldman); Dr. Richard F. Goldman, guest conductor

**May 8-10:** Territorial Music Congress, NYC, with Netherlands National Band

**Nov. 17-18:** Eastern Canadian Congress, Montreal, Canada

**Dec.:** "Today Show" and "Hi Mom" TV shows

1960　**Feb. 5:** Annual Festival, Leidzen Night

**Mar. 12-13:** Terr. Music Leaders' Councils, NYSB featured along with soloists Philip Catelinet and Staff Bandsman Derek Smith

**May 13:** Bon Voyage Concert

**June 2-25:** Tour of Great Britain, including Bandmasters' Councils and British Congress

**Oct. 30-Nov. 1:** Sayre, Pa., trip

1961　**Feb. 3:** Annual Festival, Eric Ball guest conductor

**Apr. 14-16:** Seventh Biennial Music Congress, featuring staff bandsmen soloists

**Apr. 19-23:** Carolinas tour

**June 22:** Central Park Mall Concert, Will Overton (BBC Orchestra) guest trumpet soloist

**July 1-2:** Ocean Grove weekend; 85th Anniv. Celebrations (1876)

**Nov.:** Toronto Temple Corps (Canada), 75th Anniversary

**Dec.:** Two "Today Show" appearances, including videotaped Christmas Day edition; Gary Moore "I've Got a Secret" TV show; NBC-TV "Family Show" Christmas Special

**1962 Feb. 22-27:** NYSB Ensemble in Puerto Rico for opening of Salvation Army work on the island

**Mar. 2:** NYSB 75th Anniv. Music Festival, Erik Leidzen, guest pianist

**Mar. 30-Apr. 1:** New Haven, Conn., including concert at Yale Univ.

**Apr. 7-8:** Terr. Music Leaders' Councils, NYC, with International Staff Band (London) as guests

**Apr. 25-30:** Tour of Georgia Division

**Mary 25-27:** Washington, D.C., and concert at Watergate Ampitheater

**June 30-July 1:** Ocean Grove weekend and Diamond Jubilee Staff Band Reunion

**1963 Feb. 8:** Annual Festival, Erik Leidzen Memorial

**Mar. 2-3:** Philadelphia Divisional Music Councils and concert at M.E.N.C. National Convention

**Mar. 29-31:** Territorial Music Congress, including festival at Lincoln Center

**May 21:** NYSB plays at baseball game, Yankee Stadium, in tribute to Bobby Richardson

**Sept. 21-22:** Portland, Maine, dedication of DHQ

**Oct.:** Western N.Y. tour; last engagement for B/M Holz

**Nov. 9-10:** NYSB under B/M Vernon Post plays at installation of Holz as divisional commander of Southern New England (Bristol, Conn.)

**1964** **Feb. 7:** Annual Festival with Ray Steadman-Allen, composer/conductor/pianist

**Feb. 21:** N.J. All-State Band Clinic, Mt. Holly, N.J.; and Camden, N.J., visit

**Apr. 4-5:** Territorial Music Leaders' Councils, with Tottenham Citadel Band (London, England) as guests; NYSB features winning compositions of National Composers' Competition

**July 4-5:** Ocean Grove weekend, with five staff bandmasters present

**Oct. 14-22:** Tour of Louisiana, including Grambling College and Tulane Univ.

**1965** **Feb.:** Salvation Army Centenary (1865-1965) Festival of Music; also "New York, New York" ABC-TV show

**Apr. 29-May 4:** Toronto, Canada, for Spring Festival in Massey Hall; band and Male Chorus records for "The Living Word" S.A. TV series

**May 29-30:** Indianapolis, Ind., weekend and "Indy 500" Festival Parade

**Oct. 21-25:** Eastern Territorial Centennial Congress, NYC, and Music Councils, with General Frederick Coutts, and Maisie Wiggins (Halle Orchestra), trombone soloist

**Nov. 6-8:** 80th Anniversary Celebrations, Cincinnati, Ohio

**1966** **Apr. 17:** Philadelphia Div. Music Councils and Philadelphia Roxborough Corps dedication

**May 13-15:** NYSB participates in 38-hr. non-stop open-air meeting in Times Square, NYC

**Aug. 5-7:** Old Orchard Beach Camp Meetings

**Oct. 15-16:** Territorial Music Leaders' Councils, NYC, with Govan Citadel Band (Scotland) as guests

**Fall:** Visits to Lewistown, Pa., Waterbury, Conn., and Springfield, Mass.

**1967** **Feb. 19:** NYSB's 80th Anniversary Festival

**Mar. 4-5:** N.Y. State trip, including Hartwick College and Delhi State Univ.

**May:** F.E.T. Finale with Hollywood Tabernacle Band (Calif.) and Eric Ball leading combined bands

**July 1-2:** Band featured at Chautauqua Institution Concert Series (N.Y.) and Buffalo, N.Y.

**Oct. 21:** Montreal, Canada, Expo 67

**Nov. 10-12:** Norristown, Pa., 75th Anniversary

**1968 Feb.:** Annual Festival with Philip Catelinet, tuba soloist

**Mar. 29-30:** Worcester, Mass., including clinic at Holy Cross Univ.

**Apr. 26-28:** Territorial Music Councils, NYC, NYSB featured group

**May 17-June 3:** European tour (Netherlands, Germany, Switzerland, and England), Bandmasters' Councils, Royal Albert Hall, London

**Oct. 26-27:** Kitchener, Ontario, Canada

**Dec. 19:** Hour Christmas Special taped for WABC-TV

**1969 May 9:** Annual Festival with Ken Smith (Melbourne, Australia) cornet soloist

**June 13-16:** General's Congress, commissioning, and Billy Graham Crusade

**Sept. 20-21:** Jamaica, (L.I.) N.Y., Anniv. Weekend

**Oct. 4-6:** Concord, N.H.

**Oct. 24-26:** Eastern N.Y tour; concert at Rensselaer Polytechnic Institute

**Nov. 21:** F.E.T. Staff Band Night with Eric Ball

**1970 Jan. 30:** Annual Festival with B/M Ernest Miller (Chicago Staff Band) as vocal soloist

**Mar. 2:** Washington, D.C., including American Protestant Hospital Assoc. Convention

**Mar. 21-22:** Music Leaders' Councils, NYC, with Stockholm VII (Sweden) Band as guests

**Apr. 25-26:** Suffolk County, N.Y., campaign

**May 9-10:** Sunbury, Pa., weekend

**May 22-24:** Schenectady, N.Y., trip

1971 **Feb. 26:** 84th Anniv. Annual Festival; no guest soloists

**Mar. 6-8:** Bloor Citadel, Toronto, Canada

**Apr. 24-25:** Twelfth Biennial Music Congress, NYC, with Chicago Staff Band as guests

**Sept. 10:** Band featured at International Commissioners' Conference

**Nov. 14-15:** Philadelphia trip, including performance at Temple University; band praised by Dr. David L. Stone as "the finest non-professional group ever to visit the college (of music)"

1972 **Feb.:** 85th Anniv. Annual Festival, with Arnold Burton, bass-baritone, and Charles Baker, trombone, as soloists

**Apr. 16-18:** Twelfth Biennial Music Leaders' Councils, NYC, with Major Leslie Condon guest soloist/composer/conductor; included NYSB 85th Anniv. Reunion Festival

**Summer:** B/M Post relieved of Staff Band and Music Department responsibilities; Derek Smith designated acting B/M (DB/M), first non-officer since Robert Griffith

**Oct. 20-22:** Central Territory weekend, Chicago and Milwaukee, including Northern Illinois Div. Music Councils

**Dec. 28-Jan. 2 (1973):** Western Territory tour; Tournament of Roses Parade; visits to Denver, Phoenix, Los Angeles, San Francisco, Oakland, and Salt Lake City

1973 **Feb.:** 86th Anniv. Annual Festival, featuring slides of Western tour and New Age Brass Quintet from Juilliard School of Music

**Mar. 23-25:** Bandsmen's and Songsters' Councils, NYC, with Canadian Staff Band as guests

Many local engagements during year, plus summer tour through Eastern Pa., including Allentown, Berwick, Wilkes-Barre, and Scranton

**1974** **Winter:** First of new-style band retreats held at Hillcrest Conference Center, Sharon, Mass., with Commissioner Bramwell Tripp as speaker; band played in Tremont Temple Baptist Church, Boston, and gave concert at Cambridge Citadel

**Jan. 25:** Annual Festival with Peggy Pruet, soprano, and Harvey Burgett, organ, as guest soloists

**May 18-19:** Utica and Rome, N.Y.

**Spring:** PENDEL Congress in Philadelphia

**Nov. 2-4:** Akron, Ohio, Corps 90th Anniv.

**1975** **Jan. 11:** Band plays for first time at the New York Brass Conference and receives many standing ovations (similar concerts in 1976, 77, and 80)

**Feb. 15-16:** Weekend in Doylestown, Pa.

**Feb. 21:** Annual Festival with Harvey Philips, tuba, guest soloist

**Apr. 19-20:** Philadelphia, Pa., weekend and performance at East Regional Convention of M.E.N.C.

**Oct. 17-19:** General's Congress, NYC

**Dec.:** Arlene Francis Christmas Day radio program

**1976** **Feb. 13:** Annual Festival with Terry Camsey, cornet, guest soloist; tributes given to Olof Lundgren, Wilf Cooper and Jack Phelan

**Apr. 24:** Swedish-American Bi-Centennial Salute at Avery Fisher Hall, Lincoln Center (band plays for King Carl Gustaf XVI)

**May 22-24:** Pittsburgh, Pa., weekend; Festival Salute to Philip Catelinet

**June 11-13:** Territorial Music Congress, with Gordon Hill, trombone, featured with NYSB

**Summer:** Old Orchard Beach Camp Meetings and Star Lake Musicamp

**Oct. 2-3:** Corning, N.Y. (festival at Corning Glass Center)

**Dec. 4:** Concert at American School Band Directors' Association Convention, Atlantic City, N.J.

**1977**   **Feb. 4:** 90th Anniv. Festival, Bernard Adams, guest conductor

**Apr. 14-17:** SWONEKY Division, including taping of Art Linkletter TV Christmas Special, Southwest Ohio Brass Conference, and Asbury College

**Oct. 15:** Second 90th Anniv. Festival, in Alice Tully Hall, Lincoln Center; William Himes, euphonium soloist

**Oct. 29-30:** Lockport, N.Y.

**1978**   **Feb. 3:** Annual Festival with William Broughton, trombone, and Bruce Broughton, piano, as guest soloists

**Feb. 17:** F.E.T. Tribute to Erik Leidzen

**June-July:** Participation in International Congress, London, England

**1979**   **Feb.:** Annual Festival with Charles Baker, trombone, as guest soloist

**Apr. 14-17:** Visit to Puerto Rico

**May 5-6:** Hartford, Conn., weekend

**Oct. 26-28:** East Liverpool, Ohio, 95th Anniversary, and Kent State University concert

**Dec. 15:** Concert in Symphony Hall, Newark, N.J., sponsored by Christian Arts, Inc.

**1980**   **Feb.:** 93rd Annual Festival, with Maria Ferriero, vocal soloist, and Joseph Turrin, piano; Profile II Festival in honor of Albert Jakeway

**Mar. 5:** Concert at Manhattan School of Music

**June 13-17:** Salvation Army National Congress, Kansas City, Mo.

**Aug. 1-4:** Old Orchard Beach Camp Meetings

**Sept. 20-21:** Springfield, Mass.

**Oct. 24-26:** International Staff Band in NYC as part of their American tour

**1981** **Feb.** 6 Annual Festival, with Norman Bearcroft, composer/conductor, and Philip Smith, trumpet, as guest artists

**Mar.** 7: Temple Univ. Brass Conference

**Mar.** 13: Profile III, in honor of Brindley Boon

**May** 20-22: Houghton College and Elmira, N.Y.

**June** 5-8: Toronto, Ontario/Niagara Falls trip, including "Sounds Inspiring" Festival in Massey Hall with Eric Ball, guest conductor

**1982** **Feb.** 5: Annual Festival with Commissioner Edward Carey, guest chairman

**Mar.:** Concerts at Manhattan School of Music, Asbury Park, N.J., Barrington College (R.I.), Asbury College (Wilmore, Ky.), Lexington, Ky., and Dayton, Ohio

**Apr.** 24-25: Ithaca, N.Y.

**May** 8-10: Cleveland, Ohio

**June** 23-July 26: World Tour (Norway, Sweden, Australia, and New Zealand)

**1983** **Feb.** 25: Profile V Festival, in honor of Richard E. Holz

**Apr.** 15: "Superfest" for NYSB and Stockholm VII (Sweden) Band

**May** 19-22: Western Pa. tour

**Aug.** 5-7: Old Orchard Beach Camp Meetings

**Sept.** 23-25: Boston and Lawrence, Mass. (the latter's 100th anniv.)

**Oct.** 22: Asbury Park United Methodist Church

**Oct.** 23: Bay Ridge (Brooklyn) Corps

**Nov.** 20: Gateway Cathedral, Staten Island, N.Y.

**1984** **Feb.** 24: Profile VI, in tribute to Leslie Condon

**Mar.** 2-4: International Retreat for NYSB and Canadian Staff Band, Woodlands Conf. Center, Speculator, N.Y.

**Apr.** 7-8: Middletown, N.Y.

**June** 8-11: Territorial Congress, Ocean Grove, N.J.

**1985** **Mar. 16-17:** Utica, N.Y.

**Mar. 29:** Annual festival with Derick Kane, euphonium, guest soloist; tribute to Walter Orr

**May 4-5:** Reading, Pa.

**May 9:** Nassau County Benefit Concert, Garden City High School

**May 16-June 2:** "Return to England" Tour, including Songster Leaders' Councils (6/1)

**Summer:** 100th Anniversary Old Orchard Beach Camp Meetings

**1986** **Feb. 14:** Profile VII Festival in honor of Stanley E. Ditmer

**Mar. 1-3:** Trip to Puerto Rico (25th Anniv.)

**Mar. 21:** Annual Festival with William and Sallie Broughton, guest soloists (trombone and piano)

**Apr. 19-20:** Pottsville, Pa.

**June 13-15:** Music Ministries Weekend and Commissioning; final engagement for B/M Derek Smith (who retired June 15)

**Aug. 15:** Richard E. Holz promoted to Glory

**Sept. 1:** Brian A. Bowen appointed B/M of NYSB

**Oct. 17:** Territorial welcome to General Eva Burrows, CMT

**Oct. 24:** United Nations Peace Concert

**Dec. 7:** Calvary Baptist Church (tentative)

**1987** **Mar. 20-22:** NYSB Annual Festival; Centennial Reunion Weekend

**Mar. 24-Apr. 5:** U.S.A. tour

# APPENDIX B

## Executive Officers of The New York Staff Band

("Band Leader," "Band Manager," and
"Spiritual Leader" were other titles used)

| | |
|---|---|
| Major Wray | 1887 |
| Major Charles Miles | 1888—1890 |
| Major Bryant | 1890—1891 |
| Ensign William Hunter (National Guards Band) | 1890—1891 |
| Major William Halpin | 1897 |
| Staff-Captain F. Walter Jenkins | 1898 |
| Brigadier Charles Miles | 1899 |
| Major Edward Parker | 1900—1902 |
| Lt.-Colonel Charles Miles | 1902—1903 |
| Brigadier Gustav Reinhardsen | 1903—1905 |
| Major Edward Stanyon | 1906—1908 |
| Lt.-Colonel F. Walter Jenkins | 1911—1915 |
| Lt.-Colonel Charles Miles | 1915—1922 |
| no executive officer | 1922—1933 |
| Brigadier John Allan | 1933—1940 |
| Lt.-Colonel Norman S. Marshall | 1940—1944 |
| Lt.-Colonel Edwin Clayton | 1944—1947 |
| Colonel Holland French | 1947—1953 |
| Colonel George Marshall | 1953—1956 |
| Lt.-Colonel William Maltby | 1957—1964 |
| Lt.-Colonel Paul Kaiser | 1965 |
| Colonel T. Herbert Martin | 1965—1968 |
| Colonel C. Emil Nelson | 1968—1970 |
| Lt.-Colonel Richard E. Holz | 1970—1971 |
| Lt.-Colonel William Harvey | 1971—1972 |
| Brigadier Roland Schramm | 1972—1976 |
| Lt.-Colonel Albert Scott | 1976—1978 |
| Lt.-Colonel Stanley Ditmer | 1978—1982 |
| Lt.-Colonel Wallace Conrath | 1982—1984 |
| Lt.-Colonel Edward Fritz | 1984— |

# APPENDIX C

## Band Local Officers of the New York Staff Band, 1887-1987

### Deputy-Bandmasters

| | |
|---|---|
| Edward Trumble | 1904—1906 |
| Robert Griffith | 1906—1907 |
| John Allan | 1909—1910 |
| Robert Young | 1919—1921 |
| John Allan | 1921—1924 |
| J. Stanley Sheppard | 1925—1931 |
| William Parkins | 1931—1935 |
| William Bearchell | 1936—1945 |
| Richard E. Holz | 1947—1955 |
| Vernon Post | 1955—1963 |
| Roland Schramm | 1963—1972 |
| Derek Smith | 1972 |
| Lambert Bittinger Jr. | 1975—1978 |
| Ronald Waiksnoris | 1980— |

### Band Secretaries

| | |
|---|---|
| James Durand | 1900—1902 |
| Charles Van Leusen | 1902—1912 |
| Robert Young (Correspondence) | 1912—1915 |
| J. J. Stimson (Records) | 1912—1915 |
| William Hammond (Correspondence) | 1915—1920 |
| William F. Palmer (Records) | 1915—1920 |
| Albert E. Bates | 1920 |
| John Allan | 1920—1921 |
| Albert E. Bates | 1921—1923 |
| Edgar Arkett | 1923—1927 |
| Charles Bearchell | 1927—1946 |
| Arthur Craytor | 1946—1957 |
| George Harvey | 1957—1961 |
| Robert McNally | 1961—1963 |
| Robert Bearchell | 1963—1965 |

| Albert E. Avery | 1965—1967 |
| Peter Hofman | 1967—1968 |
| Harold Banta | 1968—1971 |
| William Hood | 1971—1973 |
| William Simons | 1973—1976 |
| Howard Burr | 1976—1977 |
| Charles West | 1977—1978 |
| Charles Schramm | 1978—1979 |
| Sidney Langford | 1979—1984 |
| Norman Voisey | 1985—1986 |
| William LaMarr | 1986— |

## Finance Secretaries (Treasurers)

| Charles Van Leusen | 1912—1921 |
| Llewellyn Cowan | 1921—1946 |
| Paul Carlson | 1946—1948 |
| Roland Schramm | 1948—1957 |
| George Harvey | 1957—1963 |
| Albert E. Avery | 1963—1966 |
| Vincent Bulla | 1966—1972 |
| William Simons | 1972—1973 |
| Charles West | 1973—1978 |
| Charles Schramm | 1978—1979 |
| George Harvey | 1979—1980 |
| Vincent Bulla | 1980— |

## Property Secretaries

| Robert Young | 1915 |
| J. J. Stimson | 1915—1923 |
| Howard Margetts | 1923—1925 |
| Herbert Bartlett | 1926—1927 |
| William Bearchell | 1927—1937 |
| Paul Carlson | 1938—1946 |
| John Sarer | 1946—1958 |
| Frank Moody | 1958—1961 |
| Harold Banta | 1961—1968 |
| Charles West | 1968—1973 |
| Samuel Bennett | 1973—1979 |
| Charles Rowe | 1979—1982 |
| Thomas Scheibner | 1982—1985 |
| Charles Olsen Jr. | 1985— |

## Librarians

| | |
|---|---|
| Samuel Hodges | 1904—1905 |
| John Allan | 1905—1906 |
| Albert Norris | 1906—1907 |
| Lt. Smith | 1907—1908 |
| Ort Mitson | 1909—1915 |
| J. Stanley Sheppard | 1915—1925 |
| William Bearchell | 1925—1927 |
| George Granger | 1927—1935 |
| Edward Clark | 1935—1940 |
| Fletcher Agnew | 1940—1941 |
| Arthur Fox | 1947—1951 |
| Josef Toft | 1951—1953 |
| Robert Lundsten | 1954—1956 |
| Alfred Swenarton | 1957—1958 |
| Harry Hartjes | 1960—1963 |
| Howard Hastings | 1965—1966 |
| Eric Eliasen | 1967—1968 |
| William Geese | 1972—1975 |
| Roger Rischawy | 1975—1977 |
| William DeMoranville | 1980—1981 |
| Andrew Kelly | 1981—1983 |
| Charles Olsen Jr. | 1983—1984 |
| Darren Mudge | 1984—1986 |
| Colin DeVault | 1986— |

## Public Relations Secretaries

| | |
|---|---|
| William Gilks (Engagement Secretary) | 1921 |
| C. Emil Nelson | 1945—1948 |
| Sidney Shields | 1950—1951 |
| Ralph Miller | 1954—1960 |
| William MacLean | 1961—1962 |
| Harold Anderson | 1963—1964 |
| David Brindley | 1964—1966 |
| William Barr | 1966—1967 |
| W. Wilbur Smith | 1967—1968 |
| Russell Prince | 1969—1971 |
| Lambert Bittinger Jr. | 1973—1975 |
| Lindsay Evans | 1975—1977 |
| Ronald Waiksnoris | 1977—1979 |
| Ken Kirby | 1979—1981 |

| Charles Olsen | 1981—1983 |
| James Kisser | 1983—1985 |
| William LaMarr | 1985—1986 |
| Craig Evans | 1986— |

## Band Sergeants

| Harold Banta | 1979—1982 |
| Harold Anderson | 1984— |

# APPENDIX D

### Roster of Members:

### The New York Staff Band and Male Chorus
### 1887—1986

| Abbreviations Used: | | | |
|---|---|---|---|
| B/M | Bandmaster | FS | Finance Secretary |
| BSec | Band Secretary | | (Treasurer) |
| BSgt | Band Sergeant | MC | Male Chorus Leader |
| Comm | Commissioner | PR | Public Relations |
| DB/M | Deputy Bandmaster | | Secretary |
| EO | Executive Officer | PS | Property Secretary |
| Lib | Librarian | | |

Abram, James
Agnew, Ernest
Agnew, J. Fletcher (Lib)
Albright
Alden
Allan, John (Lib, BSec, DB/M, EO, Comm)
Ames
Anderson, Arthur
Anderson, Charles (B/M)
Anderson, Douglas
Anderson, Harold (PR, BSgt)
Anderson, Ian
Andrews, Arthur
Andrews, Dan
Andrews, George
Arbues, Roque
Arkett, Edgar (BSec)

Arkett, Leslie
Arnold, William C. (Comm)
Aspinall
Avery, Albert E. (BSec, FS)
Avery, Albert E. Jr.
Avery, Carl
Ayres, Kenneth
Ayres, Kenneth Jr.

Baillie, Albert
Baker, Charles
Baker, Isaac
Baker, Richard
Bale, James
Banks, William
Banta, George
Banta, Harold (BSec, BSgt, PS)

Barlett, W.
Barr, William (PR)
Barrett, William H. (Lt.-Comm)
Barry
Bartlett, Herbert (PS)
Barton, Robert
Bassett, Joseph Jr.
Bates, Albert E. (BSec)
Bates, B.
Bates, Claude E. (Comm)
Baugh, W.
Baxendale, Paul
Beadle, Lawrence
Bean, Martin
Bearchell, Charles (BSec)
Bearchell, Robert (BSec)
Bearchell, William (DB/M, B/M,
    PS, MC, Lib)
Beeton
Bengston, Karl Erhard
Bennett, Samuel C. (PS)
Bergh, Karl August
Bergman, Eric
Berry, Donald
Berry, William
Bessant, William
Bethune, Douglas
Binder
Bittinger, Lambert G.
Bittinger, Lambert Jr. (PR,
    DB/M)
Black, Daniel
Bleckburn
Boarston, S.
Boorman
Booth, W. Harry
Booth-Tucker, Kris
Bouterse, W.
Bovill, James
Bowen, Brian A. (B/M)
Boyd, C. H.
Bradley, Steven

Brennecke, Fred
Brenner
Bridgen, William (B/M)
Bridgen, William Jr.
Brindley, Clifford
Brindley, David (PR)
Broughton, William (B/M)
Bryant (EO)
Brundle, Charles
Bulla, Phillip
Bulla, Stephen
Bulla, Vincent "Ben" (FS)
Burgmayer, Harold
Burleigh, George
Burlew, Henry F.
Burr, Douglas A.
Burr, Howard (BSec)
Burrows, J.
Busby, John
Buzzell, William Oscar

Cameron, Warren Weston
Campbell, Clarence
Camsey, Terry
Carey, Edward (Comm)
Carlson, Arthur
Carlson, Paul (FS, PS, Comm)
Carpenter, G.
Carvill, Carl
Castagna, Lawrence
Catlin, C.
Catlin, Leslie
Chamberlain, William (Comm)
Chapin
Childs, David
Chittenden
Clarice, F.
Clark, Edward G. (Lib)
Clark, Edward Jr.
Clarke, Fred
Clarkson
Clayton, Edwin (EO)

Coles, Robert
Conrath, Wallace (EO)
Cooke, George
Cooper, Wilfred
Cowan, Llewellyn W. (FS, Lt.-Comm)
Cox, William Henry
Coy, David D.
Craig, Thomas
Cranford, Paul
Crawford, Bramwell
Craytor, Arthur (BSec)

Damery, Fred
Damon, Alexander M. (Comm)
Daniels, F.
Darby, George (B/M, MC)
Davis, Kenneth
Davis, Michael
DeMichael, Joseph
DeMoranville, William (Lib)
DeVault, Colin (Lib)
Devoto, William L.
Devoto, William Jr.
Devoto, Wreford
Ditmer, Philip
Ditmer, Stanley E. (EO, Comm)
Ditmer, Stephen
Ditmer, Timothy
Dockendorff, John F.
Doughty, Robert
Dowdell, Charles
Drury, G.
Dukeshar, Percy
Duncan, Walter (B/M)
Durand, James (BSec)
Dye

Eliasen, Eric (Lib)
Eliasen, Harold
Elliott, Frederick Jr.
Emerson

Enders
Ernest, H.
Evans, Craig (PR)
Evans, Howard
Evans, Lindsay (PR)

Fahey, John
Fairbanks, Ian
Farrar, Fred
Ferreira, Philip
Flanders, Pershing
Flory, W.
Foreman, Ronald
Forrester, George
Fossey, Paul
Fowler, Frank
Fox, Arthur L. (Lib)
Fox, William
Francis, William
Freeh, Mark
Freeman, Floyd
Freeman, Sam
French, Holland (EO, Comm)
Fritz, Edward (EO)

Gale, Wilbur M.
Galley
Garbutt, Edwin R.
Garell, Lauren
Garland, Herbert
Gearing, H.
Gearing, W.
Geese, William F. (Lib)
Gerberich, Edgar
Gifford, Rudy
Gifford, William
Gilder, Victor
Gilks, William (PR)
Gircopazzi, Felicia
Glen, Peter
Godden, Edwin
Gooding, W.

Goodliff, William
Gorham
Gorman, Thomas
Gourlay, William
Graham, Peter
Granger, George (B/M, Lib)
Gray
Green, Robert
Greetham, Masters
Gregg, Gary
Grell
Griffith, Richard (Comm)
Griffith, Robert (B/M, DB/M)
Guard, William

Hall, Albert
Halpin, William (EO)
Hammond, William (BSec)
Hansen, William M.
Hanson
Hargreaves, Thomas W.
Harris, William G.
Hartjes, Harry (Lib)
Hartwright
Harvey, Fred
Harvey, George (BSec, FS)
Harvey, Paul
Harvey, Walter
Harvey, William H. (EO)
Hastings, Howard (Lib)
Heard, Joseph E.
Heine, G.
Heine, Louis
Henderson, James
Hepburn, S.
Hicks
Higgins, Edward
Higgins, Ernest
Hillman, B.
Hillstrom, Carl
Hillstrom, Gus
Hiscock, Laurie

Hodges, Samson (Lib)
Hofman, Peter (BSec)
Hoffman, Frank
Hoffman, George
Hohn, Jacob
Holland, Thomas
Holmes, George
Holz, Ernest
Holz, Richard (B/M, DB/M, MC,
  EO, Comm)
Holz, Richard
Homer, G.
Hood, William (BSec)
Hooper, Floyd
Hostetler, Donald
Howells
Hughes, Rowland D.
Hulteen, Arnold
Humphries, R.
Hunter, William O. (EO)

Irvine, Edgar W.
Irwin

Jackson, Eric
Jackson, Fred
Jackson, Fred Jr.
Jackson, Harold
Jackson, John W.
Jackson, Lori
Jackson, Robert
Jacobsen, C.
Jenkins, Walter (EO)
Jenkins, Walter Jr.
Jenkins, William
Jimenez, George Washington
Johns, Arthur D.
Jolley, Charles
Jones, Kenneth
Joyce, Ralph
Joyce, T.

285

Kaiser, Paul (EO, Comm)
Keeler, Mark
Keep (B/M)
Keiser
Kelly, Andrew (Lib)
Kelly, Jeremiah
Keppel, J. J.
Kimball, Albert
Kimball, Frank
Kington, Leason
Kippax, Milton
Kirby, Gordon
Kirby, Kenneth (PR)
Kisser, James Jr. (PR)
Kraft

Ladlow, Fred
LaMarr, William (PR, BSec)
Lambert, John H. Jr.
Lanckton
Langford, Sidney R. (BSec)
Laurie, Andrew C.
Lenscott, Jack
Leusden
Lewis, Newell J.
Lines, Richard
Linsky
Livingston, Ronald
Ljungholm, Sven
Lock, Albert
Lock, G. W.
Lock, John William
Longino, Frank
Longland
Lopez, Efrain
Lowcock, Edward
Lundberg, Ake
Lundgren, Olof
Lundsten, Eric
Lundsten, Robert (Lib)
Lundsten, William
Lupfer, W.

Lyons

Mack, Thomas (MC)
Mackness, Horace
MacLean, William (PR)
MacMurdo, James
MacMurdo, Norman
Maginnis, Samuel
Malpass, Fred
Maltby, Fred
Maltby, William (EO)
Mantz [Broether]
Mantz
Margetts, Howard (PS)
Margetts, William L.
Marshall, George (EO)
Marshall, John F.
Marshall, M.
Marshall, Norman S. (EO, Comm)
Martin, Reginald
Martin, T. Herbert (EO)
Matheson, Chester
McAbee, Ralph
McDonald, Michael
McDuffie
McGee, John C.
McIntyre, Eldon
McIntyre, Kenneth
McLaren
McMahon, Milton
McMillan, Donald (Comm)
McNally, Charles Jr.
McNally, Robert (BSec)
Mehling, Charles
Meredith
Merritt, J. W.
Metzger, R.
Meyer, M.
Miles, Charles (B/M, EO)
Miles, Harold
Miles, W.

Millar, C. W.
Miller, Clarence
Miller, E. R.
Miller, Ralph (PR)
Miller, W.
Mills
Millward, Clifford
Mitchell, John F.
Mitson, A.
Mitson, E.
Mitson, Herb
Mitson, Ort (Lib)
Mitson, Wilbert
Moody, Frank (PS)
Moore, Daniel
Morris, Patrick
Morris, Vernon
Moss
Moulton, Arthur
Mudge, Darren (Lib)
Munroe, Karl

Narraway, Tom
Nason, A.
Nelson, C. Emil (PR, EO)
Nelson, Karl E.
Nelson, W.
Nice, Fritz
Nichol, A.
Nicholl, George
Nichols, J. H.
Nicol, Alex
Noble, Charles
Nock, Samuel
Noel, Kenneth
Norris, Albert (Lib)
North, William
Norton, Brent
Nuber, Edward J.
Nuesch, Osvaldo

Olley, Albert

Olsen, Charles F. (PR)
Olsen, Charles Jr. (Lib, PS)
O'Neill, Fred
Orr, Arthur
Orr, Walter

Packam, William Edwin
Paige [or Page]
Palmer, William F. (BSec)
Parker, Edward J. (EO, Comm)
Parkins, Stanley
Parkins, William (DB/M, Lt.-
    Comm)
Pearson, Fred D.
Peckam, W.
Perrett, Edwin J.
Perrett, William
Perry
Pertain, F.
Phelan, John
Phillips, George H.
Phillips, Walter
Pickering, Clinton W.
Pike, Alfred J.
Pike, George
Polhemus, George H.
Porter, Walter T.
Post, Vernon (DB/M, B/M, MC)
Post, Vernon Robert
Potter, W. Scott
Prestage, J.
Price, William Harrison
Priester, Don
Prince, Russell (PR)
Psaute, Frank
Pugmire, Ernest I. (Comm)
Pugmire, Joseph
Purdum, George E.

Range, Wilbur
Reid, Henry
Reinhardsen, Gustav (EO)

Rhemick, John
Rice, Kenneth
Rich, David
Rich, Ivor
Riley, David
Riley, William
Riley, William Jr.
Riley, William III
Rimer, Richard
Rischawy, Roger (Lib)
Robb, David
Roberts, Herbert
Robertson, Lawrence
Robinson
Robinson-Cooke, Chris
Robinson-Cooke, David
Rodda, Bertram
Rodda, Gordon
Roe [or Rowe], Arthur
Rombey, M.
Rombey, William
Ross, Donald
Rowe, A. L.
Rowe, Charles (PS)
Rowland, Ronald
Ryans, Jack

Salmon, N.
Sampson, Eric
Samuelson
Sanford, A.
Sarer, John (PS)
Sawyer
Scarlett, William
Scheibner, Thomas (PS)
Schofield, William
Scholin, H.
Schotter, Richard
Schramm, Charles (BSec, FS)
Schramm, Roland (DB/M, FS, EO)
Schultz, Jeffrey

Scott, Albert (EO, Comm)
Scott, James
Scott, Lloyd
Seaver, Douglas
Seiler, Paul
Seiler, Paul D. III
Sharp, Myron
Sharp, Wynbert
Sheppard, Frank
Sheppard, J. Stanley (B/M, DB/M, Lib)
Sheppard, J. William
Shields, Sydney (PR)
Shuffle, H.
Sigler
Simington, Richard
Simons, William "Wiggy" (BSec, FS)
Simonson, Lauritz Martin
Skidmore
Slater, Aubrey
Slater, William (B/M, MC)
Slaymaker, George
Smith, Derek (DB/M, B/M, MC)
Smith, Ernie
Smith, Herbert
Smith, Maro
Smith, Philip
Smith, Warren
Smith, Warren Jr.
Smith, Wilbur H. (PR)
Soule
Spencer, Donald
Squibb, Walter
Stanyon, Douglass
Stanyon, Edward (EO)
Stanyon, Harold
Starbard, Edred D.
Starbard, Leslie M.
Starbard, Raymond
Stickland, Allister
Stillwell, Railton

Stimson, J. J. (PS, BSec)
Storey, T. Henry
Strain, Jeffrey
Straubel, Charles (B/M)
Swenarton, Alfred (Lib)
Swyers, David
Sylvester, T.

Taylor, Harry C.
Thomas, Eugene
Thompson, David
Thompson, Norma (Mrs. James Durand)
Thunell, Ed
Tillsley, Mark
Toft, James (Comm)
Toft, Josef (Lib)
Toft, Samuel
Trembath, Fred
Tripp, Bramwell (Comm)
Trumble, Edward W. (B/M, DB/M)
Trumbull, Rubin
Tunmer, E.
Tunmer, Reuben

Valentine, William
Van Brunt, Kenneth
Van Leusen, Charles (BSec, FS)
Vandewater
Vaughan, Peter C.
Vaughan, Robert
Voisey, Norman (BSec)
Von Calio, Richard

Wadman, David
Waiksnoris, Ronald (DB/M, PR)
Walden, Karl August
Waldron, John (Comm)
Waller, James
Ward, Gordon
Watson, Robert
Weber, J.
Wellman, Harold
Welte, Charles
Welte, Kevin
West, Charles (BSec, FS, PS)
Whatmore, Hugh (Comm)
Whiting, Gerard
Williams, C.
Williams, Charles
Williams, F.
Williams, T. W.
Willmer, George
Willner, Benny
Wilson, A. Kenneth
Wilson, Raymond
Wood, George
Woodruff, Arthur
Wrieden, William
Wray (EO, B/M)
Wright, Bert
Wright, Harry
Wyatt, Peter

Young
Young, Herbert W.
Young, Robert (DB/M, BSec, PS)

289

# APPENDIX E

## A Chronological List of Principal Recordings of
## The New York Staff Band and Male Chorus

NOTE: This list does not include extant radio broadcast records, festival tapes/cassettes, annual spiritual crusade records, or holiday greeting soundsheets. The band did produce one 45 rpm album associated with the movie *On the Beach* (Roulette Label) containing "There's Still Time Brother" and "Banners and Bonnets" (1959).

**Year    Title/Description**

**1922**    (Vocalion Records, produced by Aeolian Co.of NYC; one 12" 78 rpm record): three hymn tunes and a hymn tune march-medley. (B/M Darby)

**1923**    (Vocalion; one 12" 78 rpm record): "Memories" played by John Allan, and "Gems from Haydn." (B/M Darby)

**1940**    (Columbia Recording Co., Halligan Studios, "Triumphonic Recordings"; three 78 rpm records, S.A. 501-503): Christmas carols, Fowler solos, cornet trio "What a Friend," and Mozart—Hawkes transcription. (B/M Granger)

**1941**    ("Triumphonic Recordings"; three 78 rpm records, S.A. 504-507): Christmas carols, Fowler solos, marches, and trombone solos by Kenneth Ayres. (B/M Granger)

**1948**    Triumphonic; two 78 rpm records, 101-102): Christmas carols, "Christmas Joy," "Christmas Tidings," and "The Heralds Angels" (arrangements by Leidzen and Holz). (B/M Bearchell)

**1949**    *Marching to Zion* (Triumphonic; five 78 rpm records, 104-109): title march, "The Valiant Heart," "Lover of the Lord" by Cornetist Edward Lowcock, trombone solo by Arthur Craytor, Fowler with MC accompaniment, etc. (B/M Bearchell)

**1950**    (Triumphonic; two 78 rpm records, 110-111): Christmas arrangements by Bearchell, Leidzen, and Holz. (B/M Bearchell)

**1951** *On the King's Highway* (Triumphonic; four 78 rpm records): title march, "Golden Jubilee," "Grand Old Gospel Songs," MC in "The Old Time Religion." (B/M Slater, MC Holz)

**1957** *The Salvation Army Presenting the New York Staff Band* (LP recording produced by R.C.A. and made by John Castagna at live performances): selections from Ohio-Kentucky tour; not an official record. (B/M Holz)

**1957** *Festival of Music* (Triumphonic): first official LP by NYSB and MC (B/M Holz, MC Post)

**1957** *Carolers' Favorites* (Triumphonic): Christmas arrangements from new carol book arranged by Erik Leidzen (B/M Holz)

**1958** *Christmas with The Salvation Army* (Westminster). (B/M Holz, MC Post)

**1959** *The Salvation Army Band Plays the Great Marches* [original entitled *Salute to E. F. Goldman]* (ABC Paramount Records). (B/M Holz)

**1959** *Great Hymns of Salvation: Jane Pickens and The Salvation Army Choir* [Male Chorus]: 15 hymn arrangements for female soloist with male choir backup. (MC Post)

**1960** *Star-Spangled Band Music* (Triumphonic LP-5): souvenir Great Britain tour record. (B/M Holz, MC Post)

**1961** *King of Kings.* (B/M Holz, MC Post)

**1962** *Classics in Brass:* 75th anniversary album. (B/M Holz)

**1962** *Songs of Victory:* 75th anniversary album. (MC Post)

**1963** *Symphony in Brass* (Word Records Inc.). (B/M Holz, MC Post)

**1963** *The Erik Leidzen Memorial Album:* NYSB and MC side 2. (B/M Holz, MC Post)

**1964** [untitled]: produced for crusade of that year. (B/M Post, MC Post)

**1965** *Marching On* (Word Records Inc.). (B/M Post, MC Post)

**1965** *Centennial Salute* (British release LRZ4009): contains one band and one Male Chorus item. (B/M Post, MC Post)

**1965** *Centennial Celebrations* (live recordings): band at Oct. 23-24 Congress in Lincoln Center and Cathedral of St. John the Divine, NYC.

**1968** *European Tour:* souvenir recording for tour. (B/M Post, MC Post)

**1971** *Triumphant Faith.* (B/M Post, MC Post)

**1973** *Bandsmen and Songster Councils,* Mar. 23-25 (live recordings): NYSB, Canadian Staff Band, and corps groups. (B/M Smith)

1974 *New York Noel.* (B/M Smith, MC Smith)

1974 *New Frontier.* (B/M Smith, MC Smith)

1975 *Sounds of Our Heritage:* bicentennial recording. (B/M Smith, MC Mack)

1976 *1976 ASBDNA Convention, Atlantic City, N.J.* (live recording). (B/M Smith, MC Mack)

1977 *Sing-a-long with the New York Staff Band* (cassette): hymn tune acompaniments. (B/M Smith)

1977 *Ninety Years.* (B/M Smith, MC Mack)

1978 *A Song to Sing:* solo album by Albert Avery with MC. (MC Mack)

1978 Three recordings released with International Congress:
*With One Accord:* NYSB, International Staff Band, Melbourne Staff Band.
*Symphony of Praise* (live excerpts): three staff bands.
*Century of Service:* several NYSB items.

1980 *Digital Brass.* (B/M Smith)

1980 *Lift Up the Banner* (double album): produced for National Congress with NYSB and MC on side 1. (B/M Smith, MC Mack)

1980 *Profile II, The Music of Albert Jakeway* (live recording): F.E.T. program.

1981 *Profile III: The Music of Brindley Boon.*

1981 *Bravo:* NYSB with Philip Smith, guest soloist. (B/M Smith, MC Mack)

1982 *The Ambassadors:* world-tour record. (B/M Smith, MC Mack)

1983 *Profile V, The Music of Richard Holz.*

1983 *The Spirit of Christmas.* (B/M Smith, MC Mack)

1984 *Greetings at Christmas from the Territorial Center, Volume I.*

1985 *Return to England:* British tour album. (B/M Smith, MC Mack)

1985 *Going to the Army* (live recording): Songster Leaders Councils at Royal Albert Hall, London, June 1, 1985.

1985 *Tell the World* (live recording): Festival in Bournemouth International Centre (during England tour).

1985 *Recorded Live on Tour* (Cassette only): various locations.

1985 *Greetings at Christmas from the Territorial Center, Volume II.*

# Endnotes

## Abbreviations Used:

AWC

*The War Cry* (American), published by National Headquarters, 1881-1921. It reported on all Salvation Army activities in the country except those of the far west.

Band Minutes

Minutes of the New York Staff Band Board meetings are extant as follows: 1911-1921, 1927, 1929, 1933 (fragments), 1938-1941, 1945 to the present. Housed in the Salvation Army Archives and Research Center, New York City.

Bearchell Coll.

Materials held by Mrs. Lt.-Colonel William Bearchell (R), Asbury Park, N.J.

B/M

Bandmaster

BOM

"Book of Memories." A compilation of letters from current and past staff bandsmen, put together by Major Charles F. Olsen as part of the band's centennial celebration.

Damon Papers

Papers of Commissioner Alexander Damon at the Salvation Army Archives and Research Center, New York City, 47-2-2.

*Dispo*

*Disposition of Forces.* First published by National Headquarters and now annually by each territorial command; includes exhaustive listings of all Salvation Army officer personnel and locations of corps, centers, etc. The National Headquarters *Dispo* listed National Staff Band personnel consistently after 1898. The Eastern Territory's *Dispo*, starting in 1921, contains membership lists of the New York Staff Band, with the exception of the years 1930-1945.

| | |
|---|---|
| EO | Executive Officer. Administrative and spiritual leader of the New York Staff Band. |
| F.E.T. | Friday Evening at the Temple series at Centennial Memorial Temple, 14th St., New York City. |
| Holz Coll. | Pictures, letters, and memorabilia held by Commissioner Richard E. and Mrs. (Ruby) Holz (R) of Neptune, N.J. |
| HQ | Headquarters |
| Interview | The author held substantial interviews with the following individuals: Lt.-Colonel William E. Bearchell, Lt.-Colonel Edward Fritz, Commissioner Richard E. Holz, Major Thomas Mack, Vernon Post, Derek Smith, and Alfred Swenarton. Results of these interviews in complete detail are housed in the New York Staff Band Archives at the Salvation Army Archives and Research Center, New York City. |
| IHQ | International Headquarters |
| ISB | International Staff Band |
| Leidzen Coll. | Papers, letters, and memorabilia donated to the Salvation Army Archives and Research Center, New York City, by Erik Leidzen's wife Maria. MS 28-5. |
| L.T.C.L. | Licentiate Trinity College London (a performance certificate). |
| LOC | *The Local Officers' Counselor* (name changed in Oct. 1926 to *The Counselor*). Monthly periodical published in New York, 1919-1931, and designed for lay Salvationists. |
| *The Musician* | If the citation refers to *The Musician* published in Britain, *The Musician* will be used in the endnotes; *The Musician* published in the U.S.A. will be signified by *The Musician* (American). |
| Nelson Coll. | Pictures, photos, and materials in the possession of Colonel and Mrs. C. Emil Nelson (R) of New York City. |

| | |
|---|---|
| NHQ | National Headquarters |
| NSB | National Staff Band |
| NYSB | New York Staff Band |
| NYSB Arch. | New York Staff Band Archives Collection housed in the Salvation Army Archives and Research Center, New York City. Includes materials submitted by this author. |
| S.A. Arch. | Salvation Army Archives and Research Center, 145 West 15th St., New York, N.Y. 10011 |
| SB | Staff Band |
| Seiler Coll. | The collection of Salvation Army memorabilia, artifacts, and papers of Colonel Paul D. Seiler (R), Ocean Grove, N.J. |
| S/L | Songster Leader |
| THQ | Eastern Territorial Headquarters, New York City |
| WC | *The War Cry*, national edition, 1970 to the present. |
| WC/E | *The War Cry,* eastern edition, 1921-1970. |

# Notes:

## Chapter 1

1. The consequences of Thomas E. Moore's desertion in 1884 were still painfully present when Ballington succeeded Frank Smith as national commander. For an excellent summary of the Army's first decade, see chapter 1 of Edward H. McKinley, *Marching to Glory: The History of The Salvation Army in the U.S.A., 1880-1980* (San Francisco: Harper & Row, 1980).

2. *AWC*, June 25, 1887, p. 8.

3. *Seventh Anniversary Songs and All About The Salvation Army* (New York, 1887), pp. 10-11.

4. *The Salvation Fight Under the Stars and Stripes, or How We Marched during Twelve Months through the United States* (New York: U.S. National Headquarters, 1888), p. 5, 6.

5. *AWC*, July 2, 1887, p. 4.

6. *AWC*, July 23, 1887, p. 4.

7. Not everyone was hostile; *AWC*, August 27, 1887, p. 8, said, "As the Marshal and his white-helmeted brass band stepped from the depot at Asbury Park, a gentleman was heard to remark, 'They look clean and smart,' whereupon another bystander observed, 'Yes, and intelligent, too.'" This quote often attributed to various other occasions in the band's history.

8. *AWC*, August 27, 1887, p. 5.

9. *AWC*, September 3, 1887, p. 5.

10. *AWC*, October 22, 1887, p. 2.

11. *Ibid.* ("Roll On Dark Streams" contained in *Brass Band Journal* #31).

12. *Ibid.* Gay mentions Keep twice in his report. No record

survives of any other involvement by a "B/M Keep of the Staff Band." A John Keep was identified as serving as accountant and receiver of funds for Moore's splinter Salvation Army of America in a Board of Trustee member's letter of January 12, 1889, that condemns Moore's policies. Part of Seiler Coll.

13. John Keep did not disappear entirely. He shows up as a Plaintiff's Witness in the case *The Salvation Army in the United States against The American Salvation Army,* Appellate Division of the Supreme Court, printed by B. Tyrrel, New York, 1908. His testimony, pages 201-206, identifies him as a public accountant residing in Brooklyn. He was connected with the Army from 1883 but did not stay long with Moore after October 1884, except in a professional capacity. Nothing further was said about his involvement with the regular Army except his willingness to stand as witness against Moore.

14. *AWC,* December 3, 1887, p. 6; *AWC,* December 24, 1887, p. 12. The artist's sketch on page one of the Dec. 24 *AWC* shows a band of seven marching into the "Salvation Temple."

15. *WC/E,* April 23, 1931, p. 7.

16. *AWC,* November 8, 1883, p. 1.

17. *AWC,* December 27, 1884, p. 6.

18. First report of an official commissioning comes with Frank Smith's visit to Alliance, Ohio, Dec. 26-28, 1885. Fall River's tradition maintains a band there from *at least* 1885. They were featured in regional meetings, 1886. McKinley identified Oakland date via photograph; he also cites Danbury, Conn., where Charles Ives' father served as band trainer (Danbury *Sun Times,* August 23, 1886).

19. *AWC,* February 20, 1886, p. 1.

20. *AWC,* April 9, 1887, p. 16, identifies bands from Fall River, Boston, Lawrence, and New York participating in Boston's Seventh Anniversary; Grand Rapids' Band is charmingly described in *AWC,* June 11, 1887, p. 12.

21. *AWC,* January 22, 1887, p. 16; *AWC,* February 26, 1887, p. 13.

22. Staff-Captain Will B. Palmer, reporting in *AWC,* April 6, 1889, p. 15.

23. *Ibid.*

24. E. S. Gerberich (staff bandsman), "The Place of Bands in Past Days," *LOC*, I, no. 13 (October 1920), p. 29.

25. *AWC*, July 6, 1889, p. 9.

26. *AWC*, September 7, 1889, p. 16.

27. Quoted in *AWC*, August 3, 1889, p. 9. A May 4th *AWC* report (p. 7) described this band on a trip to Peekskill, N.Y., as consisting of 15 members: 3 majors, 3 staff-captains, 7 captains, and 2 lieutenants.

28. *AWC*, October 12, 1889, pp. 5-6.

29. *AWC*, October 4, 1890, p. 8. No wonder B/M Charles Miles requested, and was granted, an extended sick furlough.

30. *AWC*, September 26, 1891, p. 5. The training was held at Hempstead, N.Y.

31. *AWC*, March 19, 1892, p. 8.

32. Signed "More Anon," *AWC*, January 16, 1892, p. 5.

33. *AWC*, December 10, 1892, p. 4.

34. Program of the American Jubilee Congress (October 20-27, 1894), p. 5. S.A. Arch.

35. An interesting biographical sketch is provided in *AWC*, December 30, 1893, p. 13.

36. Trumble may have had restrictions placed on him that made the band less active, less proficient, and definitely smaller during this period. We cannot document that, however. *AWC*, April 3, 1895, p. 5.

37. A picture of Trumble in the Seiler Coll. is marked "turned *traitor*, March 1896, returned April 1897."

38. An undated newspaper article titled "Ballington Abused: Bandmaster Trumble Sends a Hot Letter of Resignation" exists in the Seiler Coll. that tells Trumble's involvement in these affairs of March-April 1896. Trumble would never again be given a major responsibility when he did return "to the ranks" the following year.

39. The Victory Band was held together by Harry Taylor (See *AWC*, August 1, 1896); a description of Halpin's band called it "a splendid band, principally of NHQ officers," which rendered

service at the National Congress, November 28-December 2. See *AWC*, Nov. 14, 1896, p. 9, for account of band at Carnegie Hall in support of Armenian Relief Fund. It was not the NSB.

40. *AWC*, January 16, 1897, p. 8.

41. *Ibid.*, p. 9.

## Chapter 2

1. Summary made from chapter 3 of Edward H. McKinley, *Marching to Glory: The History of The Salvation Army in the U.S.A., 1880-1980* (San Francisco: Harper & Row, 1980), and from Commissioner Harry Williams' unpublished paper "Booth-Tucker's Contribution to the Development of The Salvation Army in the United States of America," September 1981.

2. Information supplied in a letter to the author by Douglas Anderson.

3. *AWC*, July 27, 1897, p. 12.

4. *AWC*, March 27, 1897, p. 4.

5. *AWC*, May 1, 1897, p. 3.

6. *AWC*, June 5, 1897, p. 7.

7. *Ibid.*

8. For example, see *Dispo*, July 1899, p. 3.

9. This music is discussed in greater depth in chapter 12. Anderson's return, despite his heavy load in the Finance Department, was necessary to keep continuity in the band's program.

10. "Regulations for Special Demonstrations Relative to the General's Visit in 1898" (New York, 1898), p. 14.

11. For years Stimson was featured by Evangeline Booth at annual reunion dinners for officers and Staff Band reunions. His exploits, from his "roll call" song that introduced each member of the NSB, to his "stand-up comic" abilities are now legendary. Some of this man's unique characteristics have been captured in a collection of his improvisations, entitled *Talking It Over*, published by request of Commander Evan-

geline Booth in 1934. The drum quote cited in *WC/E,* May 18, 1940, p. 13.

12. Quoted from *The Commercial Advertiser* in *AWC,* May 16, 1898, p. 6.

13. *Cleveland Press* report echoed in *AWC,* November 8, 1902, p. 5.

14. Complete report *AWC,* August 28, 1897, p. 5.

15. *AWC,* July 29, 1899, p. 12.

16. W. Scott Potter's complete report is printed in *AWC,* June 17, 1899, p. 4.

17. *AWC,* April 22, 1899, p. 5.

18. *AWC,* January 18, 1902, p. 9, features the Far-West Portion of the Continental Campaign, including a photo of Booth-Tucker and the band with their special car, "Crystal."

19. *AWC,* January 11, 1902, p. 11.

20. A feature on the press room appears in *AWC,* April 4, 1902, p. 11.

21. Letter in BOM.

22. The Canadian Staff Band rode the train all night from Toronto in order to participate in the services, as a mark of respect for this amazing woman. *AWC,* November 21, 1903, p. 8.

23. Notes on congress by Charles Anderson, *WC/E,* September 15, 1934, p. 3.

24. *AWC,* July 2, 1904, p. 12.

25. The evening concert was divided, one in First Class, one in Steerage. The Commander's pamphlet for the cruise included the full on-ship schedule and forty-eight songs which the delegates were to learn by the congress (accompanied by the NSB). *Information Issued for Delegates to the International Congress from the United States of America* (New York, 1904), p. 20.

26. *AWC,* July 30, 1904, p. 5.

27. *AWC,* July 23, 1904, p. 11. Quote from *The Times.* The band was also requested to play at Carlton Terrace House for the American Ambassador to Great Britain, Joseph Choate.

28. Anderson, *WC/E,* September 15, 1934, p. 3.

29. *Ibid.*

30. *AWC,* September 24, 1904, p. 8.

31. *AWC,* December 24, 1904. The official welcome was December 6.

32. *AWC,* April 8, 1905, p. 9.

33. *AWC,* January 27, 1906, p. 8.

34. *AWC,* March 24, 1906, p. 13. Field Notes by Lt.-Col. McIntyre reflect this major advance in band structure: "In the reorganization of the NSB Major Anderson receives valuable assistance. Major Stanyon becomes spiritual bandmaster and will preside over special meetings given by the band. Brother Robert Griffith becomes deputy bandmaster; Ensign Van Leusen still retaining secretaryship. Speaking of the SB, a few additional musicians are needed at this time. This department will be glad to aid in finding positions for any who might be coming to NYC and who could assist in this way." By Darby's era the band board would be an efficient support mechanism in the administration of the band.

35. As printed in the *AWC,* May 19, 1906, p. 8.

36. *AWC,* December 10, 1910, p. 8. Crowd estimated at over 600 inmates.

37. For example, see report *AWC,* April 28, 1910, p. 9. Similar programs were being run at the Boston People's Palace at this time.

38. Tour reports by Norris: *AWC,* September 11, 1909, p. 12; September 18, 1909, p. 8; September 25, 1909, pp. 8 and 12.

39. Nicol's candor must have been a breath of fresh air in those days! Of course the NSB was not the ISB, but Nicol could tell that there were excellent musicians here. He used the article to get in a few "pot shots" of his own at British-style banding.

**Chapter 3**

1. Staff Band Minutes of March 20, 1912, refer to a lengthy discussion concerning B/M Griffith's relationship to the band, but this is not detailed, by request, in the minutes. Minutes of

April 6, 1912, acknowledge Griffith's resignation with Darby asserting his rights to the leadership as he had been functioning as deputy since at least October 1911 (Minutes, October 5, 1911). Evangeline appointed Robert Young as bandmaster but he strongly deferred to Darby who was eventually given the band officially, though Evangeline had him listed as deputy as late as the June 1912 *Dispo.* Evangeline would have trouble making leadership decisions with the band later, too. In this case she was probably too closely connected to be objective, as Robert Griffith was her aide-de-camp's brother.

2. "Music and Its Application to Salvation Army Purposes," *AWC,* July 31, 1915, p. 10.

3. Band Minutes, January 12, 1912. Colonel Jenkins, EO, had reported that the chief secretary (second in command to Commander Booth) was favorably considering this request.

4. Band Minutes of the months preceding the concert show a real organizer at work. Darby even sent complimentary tickets to all YMCA secretaries in the Greater N.Y. area. The general themes of these board meetings were greater efficiency and greater use of the band.

5. Concert review, *AWC,* June 22, 1912, p. 9. Fowler was featured during Male Chorus items, not as a separate soloist.

6. *AWC,* June 27, 1914, p. 12. The Flint Band also played for a large, first-class audience including the former President.

7. *Ibid.*

8. *AWC,* July 11, 1914, p. 2.

9. *AWC,* July 18, 1914, pp. 15, 16.

10. *AWC,* July 25, 1914, pp. 8-13.

11. *AWC,* June 19, 1915; also similar events at Boston congress. Date of councils was June 20; there were 24 bands in the Central Province then.

12. *AWC,* October 2, 1915, p. 9. Sunday school parades, notably in Brooklyn, were notorious for causing band problems. Later the band ran into difficulty playing in them as the Musicians' Union required payment to a card carrier for every man that marched. The Band Minutes of 1915 through the early twen-

ties are filled with trivial dealing in the financial end of the parade.

13. *AWC,* December 20, 1916, p. 9.

14. These summaries were by now commonplace. The tour account appeared in *AWC,* May 19, 1917, pp. 6-7; "The Annual Report of 1917 to the Chief of the Staff" (ACC 78-25), pp. 12-13, is one of the few of its kind from this era that survives with any mention of the band.

15. *AWC,* December 29, 1917, p. 12. The Band Minutes of November 9, 1917, had called for cancellation of all but two engagements for this reason.

16. Who knows if some of the men, like Lewellyn Cowan who entered the U.S. Air Force about this time, were not positively affected by the jingoistic spirit to which they contributed. Their first event was a patriotic parade in Yonkers; *WC/E,* May 19, 1917, p. 12.

17. *AWC,* April 20, 1918, p. 8.

18. *AWC,* May 18, 1918, p. 8.

19. *AWC,* July 20, 1918, p. 10.

20. *AWC,* September 28, 1918, p. 4.

21. *AWC,* December 7, 1918, p. 8. The ISB had a similar assignment, by invitation of the Lord Mayor of London, parading through their city. See Boon, *ISB: The Story of the International Staff Band of The Salvation Army* (London: Record Greetings Ltd., 1985), p. 61.

22. *AWC,* December 14, 1914, p. 8.

23. Fourteen members had enlisted in the war; by March 1919, seven were "mustered out" and had rejoined. By mid-March the band was back to 29 members.

24. Interview at his welcome, *AWC,* September 20, 1919, p. 8.

25. The change of title to Territorial Staff Band, or Eastern Territorial Staff Band, came in October 1920, with the division of America into three territories. National Headquarters remained in New York. The band was still called "National Staff," particularly when with the National Commander. When they

were with their territorial commander, they became a "Territorial Staff Band." Until the 1930s the titles were used interchangeably.

26. *LOC,* II, no. 7 (April 1921), pp. 10-11, 15.

27. Complete *War Cry* account appeared in the *WC/E,* September 10, 1921, pp. 12-13; September 17, 1921, pp. 7, 9, 13; and September 24, 1921, pp. 7, 16.

28. "Three Bands on Tour," *LOC,* III, no. 1 (October 1921), p. 19.

29. *WC/E,* June 10, 1922, p. 13.

30. *WC/E,* June 17, 1922, p. 13.

31. *WC/E,* October 14, 1922, p. 6.

32. *LOC,* III, no. 11 (August 1922) p. 32.

33. Staff Bandmaster William Slater preserved these historic gems by transferring them to magnetic tape, now housed in the S.A. Arch. The medley included "Onward Christian Soldiers" and "Adeste Fidelis."

34. *WC/E,* February 10, 1923, p. 9.

35. This broadcast was sponsored by Bamberger Co. *WC/E,* March 10, 1923, p. 13.

36. *WC/E,* November 24, 1923, p. 9. A broadcast on WEAF from the Brooklyn Bedford Ave. YMCA (Dr. S. Parkes Cadman) in December 1925 reached an estimated audience of two million.

37. Wonderful accounts of Evangeline and the band appear in chapters 17 and 18 of Margaret Troutt, *The General Was a Lady: The Story of Evangeline Booth* (Nashville, Tenn.: A. J. Holman, 1980).

38. *WC/E,* May 23, 1925, p. 9.

39. *WC/E,* June 4, 1927, p. 9.

40. *WC/E,* March 12, 1927, p. 13.

41. *LOC* (December 3, 1927).

42. Quote from "A New Departure," *LOC,* IX, no. 5 (February 1928), p. 21. *WC/E,* December 3, 1927, had contained announcement of the appointment.

43. *The Salvation Army Brass Band Journal (U.S.A.)* appeared in 1928, the first item being William Broughton's march "Our Leader," written in honor of Evangeline Booth. The journal, and its companion *Festival Series* (with 1930 Contest Winners like "Army of God"), were released under the auspices of National Headquarters. The venture was ultimately not a financial success, and when Broughton replaced Arkett, a decision was made to stop publishing. During the Depression it was a luxury the Army could not afford.

44. *WC/E* Congress Report, November 26, 1927, p. 4. Program of congress survives in NYSB Arch.

45. *WC/E*, Program Review; February 25, 1928, p. 7.

46. Brigadier Franklin Hoffman's letter in BOM indicates the rehearsals were 12:00-2:00, the men either walking (as Leslie Starbard's similar letter in BOM states) or riding in a taxi. The temporary HQ at 14th Street and Broadway had no room for rehearsal.

47. Program in NYSB Arch. *WC/E* report, June 22, 1929, p. 8.

48. "In Concert," *LOC*, X, no. 10 (July 1929), p. 20.

49. See *WC/E*, January 18, 1930, and *WC/E*, November 22, 1930, p. 7, for further details on the ensemble.

50. Letter in Leidzen Coll., 28-5, dated December 19, 1921, Darby to Commissioner Estill. Leidzen's first wife was soon seriously ill and he was not permitted to enter training. Later, he moved to Boston to lead the famed New England Staff Band for awhile, before returning permanently to New York.

51. Letter to George Darby, in S.A. Arch., MS 28-5.

52. Congress Reports were included in *WC/E*, May 31, 1930. Other articles on the bands of the congress and on the composers' contest appeared in *LOC*, especially XI, no. 10 (July 1930), pp. 9-10. Programs of the congress, including the "Mammoth Festival," are extant and available in NYSB Arch.

53. *The Band Tune Book Supplement* did not come out until 1953. The five-part arrangements that Leidzen used were released in 1931. Another collection, as edited by Emil Soderstrom under the title *Selected Tunes for Congregational Singing Arranged for Small Bands,* was also available by 1936 (Central Territory).

54. *WC/E,* "Musical Gems," by Coles, August 2, 1930, p. 11.

55. William Parkins, 34th stanza of his "A Tone Poem," written upon completion of NYSB Canadian Tour, May 1937.

### Chapter 4

1. *WC/E,* February 7, 1931, p. 9. William Slater was also featured, in both a euphonium solo and the performance of his third-prize selection, "Our Redeemer."

2. In January the chief secretary, in his "Notes," *WC/E,* January 17, 1931, stated that Darby was ill *again,* evidently referring to problems experienced in late 1930.

3. In an interview with the author, William Bearchell and Richard E. Holz intimated that it may have been more than ill health. Evangeline had argued with Darby in recent years over his continued use of "outside" music, although he had greatly curtailed this as better Army music became more available and more abundant. He, in return, may have quarreled with her over legal matters pertaining to the High Council that deposed her brother, Bramwell. Darby lived to a ripe old age, fulfilling major administrative responsibilities, without further reference to poor health after his resignation as bandmaster. He was rarely brought back into the musical limelight, however, at least at Evangeline's bidding.

4. *WC/E,* May 23, 1931, p. 7. He did lead N.Y. No. 1 Corps for a brief time.

5. "Red" Sheppard bequeathed his substantial cornet/trumpet library to my father. It is now in my possession. Sheppard was a student of fine brass music and solo literature.

6. *WC/E,* June 20, 1931, p. 8.

7. *WC/E,* May 30, 1931, p. 9.

8. *Ibid.*

9. *WC/E,* June 27, 1931, p. 9.

10. *WC/E,* June 20, 1931, p. 4.

11. William Bearchell related to me that this was a particularly hilarious escapade. For him it was a funny homecoming, but

"Red" Sheppard had him lead the band on the Town Hall steps; he became the home boy who made good.

12. In a BOM letter, Albert Lock mentions how unenthusiastic many of the men were about the motorcade at first. Lock had just experienced a death in his family so it was doubly hard to enter into the proceedings with a joyful heart.

13. *WC/E*, April 9, 1932, p. 8. Picture of Montreal Band, with its lone sax, can be seen in *WC/E*, April 16, 1932, p. 13. Other bands in the marathon march were Brooklyn No. 1, Yonkers, and the Cadets' Band.

14. *WC/E*, June 10, 1932, p. 10.

15. *WC/E*, June 18, 1932, p. 11. At Ellis Island the band frequently was asked to play for large groups about to be deported (those who had not cleared immigration). These crowds could be in the thousands.

16. With permission from William Bearchell I have used this excerpt to tell a truthful but perplexing account of this period in the band's history. The men of the band were not exactly saints in their response to Evangeline and Broughton.

17. From an interview with William Bearchell, July 30, 1983. One more story from that interview will seal the issue: "The men were frequently rebellious. In Philadelphia once he called out for the march 'Christ Church' on parade. The band struck up to a man, with previous planning, the march 'Alabama' from the old Darby march book, memorized. Broughton then refused to march in front of the group."

18. Broughton would have further, if checkered, success as an Army music leader; first, to Pittsburgh, where Ebbs formed a Western Pennsylvania Staff Band for him. He also returned to the podium in Detroit and finally did yeoman service as territorial music secretary of the Western Territory, where his memory is rightfully revered.

19. A full report appeared in *WC/E*, November 17, 1934, p. 6.

**Chapter 5**

1. Good accounts of the "Ensemble Festival" incident between Leidzen and Evangeline are given in these two books: Edward

H. McKinley, *Marching to Glory: The History of The Salvation Army in the U.S.A., 1880-1980* (San Francisco: Harper & Row, 1980), pp. 169-170, and Margaret Troutt, *The General Was a Lady: The Story of Evangeline Booth* (Nashville, Tenn.: A. J. Holman, 1980), pp. 174-176. What is not made clear by either, but can be asserted now by a review of the Leidzen papers at the S.A. Arch., is that though Evangeline and Leidzen did have a formal reconciliation, her subordinates purposefully blocked Leidzen from official Army involvement (with or without her endorsement we do not know). Bramwell Coles played a sensitive role in keeping Leidzen tenuously connected with Army publications through a remarkable correspondence during the 1930s and 1940s. Leidzen remained bitter toward Evangeline and her "henchmen" until the last two years of her life when they did exchange some cordial greetings on the occasions of festivals produced in each other's honor.

2. A regular series of Wednesday evening holiness meetings, for instance, was started by Booth-Tucker in the fall of 1899. There were many variants of these in the years before then, too.

3. Could it be that Booth's decision to bring in Broughton as "her" composer/conductor stemmed from some professional jealousy over Ebbs' success that fall of 1932 with Leidzen and the F.E.T.? Imagine the difficult tightrope Ebbs walked in launching the F.E.T.: he must appoint the territorial commander, John McMillan as president of the Temple Fellowship and also play court to the royal Evangeline. The introductions at special occasions at F.E.T. meetings must have been interesting.

4. Samson Hodges, staff bandsman of much stature, was the original F.E.T. organist. Mrs. Harris was the first American organist to receive the L.T.C.L. diploma, in 1933, from the hands of Sir Granville Bantock, who served as examiner.

5. The quote is from a letter dated October 13, 1932, from Ebbs' office as part of a publicity campaign for F.E.T. (Holz Collection). Leidzen shared the entire story with the May 1948 F.E.T. Finale crowd (*WC/E,* June 5, 1948, p. 8). Correspondence between Leidzen and Ebbs at this time confirms that they were the initiators of the plan and were able to convince John McMillan to allow them to try it.

6. *WC/E,* February 18, 1933, p. 8.

7. Quoted in *WC/E*, June 6, 1936, p. 11.

8. The F.E.T. was intended as a major cultural event as well. Ebbs and Leidzen had envisioned that no separation need be made between the highest musical aspirations and the loftiest spiritual growth.

9. F.E.T. drew in many churchgoers other than Salvationists; noted Christian and professional performers were eager to perform at this exciting new worship experience.

10. "Staff Band Night," *WC/E*, May 18, 1940, p. 13.

11. "A Tactful Bandmaster," *LOC*, VII, no. 5 (February 1926), p. 10.

12. This assessment confirmed in interviews with many Granger-year bandsmen, including the formal interviews with William Bearchell and Richard Holz.

13. Granger constantly tried to improve his abilities, however. Richard Holz, knowing Granger to be a record collector, mentioned to him after a particularly poor reading of "Sound Out the Proclamation," that a new recording from England had arrived of this piece. Within a week Granger returned to the podium much better prepared to teach the music to the band. From Bearchell's diary, January 23, 1936, we read: "Poor Geroge Granger not quite up to the Staff B/M. Fellows sensing the situation." They helped him become a good bandmaster because they loved his kind, gracious leadership.

14. Information from official obituary and program of 1938, "Tribute to Major George Granger, Temple Corps Bandmaster" included in NYSB Arch.

15. *WC/E*, November 10, 1932, p. 9. The Thanksgiving Day Service was the first live broadcast from Centennial Memorial Temple, by WRNY, Aviation Radio Station, Inc.

16. The amalgamation of WRNY into WHN caused the new management to feel that their budget could not support the Army programs.

17. *WC/E*, July 7, 1934, p. 4. The programs were carried on short-wave, also; WZXZ (N.Y.), W3XAV (Philadelphia). Three Canadian networks also carried the CBS programs.

18. In the Depression it was amazing that this amount of air time

was granted. William L. Devoto was soon transferred to IHQ and John Allan took over the Public Relations Department duties.

19. The reason cited in *WC/E,* December 4, 1937, p. 10, was "commercial demands."

20. *WC/E,* December 5, 1936, p. 10.

21. Carbon copy of script, Holz Coll. Richard Holz provided many of the manuscript musical arrangements required for the programs.

22. "Memories: Our Canadian Trip," p. 9; booklet privately produced by William Parkins. Bearchell Coll.

23. *Ibid.,* p. 13.

24. *WC/E,* June 26, 1937, p. 12.

25. *WC/E,* June 12, 1937, p. 8, contains full tour report.

26. A picture of the Male Chorus singing in the cemetery appears in *WC/E,* June 19, 1937, p. 15.

27. Drawn from *The War Cry,* personal diaries, and Band Minutes that survive. Only confirmed engagements are listed. This is not a comprehensive list.

28. *WC/E,* March 18, 1939, p. 8. The band was a pioneer in prison visitation, of course, and J. Stanley Sheppard, by 1943, was a guest lecturer at Yale University on correctional services.

29. All three spring programs of the 1939 Fair survive. The N.Y. State Tour, *WC/E,* June 17, 1939, p. 15; Greeting Norwegian royalty, May 10, 1939, p. 10; F.E.T. with Westminster Choir, *WC/E,* May 20, 1939, p. 12.

30. *WC/E,* October 14, 1939, p. 8.

31. It could be that Damon calculated the 1891 date to coincide with his membership. In 1936, on an Ocean Grove program, the band recognized itself as one year shy of 50. During the proceedings, the famous "bicycle band" story was retold but I have not been able to substantiate that as a Staff Band activity.

32. Jubilee concert program and banquet programs are in NYSB Arch. Concert report, *WC/E,* January 3, 1942, pp. 8-9.

33. *WC/E,* January 17, 1942, p. 10.

34. In an interview with Al Swenarton, the author learned that Granger frequently relied on servicemen stationed in the area. Another problem Granger faced was the involuntary "desertion" by 1942 (for financial/employment reasons) of fine players like Farrar, Wrieden, and Orr to Leidzen's famous Arma Band. Their break with the band was not final, however, and they played from time to time in support of Granger. Walter Orr, of course, became a stalwart solo cornetist in the post-war Staff Band.

35. *WC/E,* April 5, 1941, p. 8.

36. *WC/E,* June 7, 1941, p. 13.

37. The band joined Eva for several productions in these years. At Pittsburgh they supported her at the Syria Mosque auditorium, along with the Westinghouse Male Chorus (Oscar Grosskopf) and soloist Charlotte Shallenerger, April 12, 1942. *WC/E,* April 23, 1942, p. 8.

38. *WC/E,* April 11, 1942, p. 11. They also stopped at Atlantic City for "beach ministry."

39. Brigadier Lawrence Castagna told me that Granger frequently suffered from these wounds but rarely let on that they bothered him. Some feel they contributed to his fatal illness.

40. Nearly every program from 1936 to 1951 survives in NYSB Arch. Weekend report of 1936: *WC/E,* August 22, 1936, p. 8.

41. Complete schedule included on 1936 Festival Program brochure, NYSB Arch.

42. *Ibid.*

43. Program for the 1938 Festival; of course, encores are "officially" prohibited by Salvation Army Regulations for Bands.

44. Even though he may have sent the same one to each bandsman, the thought was kind and gracious. Letter courtesy of Brigadier Lawrence Castagna.

45. Sloan was editor of *The Christian Advocate;* the band "backed him up" on the Sunday morning services in 1939 and 1940.

46. *The Musician* (American), V. no. 3 (March 1945), p. 3.

47. "Dedicated Band" in William G. Harris, *Sagas of Salvationism* (New York: The Salvation Army, 1961), pp. 177-179.

48. From December 29, 1985, interview with Alfred Swenarton. What a remarkable series of pieces, when one considers the titles and their significance to the unexpected event of Granger's death!

49. From Bearchell interview.

50. Swenarton was officially a member by 1940 but had played in the band before that. Earlier that day Granger had asked Swenarton to play but Swenarton declined because he felt out-of-shape for such a program. Swenarton asked Granger how he felt, for he noticed the bandmaster looked pale. Granger only shrugged it off as just a bit of fatigue.

51. Swenarton interview.

52. From William Parkins poem, "To George, A Bandsman's Tribute," published by *WC/E,* August 25, 1945, p. 11.

## Chapter 6

1. Credit must be given to Commissioner Ernest I. Pugmire and to his successor, Donald MacMillan, for having the faith and vision to establish the Music Department. The work began in the late fall of 1945 when Holz was finally relieved of any remaining chaplaincy duties. One of his first efforts was to get young veterans returning to corps bands, who may have learned bad habits during the war, reestablished carefully and with understanding by local leaders who might not be very patient.

2. The Hymn Society sponsored the festival. Five hundred leading organists, hymnologists, and ministers of music were present. *WC/E,* June 4, 1949, p. 8. Other information supplied in Holz interview. Program survives, as does Holz paper, in NYSB Arch.

3. The alternating Councils-Congress plan was followed till the end of the Post era. This overview, provided in interviews with Holz, Post and Swenarton, is but a highlighting of the major efforts. Many more projects were undertaken.

4. Regional leaders, like Colonel Richard Stretton of the New

England Province, or Brigadier Harold Zealley in Southwest Ohio, were also keyed into, and approved of this rebuilding program.

5. Festival Report, *WC/E*, March 16, 1946, p. 11. The band played at Colonel Walter Jenkins' funeral in February, too. Charles Miles and Charles Anderson had also died in 1945.

6. See Richard E. Holz's "Music Camps in America," *The Salvation Army Year Book, 1948* (London: Salvationist Publishing and Supplies), pp. 5-7, for an excellent summary of the American music camp program since John Allan's 1921 North Long Branch music camp.

7. *WC/E*, February 21, 1948, p. 11.

8. The band first played at Calvary Baptist Church in June 1945; they returned in November 1947. The Christmas series of concerts began in 1947. Some of the most moving moments of those long December days, filled with contrasting engagements, would come at the Detention Home.

9. Hilarious stories are told of Billy Sunday's dramatic introductions of the band, prior to their impressive march down the aisle playing a stirring hymn. The second generation bandsmen were by and large born into Christian homes; very few were like pioneer B/M Wray, our converted saloon-keeper, alcoholic and minstrel. It made good press, though, and the band dealt with men like that all the time.

10. The list of great churches where the band has ministered is endless: from Westminster Abbey to the Cathedral of St. John the Divine to the great Catholic Cathedral in Pittsburgh. As flattering as such occasions are, many bandsmen enjoy a salvation meeting in an Army hall just as much.

11. *WC/E*, February 19, 1949, p. 8, cites this engagement in "Coming Events."

12. Program was held at New Jersey State Teachers' College, Jersey City, N.J., December 8, 7:15 p.m. NYSB Arch.

13. In 1933 Goldman had called Leidzen a "genius," during the May F.E.T. Finale. The quote about "greatest arranger" came at the 1948 F.E.T. "All Leidzen" Concert. Goldman had hired Leidzen back in 1933 and the latter served the Goldman Band as its principal arranger until his death in 1962.

313

14. This is the highest rank achieved by any New York staff bandsman: second in command of the international, worldwide Salvation Army.

15. Program from Bearchell Coll. It is possible that *all* of these pieces, with the exception of "Happy All the Day" (written for Parkins before Staff Band days), were written for the Staff Band first. Even "Pressing Onward," usually thought to be a New England Staff Band piece, was first played and read from manuscript by Darby's band. They made fun of it because they found it nearly unplayable!

16. Frequently Leidzen's new pieces were played at Star Lake first, then absorbed into Staff Band repertoire: "Richmond" (1948), "Where Flowers Never Fade" (1950), "None Other Name" (1959), and many others. Coles' march "Salute to America" was premiered at the 1948 camp, too, when he and James Neilson were the guests. (Leidzen visited on the weekend.)

17. It may be difficult for younger readers to understand the significance of Leidzen's recommitment to Army music. This nationally acclaimed musician was realigning himself with his heritage. It made so many young musicians proud; many of them studied with him: Holz, Post, Evans, Ditmer. The Holz-Leidzen collaboration from 1946-1962 is well-documented and explained in Les Fossey, *This Man Leidzen* (London: Campfield Press, 1966).

18. Holz interview. The Male Chorus sang Sullivan's "The Homeland" at Eva's funeral service, Kensico Cemetery, July 20, 1950. Frank Fowler and Olof Lundgren sang solos there as well.

19. Allan declared the festival "the finest yet" in his years of hearing the band. *WC/E,* November 5, 1949, p. 11.

20. Supplied from Bearchell Coll.

21. *The Musician* (American) of May 1948, carried a full report on the congress. The previous year's Music Leader's Councils had 210 registered local music officers.

22. From critique sheets surviving in Music Bureau Archives, this report on p. 22. Six musicians served as adjudicators: W.

Slater, B. Ditmer, E. Parr, E. Lowcock, M. MacFarlane, C. Peter Carlson.

23. *Ibid.,* p. 23.

24. Bearchell was transferred to the New England Province as divisional officer and then as provincial secretary. He had been on THQ as head accountant in Trade for 27 years. His final appointment was as divisional commander in the Northeast Pa. (Scranton) Division.

25. *WC/E,* April 28, 1951, p. 14. Full tour report on page 4.

26. *WC/E,* October 27, 1951, p. 11. The first recorded TV appearance by American Salvation Army musicians was in 1931 when an ensemble from the Training College, directed by William Maltby, played on a program released over the limited-access broadcasts of that date.

27. *WC/E,* March 22, 1952, p. 10.

28. Tour report, *WC/E,* March 8, 1952, p. 8. Toronto stores and buildings were draped in black during the band's visit due to the death of King George VI.

29. *WC/E,* March 15, 1952, p. 11.

30. *WC/E,* January 12, 1952, p. 13.

31. Ms. Graham also interviewed R. E. Holz extensively about the Army's band program. *Great Bands of America* (New York: Thomas Nelson and Sons, 1952).

32. Comparing past achievements to present standards is a dangerous undertaking. An objective analysis, however, verifies this opinion.

33. Holz's version is told in his weekly column, "The Band Box" *WC/E,* March 29, 1952, p. 13. Willson told how he came to write the song in *WC/E,* April 5, 1952, p. 10. The phrase from the Cadet's Pledge—"Will you love the unloved, never reckoning the cost?" —gave him the initial idea. The song was completed after he witnessed a Salvation Army procession on a New York street which he described with the words "Marching with trumpet and drum, with Banners and Bonnets they come" (from NYSB program note by Holz).

34. *WC/E,* March 29, 1952, p. 13.

35. Band Minutes are filled every year with complaints and counter-complaints regarding the flexibility required from department heads and lost work time because of band scheduling. It is a never-ending concern.

36. For instance, the forty-five minute TV special with Margaret Arlen, December 1953, as part of Salvation Army Week (WCBS-TV).

37. *WC/E,* October 27, 1952, p. 11.

38. The radio series was dropped, for instance, with no explanation by upper administration, with a mere statement that, "Your work is done." These special efforts, for small ensembles, always carried dangers; when the full band was poor, sextets and ensembles always flourished. This could provoke jealous reaction from those not involved.

39. Extensive reports in *WC/E,* July 3 and 10, 1954.

40. Even the other four—Samuel Hepburn, Ernest Holz, John Needham, and Norman S. Marshall (who retired in Oct. 1986)—had close connections.

41. *WC/E,* November 13, 1954, p. 8. Full brief and miscellaneous programs from the tour survive in NYSB Arch.

42. There were, therefore, two deputy bandmasters for this brief time! Slater officially retired at a January 1955 Band Banquet. The annual WNYC radio broadcast in December 1954, however, was conducted by Holz with Post leading the Male Chorus.

43. Many interesting occasions were recorded by Slater over the years, preserving a treasury of band programs.

44. *WC/E,* April 18, 1953, p. 13. The "Band Box" reviewer (Holz) specifically dwelt on dynamics. Al Swenarton told me that Bill Slater would have preferred a 50-piece band along the lines of Montreal Citadel, and he liked the band loud.

45. Congress programs survive for all the congresses from 1946 onwards.

46. *WC/E,* (February issues, 1954) contain the full "Tranas Story."

47. *WC/E,* April 24, 1954, p. 8.

48. *Ibid.,* p. 15.

49. Leidzen had trained the band on several previous visits. He and Gunnar Borg were close friends. The Leidzen "Concertino" was written for Maisie Ringham (Wiggins) of the Halle' Orchestra and officially premiered with the ISB that year. The NYSB, of course, had opportunity to preview this music with Leidzen to insure all the parts were correct before sending it to England.

### Chapter 7

1. *WC/E,* January 9, 1955, p. 9.

2. Holz had several years of study at Oklahoma University, New York University, and Columbia University. He also studied privately with Erik Leidzen for several years.

3. The term "enforcer" comes from an interview with Alfred Swenarton. Swenarton observed that though Slater wanted discipline, he could not really impart it effectively; Bearchell, himself a "wit" when a bandsman, was in no particular position to suddenly reverse roles. Their bands were, relatively speaking, less intense, "easy-going."

4. When Holz took over the band there were, of course, excellent soloists like Edward Lowcock and Arthur Anderson, among others.

5. Richard Holz relates amusing anecdotes of Frank Fowler's reluctance to give up his Conn BB♭ Bass for the new Besson horn. Some of the confrontations were not so amusing, however; it was difficult to get men seriously involved in music-making, which, prior to this, had often been looked on as merely a break from office routine.

6. Congress program in NYSB Arch.; See *WC/E,* May 21, 1955, p. 8.

7. The Star Lake Musicamp groups had played on the Mall several years before but not in the context of the Goldman Band Schedule.

8. Previous celebrations had included a festive program before 2,500 people at Battery Park on March 10.

9. Quote from program notes supplied that evening; program in NYSB Arch. *WC/E,* July 16, 1955, p. 9.

10. *WC/E,* September 3, 1955, p. 8.

11. *WC/E,* December 31, 1955, p. 10. Retired band trainer and music educator Ida Widamann, now of Bowling Green, Ky., still tells of the magnificent reception the band received that night! She was one among several brass enthusiasts who brought their entire bands to the program. They were not disappointed.

12. *Ibid.,* p. 11. A good review by C. G. Dickerson appeared in Lexington's paper the next day.

13. *Ibid.*

14. Other cities visited included Lexington and Covington, Ky.; and Springfield, Dayton and Hamilton, Ohio.

15. Concert report in *WC/E,* March 10, 1956, p. 8. Program in NYSB Arch.

16. Letter in Holz Coll., dated "Lincoln's Birthday, 1956."

17. The lead singing roles were given to Jerome Hines, Lucia Evangelista, and other New York operatic professionals. Two performances were given that year, the opera first being called *Scenes from the Life of Christ.* Hines later titled it *I Am the Way.* For a report, see *WC/E,* April 21, 1956, p. 9. I remember being enchanted by this "music drama"—particularly the scene of Lazarus' resurrection—when I was seven years old. It was the main Easter Week event for several years to come.

18. *WC/E,* April 7, 1956, pp. 8-9. Congress programs in NYSB Arch.

19. *WC/E,* January 26, 1957, p. 7.

20. Festival report in *WC/E,* February 16, 1957, p. 8.

21. Other ISB soloists on the weekend included Norman Tolliday, Ronald Symons, and Brian Cooper. For a Britisher's view of the congress, see Brindley Boon, *ISB: The Story of the International Staff Band of The Salvation Army* (London: Record Greetings Ltd., 1985), pp. 242-243. *WC/E,* April 27, 1958, p. 8.

22. It is not generally known that the "best seller" album, *The Salvation Army Band Plays the Great Marches,* was originally intended as a "Tribute to E. F. Goldman", but Westminster HiFi, the initial promoter, was bought out by ABC and the recording was given a more commercial title and promotion. It worked. Tens of thousands of this record were sold.

23. *WC/E,* August 23, 1958, p. 8.

24. *Ibid.*

25. Summary from "Music Highlights: Eastern Territory—1958-59 Season" as part of that year's "Commissioners' Report." Copy in NYSB Arch. Congress programs are also extant.

26. Reports on the Netherlands National Band at the congress were carried in *WC/E,* May 30, 1959, pp. 8-10. A member of that Dutch band, Harry Hartjes, was soon to be a valued member of the NYSB and Territorial Music Department. This Dutch band also had a good male chorus, rather rare for visiting Army bands.

27. *WC/E,* June 25, 1960, p. 12.

28. Wilfred Kitching would later state that this spiritual preparation was as important to the band's success as its musical rehearsals.

29. From Band Brief and assorted reports. The band traveled 877 miles and played for live audiences totalling nearly 31,000. Many other thousands were reached via BBC-TV and radio programs.

30. Program in NYSB Arch. Several tapes of this evening are still in existence. Derek *was* flawless and the NYSB played and sang superbly.

31. Eric Ball, *The Musician,* June 18, 1960, pp. 392-393.

32. Ball's review was flattering to the New Yorkers, compared with the way he discussed the British bands. He even intimated that the ISB, though a superb organization, played nervously that evening. It is interesting to compare descriptions of the sounds of these two bands. New York, of course, was in standard concert pitch and generally played with much less

vibrato than British bands of that day; this definitely had a psychological impact. See chapter 10 for more details.

33. Bandmasters' Councils report appeared in *The Musician,* under the title "Pentecostal Power at Denmark Hill," June 18, 1960, pp. 393-94.

34. *Ibid.,* p. 394.

35. Brindley Boon, "On Tour with NYSB," *The Musician,* June 18, 1960, p. 390.

36. *Ibid.,* June 25, 1960, p. 402; quoted by Ralph Miller, who contributed that part of Boon's review.

37. *Ibid.,* from Rance's contribution to "On Tour with the NYSB."

38. *WC/E,* July 9, 1960, p. 6.

39. *Ibid.,* p. 8. Alex Thain held major responsibilities himself in Edinburgh's famous yearly festival so he had the right to assert himself in this way. He also arranged many lovely amenities for the band, special tours, sightseeing, and even a serenade by the Queen's own Highland Pipers during the "Garden" concert just below Edinburgh Castle.

40. Quoted by Brindley Boon in "Back to the Metropolis," *The Musician,* June 25, 1960, p. 405.

41. *Ibid.*

42. Brindley Boon, "Sons Come Home," *The Musician,* June 25, 1960, p. 403. Several other aspects of the tour deserve mention. Recordings were in great demand, so much so that the crowds were nearly unruly in their desire to secure a copy. Because British hosts had greatly underestimated demand for *Star-Spangled Band Music,* after Nottingham, record sales had to be by "black market," with Fred Elliott Jr. being the man to know. So many bands were gracious hosts, but the ISB and B/M Adams gave an oil painting of a London landmark to be hung in the NYSB band room as a token of respect and esteem. Regent Hall Bandsmen and wives also graciously served a meal to the band when all had gathered back on June 24 from various vacation spots just before boarding the return BOAC flight.

43. NYSB Arch.; the band board was getting more and more

sophisticated in their programs, tour brochures, and publicity releases of this period.

44. A picture of Holz and Post with "Today Show" hosts appeared in *WC/E,* December 30, 1961, p. 8. The band met Sammy Deep later that season during their Georgia tour. Then Brigadier John Needham organized that fine tour, which included Savannah, Macon, Columbus, Atlanta, and a divisional music councils.

45. See *WC/E,* March 17, 1962, p. 8, for full report. Programs are in NYSB Arch.

46. Programs in NYSB Arch. This grand event saw Slater, Darby, Fowler and Bearchell tell humorous stories of old times. Even the reunion dinner program had a spoof: Bill Schofield's and Art Anderson's pictures superimposed on an old photo of the band (then labeled 1887, but actually from 1900).

47. The Erik Leidzen Memorial Album.

48. Summary from interviews with Richard Holz and Alfred Swenarton.

49. *WC/E,* April 6, 1963, p. 10.

50. *Ibid.*

51. *WC/E,* April 20, 1963, p. 10.

52. Robert McNally, "Tribute to a Bandmaster," *WC/E,* November 16, 1963, p. 6.

## Chapter 8

1. Vernon Post supplied several interview reports at my request. This portion from "Staff Band Memories," pp. 7-8.

2. The work was the first for this combination. It is based on William Maltby's "Christ Is the Answer." Concert report, *WC/E,* March 3, 1964, p. 10.

3. *WC/E,* April 4, 1964, p. 13.

4. Derek Smith had left the band by this time. Herbert T. Martin had replaced William Maltby as EO.

5. Tour report in *WC/E,* November 21, 1964, p. 11.

6. Some Louisiana tour proograms remain in NYSB Arch., as does congress program.

7. Concert review in *WC/E,* March 13, 1965, pp. 10, 14-15.

8. *WC/E,* May 29, 1965, p. 9.

9. *Centennial Celebrations Recording,* Tri LP 10-11.

10. From full text provided on *Centennial Celebrations* record jacket.

11. Post interview, "Staff Band Memories" portion, pp. 2-3.

12. "Elegy" was published in the *Festival Series;* the others remain in manuscript.

13. In addition to administrative pettiness like these status changes, Post endured major staff problems in the department but was never able to get a reliable musical assistant such as he had been to Holz. The arrival of Captain William Simons in later years did ease the administrative load.

14. Post interview, "European Tour" section, p. 1. All was nearly lost when U.S. President Lyndon Johnson called for a curtailment of American travel, especially overseas, due to an energy crisis. Army officers responded by removing Staff Band advertisements for charter tickets that would support the band's trip. Too much effort and money, however, had been expended on both sides of the Atlantic for the Army to comply with the governmental request. Three days of renegotiation with administration brought about a restored tour, one that would have uplifting results for thousands of Salvationists.

15. "A Statistical Summary, *WC/E,* July 27, 1968, p. 16.

16. Composite from Band Brief, Post interview, and "European Tour *War Cry* Report" (typed copy) by Captain Charles West.

17. Pean was famous for his efforts to close the French Penal Colony, Devil's Island.

18. Post interview, "European Tour," p. 4.

19. *Ibid.,* p. 8.

20. Relayed to me by William Simons.

21. *War Cry* Tour Report, entry for May 27.

22. Post interview, "European Tour" section, pp. 11-12.

23. Original clipping and translation supplied by Vernon Post.

24. Post interview, "European Tour" section, p. 4.

25. Edward Gregson, "Salvation Army 90th Anniversary Festival," *The British Bandsman,* June 15, 1968, p. 2.

26. Eric Ball, "Evening Festival," *The Musician,* June 15, 1968, p. 410.

27. Henning Schon-Larsen, "Afternoon Festival," *The Musician,* June 15, 1968, p. 411.

28. Ball, "Evening Festival," p. 410.

29. *Ibid.,* p. 412.

30. European *War Cry* Report, entries for June 1, 2 and 6.

31. *Ibid.*

32. Summary from Holz and Post interviews.

**Chapter 9**

1. From Smith interview, January 1986.

2. *Ibid.* See also SB press release on Smith in NYSB Arch.

3. *Ibid.*

4. These are Smith's words. The band frequently joked with him because of his British accent and mannerisms, though these have changed greatly over the years. He told me, "I don't try to be English, but the band accepts that and also have their fun with it, respecting my background."

5. *WC,* December 30, 1972, p. 14.

6. NYSB Arch. includes several programs from the Western tour. The 1973 Annual Festival included slides and sights of the tour, a media first, as far as can be determined, on recent Staff Band programs.

7. *WC,* May 5, 1973, p. 14.

8. The weekend included programs at Tremont Temple Baptist Church and Cambridge Citadel.

9. My wife Beatrice and I were privileged to join the band, Lt.-

Colonel and Mrs. Edward Fritz, and Commissioner Orval Taylor for this last-named retreat.

10. A picture and write-up on the NYSB appeared in the 1975 *Brass Conference Booklet,* p. 88. The event for 1975 and 1976 was held at the Hotel Roosevelt, NYC. Programs in NYSB Arch.

11. The 1976 N.Y. Brass Conference rendition by Derek Smith of the cornet solo "Someone Cares" proved to be a deeply moving experience for all who heard the band that day. At the Southwest Ohio Brass Conference, the NYSB gave a full clinic to *one person,* who turned out to be Professor Douglas Smith of the Southern Baptist Theological Seminary, noted trumpeter and composer. See "A Day with Salvation Army Brass," *The Musician* (American), November 1983, pp. 1, 8-9.

12. Smith interview.

13. Programs from the International Congress are in NYSB Arch. This section is given a "reporters" view; that is, the author's, who was in attendance at all these functions.

14. NYSB Brief, National Congress, June 13-17, 1980.

15. Observations on the Staff Band at the National Congress supplied by author.

16. See Ronald Rowland's article, "Staff Bands Unite in Toronto," *The Musician* (American), September 1981, pp. 1, 5. Program in NYSB Arch.

17. Stanley Ditmer, Jacket Notes to *The Ambassadors,* TRLPS-37.

18. Most of the excerpts that follow drawn from *Reflections,* which in turn had been compiled from various *Musician* and *War Cry* reports.

19. "NYSB Bon Voyage Festival," *The Musician* (American), August 1982, p. 4.

20. *World Tour 1982—Reflections,* p. 39.

21. *Ibid.,* p. 28.

22. *Ibid.,* p. 39.

23. *Ibid.,* p. 40.

24. *Ibid.,* p. 39.

25. *Ibid.,* p. 40.

26. Cited by Ronald Rowland in his "World Tour Report," *The Musician* (American), September 1982, p. 9.

27. *Reflections,* p. 33.

28. Reprinted from *OZOOMPAH,* an Australian brass band magazine, in *Reflections,* p. 12. "Salvos" are, of course, Salvationists.

29. *Reflections, p. 36.*

30. Smith interview.

31. The NYSB played host to the ISB on a rainy weekend in October during that 1980 tour.

32. Composite from Band Brief and BOM booklet.

33. BOM, p. 24.

34. Ray Stadman-Allen, "Happiness and Harmony," *The Musician,* June 22, 1985, p. 399.

35. George Wilson, "A Day to Remember," *The Musician,* July 6, 1985, p. 424.

36. Cover story, *The Musician,* June 29, 1985, p. 401.

37. BOM, p. 8.

38. Derek's last official engagements were scheduled in June 1986.

## Chapter 10

1. Salvation Army band scores contained clarinet parts until December 1902.

2. This standard instrumentation and order of parts is followed in the Army's *General* and *Festival Series Band Journals.* Band list from March 21, 1986 Annual Festival.

3. Bass clef parts for the low brass parts are now being supplied for *American Band Journal* items. There seems to be no move away from the old treble clef tradition, however, in international publications.

4. *AWC,* February 18, 1888, p. 1.

5. *AWC,* December 20, 1890, p. 1. See photo #1 in photo section. We know they had two clarinets, but only one, Lt. Flory, is in this sketch.

6. *Dispo,* July 1897, p. 3. Anderson listed cornets as first, second, third—thus in list (3,1,1).

7. The flugelhorn was short-lived, but came back in 1907.

8. From *Dispo,* May 1904, p. 4, plus other research into names from rosters.

9. *AWC,* January 2, 1886, p. 4. This advertisement, with minor adjustments, ran for several years.

10. October 1893 Trade HQ price list, pp. 88-107. The first full set of instruments from the Salvation Army instrument factory was realized sometime in 1894. For further information, see Brindley Boon, *Play the Music, Play: The Story of Salvation Army Bands* (London: Salvationist Publishing and Supplies, 1966), pp. 172-175.

11. *The Salvation Army Price List of Publications... Musical Instruments,* National Trade HQ, 111 Reade St., n.d. Reprinted by Eastern Trade for 1980 centenary. Manufacturers not identified.

12. *AWC,* August 15, 1903, p. 15. List included cornets, altos, baritones, euphoniums, EE$^b$ bass (contra) and a BB$^b$ helicon plus slide and valve trombones.

13. See *Dispo* lists for these years. While membership numbers varied—28 in 1909, 23 in 1910—the essential grouping remained the same, including the clarinet section, with one still in the band of 1911. Staff Bandsman Taylor's helicon BB$^b$ bass of 1892 had a "63 circumference bell" and weighed 18 lbs. See *AWC,* November 3, 1895, p. 5.

14. See *AWC,* November 2, 1901, p. 14.

15. *Dispo,* June 1912, p. 3.

16. Saxophones made spotty appearances in the band from 1916 to 1929, with players in the latter year the caliber of Harold Jackson and Kenneth Ayres. The famous Chalk Farm

(London) Band (A. W. Punchard) had saxophones as late as 1936 and proudly featured a sax sextet around 1907. For a review, see letter by Ron Woodcock, *The Musician*, December 11, 1982, p. 322, and retirement pamphlet for Punchard (1894-1938) in Holz Coll., which reviews the Chalk Farm Band's instrumentation.

17. *Dispo*, June 1914, p. 3.

18. Edgar Arkett, "In Tune," *LOC*, XI, no. 1 (October 1929), pp. 13-14. The effect on congregational singing was also a great improvement, considering the relatively *high* keys used in Salvation Army tune books.

19. See, for instance, the ad in *LOC*, II, no. 9 (June 1921), p. 33.

20. *LOC*, I, no. 13 (October 1921), p. 33.

21. Swenarton interview.

22. When a Conn representative saw a typical solo horn part, he knew his marching "peck horns" would not do. Swenarton interview.

23. *Dispo*, November 1948, p. 7.

24. The band used to be a motley assortment! The Conn bases were lacquered when reconditioned in 1946. Lacquer was considered American, rather than the old British style "Silver" Band label some bands still used.

25. Slater had purchased fine-sounding Besson trombones, but the slides proved poor.

26. Imagine the reaction at the rehearsal when the new Besson cornets were given out; Orr played a Bach, Abrams a Salvation Army B/M model, Henderson a Selmer, Post a King "Master" model, and Schramm a Bach soprano! Derek Smith was allowed to use his silver-plated Besson cornet, as it matched the others in sound, if not appearance, and he was particular about what he would use for solo work.

27. For instance, the band did switch to Getzen cornets in the mid-1970s. Only scant information has been available on the band's percussion equipment and therefore I have not been able to discuss it thoroughly in this chapter.

28. SB Tour Brief, June 1960.

29. List supplied via *Dispo* and help from Vernon Post and William Simons.

30. Tour brochure, *Return to England.*

31. We are referring to bands capable of playing the most demanding *Festival Series* and manuscript compositions.

32. From the *ISB U.S.A. Tour Brochure,* 1980.

33. For the instrumentation of that 15-member group, see chapter 8. Their repertoire was marvelously diverse. With *excellent* players on each part, small groups or staff bands are possible.

34. From separate interviews with Holz, Bearchell, and Smith.

35. From the *CCSB Great Britain Tour Brochure,* 1981. I served as tour manager for this band; while not your "average" corps band, this band needed *every* player it could muster to sustain the tour and challenging repertoire.

36. These questions are addressed more fully in chapter 16. Readers interested in more technical discussions of Salvation Army band instrumentation, music journals, etc., should examine this author's *A Reference Guide to Current Salvation Army Music Publications* (New York: The Salvation Army, 1981), his dissertation on Army musical forms, and Ray Steadman-Allen's *Colour and Texture in the Brass Band Score* (London: Salvationist Publishing and Supplies, 1981), all mentioned in the Bibliographical Review.

### Chapter 11

1. Post-interview, "NYSB Male Chorus" portion, pp. 3-4.

2. *AWC,* April 27, 1889, p. 7.

3. The much-heralded "ABC Song" by the Household Troops Band was probably a band song, by either some or all of the group.

4. *AWC,* March 12, 1892, p. 11.

5. "Great Day for Newark," *AWC,* April 27, 1907, p. 8.

6. It cannot be confirmed whether they sang "a cappella" or with

piano accompaniment. Plainfield report, *AWC,* April 11, 1908, p. 12.

7. "Watch Night at Memorial Hall," *AWC,* January 16, 1909, p. 8.

8. *AWC,* November 4, 1911, p. 7.

9. Donald McMillan, "New Day Congress Musicale," *LOC,* I, no. 3 (December 1919), p. 27.

10. *AWC,* May 23, 1914, p. 7.

11. "Songs Used by the American Delegation ..." (New York: The Salvation Army, 1914). It also contained eight "special songs" by Evangeline: "Solos, Specials, and Congregational Songs." Copy in S.A. Arch., 264.2/S698ad/pam.

12. *AWC,* August 1, 1914, p. 3.

13. Sung during a "Rags" presentation at Trenton, N.J. *AWC,* April 11, 1925, p. 8.

14. Post interview, "The Male Chorus," p. 4.

15. Band Minutes, September 12, 1933, p. 2.

16. *WC/E,* May 31, 1952, p. 9.

17. That one Male Chorus had Olof Lundgren, Albert Avery, and Peter Hofman in the first tenor section!

18. BOM.

19. See Staff-Captain Lamb, "Victories of the National Singing Brigade," *Harbor Lights* III (January 1900), pp. 26-27, 32. There were six members in 1899; group lasted about six years.

20. William Knowlton, "Interview with Frank Fowler," *WC/E,* July 13, 1948, p. 7.

21. The quartet was heard in "Lead Kindly Light" during a visit to Glens Falls, N.Y., on October 1, 1905, with Commander Booth and the band. *AWC,* October 21, 1905, p. 9.

22. Knowlton interview of Fowler, *Ibid.*

23. Richard E. Holz, "My Favorite Bandsman" *WC,* March 12, 1983, pp. 8-9. This is a fine review of Fowler's life and contribution to Salvation Army music.

24. Knowlton interview of Fowler, *Ibid.*

25. Erik Leidzen composed a selection in Fowler's honor by that title.

26. Post interview, "Male Chorus" portion, pp. 5-6.

27. Story told by Richard E. Holz, then bandmaster.

28. BOM, letter from William Simons.

**Chapter 12**

1. One other early confirmed use of the *Band Journal* comes from the band's trip to Old Orchard Beach, Maine, in the summer of 1889. As they arrived at the rail depot nearby they played G.S. #84, consisting of two tunes, "A Place in the Army for All," and "Hallelujah." On the former, as was the practice then, the words of the song were printed along with the part, so that the men could sing as well:

   We'll march away, We'll march away
   We'll bravely follow where Jesus is leading
   We'll march away, we'll march away
   Until the Conquerors Crown we gain.
   Our every rank, The Lord be thanked
   Is formed by soldiers true;
   Bravely in front or rear,
   If you're prepared for war
   There's a place for you.

   See *AWC,* August 3, 1889, p. 9.

2. From advertisement, *AWC,* April 9, 1898, p. 15.

3. A new "tune book" was released in 1900, *Band Music No. 1,* as brass companion to the 1899 congregational song book entitled *Salvation Army Songs.*

4. "Analysis of the *Brass Band Journal* for 1900, Nos. 383-386."

5. "Selections" could be rendered in a similar manner with slower-moving tunes.

6. More detailed discussions of early Army music are available in the Holz dissertation, Boon's *Play the Music, Play,* and Steadman-Allen's "Evolution of Salvation Army Music" series (see Bibliographical Review). Much of this section is a paraphrase of chapter 2 of the Holz dissertation.

7. Copy in S.A. Arch, 785.067/Si59/pam.

8. *AWC,* January 2, 1904, p. 11.

9. *AWC,* June 3, 1911, p. 9.

10. Letter in BOM.

11. Many of the old Staff Band bound journals have inserted marches and selections from such series as the *Liverpool Brass Band (and Military) Journal,* published by Wright and Round, 34 Erskine St., Liverpool.

12. Quoted by Richard E. Holz, "The Lord's Trumpeter," *WC,* March 16, 1985, p. 8.

13. Quoted by Joy Steadman-Allen in "Salvation Army Music and Worship," Section I, p. 6 (unpublished paper for use at International Officers' Training College).

14. Letter of Bernard Adams to Erik Leidzen, January 31, 1955. S.A. Arch., MS28-5. The filing-in duties, as in preliminary music, were usually performed under chaotic conditions. Most typical is a *War Cry* report for a commissioning of 1925: "Salvationists gossiped while the band played"! *WC/E,* July 11, 1925, p. 9.

15. *AWC,* January 16, 1886, p. 4.

16. Damon Papers, S.A. Arch., 47-2-2.

17. The band's first Annual Festival under Darby (1912) is explained in chapter 3.

18. *AWC,* March 21, 1914, p. 8.

19. I attended this program; for me, for many staff bandsmen, and for many in the audience, it stands out as one of the most moving Salvation Army meetings ever attended.

20. Of course, what is a band program without marches? This one had two "sparklers"!

## Chapter 13

1. From interview with William Parkins. Parkins relates that Chet Mattheson, while a very technical player, would occasionally have "nerve" problems, and thus run afoul of Evangeline.

2. His Buffalo, N.Y., cornet trio received top honors, and he

received the silver medal in the soloists division, from 25 semi-finalists. *WC/E,* July 20, 1935, p. 3.

3. Robert Jackson, principal trumpet of the Charlotte, N.C., Symphony, was also in the band for a short while. Star Lake produced excellent cornetists, and Smith and Hofman were fine instructors there.

4. Holz and Parkins interviews.

5. From Parkins interview and various other articles; Band Minutes of the 1920s have frequent mention of von Calio's job positions. His service was sporadic.

6. Letter from Harold Anderson, BOM.

## Chapter 14

1. Letter from Frank Moody, BOM.

2. Letter from Frederick Clarke, BOM.

3. Letter in Holz Coll.

4. Letter from Frederick Jackson, BOM.

5. *AWC,* August 25, 1900, p. 7.

6. Letter from Paul D. Seiler, BOM.

7. Story told to me by William Bearchell and Richard Holz during Bearchell interview.

8. Letter from Jacob Hohn, BOM.

9. Letter from William B. Simons, BOM.

10. Letter from Thomas Scheibner, BOM.

11. *WC/E,* June 18, 1966, p. 19.

12. Holz interview.

13. Letter from George Harvey, BOM.

14. Letter from Roland Schramm, BOM.

15. Letter from Harold Banta, BOM.

**Chapter 15**

1. Not all, but a large majority of staff bandsmen commute from these suburban areas.

2. Much of the following concerning challenges the band faces is drawn from discussions with staff bandsmen during their January 1986 band retreat at Ladore Lodge and from an interview with Edward Fritz, EO, May 13, 1986.

3. Holz dissertation, p. 249 (see Bibliographical Review).

4. Fritz interview.

5. *AWC*, July 7, 1888, p. 8.

6. Throughout the years, Band Minutes frequently contain discussion of the need for more help with personnel, usually with regard to upper administrative assistance. Two typical samples which deal with the complexity of departmental cooperation would be the minutes of March 5, 1939, p. 2, or June 6, 1952, p. 2, each of which includes impassioned pleas for further help and support.

7. Letter from Terry Camsey, BOM.

8. Article by Will Crutchfield, "Tradition and Talent March in Yule Bands," *The New York Times* (December 20, 1985), p. C34.

9. Ronald Waiksnoris tells me that Ivor Bosanko, Vernon Post, Ray Bowes, and Robert Redhead are also working on items.

10. Letter from Harold Burgmayer, BOM.

# Bibliographical Review

Primary source materials consulted for this book may be divided into two broad categories: (1) collections housed in the Salvation Army Archives and Research Center in New York City, and (2) materials gathered from personal collections, interviews, correspondence, and the New York Staff Band's "Book of Memories" project.

The New York Staff Band has given to the Archives a substantial collection of papers, programs, band board minutes, etc., dated 1912-1979 (Acc. 83-45). To this the author will be contributing the results of his own research—a year-by-year compilation of articles, programs, memorabilia, biographical sketches/obituaries, and interviews—that will further enhance that collection.

The principal Salvationist periodicals reviewed included the following: *The War Cry* (American edition, 1881-1986, including the Eastern Territory's edition of *The War Cry*, 1921-1970) which were available to the author at the Archives in New York City and at Asbury College in Wilmore, Kentucky; *The Musician* (International, published in London, 1938-1986); and a little known but excellent magazine entitled *The Local Officers' Counselor* (or *The Counselor*) published by the Eastern Territory, 1919-1931.

While the endnotes contain more exhaustive citations from a host of sources, the following selective listing may be of help to the general reader. For other music sources, the reader is referred to this author's *Reference Guide* and dissertation, as cited in this section. Those wishing for further bibliographic listings may contact the author or consult the New York Staff Band Collection at the Archives.

## Salvation Army Literature about Music

### Books and Articles:

Avery, Gordon. *Companion to The Song Book of The Salvation Army.* 4th ed. London: Salvationist Publishing and Supplies, 1970.

Boon, Brindley. *ISB: The Story of the International Staff Band of The Salvation Army.* London: Record Greetings Ltd., 1985.

_____. *Play the Music, Play: The Story of Salvation Army Bands.* London: Salvationist Publishing and Supplies, 1966.

_____. *Sing the Happy Song: A History of Salvation Army Vocal Music.* London: Salvationist Publishing and Supplies, 1978.

Fossey, Leslie. *This Man Leidzen.* London: Campfield Press, 1966.

Holz, Ronald W. *A History of the Hymn Tune Meditation and Related Forms in Salvation Army Instrumental Music in Great Britain and North America, 1880-1980.* Ph.D. Dissertation. Univ. of Connecticut, 1981. University Microfilms 82-11-403.

_____. *A Reference Guide to Current Salvation Army Music Publications.* New York: The Salvation Army, 1981.

*Orders and Regulations for Bands and Songster Brigades in the United States of America.* New York: The Salvation Army, 1972. (currently under revision)

*Orders and Regulations for Salvation Army Bands and Songster Brigades.* Rev. international ed. London: Salvationist Publishing and Supplies, 1977.

Steadman-Allen, Ray. *Colour and Texture in the Brass Band Score.* London: Salvationist Publishing and Supplies, 1981.

_____. "The Evolution of Salvation Army Music." *The Musician* (International), July 1965 through Feb. 1966.

_____. "One Hundred Years of Music Publishing." *The Salvation Army Year Book* (1976), pp. 15-18. London: Salvationist Publishing and Supplies.

Wiggins, Arch R. *Father of Salvation Army Music: Richard Slater.* London: Salvationist Publishing and Supplies, 1945.

_____. *Triumph of Faith: Bandmaster George Marshall.* London: Salvationist Publishing and Supplies, 1958.

## Periodicals

(in chronological order of publication):

*The Local Officer, Bandsman and Songster of The Salvation Army,* published weekly, 1900-1907. London.

*The Bandsman and Songster of The Salvation Army,* published weekly, 1907-1937. London.

*The Local Officers' Counselor* (later, *The Counselor*), published monthly, 1919-1931. New York. Contains many articles about Salvation Army music of the period.

*The Musician* (International), published weekly, 1938-1986. London.

*The Musician* (American), published irregularly (monthly issues), 1937-1958. Chicago.

*The Musician* (American), published monthly, 1978 through present. New York.

# Index of Names, Musical Organizations, Instruments, and Principal Events

340

341

344

345

# Author's Biographical Summary

Dr. Ronald W. Holz currently serves as chairman of the Division of Fine Arts at Asbury College in Wilmore, Kentucky, having joined the faculty of that institution in 1981. Associate Professor of instrumental music and music literature, Dr. Holz teaches courses in music history and music theory and conducts the brass choir and stage band. Unique among colleges and universities in the United States for its Salvation Army Student Fellowship (S.A.S.F.) of approximately 100 members, Asbury College's S.A.S.F. is the only such organization with local officers commissioned by the Army's National Headquarters. Dr. Holz is the bandmaster of the S.A.S.F. Brass Band. He received his PhD in Historical Musicology from the University of Connecticut in 1981, his Master of Music in Musicology from the College-Conservatory of the University of Cincinnati in 1973, and his Bachelor of Science in Music Education from the University of Connecticut in 1970. His published work includes an extensive doctoral dissertation on Salvation Army instrumental music, various articles on brass and wind band music in scholarly journals, and *A Reference Guide to Current Salvation Army Music Publications*.